Accountability Reconsidered

The last two decades have witnessed a substantial change in the media environment, growing polarization of the two dominant parties, and increasing inequality of wealth and income. These profound changes necessitate updating our understanding of political accountability. *Accountability Reconsidered* examines how political accountability functions in the USA today given the dramatic changes in voting behavior, media, congressional dynamics, and relations between branches. With particular attention to policymaking, this volume uses original research to analyze micro-foundations of voter behavior, examining its implications for incentives and offering insight into the accountability relationships among voters, interest groups, legislators, and government bureaucracy. Combining contributions from leading experts who write about the political system synoptically with those who focus on specific elements, *Accountability Reconsidered* brings together distinct perspectives to focus on the effect of the informational environment on government officials, bridging up-to-date knowledge about accountability mechanisms with our overall understanding of political accountability.

CHARLES M. CAMERON is Professor of Politics and Public Affairs at Princeton University. The author or co-author of many articles in leading journals of political science, law, and law and economics, he is also the author of the prize-winning *Veto Bargaining: Presidents and the Politics of Negative Power* (Cambridge, 2000) and co-author with John Kastellec of *Making the Supreme Court: The Politics of Appointments 1930–2020* (Oxford, 2023).

BRANDICE CANES-WRONE is Professor of Political Science and Senior Fellow at the Hoover Institution, Stanford University. During the course of her career, Canes-Wrone has published extensively in the areas of political institutions, mass political behavior, and political economy in leading journals of political science and other social sciences. Her book, *Who Leads Whom? Presidents, Policy, and the Public* (University of Chicago Press, 2006) was awarded the Richard E. Neustadt prize by the American Political Sc⁓ ⁓ ⁓ ⁓k on the US presidency that year.

T0370938

SANFORD C. GORDON is Professor in and Chair of the Wilf Family Department of Politics at New York University and an Associated Professor (by courtesy) in the New York University School of Law. His work has appeared in *The American Political Science Review, the American Journal of Political Science, The Journal of Politics, the Proceedings of the National Academy of Sciences*, among many other leading journals.

GREGORY A. HUBER is the Forst Family Professor of Political Science and Chair of the Political Science Department at Yale University. He is the author of *The Craft of Bureaucratic Neutrality: Interests and Influence in Governmental Regulation of Occupational Safety* (Cambridge, 2007) as well as over eighty articles in leading journals of political science and related fields.

Accountability Reconsidered

Voters, Interests, and Information in US Policymaking

Edited by

CHARLES M. CAMERON
Princeton University

BRANDICE CANES-WRONE
Stanford University

SANFORD C. GORDON
New York University

GREGORY A. HUBER
Yale University

 **CAMBRIDGE**
UNIVERSITY PRESS

Shaftesbury Road, Cambridge CB2 8EA, United Kingdom

One Liberty Plaza, 20th Floor, New York, NY 10006, USA

477 Williamstown Road, Port Melbourne, VIC 3207, Australia

314–321, 3rd Floor, Plot 3, Splendor Forum, Jasola District Centre, New Delhi – 110025, India

103 Penang Road, #05–06/07, Visioncrest Commercial, Singapore 238467

Cambridge University Press is part of Cambridge University Press & Assessment, a department of the University of Cambridge.

We share the University's mission to contribute to society through the pursuit of education, learning and research at the highest international levels of excellence.

www.cambridge.org
Information on this title: www.cambridge.org/9781009168304

DOI: 10.1017/9781009168311

First published 2023
First paperback edition 2024

A catalogue record for this publication is available from the British Library

Library of Congress Cataloging-in-Publication data
Names: Cameron, Charles M. (Charles Metz), 1954– editor. | Canes-Wrone, Brandice, editor. | Gordon, Sanford Clark, 1972– editor.
Title: Accountability reconsidered : voters, interests, and information in US policymaking / Charles M. Cameron, Princeton University, Brandice Canes-Wrone, Princeton University, Sanford C. Gordon, New York University, Gregory A. Huber, Yale University, eds.
Other titles: Voters, interests, and information in United States policymaking
Description: First Edition. | New York : Cambridge University Press, 2023. | Includes bibliographical references and index.
Identifiers: LCCN 2022032961 (print) | LCCN 2022032962 (ebook) | ISBN 9781009168328 (Hardback) | ISBN 9781009168304 (Paperback) | ISBN 9781009168311 (epub)
Subjects: LCSH: Government accountability–United States. | Representative government and representation–United States. | Political participation–United States. | Communication in politics–Technological innovations. | Social media–Political aspects–United States. | Elite (Social sciences)–United States. | United States–Politics and government.
Classification: LCC JF1525.A26 A25 2023 (print) | LCC JF1525.A26 (ebook) | DDC 352.3/5–dc23/eng/20220930
LC record available at https://lccn.loc.gov/2022032961
LC ebook record available at https://lccn.loc.gov/2022032962

ISBN   978-1-009-16832-8   Hardback
ISBN   978-1-009-16830-4   Paperback

To R. Douglas Arnold –
Teacher, Colleague, Mentor, Friend

Contents

Figures

Tables

Contributors

Kathleen Bawn
Professor of Political Science, University of California at Los Angeles (UCLA)

Knox Brown
Assistant Professor of Political Science, Tulsa Community College

Charles M. Cameron
Professor of Politics and Public Affairs, Princeton University

Brandice Canes-Wrone
Professor of Political Science and Senior Fellow at The Hoover Institution, Stanford University

Nicholas Carnes
Creed C. Black Associate Professor of Public Policy and Political Science, Duke University

Daniel P. Carpenter
Allie S. Freed Professor of Government, Faculty of Arts and Sciences, Harvard University

Joshua D. Clinton
Abby and John Winkelreid Chair, Department of Political Science, Vanderbilt University

Lee Drutman
Senior Fellow, Political Reform Program, New America

Patrick J. Egan
Associate Professor of Politics and Public Policy, New York University

Alan Gerber
Dean of Social Science, Charles C. and Dorathea S. Dilley Professor of
Political Science, and Professor in the Institution for Social and Policy Studies,
of Economics, and of Public Health, Yale University

Sanford C. Gordon
Professor of Politics, and Associated Professor (by courtesy) of Law, New
York University

Justin Grimmer
Professor of Political Science and Senior Fellow at the Hoover Institution,
Stanford University

Gregory A. Huber
Forst Family Professor of Political Science and resident fellow of the
Institution for Social and Policy Studies (ISPS), Yale University

Devin Judge-Lord
Postdoctoral Fellow, Harvard University

Michael R. Kistner
Assistant Professor of Political Science, University of Houston

Frances E. Lee
Professor of Politics and Public Affairs, Princeton University

Brian Libgober
Assistant Professor of Political Science, University of California at San Diego

Angela X. Ocampo
Assistant Professor of Mexican American and Latina/o Studies, University of
Texas at Austin

Eric M. Patashnik
Julis-Rabinowitz Professor of Public Policy and Professor of Political Science,
Brown University

Shawn Patterson
Assistant Professor of Political Science, Southern Oregon University

John W. Patty
Professor of Political Science and Quantitative Theory & Methods, Emory University

Eleanor Neff Powell
Booth Fowler Associate Professor of Political Science, University of Wisconsin-Madison

Markus Prior
Professor of Politics and Public Affairs, Princeton University

John L. Ray
PhD Candidate, University of California at Los Angeles (UCLA)

Michael W. Sances
Assistant Professor of Political Science, Temple University

Mary Catherine Sullivan
PhD Candidate, Vanderbilt University

Patrick Tucker
Senior Statistician, Edison Research

John Zaller
Professor of Political Science Emeritus, University of California at Los Angeles (UCLA)

Acknowledgments

This volume is concerned with understanding the dynamics of political accountability in the contemporary United States. Its origins lie in the authors' attempts to grapple with the work of a particular scholar, R. Douglas Arnold. Doug's work on political accountability, centrally focusing on the lynchpin of the US Congress, is broadly influential to many scholars interested in this topic and the performance of the US political system more generally. Additionally, Doug is and has been a friend, mentor, colleague, and inspiration to many scholars of American politics.

In honor of Doug's forty-two-year career at Princeton and on the occasion of his retirement, we assembled a group of scholars in May 2019 to participate in a conference on the broad theme of political accountability. The chapters in this volume are a subset of those presented at the conference, revised and improved upon in light of discussions that took place at that event.

We would like to thank the conference participants and discussants, including Larry Bartels, Jason Casellas, Justin Crowe, Andrew Guess, Patricia Kirkland, Jonathan Ladd, Asya Magazinnik, David Mayhew, Adam Meirowitz, Kevin Munger, Rachel Potter, Andrew Roberts, Kodiak Sauer, Sebastian Thieme, Danielle Thomsen, Philip Wallach, and Keith Whittington. Michele Epstein and Helene Wood lent their incalculable administrative acumen to the organization of the conference itself and also helped in numerous ways as we prepared this volume for publication. Ivan Aleksandrov, Michael Pomirchy, and Jamila Ruddock provided substantial additional assistance in whipping the volume into shape. We are also grateful to the helpful suggestions of the reviewers and team at Cambridge University Press.

As for Doug, we expect he'll appreciate our directness in admitting that while we continue to be inspired by his work, we also enjoyed finding the areas where he got things wrong.

1

Introduction

Charles M. Cameron, Brandice Canes-Wrone,
Sanford C. Gordon, and Gregory A. Huber

How does political accountability function in the contemporary United States and what are the consequences for representation? The contributions in this volume provide distinct yet interrelated perspectives on this question, sharing a common focus on how the informational environment confronted by political actors affects the accountability of elected representatives and other government officials to public preferences.

What is accountability? A useful starting point is the following definition: accountability refers to actions by an actor or group of actors on behalf of another under a system of punishments and rewards at least in part under the control of the latter. As is common, we label those with the authority to offer sanctions principals, and those who are overseen as agents. From the perspective of scholars of US politics, electoral accountability is perhaps the most important subspecies of these principal-agent relationships. This type of accountability centers on the relationship between voters and elected officials, where the system of punishments and rewards is implemented primarily via the electoral mechanism.

At the same time, the electoral connection is clearly not the only politically relevant accountability relationship. Others include the relationship between private interests and candidates who seek their financial support to run for office; between elected members of political parties and their party's legislative leadership; and between unelected bureaucrats who implement policies and elected officials, the latter of whom are an intermediate link connecting the former to voters and private interests. These examples highlight that accountability relationships are layered and overlapping in the American political system. Consequently, understanding policymaking requires appreciating the complex relationships linking voters and private interests to elected and unelected policymakers and how the incentives and behavior of the former influence the incentives and behavior of the latter.

A comprehensive understanding of these relationships also brings to the fore the critical role of information, without which accountability is impossible. For example, voters may want their representatives to choose good public policy but may lack the information or expertise necessary to determine what "good" even means. Instead, if they observe anything, they may be forced to rely on imperfect proxies for incumbent performance (e.g., roll call voting), or on a third party such as a challenger to tell them what their incumbent has been up to. What are the consequences of these contexts for incumbent incentives? How might these incentives change in a world where key policymaking is often negotiated behind closed doors in advance of a highly polarized floor vote? And how does influence of outside political actors on candidate selection affect the accountability relationship between representatives and their nominal constituents?

To be sure, the underlying question of how accountability functions is not new in American politics. Canonical research highlights how voter preferences (e.g., Downs, 1957) and interest group goals (e.g., Wilson, 1980) shape policy outcomes. Moreover, electoral incentives are understood as essential for understanding the internal organization of Congress (Mayhew, 1974), the behavior of its members (Fenno, 1978), and how coalition leaders sometimes manage to overcome electoral parochialism to serve the national interest (Arnold, 1990). Similarly, some research studies the bureaucracies as agents of congressional interests (McCubbins, Noll, and Weingast, 1987) or presidential interests (Moe, 1985), while other scholarship views them as essentially ungoverned (Lowi, 1979) or acutely concerned with cultivating support from the public and special interests to pursue preferred policies in the absence of interference (Carpenter, 2001). But much of this work, even if not explicitly historical, comes from a different era of policymaking, and as such, does not reflect a contemporary political context in which the preferences of key actors have changed and the informational environment has been dramatically altered.

As a non-exhaustive list, consider four facts that have enormous implications for the contemporary informational environment and incentives of political actors:

1. The media ecosystem has fractured, and local newspapers have declined precipitously. The monolithic national television news that generated a shared understanding of contemporary politics has been replaced by cable television, offering numerous non-news outlets and more ideological content. More than ever, individuals can avoid politics altogether or choose their own ideological flavor of coverage. At the local level, the decline of local newspapers means that a key source of information about local politics, including coverage of individual members of Congress, has diminished precipitously and in some districts disappeared entirely. Each of these factors has been exacerbated by the internet and social media.

2. Political parties have grown more ideologically homogeneous at both the mass and elite levels. More polarized parties pursue more distinct policy agendas. Inside Congress, members have ceded greater control of the legislative agenda and the crafting of legislation to party leadership, often bypassing the traditional committee system. And voters are more likely to share the policy goals of the party they identify with, even while a large portion of the electorate does not officially align with either party.

3. The concentration of wealth and economic power has increased, and with it, the avenues through which economic resources may be deployed for political ends. Accompanying these changes have been concurrent ones in the legal landscape surrounding political spending by corporations and individuals. Donations from and expenditures by individuals and organizations outside of a legislator's district have dramatically altered the set of interests to which rank-and-file legislators must attend. Similarly, efforts to lobby both elected officials and unelected bureaucrats have grown in both volume and sophistication.

4. Electoral fortunes are less stable. Both major parties robustly contest national elections, with frequent changes in party control of the House, Senate, and Presidency. Parties work to recruit credible candidates for those elections that decide control of Congress, and the incumbency advantage has shrunk while primary contests have become more closely contested.

It is this evolving political context that frames our inquiry into political accountability in the United States. The chapters that follow, in addition to offering specific contributions, collectively contribute to two related themes. First, the volume joins analysis of voters' behavior with how policymakers respond to it. Often in the literature, scholarship examines internal legislative dynamics without considering voters' incentives and information, or electoral behavior without the implications for policymaking. Indeed, as the subfields of political science have become more specialized, different strands of American politics scholarship relevant for understanding political accountability and representation have developed in disparate ways.

For example, formal models of political accountability have investigated policymakers' incentives under various institutional arrangements and political contexts.[1] A rich literature on Congress has delved into internal legislative dynamics by examining the roles of parties, committees, and institutional rules for law production, roll call voting, and bureaucratic oversight.[2] Meanwhile, empirical examinations of policy responsiveness have uncovered evidence regarding the extent to which mass preferences translate into policy, and the

---

[1] See reviews by Ashworth (2012) and Gailmard and Patty (2012a) on, respectively, electoral accountability and congressional-bureaucratic relations.

[2] See, e.g., Binder (2015) for a recent review article.

"credibility revolution" has untied previously intractable debates about the antecedents of voter behavior.[3] Yet as the field has become more specialized, synthetic work that theoretically and empirically investigates policymaking as a nexus of accountability relationships has become less common or has become increasingly disconnected from the theoretical and empirical insights from more specialized research lineages. The need for such work is particularly important given the massive developments in politics and media that have occurred in recent decades.

The second theme is a consideration of political developments that may merit a reevaluation of canonical accounts of political accountability. In other words, this treatment of accountability and policymaking helps delineate what has fundamentally changed versus what has not. Indeed, several chapters are explicitly concerned with offering updates to classic research studies that, while still frequently assigned in both undergraduate and graduate courses, are dated in both the evidence they draw on and the perspectives they take. Thus, the volume serves as a bridge from these canonical studies to a more contemporary perspective. Even chapters that are not explicit updates of those studies offer important insights into the ways in which political developments reshape conventional wisdom.

No intellectual inquiry can be about everything, and so it is important to delimit the scope of the efforts of the contributors to this volume by explaining what it is *not* about. In particular, the chapters have little to say about the president, the courts, and state and local governments or many proposed institutional reforms. Issues of accountability and representation as they apply to each of these topics are critical, but beyond the purview of the current inquiry.

The volume is organized into four parts. Part I focuses on candidates running for Congress, and considers how these candidates are selected in primary and general elections in light of the information available to other political actors. Part II hones in on the media as a critical source of such information, particularly how it serves as a key intermediary between voters and both incumbents and new candidates for office. Part III again focuses centrally on information, but shifts to the perspective of government officials, to analyze how informational asymmetries in the contemporary political landscape affect policymaking. More specifically, Part III considers the policy implications of such asymmetries between voters and public officials (especially Congress) as well as between Congress and the bureaucracy. Finally, Part IV considers how interests affect policymaking in ways that are generally outside the purview of voters and thus limit voters' ability to hold officials accountable.

---

[3] See, e.g., Canes-Wrone (2015) for a recent review article on policy responsiveness and Jacobson and Carson (2019) for evidence on congressional elections.

PART I: CANDIDATE EVALUATION AND SELECTION

The chapters in this section open up the black box of congressional elections. To what degree are incumbents held accountable for their policy decisions? How do voters interpret different pieces of information when forming inferences about incumbent performance? What are the implications of different understandings of voter psychology and the informational environment for the disciplining force of elections? And what of primaries, where in the absence of party labels, voters and interest groups face much tougher challenges in choosing among candidates? Together, the chapters point to a world that moves beyond the classic perspectives such as Downs (1957), Mayhew (1974), and Arnold (1990), but also retains critical components. In particular, legislators continue to face substantial pressures that facilitate some form of electoral accountability, but the nature of those pressures differs from that detailed in the earlier perspectives.

The section opens with Chapter 2, by Josh Clinton, Michael Sances, and Mary Catherine Sullivan. This chapter considers whether voters hold incumbent House representatives accountable for policy actions in office, focusing on the context in which a representative takes a position that is unaligned with constituents' views. Two analyses are presented. First, the authors examine the universe of issues in the 2008–2017 Congressional Cooperative Election Study (CCES) surveys in which respondents' positions can be matched to a House roll call vote. Second, they conduct an in-depth analysis of recent legislative activity concerning the Affordable Care Act (ACA), including with respect to how demographic groups vary in holding members accountable for their positions. Across both tests, the results suggest that even though partisan labels exert an independent effect on voter evaluations, issue positions matter. These findings imply that despite the increasing role of partisanship in US elections, issue-based considerations as observed in roll call votes remain important with respect to voters' willingness to hold incumbents accountable.

In Chapter 3, Eric Patashnik, Patrick Tucker, and Alan Gerber continue the examination of whether and how voters hold legislators accountable. Building on behavioral research concerning the ways in which individuals evaluate policy costs and benefits, the authors employ a series of survey experiments to examine voter choice. One set investigates whether individuals are more responsive to information about the absolute size of a grant a legislator secures for the district, or instead information about obtaining a grant of above or below average size. A second set manipulates information concerning road benefits, social programs, and an abstract policy. The results suggest that citizens' sensitivity to the incidence of costs and benefits depends substantially on whether they possess a point of reference that enables them to benchmark the magnitude of policy effects. Additionally, respondents are responsive to information about changes in policy costs and benefits when the vignettes concern a specific policy but not an abstract one. Together, these findings highlight how incumbent accountability depends on the nature of the information voters receive.

Chapter 4 by Patrick Egan and Markus Prior steps back, considering how an optimizing legislator concerned both with their own policy preferences and the threat of electoral sanction would behave in light of contemporary evidence regarding voters' tighter policy agreement with their parties, their limited information about incumbents and policy outcomes, and heightened partisan-motivated reasoning. Each of these phenomena requires significant modification to our understanding of legislator incentives. Even so, the authors show that the changes do not imply Westminster-style accountability of legislators based on party labels; the real consequences of policies continue to matter to voters. At the same time, party labels and primaries matter much more than formerly, potentially weakening the incentives for cross-party cooperation to enact policies that serve the general interest.

The final chapter of this section, Chapter 5, by Kathleen Bawn, Knox Brown, Angela X. Ocampo, Shawn Patterson, Jr., John L. Ray, and John Zaller, examines the roles of voters and organized interests in congressional primaries. The authors present findings from extensive fieldwork, which involved interviews with supporters and candidates in fifty-three potentially winnable open seat House races in the 2013–2014 election cycle. They argue that groups, including sometimes local party organizations, are the key principals that monitor candidates. Both groups and voters are interested in minimizing uncertainty about a candidate's commitment to particular policy goals, competence, and competitiveness. Groups are central to reducing this uncertainty, with voters relying on groups' signals to distinguish among potential nominees. Notably, this perspective differs from the classic Downsian model in which a selectorate simply supports the candidate closest to their ideological position. In Bawn et al.'s perspective, differences in candidates' commitments or abilities to secure a group's policy goals may cause the candidate closest to the selectorate's ideological positions to lose the primary. These findings highlight the vital role of primaries and suggest an explanation as to why general election candidates do not adopt more ideologically moderate positions.

PART II: THE MEDIA AND THE INFORMATIONAL ENVIRONMENT

The second set of chapters considers how media developments shape voter knowledge about candidate actions and preferences. Because information collection is costly, rational individuals largely rely on others to provide this public good or turn to less costly heuristic substitutes, such as party labels, to inform their choices. The "media" – broadly construed to include forums as varied as local newspaper and televisions stations; national newspapers, broadcast, and cable television stations; and the internet and social media – are arguably the key source of free or low-cost information from which voters can move beyond party labels in making electoral choices. Historically, local newspapers have served as the critical source of information about congressional candidates, but local newspapers are disappearing or being hollowed out at an alarming rate while cable TV, the internet, and social media provide new outlets that bypass traditional media gatekeeping and where content is often devoid of traditional journalistic norms about coverage. These changes raise new questions about how political accountability functions in the current media environment as well as how accountability-related incentives have evolved with changes in the media. The three chapters in this section each approach these questions in different ways.

In Chapter 6, Brandice Canes-Wrone and Michael Kistner examine how local newspaper coverage affects the extent to which ideologically extreme candidates are punished at the polls, and whether this relationship has changed over time with the decline in local newspapers. Specifically, the authors exploit variation across districts and time in the congruence between House members' districts and local newspaper markets to estimate the effect of coverage on the relationship between candidate ideology and election outcomes. While for incumbents the impact is modest, for challengers, reduced coverage is associated with a substantial reduction in the penalty (reward) associated with ideological extremity (moderation). Additionally, the authors show that this effect increased during the period in which the internet, social media, and cable TV increased and the coverage of local newspapers declined.

Nicholas Carnes continues the focus on local newspapers in Chapter 7 by investigating how they cover members of Congress. A lack of information about candidates often makes it difficult for voters to learn important characteristics that could alter voting choices. Given this asymmetry, the pre-election employment history of candidates may fill in some of the gaps. Class background may be an important factor for voters to consider, for example, if they desire the expertise of candidates with a particular background and/or descriptive representation. Do local newspapers provide that information? Carnes examines the coverage of 25 House races with incumbent members running for reelection in 2006, selected to oversample those incumbents with working class backgrounds prior to taking office. Content analysis reveals that the occupational history of incumbents rarely receives much coverage. The backgrounds of challengers are more newsworthy, but overall coverage of this aspect remains modest. The findings suggest that coverage near election-time focuses on incumbent party, issue positions, and performance in office but not signals of class background. This lack of biographical information may prevent voters from obtaining descriptive representation that they desire.

Finally, in Chapter 8, Gregory Huber and Patrick Tucker reconsider the central role of local newspapers in congressional accountability given the decline in local print media, expansion of national newspapers and cable television, and growth of the internet. As the authors argue, these changes call into question whether classic works accurately characterize the current environment and the dynamics of electoral accountability. The chapter begins by discussing the theoretical relationship between developments in the quantity as well as nature of coverage and the ensuing incentives for candidates and officeholders. It then uses this theoretical framework to review prior work on the nature, frequency, and correlates of media coverage of congressional members and elections across different mediums. Finally, the authors propose an agenda for a unified cross-media data collection project on citizens' political information environments vis-á-vis Congress.

PART III: POLICYMAKING, INFORMATION PROVISION, AND ACCOUNTABILITY

Part III of the volume shifts from a focus on voters and the media to how these external pressures and other developments affect policymaking. A common thread across the chapters is the role of information in shaping policymakers' incentives. How do coalition leaders seek to build legislative coalitions that can survive in a world of stronger, more polarized parties, and how does voter information about policies and outcomes affect these incentives? Given that voters have strong motivations to delegate to others the task of bringing to light legislative malfeasance, what happens when those "fire alarms" are biased and voters know it? Finally, given the complexity of bureaucratic policymaking and an informational asymmetry that favors bureaucrats over legislators, how do legislators engender bureaucratic accountability when overseeing agencies?

Frances Lee begins this section in Chapter 9 by asking: What strategies do coalitions use in the contemporary, polarized Congress to build feasible legislative coalitions, and do these strategies differ from those in periods with less distinct and less homogenous parties? Carefully examining the two major legislative efforts of the 115th Congress (2017–2018), tax reform and the repeal and replacement of the Affordable Care Act (ACA), Lee finds that coalition leaders used many of the same policy and procedural techniques of previous periods. In particular, leaders deployed procedural tactics to break the clear linkage between congressional action and painful policy effects, reducing the traceability of their actions to voters. Similarly, coalition leaders substantially modified their proposals to reduce the costs imposed on the constituents of legislators whose votes they needed, allowing them to gather support even from reelection-minded members. When these efforts failed outright, as in the case of the ACA, the reasons were that the policy reforms afforded insufficient benefits beyond a party fulfilling a campaign promise while imposing traceable costs on constituents. Ultimately, she concludes that although polarization may have lowered prospects for major legislative success, coalition builders' optimal tactics and procedural techniques demonstrate more continuity than change.

In Chapter 10, Charles Cameron and Sanford Gordon consider the implications for political accountability of biases in the sources of information voters use to evaluate incumbent performance. Voters often depend on knowledgeable third parties, such as challengers and interest groups, to provide such information, which often comes in the form of "fire alarms" alerting voters to damaging facts about the performance of their elected officials. Groups and challengers are hardly disinterested parties, however – they have political motivations of their own. Cameron and Gordon show that the desire of incumbents to avoid triggering a fire alarm from such a biased observer may lead them to eschew actions that serve the interests of their constituents or to take actions against those interests. Thus, third-party fire alarm oversight of incumbents can create perverse policymaking incentives that undermine accountability. Incumbent credit-claiming can mitigate, but not eliminate, these distortions. In short, fire-alarm accountability is no substitute for knowledgeable voters.

Finally, in Chapter 11, John Patty investigates how principals in complex political relationships (e.g., legislators overseeing bureaucratic agencies, administrators overseeing civil servants) manage their own thorny informational problems. In particular, he asks how the selective incentives and diagnostic criteria employed by political principals account for the profound complexity of political organizations and policy decisions. Drawing on developments in behavioral economics, Patty introduces the concept of *bracketing* – how principals and agents group choices when contemplating actions. As the chapter shows, bracketing can affect the ways in which, for example, congressional members evaluate the consequences of bureaucratic choices, the flow of evaluative information available to members, and the incentives for agency officials to misallocate efforts. Patty also discusses how bracketing may consequently influence features of institutional design including ex ante controls, such as notice and comment procedures, and ex post monitoring, such as congressional oversight hearings.

PART IV: OUTSIDE THE PUBLIC EYE? PRIVATE INTERESTS AND POLICYMAKING

Moving away from a focus on voters as the chief political principal in accountability relationships, the contributions in this section focus on government officials' accountability to a different set of political actors: private interests. When policymaking takes place behind closed doors, either in the bureaucracy or, increasingly, within party caucuses, do private interests supplant voters as the primary outside influence on policy decisions? This question is central to the chapters that follow, each of which takes on a different aspect of the issue. For instance, when members of Congress communicate the interests of their constituents to bureaucratic agencies, how much do those communications reflect biases in the resources available to different groups? Are interest groups more or less powerful in the contemporary highly polarized Congress where committees and other policymaking parts of the institution have become weaker vis-à-vis party organizations? And how different from legislative policymaking is highly traceable and contested administrative policymaking in light of interest group knowledge of these actions and participation?

Chapter 12, by Eleanor Neff Powell, Devin Judge-Lord, and Justin Grimmer, considers how congressional oversight of the bureaucracy relates to constituency demands and financial contributions. Drawing on a novel dataset of over 6,000 communications between legislators and the Federal Energy Regulatory Commission (FERC) from 2000 to 2018, they reveal three important patterns. First, Republican legislators write more letters on behalf of producers and Democrats write more on behalf of individual constituents. This relationship, however, is contingent on majority status, with each party writing more pro-business letters while in control of their chamber. Second, energy sector campaign contributions are focused primarily, but not exclusively, on Republican candidates, with Democratic candidates receiving about a third as much as their Republican counterparts. Third, the authors describe a statistically significant relationship between pro-business communications by legislators and energy sector contributions. These findings are consistent with the argument that private interests are influential in congressional oversight of the bureaucracy.

Chapter 13 asks more generally whether the contemporary Congress can serve the general public interest or merely narrow, particularistic ones. Lee Drutman examines the effects of crucial changes in the contemporary Congress vis-à-vis earlier periods including increased efforts by incumbents to raise money through campaign donations, a growth in advocacy and lobbying by private special interests, and intense party polarization. In particular, he considers whether the recent developments invalidate earlier understandings of congressional representation and accountability. Perhaps surprisingly, he argues that much remains unchanged: special interests have always had the upper hand and at least on occasion, Congress is still able to pass significant, bipartisan legislation that represents diffuse interests. However, he also contends that the changes have strengthened the hands of organized groups and reduced legislators' willingness to rise above their preferences to pursue (bipartisan) policies that serve the interests of inattentive citizens.

Finally, in Chapter 14, Daniel Carpenter and Brian Libgober examine policymaking that originates in the bureaucracy, focusing on a case of newfound administrative authority generated by the Dodd–Frank Act. In this instance, key interest groups precisely understood the stakes and process of bureaucratic policymaking, rendering it highly traceable and arguably akin to interest group lobbying of Congress on major legislative enactments where policy choices are anticipated to be zero-sum. Specifically, they examine the debit card regulations issued by the Federal Reserve under the Dodd–Frank Act. The authors argue that the conditions encouraged more intense and effective interest group activity than is the case in typical administrative policymaking. To assess this argument, the chapter provides a detailed narrative of the rule's development, integrating quantitative evidence about the impact of the rule's evolution on stakeholder firms. Consistent with expectations, the analysis suggests that debit card regulation attracted more lobbying and of a more diverse kind than other Dodd–Frank regulations, including ones such as the Volcker Rule where the aggregate impact was far higher but with less readily traceable policy effects. These findings highlight that even in administrative policymaking, the traceability of policy outcomes to government officials' decisions will affect the ways in which private interests shape these decisions.

CONCLUSION: ASSESSING CONTEMPORARY ACCOUNTABILITY

Together, the contributions to this volume inform our understanding of the myriad ways in which accountability relationships function in the contemporary United States. In Chapter 15, we build on these individual contributions to consider the overall status of political accountability in the USA today. The preceding chapters indicate that incumbent behavior is still a factor in electoral outcomes, despite the informational problems that have resulted from a less vibrant local media. At the same time, members face greater barriers to producing collective, bipartisan legislation that serves diffuse interests. Likewise, in the policy implementation and agency oversight stages, financially advantaged interests continue to exercise disproportionate influence. As a whole, the findings point to a world in which incumbents shy away from taking observable actions or endorsing policies that explicitly counter voters' preferences but where inaction on issues supported by diffuse interests is also prominent. The concluding chapter considers these and other themes. In doing so, we identify key empirical and theoretical questions that are informed by the chapters and, furthermore, areas where the questions raised suggest a need for further inquiry.

PART I

CANDIDATE EVALUATION AND SELECTION

2

The Importance of Issue Representation in a Polarized Congress

Joshua D. Clinton, Michael W. Sances, and Mary Catherine Sullivan

Questions related to the nature of political representation are central to a voluminous literature in political science (Pitkin, 1967). Despite a plethora of work,[1] our understanding of the relationship between elected officials and their constituents remains unclear, and the scholarship is rife with disagreements. In light of increased polarization among elected officials (McCarty, Poole, and Rosenthal, 2006), the importance of partisanship as an influential social identity for politically active citizens (e.g., Green, Palmquist, and Schickler, 2002), and continuing disagreements over whether citizens are even able to possess issue-based preferences (e.g., Converse, 1964), characterizing the relative import of partisan and issue considerations in constituents' evaluations of their representatives is critical for assessing the nature of representation that can be expected.

The type of representation we can expect depends critically not only on the types of candidates that are selected in party primaries, as Bawn et al. in Chapter 5 in this volume discusses, but also on the incentives that those candidates who are elected representatives face when deciding what actions and positions to take (e.g., see Cameron and Gordon in Chapter 10 in this volume). If, for example, constituents care only about partisanship when evaluating their incumbent – perhaps because of a media environment that focuses on national politics rather than issues of local representation (e.g., Huber and Tucker in Chapter 8 in this volume) – representatives will have the most incentive to focus on their fidelity to party positions. If constituents care about specific issues, however, representatives are incentivized to take positions that reflect constituents on those issues. If constituents evaluate their elected officials using heuristics that are beyond the representative's control – perhaps based on the actions of the president (e.g., Rogers, 2019) or the consequence of natural

---

[1] See, for instance, extensive summaries in Jewell (1983) and Canes-Wrone (2015).

disasters (e.g., Achen and Bartels, 2016) – the inability of representatives to control their fate may result in them choosing to follow their personal preferences or the preferences of special interests and influential donors. Understanding the nature of representation requires understanding the reactions of constituents because those reactions presumably shape the expectations of elected officials, and this has important implications for whether representation is best conceived in dyadic (i.e., representative-constituency) or collective terms (i.e., party-constituency) (Weissberg, 1978).

The extent to which dyadic, issue-based representation occurs is a matter of some dispute. Some scholars argue that issues matter only insofar as they define a party brand that voters can use as a heuristic when voting (Cox and McCubbins, 2005). Recent work by Bonica and Cox (2018) and Tausanovitch and Warshaw (2018), for example, suggests that voters are more focused on party-based considerations and that members no longer pay electoral costs for being "out-of-step" with their district as earlier work argued (e.g., Arnold, 1990; Canes-Wrone, Brady, and Cogan, 2002; Canes-Wrone, Minozzi, and Reveley, 2011). But work by Griffin, Newman, and Nickerson (2019) shows that constituent evaluations respond to learning about representative positions, and work by Nyhan et al. (2012) highlights the electoral consequences of a single vote on a prominent issue.

To evaluate whether issue-based representation still matters, we identify the relative importance of issue-based and party based considerations on citizens' evaluations of their representatives. We begin by characterizing how partisan disagreement and issue-specific disagreement correlate with respondents' evaluations of their representative using responses to the Cooperative Congressional Election Surveys fielded between 2008 and 2017. Party misalignment has a predictably large effect on citizens' approval of their incumbent representative, but we also find evidence of varying, and also sometimes sizable, effects of being misaligned on specific issues. Because the observed disagreement occurs even though representatives are presumably choosing positions so as to maximize their reelection, and party leaders are also using tools to prevent members from having to take votes contrary to the party position (see, e.g., Lee in Chapter 9 in this volume), these effects presumably provide a lower bound on the importance of issue-based considerations for citizens' evaluations. Moreover, given that the importance of specific issues varies among individuals and among issues, we further demonstrate that aggregate measures of issue misalignment underestimate the importance of issue-based considerations.

After describing the general contours of issue-based representation, we explore the relative importance of party-based and issue-based representation using what is arguably the most prominent and consequential policy enacted in recent decades – the Affordable Care Act (ACA). Using characteristics presumably related to being a member of an attentive or inattentive public – including income, education, and political knowledge – we find varying effects of the importance of the ACA on incumbent evaluations. Contrary to expectations from the policy feedback literature, the evaluations of richer individuals are more responsive to representative positions on the ACA than poorer individuals despite the fact that poorer individuals are more likely to benefit from the policy benefits of the ACA. Moreover, the evaluations of poorer individuals are more likely to be affected by the positions taken by the party caucus of their elected representation than they are to be impacted by the positions taken by their representative.

ISSUE REPRESENTATION, PARTY REPRESENTATION, OR BOTH?

As noted above, the extent to which the actions of elected representatives reflect constituency preferences is a question of robust discussion and disagreement. Some scholars find a lack of issue representation in the aggregate (e.g., Bafumi and Herron, 2010) or on specific issues (e.g., Highton, 2019), while others find support for a strong relationship between public opinion and elite position-taking in the aggregate (e.g., Erikson, MacKuen, and Stimson, 2002) or at the individual level (e.g., Broockman, 2016; Nyhan et al., 2012). Moreover, the relative importance of issue-based and party-based considerations has arguably varied over time as increased disagreement among political elites has produced voting coalitions that are more homogeneous within party and more differentiated between parties (McCarty, Poole, and Rosenthal, 2006). Party leaders are also thought to use their position to promote agendas to unify the caucus and define an electorally valuable party brand (Cox and McCubbins, 2005) – especially since party leaders now believe they can gain (or lose) the majority in every election (Lee, 2016).[2] Claims regarding the increased incentives for representatives to focus on party considerations and issues where the party is unified coincide with claims about the increasing importance of partisanship among citizens. Partisan affiliation is increasingly considered as a social identity (e.g., Green, Palmquist, and Schickler, 2002). Alongside vibrant debates about whether citizens possess meaningful issue positions independent of party affiliation (e.g., Barber and Pope, 2019; Freeder, Lenz, and Turney, 2019), and whether citizens value ideology or identity considerations (Grossmann and Hopkins, 2016), the potential for citizens caring about issues independently of party-based considerations is uncertain.

Some of this disagreement may be due to the measures and methods being used. Despite a rise in the availability of measures and methods since the pioneering work of Miller and Stokes (1963), a consensus has yet to emerge about the meaning of available data. Concerns have been raised about the ability to equate responses on a public opinion survey to votes cast in Congress

---

[2] If coalition leaders in Congress focus on issues that are thought to unite the party caucus, it may be hard to distinguish the effects of partisan and issue-based representation precisely because the set of observed votes is chosen precisely so as to minimize the tension that members may face between their partisan and issue-based considerations.

(Hill and Huber, 2019) and also the ability to summarize constituency policy preferences by aggregating across issues (Broockman, 2016).

We explore the nature of issue-based representation following the framework Arnold provides in *The Logic of Congressional Action* (1990). An important insight about the nature of issue-based representation is the anticipatory nature of the representative's decisions. As Arnold notes, "The cautious legislator, therefore, must estimate three things: the probability that an opinion might be aroused, the shape of that opinion, and its potential for electoral consequences" (p. 68). The anticipatory nature of issue-based representation has important empirical consequences. First, it means that issue-based representation can occur even if constituents are unaware of how their representative voted on an issue. In particular, if incumbents correctly foresee the preferences of an inattentive constituency, this successful anticipation can result in a continued lack of attention and awareness by citizens because challengers have no incentive to publicize congruent positions. Second, issue-based representation is possible even if citizens lack well-defined policy preferences. So long as representatives are able to correctly anticipate what constituents would think about an issue if they were motivated and mobilized to do so, inattentive publics may never have an incentive to become attentive.

That said, there are also reasons to think that issue-based considerations may not be relevant for constituent evaluations. If, for example, citizens evaluate representatives based on their party and the state of societal conditions, what Arnold (1990, 41) terms the "party performance rule," representatives may be able to take positions on issues unrelated to the party platform without consequence. Citizens appear to engage in this type of decision-making when evaluating state legislators, as there seems to be very little correlation between electoral outcomes and the quality of issue representation (Rogers, 2019).[3]

Citizens may also vary in the issues they find relevant for evaluating their representative, and this variation is extremely relevant for how scholars study the nature of issue-based representation. In particular, evaluations using aggregated and summary measures of issue opinions are of uncertain worth because it is unclear whether aggregate measures can adequately reflect the importance of issues if their relevance varies both by issue and by respondent. The noise introduced by aggregating and analyzing possibly irrelevant issues is true for both constituents and elected officials. Another reason for potential variation is the importance of the various issues being considered to different core constituencies (Fenno, 1978). As Bawn et al. document in their exploration of primary nominations in Chapter 5 in this volume, the electoral process can create incentives whereby the general election candidates that emerge may be associated as the "champion" of particular constituents, and those ties may result in a legislator who prioritizes the views of a core

---

[3] "Blind retrospection" (Achen and Bartels, 2016) would similarly minimize representatives' incentive to represent constituency opinion.

constituency whose preferences may not be well captured in aggregate measures of constituency opinion.

To measure the relative importance of party-based and issue-based considerations for voters' evaluations of elected officials, we therefore examine the impact of individual policy positions. Notably, we recognize that while issue-based considerations may be driven by policy outcomes rather than positions, the impossibility of knowing how policy outcomes affect individual respondents necessitates focusing on issue positions. Moreover, we note that our ability to detect the existence of issue-based representation in the (equilibrium) behavior of representatives and citizens that is observable is imperfect. If representatives correctly anticipate their constituents' reactions, optimal representation may occur even when constituents are uncertain about their own policy preferences and unaware of how their representative voted on the issues they care about. Likewise, without knowing the perceptions of expectations of representatives, it is also impossible to determine whether the actions we observe are inconsistent with actions that were intended to give the citizens what they value.

In what follows, we therefore assume the observed behavior is equilibrium behavior and describe the extent to which the observed equilibrium patterns are consistent with issue-based representation. Do citizen evaluations of representatives covary in ways consistent with citizens basing their evaluations on the positions taken by individual members, or has the polarized landscape and increased partisanship produced a party-centered notion of representation in which positions taken by individual representatives have only limited effects on their electoral prospects?

RESEARCH DESIGN

We use the common content of Cooperative Congressional Election Surveys (CCES) conducted between 2008 and 2017 to identify the universe of issues for which we can match issue-specific respondent opinions to representatives' roll-call positions. To compare the relative importance of party-based and issue-based considerations, we focus our analysis on respondents who either self-identify with a party or who indicate that they lean toward a party. Among the 346,335 respondents to the pooled CCES data we examine, only 45,780 (13.2%) are "pure" independents. We examine the effects on independents separately in supplementary analyses, but excluding pure independents focuses the analysis on those who are arguably most invested in the political system and, at a minimum, most likely to vote based on party.

Our dependent variable is simply whether the respondent approves of their elected representative or not. To identify the effect of party-based considerations, we identify whether each respondent's self-identified party affiliation conflicts with the party of their incumbent representative (*Misaligned Party*$_i$). The estimated effect simply reflects how respondents' evaluations differ depending on whether the respondent is affiliated with the party of the incumbent or not.

Excellent work examines the relationship between healthcare issues and electoral support (e.g., Nyhan et al., 2012; Bussing et al., 2020), but we choose to focus on respondents' approval of their representative for two reasons. First, insofar as opinions on approval are prior to opinions about whom to vote for, it is useful to establish a relationship on a concept that is conceptually prior to vote choice and which is also entirely a function of the representatives' own statements and actions. By contrast, opinions regarding whom to vote for involve a choice between two candidates, and it can be hard to know whether a vote is due to the positions and actions of the representative or her opponent. To be clear, a focus on vote choice is important and informative for understanding the electoral consequences, but so too is understanding the relationship with approval as that is the relationship that the representative can more easily control and, as a result, be more attentive to. Second, because approval is asked every year but elections only happen every two years for those representatives who choose to run again, focusing on approval eliminates some complications that arise because of strategic retirements or unequal effects due to using votes of varying proximity to election day.

To identify the consequences of issue-based considerations, we determine whether party-leaning respondent i provides a contrary opinion on issue n to the position taken by the representative on the CCES-associated roll call (*Misaligned Issue$_{i,n}$*). Respondents who did not offer an opinion are coded as missing and not as being in alignment with the representative, and the decision to do so does not change the substantive results. While we exclude respondents without an opinion, nearly every respondent provides a response – among the 346,335 respondents to the pooled 2008–2017 CCES studies, only 29,492 (8.5%) fail to offer an opinion on one or more issue questions. The lack of nonresponse is surprising given the sparseness of the questions being asked. In the 2016 CCES, for example, respondents were shown five issues and told: "Congress considered many important bills over the past few years. For each of the following tell us whether you support or oppose the legislation in principle." The wording for some of these items included:

- **No Sanctuary for Criminals Act:** Withholds federal funds from states and localities that do not follow federal immigration laws.
- **Repeal Affordable Care Act:** Would repeal the Affordable Care Act.
- **American Health Care Act:** Would repeal the tax penalties on individuals for not maintaining health coverage, and on employers for not offering coverage. Would end subsidies to help people purchase insurance and would end funding for states that expanded Medicaid.
- **Kate's Law:** Increases criminal penalties for individuals in the country illegally who are convicted of certain crimes, deported, and then re-enter the US illegally.

As is clear from the questions being asked, respondents are not provided with much policy-relevant information, and it is unclear what, if anything, they know about the policies they are providing opinions on. Given how few respondents declined to answer the questions, it is hard to know if the responses measure constituents' issue preferences, but such concerns are thankfully not particularly troubling given the nature of our analysis. Insofar as the issue-specific questions are problematic – and the responses are likely to reflect guessing or the use of party cues – it should be more difficult for us to detect the presence of issue-based considerations. Likewise, although it is similarly unclear whether responses on a briefly worded question are comparable to the positions taken in the matched roll-call in Congress (Hill and Huber, 2019), it will also be harder to detect the presence of issue-based representation if the items reflect such different considerations.

To measure issue misalignment between a respondent and their representative, we compare CCES survey responses to the roll-call position taken by the respondent's representative that is associated with each CCES question. To be clear, we do not know whether the respondents are aware of how their representative voted (but see Ansolabehere and Jones 2010 for an examination of awareness in 2005 and 2006). As a result, our measure likely underestimates the impact of issue-based considerations by estimating the average effect among misaligned respondents regardless of whether respondents are aware of the misalignment. Insofar as unaware respondents contribute "noise" to the average effect of issue misalignment on the approval of a respondent's representative, the effects of issue misalignment among the (unknown) subset of respondents who were aware of the discrepancy are presumably even larger because their disapproval is presumably responsible for the estimated association. The fact that we cannot determine which constituents are aware and unaware of their representative taking a contrary position is troubling from the perspective of correctly identifying the effect of issue misalignment among voters, but it is less problematic from the perspective of assessing the potential consequences of the representative's choice. Representatives are presumably interested in knowing the overall effects of their position-taking regardless of whether their constituents are aware of their vote. If so, the effects we identify are the effects of interest because they reveal the overall impact of issue-based disagreement on constituent approval. Put differently, our focus is not on the conditions under which individual voters choose to become attentive or not, nor the mechanisms through which this attention is possible. Instead, we seek to characterize whether groups of voters appear to respond to policy in ways that may shift the incentives of the representative toward that group.

To estimate the relative impact of party and issue-based considerations on the approval of elected representatives, we estimate the following specification for CCES respondent i in district j in year t with issues n:

$$\Pr(\text{Support Rep})_{ijt} = \alpha_t + \beta_t * \text{Misaligned Party}_{ijt}$$

$$+ \sum_{n=1}^{N} \gamma_n * \text{Misaligned Issue}_{ijt}^n + \epsilon_{ijt}. \qquad (2.1)$$

The dependent variable in Equation 2.1 denotes whether respondent i in district j approves of their incumbent representative during year t. α_t identifies the average support for the representative among respondents belonging to the same party as the representative and whose issue opinions also match the representatives' positions. β_t captures the difference in support between same-party and out-party respondents, all else equal. γ_n reveals the effect of disagreement on approval for each of the n issues. This specification is estimated separately for each year – allowing the estimated parameters to vary over time because of time-varying differences (e.g., actions taken by the president, external events) – and standard errors are clustered by congressional district.

If representation is driven primarily by party-based considerations, variation in respondent evaluations of their incumbent representative should be driven by the party-correlated considerations captured by the average effect β. If issue-based considerations matter for constituent evaluations, we should observe statistically distinguishable and substantively sizable effects for at least some of the n issues (γ_n).

To focus on the relationship in more detail, we also probe the relationship deeper using opinions on the ACA over time – that is, we restrict the issues we analyze using Equation 2.1 to the ACA-related issues. In so doing, we examine whether the effects of issue-based considerations vary by respondent traits that are likely correlated with policy awareness and beneficiary status to determine the extent to which such traits may condition the importance of issue-based considerations.

To account for the possibility that the effects of issue disagreement are multiplicative rather than additive – that is, the effect of disagreement on three issues exceeds the separate additive effects of each issue – we also summarize the effect of increasing issue misalignment on a citizen's approval using the percentage of issues that the respondent disagrees with the representative (*Pct Misaligned Issues*). Doing so risks the previously discussed problems associated with issue aggregation, but it is still useful to examine whether such effects occur. As Arnold (1990, 61) notes, "The question facing a legislator is seldom whether a specific roll-call vote might cost him the next election … yet small effects can quickly add up to become large effects when summed over the many issues that Congress considers each year."

An aggregate measure is also required to estimate the average effect of issue misalignment over time because of the fact that different issues are asked about in the different CCES surveys. To estimate the average relationship over the entire time period, we estimate:

$$\Pr(\text{Support Rep})_{ijt} = \alpha + \beta * \text{Misaligned Party}_{ijt} + \kappa * \text{Pct Misaligned Issues}_i$$
$$+ \gamma * \left(\text{Misaligned Party}_i \times \text{Pct Misaligned Issues}_i\right)$$
$$+ \delta_t + \epsilon_{ijt}. \tag{2.2}$$

Variation in the number and importance of issues being asked by each CCES will obviously impact the meaning of the effect being attributed to κ – the average marginal effect of a one-unit increase in issue disagreement (i.e., the effect of going from 0% agreement to 100% agreement). We employ year fixed effects δ_t to partially control for this possibility. The interaction effect γ identifies whether the importance of issue misalignment varies depending on party misalignment – conditional on party alignment, are same-party respondents more or less responsive to issue disagreement than out-party respondents?

To address claims that the nature of representation varies between the Democratic and Republican parties because of supposed differences in what members of each party care about, we estimate the relationship separately for Democrat and Republican respondents. Grossmann and Hopkins (2016) articulate this perspective when they argue: "The Republican Party is best viewed as the agent of an ideological movement whose members are united by a common devotion to the principle of limited government ... In contrast, the Democratic Party is properly understood as a coalition of social groups whose interests are served by various forms of government activity. Most Democrats are committed less to the abstract cause of liberalism than to specific policies designed to benefit particular groups." This perspective has consequences for the use of aggregate measures – suggesting that the meaning of an aggregate measure is less informative for Democrats than Republicans, but the consequences for the issue-specific measures is less clear. Even if the meaning of issue misalignment may vary, the first-order question is whether the possibility that citizens care about different considerations produces variation in how citizens react to issue misalignment when it occurs.

Estimating Equations 2.1 and 2.2 reveals the extent to which respondent evaluations depend on party-based and issue-based considerations, but three important caveats are worth noting. First, our assessment of the relative importance of issue-based and party-based representation obviously depends on the issues that the CCES has chosen to ask about. Insofar as the issues being asked about are unrepresentative of citizens' concerns, then it is difficult to characterize the importance of issue-based considerations. Moreover, if the CCES-chosen issues were chosen because those were issues on which the parties devoted considerable attention and resources, it may be hard to distinguish issue-based and party-based considerations given the mobilization of party-based considerations and resources among elites and the mass public.

Second, the effects of issue disagreement being identified are conditional on the existence of issue disagreement. Insofar as representatives are strategic in their position-taking, the disagreement we observe is a consequence of the fact that the alternative position would presumably be even worse. The disagreement we observe in the data is a consequence of intentional choices being made by the representative in terms of which respondents they choose to represent, and issue misalignment is certainly not "randomly assigned." Thankfully it is possible to sign the bias in the estimated effects – insofar as representatives are maximizing their expected electoral returns by the positions they choose to take, the effects of disagreement that we observe must *underestimate* the true expected effect of issue disagreement.

Underestimating the effects of issue-based representation has asymmetric effects on our ability to interpret the nature of representation. Because we underestimate the effects of issue-based representation, finding evidence of issue-based consequences among those citizens that the representative chooses to ignore suggests that the actual effects of issue-based considerations are even higher. In contrast, null effects are hard to interpret. A null effect may reflect the possibility that the representative chose to take the position of the citizens who care enough about the issue to punish the representative on the issue or it may reflect the possibility that issues are irrelevant for respondent evaluations. It is an unavoidable complication that it is hard to make inferences about the importance of issues for citizens who agree with the representative using only the reactions of respondents who disagree with the representative.

THE CONSEQUENCES OF ISSUE MISALIGNMENT

Figure 2.1 begins by summarizing the extent to which respondents' CCES responses differ from the positions taken by their representative. Most respondents offer an opinion on the issue questions, and most opinions appear to be consistent with the positions taken by their representative (Ahler and Broockman, 2018). The fact that so many respondents disagree with their representative's position is a consequence of the partisan divides on the issues being asked about – insofar as opinions correlate with partisanship, we would expect to find fairly large levels of disagreement if citizens are not perfectly sorted into districts according to their partisanship. Even if so, it is difficult to know whether the survey responses reflect strongly held policy preferences (Zaller, 1992). In 2008, for example, respondents were given a "not sure" option that resulted in a much higher level of non-opinions.[4]

Figure 2.2 summarizes the results of separately estimating Equation 2.1 for each CCES using a binary indicator for approval (1) vs. disapproval (0).[5] Ten separate regressions are presented in Figure 2.2, and Tables 2.A.1 and 2.A.2 of the Appendix report the associated point estimates from each of the ten specifications.

The results are immediately revealing regarding the extent to which issue-based considerations impact the approval of representatives. The effect of party misalignment is unsurprisingly large, and the average effect of party misalignment exceeds −0.4 across the ten specifications summarized in Figure 2.2. A magnitude of this effect is sufficient to produce a predicted evaluation of near indifference (i.e., a predicted approval of around 0.5) given the estimated intercepts among party-misaligned respondents. Party misalignment is alone sufficient to cause respondents' approval to shift from complete approval to mere indifference.

[4] In some years the CCES did not ask all respondents each issue question, resulting in higher missing values.
[5] A five-point scale provides substantively similar results.

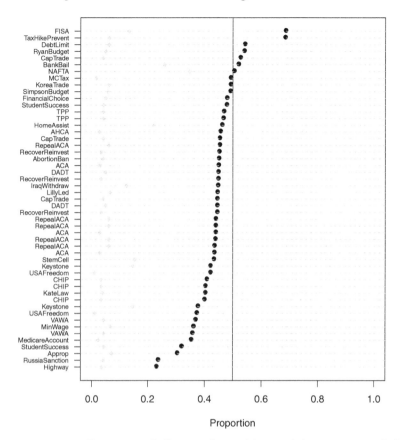

FIGURE 2.1 Percentage of all respondents with an opinion contrary to their representative on each issue (black) or without an opinion (gray), by issue

Pure independents included. The 2008 CCES included a "Not Sure" option that is coded as no opinion.

More surprising, given the previously noted measurement issues, is the fact that issue-based considerations also appear to matter for respondent evaluations of their representative. Among the fifty issues that were asked about, thirty-eight had effects that were statistically distinguishable from zero at conventional levels. Moreover, the effects of issue disagreement is sometimes considerable – respondents who disagreed with the positions taken by their representative on the ACA, for example, were between 0.1 and 0.2 less likely to approve of their representative on the 0–1 scale relative to a respondent who agreed with the representative's position. While the effect of partisan misalignment is obviously considerable, the results clearly suggest that issue misalignment also matters for respondents' evaluations of their incumbent.

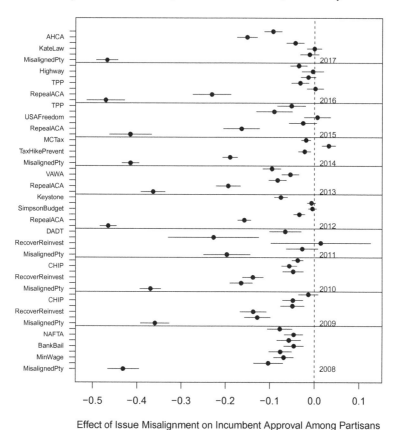

Effect of Issue Misalignment on Incumbent Approval Among Partisans

FIGURE 2.2 Issue (γ_n) and party (κ) misalignment effects, by year

95% confidence intervals clustered by congressional district. Estimates computed separately for each CCES year.

We can also consider the aggregate effect of issue misalignment by calculating the percentage of issues on which the respondent disagrees with the representative. Pooling across time to estimate Equation 2.2 reveals the extent to which partisans differ in terms of the impact of issue misalignment. Figure 2.3 plots the resulting coefficient estimates. (Table 2.A.3 in the Appendix reports the full set of coefficient estimates.)

Several conclusions emerge from Figure 2.3. First, although party misalignment continues to have the largest negative effect on a respondent's evaluation of their incumbent representative, issue misalignment also matters. In fact, the marginal effect of increased issue misalignment among respondents in alignment with the party of their incumbent is nearly identical between partisans (−0.197 for Republicans and −0.219 for Democrats). Because the measure of issue-misalignment measures the fraction of votes with

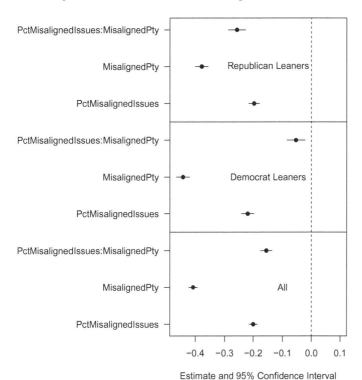

FIGURE 2.3 Effect of overall misalignment on approval of representative among partisan leaners (2008–2012)

Effects being plotted are β, κ and γ from Equation 2.2 estimated using all partisan leaners (bottom), Democrat leaners (middle), and Republican leaners (top). 95% confidence intervals clustered by congressional district. Full results reported in Table 2.A.3.

disagreement, the effect of issue disagreement is somewhat muted relative to the individual issue effects noted in Figure 2.2 – the difference in approval between a respondent who completely agrees and completely disagrees with the positions taken by the representative is 0.2 on the 0–1 approval scale (i.e., about the same effect as disagreeing with the representative on just the ACA when estimating the effect of individual issues). The fact that issue misalignment matters controlling for partisan misalignment suggests that issue-representation is indeed a relevant consideration for representatives. Issues appear to still matter for citizens' evaluations.

The interaction effect between party misalignment and issue misalignment also reveals that there are effects of issue misalignment above and beyond the effects attributable to party-misalignment and misaligned voters are actually slightly more responsive to changes in the level of overall issue-misalignment. Among Republicans in a district with a Democrat incumbent, a 100% change in the percentage of misaligned issues results in a −0.45 effect on approval.

Among Democrats in a district with a Republican incumbent, the same 100% shift would produce a −0.27 effect. As a result, insofar as there are differences in the importance of issues by partisanship as some claim, it is a difference that only seems to emerge among partisans living in misaligned districts. Moreover, the party-related difference in the importance of issue-based considerations is relatively modest.

ISSUE MISALIGNMENT AND THE ACA

Having provided evidence that issue-based representation appears to be of continued relevance, based on how citizens' evaluations of their incumbent representative vary depending on issue-misalignment, we now focus on the importance of issues using the Affordable Care Act. This is an appropriate focus not only because of how consequential the law has been both in terms of policy and political effects, but also because congressional action appears to satisfy the conditions Arnold (1990) and others identify as enabling issue-based representation. Not only did elected officials choose to publicize their actions on the Affordable Care Act (as well as those of their opponents), but a host of explanations were also offered to citizens about the consequences of the actions being taken. Moreover, given the importance of the ACA for political debates and elections, it was nearly impossible for legislators to avoid taking an explicit position on the ACA and its closely associated policies (e.g., Medicaid expansion).

While the ACA offers an important opportunity to evaluate the consequences of issues for citizens' evaluations because of its impact and importance, the fact that it was so partisan may make it harder than usual to detect the importance of issue representation due to observational equivalence. Both parties actively positioned themselves on the issue and coalition leaders tried to keep their party caucuses united – especially when they were in control of the agenda (see Lee, Chapter 9 in this volume). Combined with how the media covered the ACA and the prevalence of motivated reasoning among voters (see, for example, Egan and Prior, Chapter 4 in this volume) it may be hard to imagine that there was any role for issue voting above and beyond the impact of partisanship. Precisely because of how prominent and important the issue was – and how much the parties chose to use the issue to define themselves – the ACA arguably presents a hard case for finding evidence of issue-based representation given the importance of party representation on this issue as well. To disentangle the potential effects of issues and partisanship, we leverage the reactions of issue-misaligned voters in each party combined with the variation in position-taking among representatives belonging to the same party.

More specifically, we build upon the analyses of the prior section to focus on the effect of issue misalignment on citizens' evaluations of their representatives among those with misaligned preferences. Because politics at the national level is extremely partisan and exhibits very little variation, within-party variation

TABLE 2.1 *Votes on Affordable Care Act and repeal efforts*

Bill	Bill Title	Data	Vote
HR 1628	American Health Care Act	5/4/2017	(217-213)
HR 3762	2017 Budget Resolution	1/6/2016	(240-81)
HR 596	To Repeal the Patient Protection and Affordable Care Act	2/3/2015	(239-186)
HR 45	To Repeal the Patient Protection and Affordable Care Act	5/16/2013	(245-189)
HR 2	Repealing the Job-Killing Health Care Law Act	1/19/2011	(245-189)
HR 3590	Patient Protection and Affordable Care Act	3/21/2010	(219-212)

in opinions regarding the ACA largely occurs at the citizen-level and our investigation describes how citizens react when their representatives take a contrary position in Congress. Put differently, we ask: which respondents are likely to have misaligned preferences from their representative (who is likely following the party line given the partisanship of the ACA), and what are the consequences of that misalignment on the respondent's evaluation of their representative?

Table 2.1 describes the set of roll-call votes that the CCES asked respondents about. These are the opinions that we analyze in the analysis that follows using three questions on the vote related to the ACA (in the 2009, 2010, and 2011 CCES), five CCES questions on votes to repeal the ACA (in 2012, 2013, 2014, 2015, and 2016), and one question on the vote to pass the Republican alternative (the AHCA) in 2017.

Support for the ACA

To begin, we start by examining whether the effect of issue-misalignment on the ACA varies depending on the income level of constituents. Because the benefits of the ACA were intended to primarily help the less fortunate obtain health insurance through subsidies and the expansion of Medicaid, it is of interest whether these policy benefits mobilized and incentivized the less fortunate to monitor the actions taken by their representatives on this issue. Moreover, as Patashnik, Tucker, and Gerber (Chapter 3 in this volume) demonstrate, citizens' reactions to legislative credit claiming on polarized policies depend on the frame of reference they possess when trying to evaluate the magnitude of policy effects they perceive and experience.

The potential meaning of differences based on income are somewhat hard to interpret. Some have argued that roll calls are more likely to reflect the opinions of wealthier individuals (Bartels, 2008; Gilens, 2012; Gilens and Page, 2014). If so, wealthier individuals may be more likely to react negatively to issue misalignment. On the other hand, given that wealthier individuals are more likely to participate, follow politics and contribute to campaigns (Schlozman, Verba, and Brady, 2012), representatives may be more likely to account for those views when deciding which position to take and the effect of issue-disagreement among those individuals that the representative chooses to disobey may be harder to extrapolate from. Even so, separately estimating the relationship for citizens making more than \$120,000 and less than \$30,000 helps examine whether the effects of the wealthy differ from those with below-average incomes. Moreover, given that the policy benefits of the ACA were targeted towards those making less than the 147% of the federal poverty limit, the investigation also reveals whether issue disagreement had larger effects among the set of respondents who were more likely to benefit from the effects of the ACA.

Because issue misalignment may reflect three different circumstances – (1) being misaligned with both their representative and party (measured by a majority of representatives in the party) on the issue, (2) being misaligned with their representative but not their party (i.e., their representative voted against a majority of their party caucus), and (3) being misaligned with their party caucus but not their representative (i.e., their representative took a position that was consistent with the respondent contrary to the party caucus) – we decompose misalignment on the ACA into groups depending on whether the citizen is: misaligned with the representative's position and party (*Both*), misaligned with the representative's position but not with a majority of the representative's party caucus (*JustRep*), and misaligned with a majority of the representative's party caucus but not the representative's position (*JustParty*). Because of the partisan nature of the roll-call votes on the ACA, the number of citizens who are in districts where the representative's position varied from that of their party caucus is small: roughly 45,000 citizens were in districts where they agreed with the position taken by both their representative and the representative's party caucus, 35,000 citizens were in districts where they disagreed with both their representative and their representative's party (*Both*), 2,900 respondents disagreed with just their representative (*JustRep*), and 3,500 respondents only disagreed with the party caucus of their representative (*JustParty*). The first two possibilities should presumably decrease citizens' support for the representative, but respondents may choose to reward representatives taking a position that matches the respondent's opinion rather than the opinion of the party caucus.

To recover these effects we use votes supporting the ACA to estimate:[6]

$$\Pr(\text{Support Rep})_{ij} = \beta * \text{Misaligned Party}_{ij} + \gamma_1 \text{Both}_{ij}$$

$$+ \gamma_2 \text{JustRep}_{ij} + \gamma_3 \text{JustParty}_{ij} + \epsilon_{ij}, \qquad (2.3)$$

where *Both* indicates whether the respondent has a different opinion than the representative and a majority of the representative's party caucus in Congress,

[6] Replicating the results for votes repealing the ACA reveals qualitatively identical relationships.

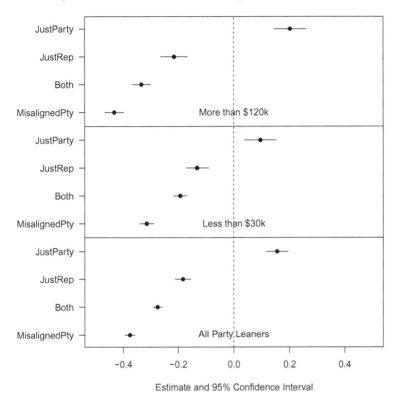

FIGURE 2.4 Effect of misalignment on ACA votes by income

Effects are estimated using all partisan leaners (bottom), partisan leaners with incomes less than $30,000 a year (middle), and partisan leaners making more than $120,000 a year (top). 95% confidence intervals clustered by congressional district.

JustRep indicates that the respondent disagrees with the representative but agrees with a majority of the representatives' fellow congresspeople, and *JustParty* indicates that the respondent agrees with the representative but disagrees with a majority of the representatives' fellow congresspeople. Figure 2.4 plots the estimates for estimating Equation 2.3 for various subsets of the data based on the respondent's income. (The effect of party mis-alignment (β) is only needed for the pooled results in the bottom graph of Figure 2.4 because the results graphed in the top two graphs condition on party alignment when estimating the relationship.)

The results plotted in Figure 2.4 are consistent with issue-based accountability in that an individual's approval of the representative is associated with the representative's alignment on the ACA. At the same time, however, those with the most to gain from the ACA, lower income voters, were not more likely to punish representatives for misalignment than those with higher incomes.

Despite the publicity and attention given to the ACA by the media and elites, the fact that we do not see much evidence that poorer citizens were especially incentivized to engage in issue-based evaluations involving the ACA suggests that the conditions required for strong policy feedback effects may be unlikely to obtain. This is troubling from the perspective of policy feedback, as it seems hard to imagine an issue for which position-based evaluations would be more accessible and available than the ACA.

To be clear, the effects we are characterizing are the overall average effects and they do not account for the many ways that income may affect the conditions under which issue-based accountability is possible or not (e.g., differences in education, attention to politics, access to media coverage, and campaign effects), some of which are discussed elsewhere in this volume (e.g., see the chapters of Canes-Wrone and Kistner, Chapter 6; Egan and Prior, Chapter 4; Huber and Tucker, Chapter 8; and Patashnik, Tucker, and Gerber, Chapter 3). Our results are silent as to the mechanisms by which issue-based accountability may occur and whether some voters are more attentive (and why). Probing for potential differences is clearly important for understanding why some lower-income voters may be more attentive than others, but this is a slightly different focus than our investigation. We are primarily interested in whether the ACA appeared to shift the incentives for representatives by creating an "attentive public" of lower-income voters whose evaluations were affected by positions taken on the ACA. What we show is that even if there were some voters who became more attentive, there does not seem to have been a widespread shift that is consistent with creating an incentive for representatives to account for the policy views of those lower-income voters who were most likely to benefit (relative to higher-income voters). Why this effect did not occur, and the conditions required to produce an effect are important questions that are worthy and deserving of continued study, but our point is simply that the policy effects of the ACA were insufficient for creating the conditions required for issue-based accountability among the population of voters who were most likely to be affected by the policy effects.

Figure 2.5 allows the effects of issue misalignment to vary by partisan misalignment for votes related to the ACA (black) and repeals of the ACA (gray) to examine whether party-related differences emerge by estimating Equation 2.3 separately for Democrat-leaning and Republican-leaning respondents.

The bottom graph summarizes the effect of issue misalignment regardless of the respondent's partisanship. The effects are sizable – resulting in a change in predicted probability of −0.37 in terms of whether the citizen approves of the representative for votes associated with the ACA (and slightly larger for votes on repealing the ACA) – but issue-based considerations also matter. There is also a considerable effect associated with being misaligned with the position of the representative and the representative's party caucus (*Both*). Having a different opinion on the ACA from the position taken by the incumbent representative and a majority of the representative's party caucus

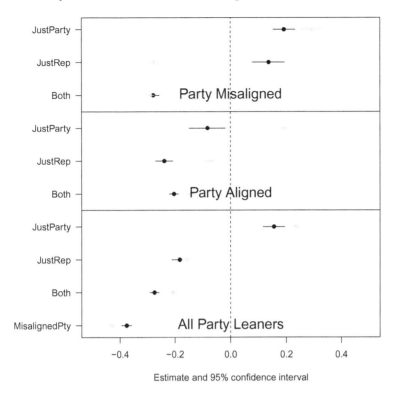

FIGURE 2.5 Effect of misalignment on ACA votes and votes to repeal the ACA by Partisanship

Effects are estimated using all partisan leaners (bottom), partisan aligned citizens (middle), and partisan misaligned citizens (top). Effects for the ACA are plotted in black and the effects for Repealing the ACA are plotted in gray. 95% confidence intervals clustered by congressional district.

decreases the probability of the respondent approving of the representative by roughly −0.29. This sizable effect is notable as it is only slightly smaller than the effect size associated with partisan misalignment – suggesting that issue-based considerations can have a sizable effect on citizens' evaluations of their representative.

The effects for *JustParty* and *JustRep* are also broadly consistent with issue-based representation. Instances in which the citizen is misaligned with the representative but not the party caucus of the representative (*JustRep*) is also associated with increased disapproval of the representative. Circumstances where the representative's position matches the respondent's opinion but not a majority of the representative's party (*JustParty*), however, does not result in less approval. This strongly suggests that not only are respondents able to distinguish between the position of the representative and the position of the representative's party caucus, but that they also reward the representative who follows their opinions with higher evaluations. The estimated effects on efforts to repeal the ACA (gray) are qualitatively similar.

Estimating the effects separately for citizens who are party-aligned (middle graph) and party-misaligned (top graph) with their representative reveals broadly similar effects, although there are some differences depending on whether the votes are related to the ACA or repealing the ACA. However, given the extremely partisan nature of elite voting, relatively few representatives (and therefore respondents) are associated with the *JustParty* and *JustRep* conditions.

Among party-aligned respondents (middle graph), respondents were less likely to approve of their representative if they disagreed with the position taken by the representative and a majority of the representatives' party in Congress (*Both*). However, if respondents agree with the representative's position and disagree with the position of the representative's party caucus (*JustParty*) they are more likely to approve of the representative on votes related to repealing the ACA. (For ACA votes the relationship is indistinguishable from zero.) There are relatively few cases where the representative took a position contrary to their party caucus and public opinion (*JustRep*) related to the ACA, but respondents in these districts were more likely to evaluate the representative negatively in response. In general, the pattern is consistent with issue-based representation and the ability of respondents to hold their representative responsible for issue disagreement involving the ACA when evaluating the representative's job performance.

The relationship among party misaligned voters (top graph) reveals a similar pattern. Party misaligned voters unsurprisingly punish representatives with lower evaluations when they disagree with the position taken by the representative and their party (*Both*). However, respondents are more likely to approve of the representative when the representative votes in accordance with citizens' opinions but a majority of the representative's party caucus does not (*JustParty*). Although it is an admittedly odd situation, when the representative votes contrary to the citizens' opinions on votes involving the ACA (*JustRep*) and the misaligned respondent agrees with a majority of the representatives' partisans in Congress, the representative's approval surprisingly increases, suggesting that citizens are perhaps incorrectly rewarding the representative for the actions taken by the representative's party (or else that the odd circumstances in which this pattern occurs makes it hard to generalize the effects). Suggestive of the fact that this relationship may be driven by a few districts, respondents (correctly) punish the representative with lower evaluations when the representative votes contrary to both their own party caucus and respondents' opinions on votes involving the attempts to repeal the ACA.

Overall, the results that emerge when analyzing the effects of issue-disagreement involving the ACA and its attempted repeal suggest that issue-based considerations matter for citizens' evaluations even for a highly partisan issue with lasting policy and political effects. While individuals who were most likely to benefit from the policy do not appear to be more likely to engage in issue-based evaluations relative to those with considerable means, respondents' evaluations are sensitive to whether the respondent agrees with the representative's position on the ACA.

CONCLUSION

An extensive literature employs a myriad of measures and approaches to characterize whether and how elected officials' positions reflect constituency opinion (e.g., Clinton, 2006; Bafumi and Herron, 2010). We focus on a slightly different question: to what extent does constituency approval of their representative vary by issue and party misalignment? Are voters less likely to support a representative who takes a recorded roll call that is at odds with the opinion they express? How does the effect of issue misalignment compare to the effects of partisan misalignment on citizens' evaluations of their representative and is there evidence that the importance of issues varies among issues and constituents?

Huber and Tucker (Chapter 8, this volume) describe how coverage of individual representatives and their actions has decreased. Given the relative lack of coverage as well as the information required to connect outcomes to policy actions highlighted by Patashnik, Tucker and Gerber (Chapter 3, this volume), it is unclear whether one should expect meaningful issue-specific accountability to exist – especially for highly partisan issues in which coalition leaders may be minimizing the need for partisans to defect from the party coalition and distinguish themselves relative to the party "brand" (see, for example, Lee in Chapter 9, this volume). In particular, because re-election seeking representatives will consider the consequences of their actions and minimize their electoral risks, it is critical to examine how representatives are likely to perceive the electoral risks of being misaligned with their constituents. If constituents evaluate the representative based purely on partisan considerations, for example, then there is little incentive for the representative to follow constituency opinion so long as they are able to maintain their party brand. In contrast, if voters can distinguish between issue-based and party-based representation then this can affect how representatives vote in the hopes of maintaining (or gaining) the approval of those respondents.

Complications emerge because of the difficulty of estimating the counterfactual when we only observe presumably equilibrium behavior. As Arnold (1990) highlights, the actions we observe are a consequence of representatives' anticipation of the response of inattentive publics when deciding how to vote. As a result, the issue-disagreement we can detect is the disagreement that the representative chooses to allow. The assumed optimality of representative behavior means that the effects of issue-disagreement are almost certainly a lower bound – insofar as issue-based representation matters for the set of respondents whose opinions are being consciously ignored, it follows that the effects of issue-based representation likely matter even more for the respondents whose views the representative is choosing to represent. It is difficult to identify precisely how much issue-based considerations matter for respondents given that the logic of congressional action suggests that we are almost certainly underestimating the impact by looking at the effects among those respondents that the representative chooses to ignore.

Even so, we are able to evaluate how issue-disagreement impacts citizens' evaluations of representatives *conditional on representatives choosing to disagree with those citizens* on specific issues by comparing the effects of issue-misalignment and party-misalignment on respondents' approval of their representative. We conduct this analysis on a range of issues and then provide a detailed examination of votes related to the Affordable Care Act. As well, we analyze an aggregate measure of issue-alignment.

Our investigation reveals that issue-based considerations matter for respondent evaluations of their elected representative even despite the shortcomings of the issue-specific opinion measures. We show that respondents rely on more than just partisanship when evaluating their representative. Moreover, there is considerable variation in the importance of issue-based considerations across the issues that respondents were asked about on the CCES. As a result, investigations relying on aggregate measures of issue-misalignment (or summary measures of ideology) almost certainly underestimate the importance of issue-based considerations for voters (and therefore also for representatives). Whereas misalignment on votes related to the ACA is associated with a 0.2 decrease in representative approval, the effect of going from 0% to 100% misaligned on the entire set of CCES issues is also only 0.2. Ignoring the between-individual and between-issue differences appears to dramatically understate the importance of issues – a point forcefully made by Arnold (1990).

That said, several caveats are important to note. First, our analysis focuses only on the set of issues and votes that were sufficiently publicized such that scholars were inclined to ask the public about their opinion on the specific votes. The importance of issues on votes that were less publicized is unclear. Second, our analysis is looking at the difference in approval between constituents that the representative is consciously choosing to agree and disagree with. Representative positions are not randomly chosen and the fact that representatives are seeking to minimize the electoral backlash suggests that our estimated effects surely underestimate the importance of policy positions among voters. Still, the fact that we detect a relationship between issue misalignment and policy views above and beyond the impact of partisan identity in a contemporary congress where partisan coalitions are actively cultivated and maintained by coalition leaders, and where the media environment is focused on national rather than local actions and actors, suggests that the relationship between a representative and her district still matters.

2.A APPENDIX: ADDITIONAL RESULTS

TABLE 2.A.I *Full results: CCES 2008–CCES 2012*

	Dependent variable:				
	RepApprove				
	(2008)	(2009)	(2010)	(2011)	(2012)
MisalignedPty	−0.430***	−0.360***	−0.370***	−0.197***	−0.464***
	(0.013)	(0.012)	(0.006)	(0.018)	(0.006)
MA_IraqWithdraw	−0.103***				
	(0.013)				
MA_MinWage	−0.069***				
	(0.011)				
MA_StemCell	−0.077***				
	(0.011)				
MA_BankBail	−0.047***				
	(0.010)				
MA_HomeAssist	−0.058***				
	(0.011)				
MA_NAFTA	−0.047***				
	(0.010)				
MA_FISA	−0.078***				
	(0.011)				
MA_ACA		−0.128***	−0.165***	−0.227***	
		(0.011)	(0.006)	(0.027)	
MA_RecoverReinvest		−0.137***	−0.138***	0.015	
		(0.011)	(0.006)	(0.029)	
MA_CapTrade		−0.050***	−0.048***		
		(0.010)	(0.005)		
MA_CHIP		−0.049***	−0.057***	−0.028*	
		(0.009)	(0.004)	(0.015)	
MA_LillyLed		−0.014			
		(0.010)			
MA_DADT			−0.038***	−0.065***	
			(0.005)	(0.015)	
MA_RepealACA					−0.157***
					(0.006)
MA_RyanBudget					−0.034***
					(0.005)
MA_SimpsonBudget					−0.005
					(0.005)
MA_KoreaTrade					−0.007
					(0.005)
MA_Keystone					−0.075***
					(0.005)
Constant	0.982***	0.922***	0.911***	0.786***	0.917***
	(0.010)	(0.007)	(0.003)	(0.010)	(0.005)
Observations	6,356	9,050	38,239	4,846	29,136
R^2	0.386	0.363	0.470	0.170	0.374
Adjusted R^2	0.385	0.363	0.470	0.169	0.373
Residual Std. Error	0.385	0.389	0.361	0.452	0.386
F Statistic	499.049***	858.936***	5,654.945***	198.621***	2,894.776***

Note: *$p < 0.1$; **$p < 0.05$; ***$p < 0.01$.

TABLE 2.A.2 *Full results: CCES 2013–CCES 2017*

	Dependent variable:				
	RepApprove				
	(2013)	(2014)	(2015)	(2016)	(2017)
MisalignedPty	-0.364^{***}	-0.414^{***}	-0.415^{***}	-0.470^{***}	-0.467^{***}
	(0.011)	(0.007)	(0.019)	(0.013)	(0.010)
MA_RepealACA	-0.194^{***}	-0.190^{***}	-0.164^{***}	-0.231^{***}	
	(0.011)	(0.007)	(0.018)	(0.013)	
MA_AbortionBan	-0.083^{***}				
	(0.009)				
MA_VAWA	-0.054^{***}		-0.026^{*}		
	(0.009)		(0.015)		
MA_StudentSuccess	-0.095^{***}			-0.036^{***}	
	(0.009)			(0.009)	
MA_TaxHikePrevent		-0.022^{***}			
		(0.005)			
MA_DebtLimit		0.033^{***}			
		(0.005)			
MA_MCTax		-0.019^{***}			
		(0.005)			
MA_USAFreedom			0.007	0.002	
			(0.015)	(0.009)	
MA_Keystone			-0.090^{***}		
			(0.018)		
MA_TPP			-0.052^{***}	-0.033^{***}	
			(0.015)	(0.008)	
MA_MedicareAccount				-0.014	
				(0.009)	
MA_Highway				-0.004	
				(0.011)	
MA_RussiaSanction					-0.011
					(0.010)
MA_KateLaw					-0.0004
					(0.008)
MA_Approp					-0.044^{***}
					(0.009)
MA_AHCA					-0.151^{***}
					(0.010)
MA_FinancialChoice					-0.093^{***}
					(0.009)
Constant	0.908^{***}	0.868^{***}	0.903^{***}	0.899^{***}	0.918^{***}
	(0.007)	(0.006)	(0.015)	(0.009)	(0.007)
Observations	9,407	26,326	3,009	7,814	9,794
R^2	0.366	0.332	0.342	0.442	0.384
Adjusted R^2	0.365	0.331	0.341	0.441	0.384
Residual Std. Error	0.394	0.398	0.397	0.370	0.384
F Statistic	$1,083.661^{***}$	$2,611.173^{***}$	260.184^{***}	882.327^{***}	$1,016.448^{***}$

Note: $^{*}p < 0.1$; $^{**}p < 0.05$; $^{***}p < 0.01$.

TABLE 2.A.3 *Full results: aggregate misalignment by party*

	Dependent variable:		
		RepApprove	
	(Pooled)	(Dem)	(Rep)
Pct. Misaligned Issues	-0.200^{***}	-0.219^{***}	-0.197^{***}
	(0.005)	(0.007)	(0.007)
Misaligned Party	-0.408^{***}	-0.443^{***}	-0.378^{***}
	(0.004)	(0.006)	(0.006)
2009	-0.003	-0.002	-0.006
	(0.005)	(0.007)	(0.007)
2010	-0.044^{***}	-0.040^{***}	-0.046^{***}
	(0.004)	(0.005)	(0.005)
2011	-0.025^{***}	-0.108^{***}	0.075^{***}
	(0.004)	(0.006)	(0.006)
2012	-0.013^{***}	-0.020^{***}	-0.011^{**}
	(0.004)	(0.005)	(0.005)
2013	-0.044^{***}	-0.039^{***}	-0.053^{***}
	(0.005)	(0.007)	(0.007)
2014	0.005	0.009^{*}	0.002
	(0.004)	(0.005)	(0.005)
2015	-0.029^{***}	-0.021^{***}	-0.043^{***}
	(0.005)	(0.007)	(0.008)
2016	-0.058^{***}	-0.052^{***}	-0.064^{***}
	(0.004)	(0.005)	(0.005)
2017	-0.047^{***}	-0.053^{***}	-0.031^{***}
	(0.005)	(0.007)	(0.007)
Misaligned Interaction	-0.156^{***}	-0.053^{***}	-0.257^{***}
	(0.007)	(0.010)	(0.010)
Constant	0.915^{***}	0.918^{***}	0.919^{***}
	(0.003)	(0.005)	(0.005)
Observations	226,078	121,819	104,259
R^2	0.337	0.320	0.366
Adjusted R^2	0.337	0.320	0.365
Residual Std. Error	0.400	0.406	0.389
F Statistic	$9,593.945^{***}$	$4,785.444^{***}$	$5,005.356^{***}$

Note: $^{*}p < 0.1$; $^{**}p < 0.05$; $^{***}p < 0.01$.

TABLE 2.A.4 *Full results: aggregate misalignment by party and income*

| | Dependent variable: | | | | | |
| | | | RepApprove | | | |
	Low Income	Low Income Dem	Low Income Rep	High Income	High Income Dem	High Income Rep
Pct. Misaligned Issues	−0.147***	−0.252***	−0.143***	−0.168***	−0.295***	−0.236***
	(0.011)	(0.011)	(0.015)	(0.018)	(0.017)	(0.015)
Misaligned Party	−0.319***	−0.515***	−0.349***	−0.281***	−0.541***	−0.506***
	(0.009)	(0.009)	(0.012)	(0.015)	(0.015)	(0.012)
2009	0.010	−0.010	0.036**	−0.028	−0.009	−0.010
	(0.012)	(0.010)	(0.016)	(0.019)	(0.016)	(0.014)
2010	−0.050***	−0.040***	−0.019	−0.091***	−0.044***	−0.036***
	(0.010)	(0.007)	(0.013)	(0.015)	(0.011)	(0.009)
2011	−0.056***	−0.021**	−0.091***	0.013	−0.123***	0.075***
	(0.011)	(0.010)	(0.014)	(0.017)	(0.015)	(0.014)
2012	−0.017*	−0.014*	0.004	−0.053***	−0.024**	−0.011
	(0.010)	(0.008)	(0.012)	(0.015)	(0.012)	(0.010)
2013	−0.046***	−0.060***	−0.029*	−0.068***	−0.066***	−0.056***
	(0.012)	(0.011)	(0.015)	(0.019)	(0.017)	(0.015)
2014	−0.004	0.006	0.017	−0.032**	0.017	−0.003
	(0.010)	(0.008)	(0.012)	(0.015)	(0.012)	(0.011)
2015	−0.024*	−0.040***	0.007	−0.075***	−0.025	−0.059***
	(0.013)	(0.012)	(0.017)	(0.021)	(0.019)	(0.017)
2016	−0.057***	−0.056***	−0.027**	−0.098***	−0.054***	−0.057***
	(0.010)	(0.008)	(0.013)	(0.015)	(0.012)	(0.011)
2017	−0.052***	−0.043***	−0.031**	−0.072***	−0.033**	−0.052***
	(0.012)	(0.011)	(0.015)	(0.019)	(0.015)	(0.015)
Misaligned Interaction	−0.161***	−0.095***	−0.088***	−0.283***	0.013	−0.158***
	(0.017)	(0.017)	(0.022)	(0.027)	(0.026)	(0.022)
Constant	0.867***	0.953***	0.842***	0.910***	0.959***	0.954***
	(0.009)	(0.007)	(0.012)	(0.014)	(0.011)	(0.009)
Observations	42,643	36,854	27,065	15,578	16,992	19,862
R^2	0.219	0.467	0.211	0.243	0.446	0.490
Adjusted R^2	0.219	0.467	0.210	0.242	0.446	0.490
Residual Std. Error	0.433	0.360	0.437	0.424	0.367	0.352
F Statistic	995.089***	2,687.075***	602.085***	415.820***	1,139.677***	1,590.502***

Note: $^*p < 0.1$; $^{**}p < 0.05$; $^{***}p < 0.01$.

TABLE 2.A.5 *Roll-call votes*

Bill	Bill Title	Data	Vote
HR 3364	Countering America's Adversaries Through Sanctions Act	7/25/2017	(419-3)
HR 3003	No Sanctuary for Criminals Act	6/26/2017	(228-195)
HR 3004	Kate's Law	6/26/2017	(257-167)
HR 10	Financial Choice Act	6/8/2017	(233-186)
HR 1628	American Health Care Act	5/4/2017	(217-213)
HR 244	Consolidated Appropriations Act of 2017	5/3/2017	(409-1)
HR 2353	Highway and Transportation Funding Act	5/19/2016	(287-35)
HR 2	Medicare Accountability and Cost	3/26/2016	(392-37)
HR 3762	2017 Budget Resolution	1/6/2016	(240-81)
S 1	Keystone Pipeline	12/11/2015	(270-152)
S 1177	Every Student Succeeds Act	12/2/2015	(359-64)
HR 1314	Bipartisan Budget Act of 2015	10/28/2015	(266-167)
HR 2048	USA Freedom Act	5/13/2015	(338-88)
HR 596	To Repeal the Patient Protection and Affordable Care Act	2/3/2015	(239-186)
HR 5771	Tax Hike Prevention Act	12/3/2014	(378-46)
HR 5	Student Success Act	7/19/2013	(218-213)
HR 1797	Pain-Capable Unborn Child Protection Act	6/18/2013	(228-196)
HR 45	To Repeal the Patient Protection and Affordable Care Act	5/16/2013	(245-189)
S 47	Violence Against Women Act	2/28/2013	(286-138)
HR 325	Debt Ceiling	1/23/2013	(285-144)
HR 112	Simpson-Bowels Budget Agreement	2/28/12	(382-38)
HR 3630	Middle Class Tax Cut Act	12/13/2011	(234-193)
HR 3080	US Korea Free Trade Agreement	10/12/2011	(278-151)
HR 1938	Keystone Pipeline	7/28/2011	(293-126)
HR 34	Establishing the Budget for the United States Government for Fiscal Year 2012	4/15/2011	(235-193)
HR 2	Repealing the Job-Killing Health Care Law Act	1/19/2011	(245-189)
HR 3590	Patient Protection and Affordable Care Act	3/21/2010	(219-212)
HR 4173	Dodd-Frank Wall Street Reform and Consumer Protection Act	12/11/2009	(223-199)
HR 2965	Don't Ask, Don't Tell Repeal Act	7/8/2009	(230-194)
HR 2454	American Clean Energy and Security Act	6/26/2009	(218-212)
HR 1	American Recovery and Reinvestment Act	1/28/2009	(244-188)
S 181	Lilly Ledbetter Fair Pay Act	1/27/2009	(247-171)
HR 2	State's Children Health Insurance Program	1/14/2009	(289-139)
HR 1424	Troubled Asset Relief Program	10/3/2008	(262-171)
HR 3221	Housing and Economic Recovery Act	7/23/2008	(239-169)
HR 976	State's Children Health Insurance Program	9/25/2007	(262-156)
S 1927	Protect America Act	8/4/2007	(292-129)
HR 2956	Responsible Redeployment from Iraq Act	7/12/2007	(169-247)
S 5	Stem Cell Research Enhancement Act	6/7/2007	(243-171)
HR 2	Fair Minimum Wage Act	1/10/2007	(306-114)

3

Can Citizens Assess Policies Based on Programs' Costs and Benefits? The Role of Yardsticks and Contextual Information in Democratic Accountability

Eric M. Patashnik, Patrick Tucker, and Alan S. Gerber

One of the most important questions for political representation is whether citizens can deliver sensible rewards and punishments to politicians for their performance. One way that citizens could control their elected officials is by carrying out a cost-benefit analysis on each government decision and punishing politicians for producing policies in which the present discounted value of the costs exceed the present discounted value of the benefits. Of course, this model of political behavior may be unrealistic because citizens do not notice most policy costs and benefits. But if citizens can *perceive* costs and benefits, then the idea that citizens perform cost-benefit analyses to deliver rewards and punishments is plausible. This may occur, for example, when the magnitude of costs and benefits is large (especially in relative terms), when the distribution of costs and benefits is more narrowly concentered across groups and communities, and when costs and benefits occur in the near-term rather than in the distant future (Arnold, 1990).

A second way that citizens could hold politicians accountable is by evaluating how well they perform compared to other public officials. This is the basic idea of "yardstick competition" in labor economics, in which the rewards that an actor (such as a firm or worker) receives is based on their performance relative to a benchmark or to the performance of similar actors (Shleifer, 1985; Besley and Case, 1995). Both Arnold's theory of citizen responses to the incidence of perceived costs and benefits and yardstick competition suggest that contextual information plays an important role in enabling citizens to make reasonable assessments of government performance.

In this chapter, we conduct several survey experiments to examine how citizens assess policies and their advocates based on programs' costs and benefits. The first section extends experiments from Grimmer, Messing, and Westwood (2012, 2015) to examine how citizens respond to information about both the absolute and relative size of project grants delivered by legislators. The next section investigates voter responses to programmatic costs and benefits through three experiments. The first examines subjects' response to a gas tax targeted for road improvements. The second examines responses to a social safety net program, funded by the revenue from a broad tax. The third experiment uses an abstract vignette to see how subjects respond to policies when they are not provided contextual information to make their assessments easier. We experimentally manipulate the incidence of policy costs and benefits in each of the three studies.

Overall, our experimental results provide evidence that citizens can make reasonable assessments when they are given a yardstick or another simple reference point that enables them to readily grasp the magnitude of policy effects. However, public responses are mediated by well-known biases identified in the social psychology and behavioral economics literature. Consistent with research on negativity bias (Boydstun, Ledgerwood, and Sparks, 2019) and loss aversion (e.g., Kahneman and Tversky, 1979), we find that citizens punish incumbents who underperform relative to other lawmakers. We also find some evidence that citizens negatively evaluate policies that concentrate benefits and harms among a small slice of the population. The concluding section of the chapter discusses broader implications.

ASSESSING POLITICIANS' GRANT DELIVERY PERFORMANCE

Legislative credit-claiming for the delivery of grants and other particularistic benefits is a common setting in which voters evaluate policy attributes. Credit claiming involves "generating the belief among constituents or other relevant actors that a legislator is personally responsible for delivering a valued good" (Arnold, 2017, 21; see also Mayhew, 1974). Such public beliefs may not be grounded in reality. Grimmer, Westwood, and Messing (2015) demonstrate that legislators are rewarded for convincing voters that they are responsible for district spending, even when their role in securing expenditures is limited or absent. Legislators can often get away with this deception because voters lack the time and incentives to track what legislators actually do. Using a series of survey experiments, Grimmer, Westwood, and Messing also show that "constituents are largely unresponsive to the amount of money that legislators claim credit for securing" (2015, 3). That is, citizens reward legislators for boasting about delivering small projects about as much as for boasting about delivering large ones. The implication is that the magnitude of policy benefits has little influence on how citizens reward legislators for credit claiming activities, raising concerns for democratic accountability.

One possible explanation for the insensitivity of constituent evaluations to the amount of spending is innumeracy, meaning the inability to make sense of numbers and process mathematical operations (Peters, 2012; Paulos, 1988), which would severely limit the mass electorate's capacity to form independent judgments of officeholder performance. Another possible explanation is that people's use of numbers depends on the context in which they are communicated. If numbers are presented in a way that renders them abstract or difficult to understand, people will ignore them in their decision-making. However, people will attend to numbers and use them in reasonable ways, when given a benchmark to put quantitative information into a graspable context.

Credit Claiming and Yardstick Competition

Gerber, Patashnik, and Tucker (2022) previously extended the work of Grimmer, Westwood, and Messing (2015). In the original Grimmer, Westwood, and Messing (2015) study, respondents read a newspaper story about a representative claiming credit for a grant from a justice assistance program to hire and train new police officers. The experiment randomized the size of the grant (between \$10,000 and \$10 million) for which legislators claimed credit. (The legislator's party was also randomized). After seeing the newspaper article, respondents were asked to assess the legislator on a feeling thermometer (0 to 100 scale). While lawmakers experience a small bump in approval for securing bigger grants, the marginal return in constituent approval for securing larger amounts vanishes around \$1 million.

Gerber, Patashnik, and Tucker (2022) replicated this finding using the identical experimental vignette and manipulation of the grant size, demonstrating the absence of a statistically significant relationship between the dollar amount of the credit-claim and the survey respondents' evaluation of the legislator on a 0 to 100 favorability scale. In the replication, the authors once again found little evidence that citizens are responsive to the absolute dollar amount of the grant announced by a legislator. Rather, the effect on approval of the grant's dollar amount is statistically indistinguishable from zero.

To test the influence of an informational intervention, Gerber, Patashnik, and Tucker (2022) extended this experiment in a separate sample with 816 Amazon Mechanical Turk workers. In the extension, subjects read the same news story as in the replication experiment, except for an addendum at its conclusion stating how large the grant is relative to the average grant awarded by the agency that year, ranging from "50 percent smaller than the average grant" to "200 percent larger than the average grant." Subjects then evaluated the legislator on a 0 to 100 scale. The authors found that providing contextual information about the relative grant size significantly influences ($p < 0.01$) respondents' evaluations of the legislator. This effect was asymmetric. Respondents who were informed that the grant was less than average significantly lowered their evaluations of the legislator relative to respondents who were informed that the grant was average size, but respondents who were informed that the grant was larger than the average grant increased their evaluations of the legislator by only modest amounts.

It remains unclear, however, whether the nature of the grant in this experiment – a law enforcement grant – might have some effect. While certain

TABLE 3.1 *Measuring constituent responsiveness to the dollar claimed: Extension of Grimmer, Westwood, and Messing (2015) with climate change education scenario*

Headline:	Representative : (D/R —| State) Secures |amount to Increase Funding for Climate Change Education
Body:	Representative : (D/R —| State) secured |amount today to develop curricula that focus on the causes and consequences of human-caused climate change. The money, which is from the North American Association for Environmental Education (NAAEE), will provide local public school educators with resources to develop courses addressing climate change, as well as strategies for integrating climate change fighting applications in existing courses. When asked for comment, Representative said "It is critical that we ensure young people are aware of the current environmental crisis and that they are equipped to confront the climate change problems of the future. I am pleased to announce |amount for our local students." *The NAAEE assists public school districts across the country. The |amount grant secured by Representative is |context the average award distributed by the NAAEE this year.*
Treatments:	**Money:** |amount **Party:** [D/R] **Grant Context:** |context

The table presents the extension to Grimmer, Westwood, and Messing (2015) using a climate change education scenario. The text in italics presents the portion of the extension in which grant context is included.

police activities have become controversial in recent years, most citizens still believe governments should fund public goods such as a well-trained police force. Other policy areas associated with credit-claiming may generate less consensual responses among the electorate, with clear divisions along partisan lines. For example, Republicans may welcome grants to build a border wall, while Democrats may resist such projects.

For this reason, we conducted an experiment in which we used the same research design as in the original Grimmer, Westwood, and Messing (2015) study while changing the nature of the grant. We used a vignette about a legislator obtaining a grant to develop curricula for public schools to educate students about the causes and consequences of human-caused climate change. Table 3.1 displays the language for this extension. In addition, we performed an experiment in which we experimentally manipulated information provided to subjects about the relative size of the grant. The italicized text in Table 3.1 provides language for the relevant vignette.

We regressed the subject's evaluation of the legislator on the size of the grant, as well as an indicator for matching party identification using ordinary least squares. We operationalized the grant amount as the total of the grant in millions of dollars (values range from 0.01 to 10). Possible values for the context of the grant range from 50% less than average to 200% greater than average. We set the context variable for a grant of "average" size as equal to 1. Thus, 50% less than average corresponds to a grant context value of 0.5 and 200% greater than average corresponds to a grant context value of 3. The partisan identification match variable is coded as 1 when the respondent and the legislator have the same party identification, −1 when the respondent is a Democrat [Republican] and the legislator is a Republican [Democrat] and coded as 0 when the respondent is an independent. We repeated this exercise two more times, keeping the absolute dollar size of the grant the same but varying the information provided about the relative size of the grant. Subjects then provided their evaluation of the legislator on the 0 to 100 thermometer scale after each round. Thus, we include dummy variables indicating if the observed value was the second or third round (the first round serves as the baseline). In these regressions, we cluster the standard errors by respondent.

Results

The results of these regressions can be found in Table 3.2. The first column displays the results for the baseline experiment in which contextual information about the relative size of the climate change education grant was not provided. In this extension, we find no significant effect of the size of the dollar amount of the grant on the respondent's evaluation of the legislator (effect = −0.358, SE = 0.303). In fact, the direction of the effect is negative, again suggesting that citizens do not give greater rewards to legislators for claiming credit for larger projects. The second and third columns provide the results for the extension in which subjects received information about relative grant size. As the second column shows, the dollar amount of the grant has no significant relationship to the evaluation, yet the relative size of the grant is significantly and positively related to the evaluation. The results suggest that a subject who is informed that the legislator secured a grant that is 200% greater than average will rate the grant 17.66 points higher than a respondent who is informed that the legislator secured a grant that is 50% less than average. Column 3 explores the asymmetry of this effect. The results show that if a subject learns that a grant is smaller than average, support declines by 11.13 points relative to learning the grant is average (the baseline category). Being informed that the grant is larger than average increases the evaluation only by 2.83 points relative to learning the grant is average size.

We find that the climate change education issue is indeed polarized. Figure 3.1 displays the predicted level of favorability of the legislator when the absolute size of the grant is held at its mean, partisanship of the respondent is held fixed, and the relative size of the grant varies on the x-axis (corresponding to Column 3 of Table 3.2.). Republicans and Democrats respond quite differently from one another to the grant at all three categorical levels. For

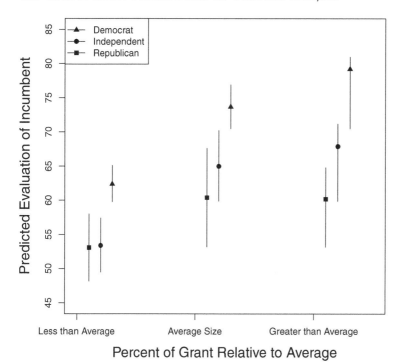

FIGURE 3.1 Predicted evaluation by respondent party ID and grant context

Figure 3.1 displays the predicted level of favorability, averaging over the grant amount and varying the context of the grant, while holding the party identification of the respondent constant. The y-axis displays the predicted level of legislator favorability and the x-axis presents the relative size of the grant, restricted to three categories based on their relation to an average grant, as in Column 3 in Table 3.2. Triangles represent the predicted mean favorability for Democratic subjects, circles represent the predicted mean favorability for Independent subjects, and squares represent the predicted mean favorability for Republican subjects. Lines represent the 95% confidence intervals.

example, when the grant is less than average size, Democrats rate the incumbent more positively than Republicans by roughly 9 points. Interestingly, we also find that the slope across the categories is much more positive for the Democratic respondents than for Republicans. For grants that are greater than average, the gap between Democrats and Republicans is predicted to be 19 points. Democrats respond much more enthusiastically to relatively larger grants, while Republicans, and to a lesser extent Independents, do not significantly increase their ratings from the predicted evaluation of an average sized grant for grants of greater than average size.

To investigate whether conservatives are more responsive to information about the relative size of grants than liberals, we reexamined the data from Gerber, Patashnik, and Tucker (2022) and estimated regressions similar to

TABLE 3.2 *Relative, not absolute, size influences subjects' evaluations: climate change education vignette*

	No context	Context Provided	
Grant Amount (in Millions)	−0.358	0.436	0.457
	(0.303)	(0.276)	(0.273)
Context of Grant		7.065***	
		(0.745)	
Less than Average Context			−11.128***
			(1.553)
Greater than Average Context			2.825**
			(1.404)
Partisan Identification Match	0.853	1.471	1.391
	(1.059)	(0.961)	(0.954)
Second Round		−4.302***	−4.256***
		(0.711)	(0.694)
Third Round		−4.740***	−5.078***
		(0.718)	(0.715)
Constant	73.251***	57.517***	69.114***
	(1.742)	(1.882)	(2.044)
Clusters		798	798
Observations	761	2,394	2,394
R^2	0.026	0.035	0.066

Standard errors in parentheses.
*$p < 0.1$; **$p < 0.05$; ***$p < 0.01$.
Dependent Variable = Legislator Rating on 0 to 100 thermometer scale. Context of Grant variable is the size of the grant relative to the average grant awarded. The values range from 0.5 (i.e. "50% less than average") to 3 (i.e. "200% greater than average"). Column 1 presents the findings from our replication of Grimmer, Westwood, and Messing (2015), while columns 2 and 3 present the results for the extension. In the extension each respondent was shown three scenarios, the second and third of which kept the partisanship of the legislator and Grant Amount in dollars the same as the first, but they were presented with new random draws for the Context of the Grant. Thus, we have three possible observations for each respondent in the extension sample. We cluster the standard errors in these models by the respondent.

those in column 2 of Table 3.2, but we subdivided the respondents by their self-identified ideology. Figure 3.2 shows that conservatives were much more responsive to the relative size of the police training grant than were liberals. The estimated effect of the contextual information is almost 8.0 for both conservatives and extreme conservatives, while the effect among liberal respondents is estimated to be just 1.4. This finding suggests that if conservatives learned that a grant is 100% larger than average, they would increase their evaluation of the legislator by about 16 points on the thermometer scale, while liberals would increase the rating by only 3 points.

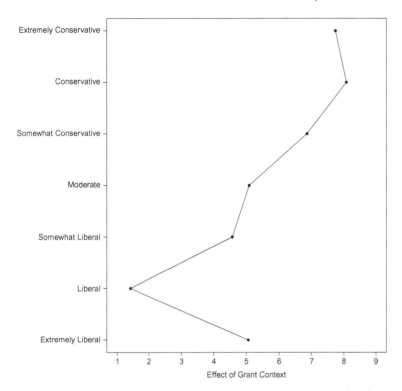

FIGURE 3.2 Conservatives are More Responsive to Contextual Information about Relative Grant Size than Liberals

Figure 3.2 presents the effect of the grant context variable for the police assistance program (Gerber, Patashnik, and Tucker, 2022). We estimated regressions for each category of survey respondents' self-identified ideology on a traditional 7-point scale. The y-axis presents the 7 ideological categories, and the x-axis presents the estimated effect of the grant context on legislator favorability for the given level of ideology. The figure demonstrates that the effect of grant context on the evaluation of the legislator is much stronger for conservatives than it is for liberals.

Discussion

Why might conservatives be more responsive to contextual information about a lawmaker's performance in delivering grants than liberals? Our analysis is necessarily speculative, but two possible reasons come to mind. First, liberals might be more likely to believe that government spending on projects is intrinsically desirable, and that a lawmaker who generates even relatively small projects has accomplished something of value. On a related note, Grimmer, Westwood, and Messing (2015) show in a survey experiment that strong liberals reject nonpartisan criticism of grant projects as being wasteful and contributing to budget deficits, whereas more conservative subjects have a negative response to this budget criticism, lowering their ratings of legislators when they learn of the fiscal consequences of the spending (see also Ellis and Stimson, 2012). Second – and more speculatively still – conservatives might be more likely to adopt an individualistic prism for evaluating a legislator's relative success in generating grants, assuming that the representative's performance is primarily a function of his or her skill or effort, whereas liberals might be more inclined to attribute relatively good or poor performance to luck or other circumstances beyond any single lawmaker's control. These questions require further analysis to resolve.

Taken together, these findings suggest that innumeracy does not prevent voters from delivering sensible rewards and punishments to legislators for their credit-claiming performance, even in the context of a polarized issue. The results are largely congruent with the logic of "yardstick competition" in which actors are rewarded based on their performance relative to one another (Shleifer, 1985; Besley and Case, 1995). The results underscore that citizens can make reasonable assessments about government performance if they are given information that helps them to put the magnitude of policy effects into context. In *The Logic of Congressional Action*, Arnold claimed that "[t]he relative magnitude of a specific cost or benefit appears to be more important than its absolute magnitude" in determining whether a citizen would notice it and acquire an intense preference on the matter (1990, 28). Arnold supported this claim through a detailed analysis of taxation and other cases of domestic policymaking. Our survey experiment provides additional evidence for this insight.

CREDIT-CLAIMING AND MESSAGE FREQUENCY

In related work, Grimmer, Messing, and Westwood (2012) test whether the number of messages a legislator disseminates about their credit-claiming activities improves their reputation. Similar to our extension regarding the benchmarking of information, the intensity of political communication regarding performance may have greater influence on citizen evaluations than the actual amount of money a legislator is able to secure. Research and observational evidence have long suggested that strategic legislators value the opportunity to claim credit for small grants (Arnold, 1979; Ferejohn, 1974), but the responsiveness of constituents to message frequency remains an empirical question. Grimmer, Messing, and Westwood (2012) divide an online sample into four treatment groups. The first group was assigned to receive a single news story through email that highlighted a grant secured by a member of Congress for $15,000 (single email message, small award). The second received a single email that highlighted a grant of $1,500,000 (single email message, large award). The third received one news story for five consecutive days regarding small grants (between $15,000 and $85,000, totaling $176,000) the

TABLE 3.3 *Treatment conditions for survey experiment extension on message frequency*

Five Messages; Large $ Award, Higher than Average	Single Message; Large $ Award, Higher than Average	Five Messages; Small $ Award, Higher than Average	Single Message; Small $ Award, Higher than Average
Five Messages; Large $ Award, Smaller than Average	Single Message; Large $ Award, Smaller than Average	Five Messages; Small $ Award, Smaller than Average	Single Message; Small $ Award, Smaller than Average

legislator secured (five email messages, small awards), while the final group received five emailed news stories for five consecutive days that mentioned large grants (between $1,500,000 and $8,500,000, totaling $17.6 million) that the legislator secured (five email messages, large awards). Following treatment exposure, each subject was asked to evaluate the legislator on a feeling thermometer as well as to indicate their perception of the legislator's effectiveness at delivering federal money to the district. The authors found that "increasing the number of messages cultivates more support than increasing the amount claimed" (Grimmer, Messing, and Westwood, 2012, 713). Subjects rated the legislator who brought home $176,000, about whom they heard five stories, more favorably than the legislator who secured $1.5 million, about whom they heard one story. That is, while the amount of money claimed in the messages did not significantly increase the subjects' evaluations of the legislator, increasing the number of messages substantially improves support.

We extend this research in a similar fashion to our first experiment described above. Using an online sample provided by Lucid, we first perform a pseudo-replication. Rather than send emails to our experiment subjects, we display one or five stories regarding legislator secured grants within an online survey. Following the display of the stories, respondents answer the same questions as in the Grimmer, Messing, and Westwood study (2012). For consistency, we use the same stories and the same dollar values. We include an additional treatment variable, contextual information about the relative size of the grant(s), to create a 2 × 2 × 2 design. In each of these additional eight conditions, we randomly assign respondents to be told that the legislator delivered either a large or small award, receive one or five messages, and to be informed that the grant(s) mentioned in the email was either larger or smaller (in percentage terms) than the average grant awarded by the relevant agency that year. Table 3.3 displays the eight treatment conditions.

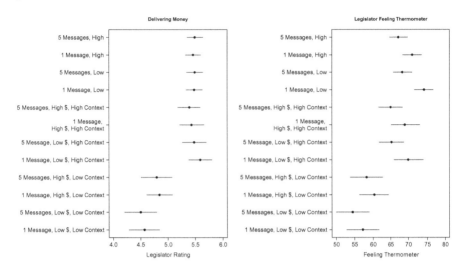

FIGURE 3.3 Subjects are responsive to information that a legislator's grants are smaller than average funded

The left panel of Figure 3.3 presents subjects' mean legislator rating for the vignette's politician to deliver money to their district. The right panel displays the subject's mean feeling thermometer rating of the vignette's politician. The rows represent the 12 experimental treatment assignments. Each row displays the number of messages the subject received, if they received a high or low dollar value message, and if they were informed whether the grant was less than average or greater than average. The first four rows represent scenarios in which panelists did not receive grant context information, while the final 8 rows represent those scenarios in which subjects received contextual information.

Results

Figure 3.3 displays the mean survey respondents' ratings of the legislator. The left panel of the figure presents the mean score for the legislator's perceived effectiveness at delivering money to the district, while the right panel presents the mean score of the legislator on a feeling thermometer in which 100 represents extremely favorable. The points represent the mean for each condition as denoted by the y-axis labels, while the bars represent the 95% confidence intervals of the mean estimate. The means and relevant standard errors are available in Tables 3.4 and 3.5 for the effectiveness rating and feeling thermometer scale.

The highest four points in both the left and right panels represent the estimates from our replication of the original study in which no contextual information about the grant size relative to the average district was provided. As in Grimmer, Messing, and Westwood (2012), there is no significant difference between the large and small award conditions when the number of messages is the same on either ratings of effectiveness or the feeling thermometer. That is, for a given number of messages, increasing the absolute amount of dollars secured does not significantly improve the lawmaker's reputation.

While Grimmer, Messing, and Westwood (2012) found that increasing the number of messages boosts support, we find little evidence that reading five stories is associated with higher levels of approval. With respect to perceptions of the legislator's effectiveness at delivering money to the district, the legislator ratings are essentially unchanged across vignettes. With respect to the feeling thermometer rating, we find higher levels of legislator approval with fewer messages. That is, respondents had more positive opinions of those legislators about whom they only read one story rather than five. Although this result is unexpected, it bears repeating that the messages in Grimmer, Messing, and Westwood (2012) were sent over the course of five days through email and our messages were conveyed in rapid succession during a fifteen-minute survey experiment. While we replicate Grimmer, Messing, and Westwood's core empirical finding that citizens are insensitive to the absolute magnitude of grant size, the differences between our two studies may explain why we did not find that an effect for the number of stories. Some research suggests that survey experiments lack the capacity to test the influence of certain manipulations, such as political phenomena that repeat over longer periods of time (see Gaines, Kuklinski, and Quirk, 2007). Furthermore, the Grimmer, Messing, and Westwood (2012) design of emails over five days may represent a different form of intensity in communication strategy than five rapid messages in an online survey. Whereas the former may signal consistent legislative performance to subjects, the five vignettes may simply irritate respondents wishing to complete the survey.

When we consider the contextual information conditions in which subjects are told that grants are of larger than average size (the next four points in each panel), we find interesting and somewhat surprising results. This condition's effect on rating the legislator's effectiveness at delivering funds to the district is again essentially unchanged. Legislator ratings remain steady around 5.5 on the 7-point scale. Although we find similar differences that do not reach statistical significance for the feeling thermometer, each condition produces a slightly lower rating on the 100-point scale. This result is surprising in that it suggests providing contextual information about a legislator securing a larger than average grant generates little to no boost in support compared to the conditions in which such contextual information is absent.

While this result might suggest that these lawmakers possess no incentive to work hard at delivering grants, the results of the final four conditions of the experiment suggest that subjects are indeed responsive to contextual information about comparatively poor legislative performance. These conditions inform subjects that a particular legislator delivered grants that were smaller than the average funded by the agency that year. We find that this information causes subjects to give substantively and statistically lower ratings to the legislator on both the effectiveness and feeling thermometer scales.

TABLE 3.4 *Means and standard errors across conditions: delivering money*

	Low Grant Value	High Grant Value
1 message	High Context: 5.60 (0.11)	High Context: 5.43 (0.11)
	No Context: 5.48 (0.07)	No Context: 5.47 (0.08)
	Low Context: 4.57 (0.14)	Low Context: 4.84 (0.12)
5 messages	High Context: 5.48 (0.11)	High Context: 5.39 (0.10)
	No Context: 5.49 (0.07)	No Context: 5.49 (0.07)
	Low Context: 4.50 (0.15)	Low Context: 4.79 (0.14)

TABLE 3.5 *Means and standard errors across conditions: feeling thermometer*

	Low Grant Value	High Grant Value
1 message	High Context: 69.95 (2.02)	High Context: 69.06 (1.99)
	No Context: 74.13 (1.29)	No Context: 71.02 (1.28)
	Low Context: 57.22 (2.21)	Low Context: 60.33 (2.03)
5 messages	High Context: 64.99 (1.76)	High Context: 65.23 (1.81)
	No Context: 68.38 (1.31)	No Context: 67.25 (1.30)
	Low Context: 54.44 (2.27)	Low Context: 58.25 (2.25)

For example, consider a legislator who secures five grants for large amounts. In our experimental replication, we find this legislator would have an average rating of 67.25 on the thermometer scale. Informing constituents that the five grants were higher than the average given out by the agency leaves the rating essentially unchanged (the rating falls to 64.99, a difference not statistically distinguishable from zero). However, when subjects are informed that the grant delivered by the legislator is in fact much smaller than average, the rating declines significantly to an average rating of 58.25. If we consider the subjects in the replication experiment (who did not receive contextual information) as a control group, the average treatment effect of the negative contextual information is approximately a 9-point decrease in approval on the thermometer scale when the subject receives five messages about high dollar awards. On the effectiveness scale, the average treatment effect is a 0.7 decrease on a 7-point scale. In summary, our results again point to an asymmetric effect. Citizens are more inclined to punish legislators for securing smaller than average grants than they are to reward legislators for securing larger than average grants.

Pooling over all conditions, the mean thermometer rating of the policy is 66.51 with a standard deviation of 24.51. When we pool over all conditions in the baseline set of conditions (i.e. those conditions in which no context is given), the mean level on the policy scale is 70.10. Pooling over the four contextual conditions in which subjects are informed that grants are of below average size, the mean is roughly 57.52. That is, the differences in means between the two pooled groups is about one-half of a standard deviation of the outcome variable for the entire population.

Discussion

The observed asymmetry in responsiveness to information that a legislator has delivered a smaller than average grant is broadly consistent with the concept of loss aversion in cognitive psychology (Kahneman and Tversky, 1984). Expressed preferences are often influenced by a reference point for value (Tversky and Kahneman, 1991). In this instance, that reference point appears to be the average level of performance. When taken in tandem with our previous findings, citizens appear to be particularly sensitive to negative information. This result is consistent with political science research showing that negatively valenced frames "stick in the mind" more than positively valanced frames (Boydstun, Ledgerwood, and Sparks, 2019; Soroka, 2014). For example, in a recent paper, Butler et al. (2019) show that when constituents are informed that their representative is a "highly effective" lawmaker, they are 10 to 20 percentage points more likely to approve of the representative's job performance, but when they learn that the representative is "highly ineffective," they are about 25 percentage points less likely to approve of the job they are doing.

CITIZENS' POLICY PREFERENCES AND THE INCIDENCE
OF COSTS AND BENEFITS

In the previous section we investigated how voters evaluated the performance of politicians in delivering grants to the district. Such assessments are critical to democratic accountability, increasing the probability that relatively low-performing officeholders will face a heightened risk of being defeated at the polls. In this section, we examine citizens' assessment of the design and effects of public policies themselves. Arnold (1990) suggests that lawmakers' policy decisions are constrained partly by their anticipation of how citizens will react to them, and that this anticipation can ensure a measure of democratic responsiveness under certain conditions, even though ordinary citizens typically engage in a lower degree of mobilization than organized interest groups. In particular, Arnold argues that citizens' policy preferences "relate directly to two attributes of policies: the incidence of costs and benefits and the nature of the causal chain that links a policy instrument with policy effects" (13). We focus on the former policy attribute. The incidence of costs and benefits refers to (1) "who would profit and who would pay under a proposed policy" and (2) "how much the beneficiaries would reap and the contributors would suffer" (25). How sensitive are citizens to costs and benefits, and how does information about their distribution affect public support for policies and evaluations of legislators?[1]

Ideally, this topic would be explored in a real-world setting through natural experiments that leverage changes in the resource flows of actual programs. As a decidedly second-best research design, we perform three online survey experiments through Lucid that allowed us to control variation in incidence of costs and benefits. Each experiment presented respondents with a policy that would have winners, who would benefit, and losers, who would be harmed. (See Appendix for summaries of the vignettes.)

We designed three vignettes to explore whether citizens' responsiveness to the distribution of costs and benefits is mediated by the nature of the policy. In the first vignette, we presented respondents with an abstract policy that lacked content; we simply informed subjects that a policy was being considered in which a certain percentage of the population would benefit and another would be harmed. This vignette provides a benchmark for measuring citizen responsiveness to costs and benefits that is not colored by issue preferences over a given policy domain. The other two vignettes are intended to capture different types of policies that citizens should find relatively straightforward and familiar. The first policy focuses on a gas tax that funds road improvements. Using Wilson's (1980) well-known typology, this is a majoritarian program

---

[1] Arnold makes clear that the test of his precepts about how policy attributes affect public preferences is whether legislators use them in their decision-making, not whether the precepts exactly mirror the real-world dynamics of public opinion formation (1990, 36). Nonetheless, we believe that survey experiments offer a useful tool for examining how citizens respond to information about costs and benefits.

with diffuse benefits and diffuse costs; many Americans have experience paying gas taxes themselves, and most Americans drive. We randomized the tax to vary between a 1 cent and $1.72 increase per gallon. The benefits of the gas tax project would be fewer minutes spent in traffic as a result of road improvements financed by the tax hike. The next vignette (an example of what Wilson would call a clientele program) involved a social safety net program targeted at the poor, with spending funded out of general taxes. We chose this design because we were interested in how citizens would respond to a redistributive program with concentrated benefits and diffuse costs. Policies such as gas taxes and social safety net spending should be relatively graspable to the average citizen.

Within each cost and benefit experiment, we randomly assigned the share of the people harmed by the policy and share of the people benefiting (10%/ 90%; 25%/ 75%; 50%/ 50%; 75%/ 25%; and 90%/10%, respectively), the size of the population affected (1,000; 10,000; 100,000; and 1,000,000), the size of the average cost per person among the harmed ($1; $10; $100; and $1,000), and the size of the average benefit per person among the those benefiting ($1, $10, $100, and $1,000). We also randomly assigned respondents to conditions varying the concentration of the benefits and costs: one-third of respondents were told that the policy had benefits and costs distributed equally (that is, all citizens received a benefit, received the same benefit and all citizens who endured a cost, endured the same cost); the other two-thirds were told that the benefits [costs] were distributed equally, but that the costs [benefits] were distributed unevenly.[2] For those assigned to the unequal distribution scenarios, we randomly assigned the distribution of costs or benefits, respectively. Subjects were informed that most of those in the group had a cost or benefit that was close to the overall group average, but a small minority had a cost or benefit that was much more. We randomly assigned subjects in these groups to one of five distribution conditions (0.1%/ 99.9%; 1%/ 99%; 5%/ 95%; 10%/ 90%, and 20%/ 80%, respectively), where the minority bears a much larger cost or enjoys a much larger benefit than the others. The number of people hurt or harmed by the policy was randomly assigned across 4 values (1,000, 10,000, 100,000, and 1,000,000). In the safety-net vignette only, the raw number of people helped by the policy was displayed to subjects, rather than the percent of people helped.

After subjects read each vignette, they were asked to evaluate the policy on a feeling thermometer that ranged from 0 (extremely unfavorable) to 100 (extremely favorable). Subjects also were asked that if a hypothetical legislator voted in support of the policy, how likely would it be that the legislator was doing a good job. Responses ranged from 1 (very unlikely) to 7 (very likely).

---

[2] We also conducted an experiment in which costs and benefits were distributed equally among the harmed and the benefiting, but average costs and benefits were not revealed to the subjects. We omit that study from this analysis.

Results

We regressed the rating of the policy and the legislator on the distribution variable, as well as a series of covariates. Figure 3.4 shows the predicted thermometer ratings for the policy and the likelihood of "doing a good job" ratings for each vignette, given the incidence and distribution of costs and benefits each of the three policies (abstract policy, gas tax, and social safety-net), averaging across the average cost of the policy displayed to the respondent and holding key demographics, such as ideology, race, education, income, and party ID at the median. We treat the distribution variable as an 11-category variable. Table 3.6 provides the results of the policy thermometer regressions.

The first row of Figure 3.4 displays the results for the abstract policy vignette. In a regression (see Table 3.6), we found that the magnitude of the average harm borne by members of the harmed group has a negative effect on approval of the policy. However, as the figure demonstrates, there is little evidence that an unequal distribution of costs and benefits significantly changes support for the policy relative to scenarios in which costs and benefits are equally distributed.

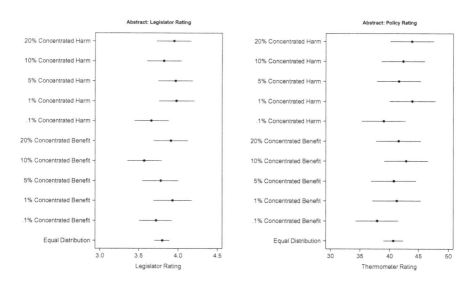

FIGURE 3.4 Predicted legislator and policy ratings across vignettes

The left column of Figure 3.4 displays the predicted legislator rating for each vignette from Section 2. The right column of Figure 3.4 displays the predicted policy rating for each vignette from Section 2. The first row of panels displays the predicted values from the abstract vignette, the second row (see next page) displays the predicted values from the gas tax vignette, and the third (next page) displays the predicted values from the safety net vignette. The x-axis of each panel displays the predicted rating, while the y-axis displays the experimental distribution scenario. The results hold demographics in the regression at their median and average over the total costs and benefits of the policy. Rows 2 and 3 provide some evidence that benefits and costs concentrated on 0.1% are less favorable than the equal distribution scenario. The incremental differences between the equal distribution scenario (the last row in each figure) are associated with the coefficients produced in Table 3.6.

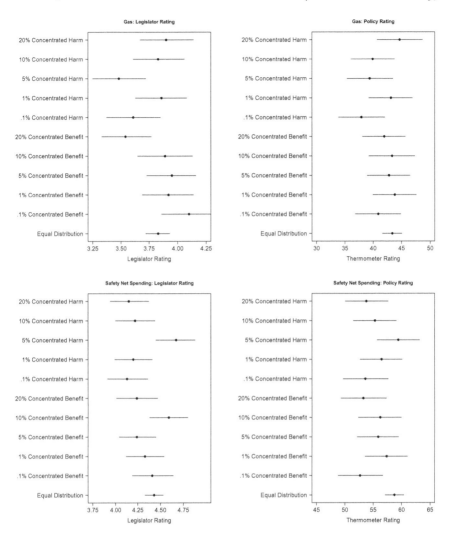

FIGURE 3.4 (Continued)

The average legislator rating in which the distribution of costs and benefits is equal is not statistically distinct from any scenario in which there is an unequal distribution of costs and benefits. This result holds when considering the policy rating.

To better understand Figure 3.4, consider a subject who is told that the abstract policy has equally distributed costs and benefits. When we hold the values in Table 3.6 at their medians, the model predicts that this individual will rate the policy about 40.3, as shown in the final row of the left panel of the top

TABLE 3.6 *Predicting policy approval by distribution of benefits and costs*

Variables	(1) Abstract Policy Thermometer	(2) Gas Policy Thermometer	(3) Safety-Net Spending Policy Thermometer
0.1% Concentrated Benefit	−3.248	−1.661	−6.625***
	(1.975)	(2.242)	(2.245)
1% Concentrated Benefit	−0.284	−0.539	−2.050
	(2.312)	(2.198)	(1.899)
5% Concentrated Benefit	0.970	−0.544	−2.422
	(2.191)	(2.301)	(1.977)
10% Concentrated Benefit	1.555	0.362	−3.400
	(2.158)	(2.361)	(2.079)
20% Concentrated Benefit	1.377	−1.297	−5.041**
	(2.177)	(2.210)	(2.146)
0.1% Concentrated Harm	−1.290	−5.422**	−6.503***
	(2.091)	(2.342)	(2.216)
1% Concentrated Harm	3.140	−1.804	−3.356
	(2.202)	(2.194)	(2.060)
5% Concentrated Harm	0.127	−3.827	0.021
	(2.123)	(2.336)	(2.070)
10% Concentrated Harm	2.004	−2.276	−3.120
	(2.035)	(2.337)	(2.012)
20% Concentrated Harm	3.843*	1.258	−5.614***
	(2.152)	(2.318)	(2.062)
Average Harm	−0.007***	−0.012***	−0.004***
	(0.001)	(0.001)	(0.001)
Conservatism	−1.408***	−2.677***	−3.937***
	(0.461)	(0.475)	(0.424)
White	−9.948***	−3.291**	−2.335*
	(1.351)	(1.403)	(1.275)
College Degree	−1.462	1.223	−1.052
	(1.220)	(1.303)	(1.196)
Household Income	0.137	0.272**	−0.072
	(0.103)	(0.108)	(0.0986)
Female	−4.104***	−4.902***	−0.788
	(1.226)	(1.278)	(1.172)
7-Point Party ID (1 = Strong Dem.)	0.673*	0.033	−1.208***
	(0.363)	(0.369)	(0.328)
2nd Round	1.245	−2.817***	0.638
	(0.863)	(1.004)	(0.827)
Proposed Gas Tax		−6.516***	
		(1.411)	
Constant	54.46***	65.71***	83.86***
	(2.176)	(2.411)	(2.054)
Observations	3,376	2,982	3,359
R^2	0.046	0.079	0.102

row of Figure 3.4. Now consider a respondent with the same demographic traits who is informed that the benefits of the abstract policy are distributed evenly among those benefiting, but that 0.1% of those harmed endure a significantly larger cost. The model predicts that the respondent's rating of this policy will be about 39.0, a decrease of about 1.29 points compared to the rating of the policy with an equal distribution of costs and benefits.

The results in the second row of Figure 3.4 and second column of Table 3.6 provide some evidence that concentrating the harm on a smaller subset of individuals decreases the popularity of the gas tax policy. The estimated effect of the 0.1% of the harmed bearing a larger cost is −5.422 and statistically reliable ($p < 0.05$). As the right panel of Figure 3.4 demonstrates, this results in about a 5-point decrease in approval from the equal distribution scenario. That is, all else equal, respondents rated the gas tax policy 5 points lower, relative to the gas tax scenario in which each member of the harmed group shares the gas tax burden equally. This effect may be distinct from the baseline, but it is not significantly distinct from all other conditions. Nonetheless, the estimate is of a relatively large magnitude.

Column 3 of Table 3.6 and Row 3 of Figure 3.4, which report the results of the social safety-net experiment, show an even tighter relationship between the incidence of costs and benefits and policy support. Approval of the policy declines significantly when the burdens and benefits are concentrated on minuscule groups. For both the 0.1% benefit and the 0.1% harm conditions, the estimated decrease in support is significant at the 0.01 level and of roughly similar magnitudes. That is, a policy that redistributes wealth for social welfare spending by focusing heavily on a few winners or a few losers is much less popular than one that includes equal distribution. Figure 3.4 demonstrates this difference. Once again, note that equal distribution of costs and benefits is estimated to produce a favorability rating of roughly 58.7. Yet, when subjects are informed that the benefits of the policy will be much greater for 0.01% of those benefiting, approval drops by more than 6 points, as is seen in Column 3 of Table 3.6. A slightly smaller, but similar effect is seen when considering the scenario in which a respondent is informed that 0.01% of those being harmed will bear a significantly higher cost than the rest of those being harmed. Surprisingly, we also find that the least unequal distribution of the policies, in which 20% bear the steepest cost or receive the more generous benefits, also produces significantly lower appraisals of the policy.

CONCLUSION

The ability of low-information voters to control their representatives is a fundamental concern in a democracy (Bartels, 1996). One of the most important contributions of Arnold's seminal book *The Logic of Congressional Action* (1990) is to demonstrate that legislators base their policy decisions partly on the assumption that voters can perceive certain costs and benefits, and that they will punish officeholders who make policy decisions they dislike. He emphasized that several factors affect the probability that a citizen will detect a cost or benefit, including magnitude, timing, proximity, and the availability of an instigator to help reveal citizens' stakes in the outcome. In this chapter, we have focused on the first factor, magnitude, because we believe it is fundamental to preference formation, but future research using survey experiments should explore the influence of the other three factors as well.

Replicating studies by Grimmer, Messing, and Westwood (2012, 2015) on legislator communication, we show that subjects are insensitive to the absolute magnitude of benefits in allocating credit for the delivery of grants in the base-line condition. However, consistent with Arnold's claim about the importance of relative benefits and costs, we find in our experimental extensions that constituents are highly sensitive to information about how large or small the grants are in comparison with the average grant distributed. Consistent with the findings of the literatures on negativity bias and loss aversion, we find an asymmetry of responsiveness to contextual information. Subjects are more inclined to punish a legislator for securing a smaller than average grant than to reward a legislator for securing a larger than average grant. The results of our grant-delivery experiments suggest that the policy effects that legislators produce may indeed have consequences for public support – provided voters possess the information they need to put policy effect sizes into a context they can grasp.

Our survey experiments on public responses to changes in the incidence of costs and benefits in two substantive policy areas (gas tax and social safety-net) provide additional evidence that citizens are broadly responsive to policy attributes. In both cases, the vignettes were fairly concrete, and subjects decreased their support in response to increases in the average amount of harm each policy imposed. In the social safety-net vignette in particular, we found that public support for government spending was greater when benefits and harms were distributed equally among the affected population than when they were concentrated on a few winners and losers. This may reflect a preference among the public that social policies designed to promote economic security be majoritarian and universalist rather than client-based, but the finding requires further study (Wilson, 1980). While the experiments were not designed to tease out the influence of self-interest versus other-regarding or sociotropic factors in public opinion (see Kinder and Kiewiet, 1981), they provide at least suggestive evidence that people are attentive not only to the goals of a policy but also to how the policy allocates benefits and harms across groups within society.

Another interesting finding that we believe requires further scrutiny is the insensitivity (in the gasoline tax vignette) of public opinion to changes in the size of the population bearing an extremely high level of costs. That is, the public's reaction to a policy that imposes very large per capita costs on small subsamples of the overall population affected by this policy does not change when we inform subjects that the number of persons in this worst-off group varies greatly (in some cases by a factor of 10,000). In other words, a policy that imposes very large per capita costs on 1 person is judged as no better than a policy that imposes the same very large per capita costs on 10,000 people, a significantly bigger population. This is puzzling since the latter policy is worse from an overall social welfare perspective.

One possible explanation for this finding is that constituents may develop a picture in their heads about who the "typical" person is who is helped or harmed by a policy, which may not be sensitive to how numerous such people are or whether they are in fact statistically representative of winners or losers. For example, in evaluating whether they support or oppose an immigration policy that would make it harder for people to enter into the United States, constituents might focus on the impact of the policy on children detained at the border wall, and this might equally be true whether the number of such children is 1,000, 10,000 or 100,000. This idea relates broadly to availability and representativeness biases that have been identified by social psychologists but may operate through a different mechanism. More generally, we believe that combining insights from social psychology (for an overview, see Gilovich, Griffin, and Kahneman, 2002) with Arnold's 1990 ideas about how citizens form policy preferences is a promising direction for future research.

Subjects were much less responsive to changes in the distribution of benefits and costs when they were asked to evaluate an abstract policy. It appears that if policy information is detached from a real-life practice with which they are familiar, citizens will struggle to grasp it.

More broadly, our analysis suggests that the degree to which citizens are responsive to the costs and benefits of policies is mediated by several factors, including the substantive content of policy, the nature of the issues at stake, and whether citizens possess the ability to notice make sense of policy impacts. A better understanding of these issues will help illuminate the informational conditions under which knowledge-poor constituents can hold legislators accountable for complex policy effects in an era of activist government (Pierson, 2001).

The findings discussed in this chapter are both hopeful and concerning from the standpoint of democratic accountability. On the one hand, they point to a citizenry that can make reasonable assessments of legislative performance when they are given a yardstick and a familiar context. This result is fairly robust across policy issues and research designs. On the other hand, the results consistently show that responsiveness to legislative performance is most acute when a politician is underperforming and that a high-performing legislator gains little return performing better than her colleagues. A well-functioning political reward system should incentivize the pursuit of significant policy accomplishments, but public opinion may give lawmakers little reason to exert the energy necessary to do better than average.

Democratic accountability for under-performance depends upon an active, watchful press. Without high-quality analytical reporting of what lawmakers actually do – which depends largely upon local newspapers (Arnold, 2004) – citizens may be left with little information beyond what their legislators self-report, which is sure to be overly positive. Less scrupulous politicians, if unchallenged by the press or rival candidates, could simply exaggerate or even fabricate their own performance. These findings have important implications for representative government, particularly in view of trends in print and digital media. As Huber and Tucker observe in Chapter 8, local print media presence is declining at a rapid rate. Furthermore, as Carnes (2021) identifies, local print coverage of representatives is often shallow and lacks analysis. The kinds of benchmarks and policy information that we identify in this chapter as being of critical importance to political representation are often not provided to voters, and the situation may well deteriorate further as more and more local papers go out of business and the remaining ones cut their journalistic staffs and devote fewer pages to in-depth coverage of the performance of officeholders. Increasingly, incumbents may be able to establish their own performance benchmarks that may insulate them from democratic accountability. Like a ventriloquist's dummy, newspapers may simply repeat what politicians say verbatim (Grimmer, 2013). In turn, incumbents could be further disincentivized from producing "good public policy" by setting low benchmarks for their actions.[3] In the context of Egan and Prior's (Chapter 4 in this volume) discussion of a declining congruence between the policy decisions of representatives and the preferences of the median voter due to polarization and "leapfrog" representation, the future is potentially quite dispiriting.

Our findings also have important implications for how advocates characterize the effects of public policies. While our evidence is not overwhelming, we find that policies in which the benefits or costs are borne by a very small proportion of the population tend to be less well-received by the public. Entrepreneurial political actors could highlight the impact of the policies on discrete groups, and direct attention away from the policies' broader consequences. The result may be a debate that focuses on "us" versus "them" rather than on whether the policies are good or bad for society.

The evidence presented here has some limitations. Our results suggest that citizens would be sensitive to information about the relative size of grants delivered by legislators. This is the type of information that could in theory be communicated by the media or challengers but we are unable to demonstrate that such contextual information is conveyed during the course of actual election campaigns. Further, our vignettes on the public responses to information about the distribution of benefits and costs cannot demonstrate how robust our findings would be in the face of counter-arguments by opponents of these policies, especially in today's highly polarized political environment. In general, survey experiments may not capture political dynamics as they play out in a real-world context. And our results examine only public opinion. We are unable

---

[3] It remains to be seen whether the many Republicans who took credit for pandemic relief projects they voted against will be called out by the media or challengers.

to directly test Arnold's theory about how legislators anticipate potential public preferences when making policy decisions.

With these limitations in mind, our survey experiments do demonstrate that information about the incidence of costs and benefits can influence public opinion under some conditions. How coalition leaders, legislators, and advocates manipulate this information is at the heart of Arnold's 1990 analysis and merits attention from scholars using a variety of research approaches.

3.A APPENDIX: EXPERIMENTAL VIGNETTES

	Abstract	Gas	Safety-Net Spending
Introduction	Suppose you learned the following about a policy that is being considered for adoption. It would affect [X] people, of whom [Y] percent would benefit and [Z] percent would be harmed.	Headline: Governor [redacted] Proposes Gas Tax Hike to Pay for Road Repairs Body: Facing a shortfall in funding for new highway projects and maintenance, [redacted] lawmakers are considering the first hike in the state's gas tax in more than a decade. Currently at 28 cents per gallon, Governor [redacted] is proposing to increase it to [29, 32, 36, 40, 44, 48, 75, 100, 200] cents per gallon. The Governor said an "impending infrastructure crisis" may be near if more tax revenues aren't collected. Three years ago, lawmakers cobbled together a short-term fix to infrastructure funding shortfalls by borrowing funds against future revenues from turnpike tolls. That money, however, has already been spent.	Intro: Here is an example of a kind of story you might read in a newspaper. Committee to hold hearing on federal safety-net programs Washington, DC – The Ways and Means committee will hold a hearing next Tuesday on support for federal safety-net programs in next year's budget. The hearing witnesses will include members of Congress, academic experts, and representatives of labor unions, small businesses, and advocacy organizations. Variant 1 Washington, DC – Representative [Name Redacted] released the following statement in support of increased spending on federal safety-net programs "I look forward to the Ways and Means Committee's upcoming hearing on next year's budget. I strongly support an increase in federal spending on safety-net programs. These programs provide vital assistance to Americans who live in poverty. The United States is a wealthy and generous nation, and we can afford to ensure that all Americans have a warm, dry place to live and enough to eat."

	Abstract	Gas	Safety-Net Spending
(Introduction)		Over the years, gas tax revenues have been slowly undercut by more fuel-efficient vehicles, hybrids and rising inflation. With less money to go around, as many as 20 major road projects across the state designed to reduce traffic congestion and repair crumbling roads could be put on hold, state officials said. According to a transportation department study of the net impact of increasing the gas tax and using the money for highway projects on the state's drivers, the policy would affect [X] drivers, of whom [Y] percent would benefit and (Z) percent would be harmed.	"More than ten years after the Great Recession and the weak recovery that followed, too many Americans survive on meager incomes. In 2016, the poverty line–for an individual was $12,228. For a family of three, it was $19,100. The official poverty rate in 2016 was 12.7 percent. 40.6 million people were classified as being in poverty in 2016." "To give every citizen a fair chance of life success, we should increase funding for basic safety net policies. These program expansions would help [Y] people in poverty, and could be paid for by additional taxes on [Z] people with higher incomes."
Equal Distribution	Assume that prior to the adoption of the policy, all [X] people have equal incomes. For the people who would benefit from the policy, the average benefit is [N]. Suppose that among all those who benefit, they all benefit equally. For the people who would be harmed by the policy, the average cost is [M]. Suppose that among all those who are harmed, they are all harmed equally.	For drivers who would benefit from the policy, the average benefit would be [N] minutes less time in traffic per year. Suppose that among all those who benefit, they all benefit equally. For the drivers who would be harmed by the policy, the average cost would be [M] increase in gas taxes per year. Suppose that among all those who are harmed, they are all harmed equally.	The poor people who would be helped by my proposal would receive an average increase in social benefits of [N]. Suppose that among all those who benefit, they all benefit equally. For the people who would pay higher taxes under my policy, the average cost would be [M]. Suppose that among all those who are harmed, they are all harmed equally.

	Abstract	Gas	Safety-Net Spending
Unequal Costs	Assume that prior to the adoption of the policy, all [X] people have equal incomes. For the people who benefit from the policy, the average benefit is [N]. Suppose that among all those who benefit, they all benefit equally. For the people who would be harmed by the policy, the average cost is [M]. Those who are harmed can be divided into 2 groups: for [p] percent the cost will be [H] and for [1-p] percent the cost will be [H'].	For drivers who would benefit from the policy, the average benefit would be [N] minutes less time in traffic per year. Suppose that among all those who benefit, they all benefit equally. For the drivers who would be harmed by the policy, the average cost would be [M] increase in gas taxes per year. The study also found that those who are harmed can be divided into groups: for [p] percent of drivers being harmed by the policy, the cost will be a [H]increase in gas taxes per year and for [1-p] percent, the cost will be a [H'] increase in gas taxes per year.	The poor people who would be helped by my proposal would receive an average increase in social benefits of [N]. Suppose that among all those who benefit, they all benefit equally. For the people who would pay higher taxes under my policy, the average cost would be [M]. The amount of extra taxes that people would pay would be based on their incomes. For the richest [p] percent of the people who would bear tax increases, primarily people with yearly incomes over $500,000, the cost will be [H] and for the other [1-p] percent, the cost will be [H'].
Unequal Benefits	Assume that prior to the adoption of the policy, all [X] people have equal incomes. For the people who benefit from the policy, the average benefit is [N]. For the people who would be harmed by the policy, the average cost is [M]. Suppose that among all those who are harmed, they are all harmed equally. Those who benefit can be divided into 2 groups: for [p] percent the benefit will be [H] and for [1-p] percent the benefit will be [H'].	For drivers who would benefit from the policy, the average benefit would be [N] minutes less time in traffic per year. For the drivers who would be harmed by the policy, the average cost would be [M] increase in gas taxes paid per year. Suppose that among all those who are harmed, they are all harmed equally. The study also found that those who benefit can be divided into 2 groups: for [p] percent of drivers benefitting from the policy, the benefit would be [H] fewer minutes in traffic per year and for [1-p] percent, the benefit would be [H'] fewer minutes.	The poor people who would be helped by my proposal would receive an average increase in social benefits of [N]. For the people who would pay higher taxes under my policy, the average cost would be [M]. Suppose that among all those who are harmed, they are all harmed equally. The size of the benefits that people would receive would depend upon how vulnerable they are. For [p] percent of the eligible people, primarily young children living in deep poverty, the benefit would be [H] and for the other [1-p] percent, the benefit would be [H'].

4

Logic with Polarized Parties, Changing Media, and Motivated Reasoners

Patrick J. Egan and Markus Prior

Constituents have frequent opportunities to voice discontent with their representatives and kick them out of office. Yet they often decline these opportunities, out of a lack of concern or to avoid the cost of participation. Because constituents could switch to more active involvement at any time (and any election), representatives must remain aware of their voters' political moods. This link between representatives and constituents raises two deceptively simple questions critical to timeless scholarly debates about accountability: What do elected officials think their voters want? And under what circumstances do lawmakers believe they must pay attention to their voters' preferences? The inclusion of the words *think* and *believe* in these questions highlights an important departure from the approach taken by most studies of accountability and representation, in that the focus is on elected officials' perceptions. These perceptions are influenced by facts on the ground, including most fundamentally voters' preferences as expressed in polls, town hall meetings, lobbying and other in-person conversations, and letters and emails. But politicians' perceptions incorporate more than just the kind of feedback that might be voiced by their constituents. They also include a sense of just how firm expressed opinion is on any particular issue, the possible distribution of currently latent public opinion that may exist on issues that are not salient, and the likelihood that constituents will become aware of – and properly assign credit and blame for – laws and policies that the politician works to enact.

The challenges of measuring and modeling politicians' perceptions has meant that empirical political science on representation and accountability has largely shied away from these themes. This is despite the fact that the earliest empirical research on representation, Warren E. Miller and Donald E. Stokes's path-breaking 1963 article "Constituency Influence in Congress," specified these perceptions as key mediators of the opinion-policy relationship and assessed them with surveys of legislators (Miller and Stokes, 1963). It is only recently that empirical scholars have returned to this theme with large-scale efforts measuring the perceptions of legislators and their staffs and experiments exposing legislators to information about their constituents' opinions in order to assess the impact of lawmakers' perceptions of constituency opinion on their actions. But these efforts to take perceptions into account are few in number. For the most part, scholars of representation have instead focused on assessing the strength of the relationship between constituency preferences expressed in opinion polls and politicians' actions as a meaningful indicator of whether the public is holding lawmakers accountable.

Three critical building blocks for a theory of accountability have often been treated in separate scholarship: mostly conceptual work on "latent public opinion" (Key, 1961), models of retrospective evaluations and candidate selection (e.g., Ferejohn, 1986), and accounting of costs and benefits associated with a representative's action in office. A notable exception that draws on all three building blocks is R. Douglas Arnold's *The Logic of Congressional Action* (1990), which offers a systematic theoretical treatment of lawmakers' perceptions of their voters' desires and the implications of these perceptions for accountability and representation. Arnold's "principal concern is to show how legislators anticipate citizens' acquisition of policy preferences ... The aim is to show how legislators *think* citizens might react" (18, emphasis in original). Arnold's book takes lawmakers' perceptions seriously and weaves them into a model laying out the conditions under which constituents' preferences affect the decisions of their elected officials. Its innovation is to show how voters' attention can be aroused by policies that distribute costs and benefits in particular ways, and how voters impose electoral consequences on legislators when the effects of costly policies can be traced back to their actions. Arnold provides the microfoundations for his theory with four decision rules detailing how voters render evaluations of their representative and their representative's party on the basis of the performance and the positions of each.

The purpose of this chapter is to adapt *Logic* for the 21st century. US politics – and therefore congressional action – has changed quite a lot since the book's publication more than three decades ago. In addition, over this period, political science has made and extended a host of discoveries about how Americans get information, evaluate the state of the world, and make voting decisions in an increasingly polarized political landscape. Arnold himself raises the question of *Logic*'s applicability to other contexts, describing his theory as appropriate for "a Congress where most members seek to be reelected, where parties are relatively weak, and where members face repeated demands to stand up and be counted on roll-call votes." These necessary conditions, he writes, mean his theory fits the Congresses of the 1970s and 1980s "quite well," with the fit to those of the 1950s and 1960s "less perfect," and before that "relatively poor" (1990, 15, n 18).

Here we ask how good *Logic*'s fit is for the Congresses of the 2010s and 2020s and suggest some adaptations to the theory where its fit is found to be lacking. We do so by delineating and distilling Arnold's four rules – in some cases with graphics and others with formal equations – in order to isolate in a precise way the elements of his system. With this delineation in place, we then examine what's changed since the era, forty or fifty years ago, that *Logic* sets out to illuminate. We consider three broad categories of change: increasing partisan polarization of US politics among elites and masses; shifts in supply and demand for media that provide news about politics and public affairs; and the clear demonstration by scholars of motivated reasoning about politics, which for our purposes includes partisans' differing perceptions of objective conditions as well as their uptake of elite cues regarding public policies.

We then rewrite the four rules to reflect the changes we identify and consider the implications of these changes for Arnold's theory. After updating *Logic*'s basic framework with these changes, we assess that the theory remains valuable for understanding the circumstances under which Congress is accountable to the public, particularly if the decision rules are extended to primary elections. The theory and empirical evidence lead us to conclude that the conditions for accountability have not improved since *Logic*'s publication and have likely declined. They still exist, however, and the foremost contribution of *Logic*, and – we hope – our modernization of it, is to provide a road map for future scholarship to assess the accountability of legislators in a systematic way. (For more thoughts about the relevance of *Logic* to our times, see also Drutman, Chapter 13 and Lee, Chapter 9 in this volume.)

TRACEABILITY AND TWO KINDS OF ACCOUNTABILITY

Given the design of Congress and a public that is largely inattentive to politics, victories enjoyed by concentrated, group interests (whether groups are defined by people or geography) are unsurprising. Thus, perhaps the most enduring contribution of *Logic* is that it identifies more unusual circumstances under which diffuse, general interests are promoted by Congressional action. This question is not only an empirical puzzle; it's also of normative importance, as most efforts to improve general welfare require this kind of policymaking. As examples of these welfare-improving policies, Arnold (1990, 4) lists – and proceeds to examine in detail – "environmental and safety legislation, efforts to reduce the federal deficit, and the deregulations of the airline, trucking and telecommunications industries," all examples of legislation that imposed concentrated costs to advance the interests of the diffuse public.

Arnold developed his model in the late 1980s, a time when empirical scholars of Congress were skeptical that voters held meaningful policy preferences that they could use to evaluate the actions of their elected officials. His insight was that just because voters cannot be expected to know intricate details about the policymaking process – and incumbents rarely lose because of votes they cast on legislation – doesn't mean that citizens' preferences are ignored by Congress. Rather, fundamentally risk-averse members of Congress are always anticipating and usually forestalling the dreaded moment when the inattentive public is aroused from its slumber by an inopportune decision made in office.

The challenge is that these difficult roll-call votes are often exactly what's required for policymaking that favors general over group interests. Safely storing nuclear waste, shuttering unneeded military bases, and closing tax loopholes – all make the general public better off while exacting costs on particular people or places. The general public is unlikely to be aware of these efforts or to reward legislators for them, whereas group and geographic interests incur the pain of these policies and are likely to impose electoral punishment for them. Members of Congress are therefore loathe to cast these votes, and Arnold argues that when they do it's generally because the policies (and the policymaking process) have been designed to minimize their "traceability" – that is, the chances that affected voters will link the costs they are experiencing with the policy and lawmakers that imposed the costs. (For additional thoughts on the notion of traceability, see Carpenter and Libgober, Chapter 14 in this volume.)

If we consider "accountability" as the extent to which legislators prioritize the diffuse public interest over concentrated special interests, the normative implications of Arnold's traceability theory are quite profound. General welfare-enhancing policies are less likely to emerge from Congress when its actions are transparent, because transparency makes it easier for concentrated interests harmed by these policies to penalize incumbents for their roll-call votes. To borrow terminology from the representation literature, traceability can lead members of Congress to act like delegates when big policy problems necessitate that they act as trustees.

The distinction between delegate and trustee representation is a reminder that Arnold is largely silent about a different and equally important notion of accountability that has been the focus of much recent empirical political science research on representation. In this line of work, accountability is tied to the question of whether legislative representation reflects Robert Dahl's maxim that democracy be characterized as "the continuing responsiveness of the government to the preferences of its citizens, considered as political equals" (Dahl, 1971, 1). The typical empirical approach, following in the vein of Miller and Stokes, is to examine whether a constituency's average preferences are reflected in its representative's roll-call votes – in other words, how well legislators conform to the delegate model. The primary normative concern of this work is that lack of accountability can allow members of Congress to amass records that are more ideologically extreme than desired by their district's voters. For this notion of accountability, the conditions Arnold identified as conducive to traceability – a strong media, dogged challengers, engaged voters – are thought to be helpful.

Traceability thus has potentially opposite implications for these two kinds of accountability. Traceability makes it easier for special interests to prevail over efforts to enact policies that help general interests, but traceability also makes it harder for legislators to ignore their districts' median voters and compile ideologically extreme records. We return to a consideration of this tension at the end of our chapter.

DELINEATING THE LOGIC OF *LOGIC*

Arnold's four rules lay out the conditions under which voters' awareness of the activities of legislators lead them to reward or punish incumbents for the policy consequences of the actions they take in office. (We use the term "voter" here, although as will be seen the decision to vote is of course itself endogenous to lawmakers' actions.)

In this section, we delineate and distill Arnold's four rules – which have many component parts – using graphics and equations. According to Arnold, lawmakers *perceive* their constituents applying these rules as they choose how to vote in Congressional elections. As laid out, the rules are decision-theoretic: they specify how voters are perceived to respond to a given set of actions by elected officials. But these decisions take place within *Logic*'s game-theoretic framework, which incorporates how the actions of lawmakers and others can affect the extent to which the rules operate in constituents' minds.

On its surface, the logic of *Logic* is simple: voters render evaluations of both their representative in Congress and their representative's party on the basis of the performance and the positions of each. These evaluations are made according to four rules that each yield running tallies, weighted to different degrees, that together produce a decision about whether to support the incumbent or the challenger in the general election.

This decision is depicted in Figure 4.1, with each of the four rules contributing to the evaluation of the incumbent legislator. Arnold is unspecific about the relative magnitudes of the rules' weights; we discuss this further below. Arnold also mentions what he calls a "host of other factors" (57) that can matter but are distinguished from the four rules by virtue of being "non-policy-related" (58). These factors include candidates' familiarity and accessibility to voters, the impact of their communications, and their constituency service.

The Performance Rules

The first two of the four decision rules in Arnold's account have to do with the performance of the incumbent's party and that of the incumbent him- or herself. Although Arnold never uses the term, performance here is defined with regard to "valence" issues that have to do with generally agreed-upon end states, such as prosperity or support for local economic opportunity. The evaluations voters render via these rules are retrospective in that they have to do with particular conditions and the extent to which the incumbent and the incumbent's party is believed to be responsible for these conditions.

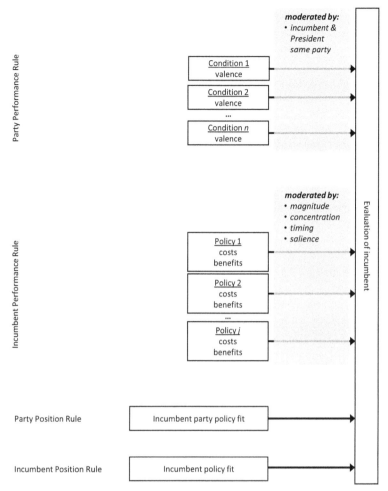

FIGURE 4.1 The four voter decision rules in *The Logic of Congressional Action*

The *party performance rule* requires that voters "first evaluate current conditions in society, decide how acceptable those conditions are, and then either reward or punish the governing party by supporting or opposing its legislative candidates" (41). This rule is depicted at the top of Figure 4.1, where voters reward or punish the incumbent based on a total of N conditions depending on (as indicated by the shaded part of the diagram) whether the incumbent's party controls the presidency. These conditions are almost entirely out of individual legislators' hands, but incumbents' electoral fortunes rise or fall with them anyway. The state of the economy is typically the most influential of these conditions; others might include the success of military operations abroad – or, to apply the rule to a more recent circumstance, the government's success at combating a nationwide epidemic.

Like the party performance rule, the **incumbent performance rule** again requires that voters evaluate current conditions in society and decide how acceptable these conditions are. But what is different is that voters then proceed to evaluate incumbent legislators for their individual actions – as distinguished from those of their party – that they can link to current conditions. Such conditions need not be present in the incumbent's district: group costs, for example, can lower evaluations of an incumbent even when most of the group members live outside the incumbent's district.

Executing the incumbent performance rule isn't easy: voters must be able to perceive effects of a policy and associate them with a government action tied to their particular legislator. The pursuit of what Arnold calls this "traceability chain" by inattentive publics is thus a rather tall order, and most lawmakers' actions go unnoticed. Election challengers and any groups negatively affected by legislators' actions work hard to make connections for voters that reflect poorly on the incumbent. An officeholder, conversely, will attempt to increase traceability for actions that she believes will be seen positively. Arnold observes that certain kinds of policy effects are easier to trace to their sources, including those that happen early after the policy is made, rather than later; those tied to simple actions rather than complex ones, those that exact costs rather than bestow benefits, and those that result from action rather than neglect (47–51).

Both the actual costs and benefits of policies and their salience to potential voters are central explanatory constructs in Arnold's theory, making the incumbent performance rule the most complex of the rules. The diagram reflects this complexity by denoting (in the shaded part of the figure) that costs' and benefits' impact on evaluations can be moderated by their magnitude, their concentration – that is whether the costs and benefits are general, geographic, or group-specific – their timing, and the extent to which actions by the incumbent and other political actors affect their salience.

Different types of costs or benefits are thought to affect constituents to different degrees. For example, group-specific benefits tend to have larger effects than general benefits. The principle of loss aversion tells us that costs often weigh more heavily than benefits. The moderating impact of the timing of costs and benefits accords with the disproportionate impact events have on many kinds of evaluations, a common finding in research on the effects of advertising, frames, and economic conditions. Arnold's argument about timing also suggests another kind of time dependence: policy effects will be more traceable when they occur in close proximity to the actions that caused them

The distinction between attentive and inattentive publics is critical to Arnold's way of thinking about political accountability. There is a "probability that the potential preferences will be transformed into real preferences" (84), but Arnold is not specific on how this transition occurs. The properties of costs and benefits can precipitate the transformation in real preference. But it also depends on the extent to which the actions of incumbents (most importantly, their floor roll-call behavior, but also bill sponsorship, committee votes, etc.) and instigators (challengers who work to raise salience of unpopular incumbent actions; interest groups; journalists) raise the salience of particular conditions and policy effects. Lastly, salience can also be affected by how much attention voters routinely pay to particular policy issues. Research in voting behavior has often referred to this proposition with reference to "issue publics." It is an interesting empirical question how much of what is usually thought of as individual-specific issue salience is in fact explained by policy-specific properties, such as concentrated costs. Of course, changes in individuals' general level of awareness could affect salience across issues and transform potential into real preferences, although this mechanism might be the least common given how stable most people's political interest turns out to be (Prior, 2018).

The Position Rules

The two remaining decision rules have to do with the positions taken by the incumbent and the incumbent's party on the issues of the day. Arnold conceptualizes voters' evaluations of these positions as prospective, based upon candidates' and parties' promises and platforms. In Figure 4.1, we denote these rules as operating via the distance between a voter's policy preferences and those of the two parties and the candidates vying for office. Below we formalize these rules in a straightforward manner using the proximity voting framework that is standard to spatial models of politics.

To use the *party position rule*, a voter must "identify the party that offers the most pleasing package of policy positions and then support the legislative candidate wearing that label" (Arnold, 1990, 52). In Equation 4.1, we write this as a voter i assessing the relative fit on each issue j between i's own position x_{ij} and the positions taken by the incumbent's and the challenger's party. These relative distances are summed over all j, with each issue given a weight φ_j, yielding a balance (*INCPARTY_POS*) that if positive favors the incumbent's party and if negative favors the challenger's. Arnold expects that few voters will rely on this rule because they lack information about party positions on many platform items, meaning that φ_j will equal 0 for most issues.

$$INCPARTY\_POS_i = \sum_{j=1}^{J} \varphi_j \left(\left| x_{ij} - x_j^{CHALPARTY} \right| - \left| x_{ij} - x_j^{INCPARTY} \right| \right). \quad (4.1)$$

The *candidate position rule* is analogous to the party position rule with the evaluation rendered on the incumbent and the challenger rather than their parties. The voter "decide[s] which candidate to support by comparing the candidates' positions on the issues and then choosing the candidate with the most pleasing package of positions" (Arnold, 1990, 54). We write this rule in

Equation 4.2 in the same fashion as the party position rule, except that voter i considers the relative fit between her own position and the positions taken by incumbent and challenger, not their parties, with weights on each issue j now denoted ψ_j. The balance, INC_POS_i, favors the incumbent if positive and the challenger if negative. Informational requirements for the application of this rule are typically even more demanding of voters than for the party position rule because it takes greater effort to learn about candidate positions, again making the weights ψ_j equal to or near zero for most j.

$$INC\_POS_i = \sum_{j=1}^{J} \psi_j \left(\left| x_{ij} - x_j^{CHAL} \right| - \left| x_{ij} - x_j^{INC} \right| \right). \qquad (4.2)$$

WHAT'S CHANGED SINCE *LOGIC*

Arnold's voter decision rules do not capture several recent changes in American politics and discoveries in political science since *Logic*'s publication. Here we propose modifications of the rules that reflect the changes to guide future scholarly efforts. Three changes stand out: polarized parties, changing media and motivated reasoning.

Voters and Elites Have Polarized along Party Lines

The Congresses of the 1970s and 1980s described in *Logic* took place during what turned out to be the conclusion of a decades-long period of relatively low levels of partisan polarization in US politics. Arnold explicitly dismissed the idea that constituents vote "blindly on the basis of party," saying that "although this was once a reasonable view of congressional elections, it no longer fits the facts." He noted that "in some recent years nearly a quarter of all voters who identified with one of the major parties voted for the opposite party's candidates in elections to the House" (38).

As Figure 4.2 illustrates, what is "a reasonable view of congressional elections" has once again shifted. The rate at which people vote for different parties in presidential and congressional elections has dropped from its level of the 1970s and 1980s. Since then, split-ticket voting declined as local contests increasingly came to reflect national politics (Hopkins, 2018). This is just one manifestation of the extent to which politics became polarized along party lines after *Logic*'s publication. Roll-call voting scores such as NOMINATE show inter-party differences in House voting beginning to rise in the early 1980s. The strength of partisanship as a predictor of voting behavior in presidential and congressional elections began to climb dramatically over the same period (Bartels, 2000). Defections of conservative white Democrats – particularly in the South – into the Republican fold played an important role in making the two parties more ideologically homogeneous (Levendusky, 2009).

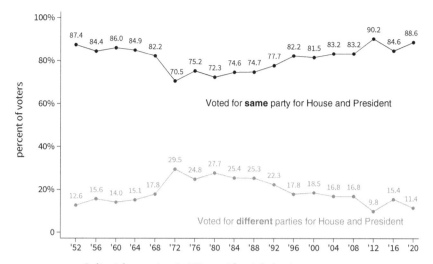

FIGURE 4.2 Split-ticket voting in US presidential elections, 1952–2020
Source: American National Election Studies (conducted with in-person interviews with the exception of 1984,1992, 1996, 2000, 2012, 2016, and 2020, which include telephone and Web-based interviews in various of these years).

So did the rise of a consistent Republican ideology that made it into a true opposition party after decades of offering policies that often mirrored those of the Democrats. Championed by Ronald Reagan in his 1980 presidential campaign and implemented in Congress when Republican Newt Gingrich took over as Speaker after the 1994 elections, the new G.O.P. philosophy successfully linked the party's traditional tax-averse, government-skeptic wing with the burgeoning Religious Right.

Logic reflected the focus of classic accounts of Congress at the time that emphasized legislators' role as independent agents (e.g., Mayhew, 1974). But the current versions of America's two main political parties look much more like ideologically-unified teams that allow for little autonomy. "Intense policy demanders" who are key to the parties' coalitions require fealty with regard to roll-call votes and policy priorities (Karol, 2009; Bawn et al., 2012; Egan, 2013; Noel, 2014), meaning that lawmakers at all levels increasingly weigh the preferences of their own party's voters as much or more than those of their median constituent (Clinton, 2006). This has created a pattern where a change in party control of a Congressional seat usually results in the new legislator "leapfrogging" over the median voter to take equally extreme positions on the other side of the political spectrum (Bafumi and Herron, 2010). As for voters, evidence suggests that partisanship has taken on the characteristic of a social identity. Partisan sentiment now features in-group favoritism and out-group antipathy and bias (e.g., Mason, 2018; McConnell et al., 2018) that can override other social identities (Egan, 2020) and extend far beyond shared policy preferences represented by an emotionally neutral brand label. All of this has unfolded as party organizations have become unambiguously weaker. Traditional party gatekeepers have less control over which candidates are nominated and what issues are prioritized, but nevertheless citizens and legislators vote increasingly in lockstep with their parties.

The Supply and Demand for Media Has Changed

The concept of traceability in Arnold's theory casts emphasis on the generation and dissemination of information about congressional incumbents. Even though news media became a central focus for Arnold only in his later work (Arnold, 2004), he was already delineating their function in *Logic*: "If legislators were careless in how they voted, they might find that journalists would cover their actions more extensively than before and that the increased coverage would focus on the issues" (39). Dramatic technological innovation since then has changed the business of journalism so much so that it bears asking if the journalists Arnold had in mind even still exist, and to what extent they still cover congressional politics.

Research has found politicians to be more accountable to their constituents when they are covered by the news media (e.g., Cohen, Noel, and Zaller, 2004; Snyder and Strömberg, 2010). It is difficult to determine if changes in the provision of information about congressional candidates have increased or decreased over the last few decades. Cable channels, Web-based news providers, online databases (Schudson, 2010), and amateur journalists (Bentley, 2008) add new sources of information, but declining advertising revenue has led many newspapers to close or reduce news coverage (Abernathy, 2018). There are strong indications that the balance is negative when it comes to local public affairs coverage in many state capitals and congressional districts (Peterson, 2021b). While there was always variation in the extent to which local news media covered the member(s) of Congress representing parts of their circulation area, the ongoing wave of newspaper closures reduces monitoring of representatives further (Darr, Hitt, and Dunaway, 2018). Recent consolidation of local TV station ownership has had similar effects (Martin and McCrain, 2019). For additional observations on how the contemporary media environment affects accountability, see Gregory Huber and Patrick Tucker, Chapter 8 in this volume.

Another shift with important implications for (paid) communication about legislators' performance stems from a dramatic rise in the real cost of congressional campaigns. Data from the Center for Responsive Politics show that in 2018, the average House election winner spent $2 million on her campaign. In 1990 the same figure was $783,000 (in 2018 dollars), meaning that the real cost of running a typical winning campaign rose more than 150% over this three-decade period (Center for Responsive Politics, 2019).

Voters have been discovered to be motivated reasoners

A growing body of research shows that on many issues, most Americans take cues from parties and candidates in forming their views about policies, rather than the other way around. Scholars were just beginning to identify the power of elite cues to affect partisans' attitudes as *Logic* was being written: for example, John Zaller was documenting the phenomenon in a series of articles in the late 1980s and early 1990s, which he then systematized in his *The Nature and Origins of Mass Opinion* in 1992. Influential work that followed in this vein includes Rahn (1993), Gilens (2001), Lenz (2012) and Bullock (2011), all of which documented in various ways the conditions under which partisans adjust their expressed policy preferences to better align with elite party cues. In an era of greater elite polarization, the strength of these signals has persisted (Barber and Pope, 2019); they are arguably even stronger than when *Logic* was published. In contrast to the emphasis in this work that voters often automatically accept or reject issue positions based on source cues, Arnold instead makes the implicit assumption that voters' policy preferences reflect how policies affect their objective interests.

To be clear, the phenomenon of cue-taking from elites does not give candidates unlimited leeway, indicating that position rules are still very much in effect. Influential work published since *Logic* has confirmed that, ceteris paribus, extreme candidates fare worse at the ballot box than moderate candidates (e.g., Canes-Wrone, Brady, and Cogan, 2002; Hall, 2015). This reassuring finding is tempered by the fact that most estimates of the magnitude of the electoral penalty incurred by extreme liberals or conservatives are not particularly large. A concurrent research agenda has focused on the phenomenon of partisan motivated reasoning, a process by which people more readily accept information that is congenial to their partisan affiliation. Reliance on partisan stereotypes ("schemas"), selective exposure and attention, and motivated processing of information may lead partisans to hold beliefs about the state of the world – some accurate, some not – that are in line with their partisanship (Lodge and Hamill, 1986; Rahn, 1993; Taber and Lodge, 2006). Voters' own positions and their perceptions of where the parties stand on issues are often distorted. Their own positions can be distorted by rationalization, and their perceptions of party positions can be distorted by projection (e.g., Brady and Sniderman, 1985).

Motivated reasoning has been found to diminish accurate judgements of party and incumbent performance and distort objective assessment of facts about public affairs. Although an original feature of *The American Voter*'s psychological theory of party identification (Campbell et al., 1960), the distorting influence of the "perceptual screen" has recently received greater attention, due in part to demonstrations that it can extend to perceptions of objective conditions (e.g., Bartels, 2002). The literature on motivated reasoning (e.g., Taber and Lodge, 2006) reinforced this insight by integrating the perceptual screen into a broader framework of belief maintenance bolstered by confirmation and disconfirmation biases. One manifestation of this development in the aggregate is that unlike approval ratings of presidents in prior decades, evaluations of Presidents Obama and Trump were less strongly (and perhaps not at all) related to changing true economic conditions (Sides, Vavreck, and Tesler, 2018).

All three of these developments – partisan polarization, Americans' changing media consumption, and the discovery (and perhaps acceleration) of motivated reasoning in politics – have important implications for Arnold's theory. To pinpoint how these changes affect *Logic*'s conclusions, we return to our delineation of the book's rules to precisely specify what has shifted. Figure 4.3 presents a modification of our previous diagram with these changes denoted in bold.

Considering the four rules together, the shifts described above toward partisanship and away from split-ticket voting suggest that it has become increasingly more difficult for incumbents to separate themselves from their parties. These trends would likely manifest themselves in greater voter reliance on the party performance and party position rules at the expense of the analogous incumbent rules. Downweighting may also apply to all other factors unrelated to policy, as it is possible that the importance of candidate familiarity or constituency service has declined to lower the value of incumbency relative to the party label. Perhaps not coincidentally, the advantage enjoyed by incumbents in House elections has declined precipitously over the past few decades (Jacobson and Carson, 2019, 44).

Revised Performance Rules

We revise the performance rules to account for the facts that partisans can misperceive objective conditions and that most voters myopically discount the past and heavily weight recent events when evaluating incumbent performance.

Our more realistic version of the ***party performance rule*** reflects that voters do not observe actual conditions, but rather assess the incumbent's party performance based on their perceptions of these conditions. Figure 4.3 shows that these perceptions are a function of actual conditions, which are distorted by two psychological distortions that have dominated research on perceptions of objective conditions: myopia and partisan bias. Voters give much greater weight to economic conditions during the election year when evaluating an incumbent president, and hardly any weight to the first half of the term (Bartels, 2008; Healy and Lenz, 2014). Partisan bias in perceptions of national conditions derives directly from motivated reasoning. Nevertheless, this screen is not completely opaque: stark realities with regard to the economy and other national conditions do tend to get noticed (e.g., Bisgaard, 2015).

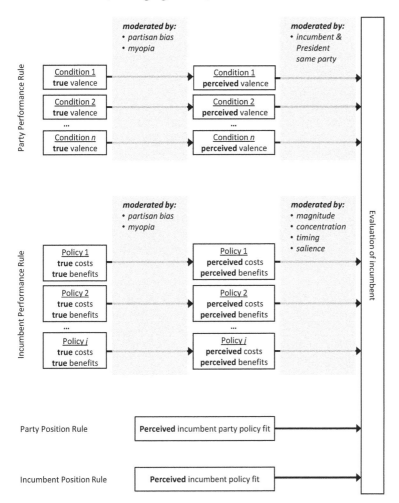

FIGURE 4.3 *Logic*'s decision rules revised to reflect polarized parties, changing media, and motivated reasoners

Our revised version of the ***incumbent performance rule*** explicitly incorporates voters' perceptions of costs and benefits. Arnold defines "policy effects [to] refer to conditions in society that are somehow attributable to governmental action or inaction" (40). The definition implies that performance considerations include not only changes in costs and benefits imposed by recent policies, but also cost-benefit implications of conditions that remain unaddressed by policy. To the extent that an incumbent could have done something to prevent adverse conditions, voters will downgrade her even in the absence of policy change.

Although perceptions can be affected by information about objective conditions, inferences and attributions about the state of the world are ultimately subjective judgements made by voters – and evidence is now abundant that they are not always particularly systematic (e.g., Achen and Bartels, 2016). Arnold discusses the possibility that constituents misperceive costs and benefits, but does not elaborate the psychological reasons for misperception. Arnold's original account partially incorporates perceptions when it comes to policy effects: the disproportionate importance of proximate policy effects and changes in the salience of costs and benefits imply that perceptions matter. Yet, this formulation is limited by not allowing for partisan motivated reasoning.

Our revised model incorporates motivated reasoning in the perception of costs and benefits in much the same way as we handled motivated reasoning in consideration of societal conditions in the revised incumbent performance rule. For each type of cost and benefit, we now specify that myopia and partisan bias can distort the translation of true costs and benefits to the voter's perceptions of them. Motivated reasoning posits that constituents with a preference for, or a shared partisan identity with, the incumbent will exaggerate the benefits for which she is responsible and downplay the costs. It is possible – but has been difficult to establish empirically – that these distortions have been exacerbated by the widespread availability of politically congenial news on cable television, the Internet, and social media (e.g., Prior, 2013; Allcott et al., 2020; Levy, 2021). Especially when it comes to learning, increasingly biased selection (and omission) of facts by partisan outlets may hurt perception of true costs and benefits.

Even with motivated reasoning, we expect true costs and benefits to retain some impact. There are several reasons to expect an attenuated impact of true conditions, however. First, reduced local news coverage is bound to lower the salience of many issues, especially for group- (and in particular, district-) specific policy effects, and especially for costs. With less monitoring by independent actors, incumbents have a greater chance at getting away with imposing costs on inattentive publics in their district and fewer incentives to secure benefits for the district because they will not receive as much attention as in the past. Waste or corruption are less likely to be exposed, reducing the probability that those costs will be attributed to the incumbent. Past research has typically found that while more challenging communication environments hurt both incumbents and challengers, they affect challengers more, so the net effect benefits incumbents (Campbell, Alford, and Henry, 1984; Stewart and Reynolds, 1990; Prior, 2007). Second, better-funded incumbents, challengers, and interest groups may spend greater resources on manipulating salience with their ideological or particularistic goals in mind. A shift of resources from general-interest to particularistic actors should exacerbate the already tough challenge Arnold identifies of imposing group-specific costs in order to provide general benefits. Finally, insofar as greater media choice has reduced exposure to politics among constituents with low levels of political interest who used to encounter politics only for lack of more entertaining options (Prior, 2007), there is likely a reduction in the probability of activating inattentive publics.

(Note, however, that Allcott et al. (2020) find a net positive effect of Facebook on knowledge of national news.)

Revised Position Rules

What's most striking about *Logic*'s position rules is their lack of incorporation of what political scientists see as one of the most fundamental tenets of US politics today: on many issues, partisans' policy preferences are strongly influenced by cues from party elites. This calls into question the notion that citizens hold fixed ideal points from which they measure the distance to candidates' and parties' platforms, objectively assessed. We revise the position rules accordingly.

In Equation 4.1 we modeled the *party position rule* as a simple spatial voting function where voter i sums up how far she is in the policy space from the two parties over all issues j. We modify this by allowing both the voter's ideal point and the positions of the incumbent and challenger parties to be distorted in ways that reduce the perceived distance between the voter and the position taken by her preferred party. Our new Equation 4.3a substitutes these distorted positions into the spatial voting function. The positions of the incumbent and challenger parties now have "hats" and an i subscript to indicate that they are individual i's perceptions of the parties, not official or universally recognized positions. Voter i's own position on issue j is now a combination of her true position plus "distortion," as shown in Equation 4.3b.

$$INCPARTY\_POS_i = \sum_{j=1}^{J} \varphi_j \left(\left| \widehat{x}_{ij} - \widehat{x}_{ij}^{CHALPARTY} \right| - \left| \widehat{x}_{ij} - \widehat{x}_{ij}^{INCPARTY} \right| \right) \quad (4.3a)$$

$$\widehat{x}_{ij} = x_{ij} + distortion_{ij}. \quad (4.3b)$$

As in the case of the party position rule, we modify the *incumbent position rule* to incorporate rationalization of i's own positions and projection of i's positions onto candidates. Equation 4.4a rewrites our original Equation 4.2 with i's distorted ideal point and her distorted notions of the two candidates' positions; as before, Equation 4.4b expresses her perceived ideal point as a function of her true position plus distortion.

$$INC\_POS_i = \sum_{j=1}^{J} \psi_j \left(\left| \widehat{x}_{ij} - \widehat{x}_{ij}^{CHAL} \right| - \left| \widehat{x}_{ij} - \widehat{x}_{ij}^{INC} \right| \right) \quad (4.4a)$$

$$\widehat{x}_{ij} = x_{ij} + distortion_{ij}. \quad (4.4b)$$

For both of the position rules, the political science research and recent developments in US politics discussed above indicate that distortion reduces the perceived distance between i and her preferred party and increases the distance between i and the other party. Our sense is that this distortion, long a factor in how voters assess parties and candidates, is stronger now than in the past.[1] The result is that, in contrast to the relatively sanguine view of spatial voting laid out in *Logic*, US voters today may be more forgiving of extreme positions taken by their preferred parties and candidates, and likely less willing to reward out-party candidates for attempts they make at moderating their policy stances.

Experimental studies that vary the presence of information about candidates' issue positions illustrate the potential consequence of declining local news coverage for the candidate position rule. When participants see such information, party labels predict their vote intention less powerfully and they are sensitive to issue congruence (Gilens, 2001; Bullock, 2011). According to these studies, candidate-specific policy information provided by the media could affect candidate choice even in an information environment that emphasized party affiliations. There are two caveats to this argument. First, the experiments generally give subjects no ability to select out of exposure to information. Hence, these studies are more informative with respect to people's reasoning capabilities than their actual reasoning because people may not seek out the information (or give less attention to it than research participants do). Second, not all studies find effects of policy information. Rahn (1993) and Peterson (2017), for example, found issue congruence to be overwhelmed by party identification when party labels were present.

IMPLICATIONS FOR ACCOUNTABILITY

What are the consequences of the changes outlined here for the two notions of accountability discussed at the beginning of this chapter? We first considered accountability as the extent to which Congress takes the unusual step of enacting laws that improve the welfare of the diffuse public while imposing costs on concentrated interests. Arnold's theory holds that all things being equal, reduced traceability should enhance the accountability of Congress to the general public. Many of the changes we identify – including partisan polarization and motivated reasoning that distorts voters' judgments, and weaker media that makes lawmakers' actions less salient – would on their face appear to reduce traceability. Has this sort of accountability therefore improved? If anything, the evidence suggests the opposite. Mayhew's updated list of important legislative enactments has about as many entries per Congress in recent years as it did in past decades. Using *New York Times* editorials to identify salient policy problems, Binder (2015) finds a drop in the share of important issues that were resolved by Congress in legislative sessions

---

[1] Assessing whether this is the case is made very difficult by the fact that the positions taken by the Democratic and Republican parties and their candidates have been moving further apart over time. Thus it might be quite difficult to empirically distinguish between over-time shifts in the placements by two hypothetical voters – one perfectly objective and one affected by distortion – of candidates and parties on the left-right scale.

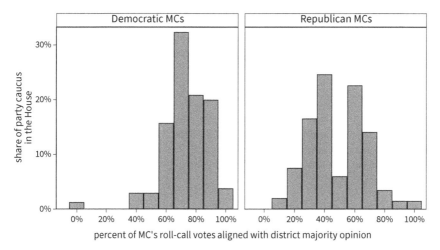

FIGURE 4.4 Representation and roll calls in the House, 2007–2008

since World War II. Curry and Lee (2019) examine the majority party's agenda instead, and also find a decline in the degree to which Congresses enact those agenda items. Overall, while a reduction in traceability may have provided a way for Congress to enact legislation that serves diffuse interests, polarization has reduced the will for the kinds of broad, bipartisan bargains that characterized the general-interest bills to which Arnold pointed as examples.

The consequences of reduced traceability for the second notion of accountability – that of members of Congress to their districts' median voters – is also disheartening. To illustrate, Figure 4.4 displays an analysis of the rich set of data collected by the 2008 Cooperative Congressional Election Study (CCES) to assess the rate at which members of the House voted with their district's majority opinion on a set of important roll-call votes in the 2007–2008 session. The 2008 CCES included a series of questions asking respondents how they would have voted on nine roll-call votes actually held during the legislative session. The CCES's large national sample permits the estimation of relatively precise measures of majority preferences at the district level. In Figure 4.4, members of Congress (MCs) are the unit of analysis. Displayed are histograms of each party's members by the share of the nine roll-call votes (ranging from 0 to 100%) that the member cast that matched district majority opinion. This comparison of district opinion with the votes actually cast by representatives provides a measure of the extent to which representatives were accountable to majority opinion during the session.

The picture is dispiriting for those hoping to see Congressional representatives acting as delegates. On average, members of Congress cast roll-call votes in accordance with their districts' opinion only 61% of the time. The figure was higher for Democrats (72%) than Republicans (49%), likely due in part to the fact that Democrats' control of the House in the 2007–2008 session made it easier for them to bring votes to the floor that forced Republican members to choose between their ideological principles and their districts' preferences. The fact that district majorities get their way just slightly more often than would be expected by chance suggests that current conditions are not particularly conducive to holding legislators accountable to their median voters. We unfortunately do not have historical data that would allow us to know whether this phenomenon is on the rise. But it leads us to the discomfiting conclusion that with regard to accountability, we are witnessing many of the costs *Logic* anticipates when traceability changes, but few of the benefits.

CONCLUSION

The three changes we identify in American politics since *Logic*'s publication all threaten citizens' ability to monitor and objectively evaluate lawmakers' actions. First, elite polarization, sorting in the mass public, and the growing impact of partisanship in elections have reduced constituents' inclination or ability to look beyond party. Second, vigorous, impartial media are on the decline, especially at the local level, making it harder for voters to trace policy effects back to the decisions of elected officials. Third, motivated reasoning is biasing constituents' assessments of the state of the world and their judgment of the extent to which elected officials should be held responsible for current conditions.

That said, there are limits to the changes we have outlined. Despite elite polarization and voter sorting, Congress has not evolved into a lock-step Westminster-style legislature. A bicameral system with staggered elections continues to exert moderating influence, and some important bipartisan legislation still passes. Local political journalism has not entirely disappeared, other actors in Arnold's model have incentives to increase traceability, and constituents need not routinely follow news reporting for it to inform them about key policy decisions and their consequences. Last, there are limits to motivated reasoning. Elections in our current era indicate that ideologically extreme incumbents still lose their bids for reelection – and moderates can enjoy high approval ratings – due in part to their records in office. Economic conditions continue to be strong predictors of election results and individual voting decisions (Lenz, 2012; Sides, Vavreck, and Tesler, 2018) and many people take notice when economic conditions change, regardless of their partisanship (Bisgaard, 2015; Khanna, 2019).

Even though Lenz (2012) finds a form of motivated reasoning on many policy issues (such that people who evaluate a candidate favorably typically change or adopt issue positions that are consistent with their candidate preference), his analysis of economic perceptions demonstrates that the impact of economic performance on vote choice increases over the course of an election campaign.

Backlash effects that lead people to update their attitudes in the direction opposite to new information or compelling arguments are rare (Chong and Druckman, 2010).

The operation of a perceptual screen does not fully cut the link between objective conditions and people's perceptions of them. Observed divergence in partisans' beliefs about objective facts is at least partly a consequence of partisan cheerleading that may be specific to the survey response rather than reflecting deeply held incorrect beliefs (Prior, Sood, and Khanna, 2015; Bullock et al., 2015). In short, while the changes we describe have likely raised the importance of policies' symbolic or psychic effects (such as seeing one's partisan "team" win election or thwart the other side's legislative efforts), real consequences of policy change continue to matter.

One corollary of the changes we emphasize is that primary electorates have become more extreme and more important compared to general electorates. Most congressional districts are uncompetitive, making victory in the dominant party's primary tantamount to election. In a weak-parties environment, party organizations have less power to overcome outside money and a fragmented media environment that can provide a lift to extreme primary challengers, giving incumbents good reason to fear challenges from their party's ideological flanks.

Arnold does not consider primary elections, but in fact *Logic*'s decision rules might very well apply to them. In primaries, the party performance and position rules are put aside, leaving only the incumbent performance rule and the incumbent position rule (with an in-party, rather than out-party, challenger). The incumbent performance rule predicts that incumbents will be penalized in primaries if they are associated with traceable policies that exact costs on important party interest groups (such as public-sector unions for the Democrats or the oil and gas industry for the Republicans). Applied to primaries, the incumbent position rule leads to the expectation that the party's intense policy demanders – for example, Republican activists who require that every candidate take a "no new taxes" pledge or Democratic activists who demand fealty to the party's health care agenda – raise the salience and therefore the weights primary voters place on the positions taken by incumbents and challengers on these and other issues the party "owns" (Egan, 2013). To the extent that they correctly anticipate these dynamics, incumbents can overcome primary challenges or stave them off entirely. Having secured their party's nomination, it would seem that incumbents in safe districts can then proceed to operate with considerably less constraint with regard to the general electorate than indicated by Arnold's four original decision rules.

Starker, more one-dimensional choices between parties, reinforced by cue-taking and motivated reasoning, have had mixed effects on electoral competitiveness. While recent presidential elections have tended to be competitive, the campaigns have largely focused on barely a dozen battleground states. In the majority of states and districts, incumbents have good reason to fear challenges from their party's extreme flanks more than a viable opponent in the general election.

To sum up, the incentives and political calculations collected in *Logic* still apply, even in an era of polarization, changing media, and motivated reasoning. In this chapter, we have argued that recent political changes have likely modified the weights that different considerations receive. Yet, none of our modernizations overturn the principles Arnold explained. Parties and voters have diverged on the main dimension of American political competition, but important laws still receive supermajorities in Congress. New technologies have multiplied media options and added many political extreme voices, but plenty of people continue to be exposed to moderate, lightly political news. Motivated reasoning pervades Americans' assessments of politics, but not to an extent that rules out counter-attitudinal updating of beliefs.

For political science, the continued relevance of the modernized *Logic* raises a challenge: the key questions empirical political research must address do not pertain to either-or matters of whether parties have polarized, voters followed them blindly, and media pushed them to further extremes. Rather, we need to better understand when and why parties compromise, voters lead, and media inform. *Logic*, and our modernizations of it, can provide theoretical guidance for such an effort, but answers will ultimately come from painstaking empirical work that is grand enough to systematically pick up these conditional effects.

5

Groups, Parties, and Policy Demands
in House Nominations

Kathleen Bawn, Knox Brown, Angela X. Ocampo,
Shawn Patterson, Jr., John L. Ray, and John Zaller

Congressional scholarship has paid little attention to organized interests in House primaries, viewing them as "candidate-centered" races whose outcomes depend on the skills and energies of the individual contestants (Herrnson, 2012). Work in the tradition of Downs (1957), including the vast literature on polarization, likewise overlooks organized effort, focusing instead on the spatial locations of voters and candidates.

In a challenge to both traditions, a 2012 paper by Bawn et al. proposed a group-centered theory of political parties in which nominations are controlled by groups seeking representation for their agendas. The paper reports only modest empirical support for its theory but has nonetheless attracted scholarly attention, both critical and laudatory (see McCarty and Schickler, 2018).

We aim in this chapter to add needed empirical flesh to the bare theoretical bones of the group-centric approach and thereby to address some of the criticism against it. We do so with evidence from a study of fifty-three winnable open seat primaries (WOSPs) for the House of Representatives in the 2013–2014 election cycle. Members of our research group conducted interviews with local observers and participants in forty-eight of the WOSPs. We also conducted exit polls of voters in four primaries and collected public information on the full set of fifty-three WOSP primaries. Our principal observation from this study is that most winning candidates anchored their campaigns in a single group or party organization. By this we mean that the group or party provided support sufficient to endow the candidate with a good chance of winning. The groups were the usual suspects of American interest group politics – business, manufacturing, finance, energy producers, and churches on the Republican side;

We thank Larry Bartels for constant advice and encouragement. We thank the Dean of Social Sciences at UCLA and the Department of Political Science at Vanderbilt for financial support. We alone are responsible for any errors in this paper.

labor, rights groups, and environmentalists on the Democratic side. National Political Action Committees, such as Club for Growth and EMILY's List, were also sometimes important.

The parties that anchored campaigns took several forms – modern patronage machines, group dominated party committees, informal associations of party activists and leaders, and the parties' congressional campaign committees (DCCC or NRCC).

By rough accounting, about 47% of primary winners anchored their campaigns in an interest or values group and another 34% in some form of party. We must add, however, that the two categories overlap, since parties regularly act as managers of group interests (Karol, 2009). But whatever the division of labor, the total influence of groups and parties on nominations appeared from our field research to be large.

Groups and parties might have simply backed candidates likely to win anyway, hoping thereby to ingratiate themselves with future lawmakers. But this is not what we observed. Groups and parties wanted candidates capable of winning, but they also wanted politicians with records of commitment to group issues and competence in dealing with them. To ensure that candidates met these requirements, groups developed arrangements that we describe as "vetting and vouching networks." They consist of leaders who knew or investigated candidates and made recommendations to group members who often acted on them. Vetting and vouching networks were a common means by which groups and parties mobilized their ranks in support of preferred candidates and hence a major element of candidate success.

Candidates seldom emphasized the agendas of their group and party sponsors in campaigns. But support for sponsors' goals was nonetheless often the reason that winning candidates had the support they did. In this basic sense, group and party agendas organized competition in a majority of our fifty-three individual House primaries.

These agendas fell into one of two broad classes. Some groups and most parties wanted narrow, material benefits; others had broader, values-based goals. Among Republicans, this difference took the form of fierce factional divisions between "establishment" and "insurgent" candidates. There was more consensus on the Democratic side in 2014, but this comparative agreement was as significant as disharmony (as has lately emerged) would have been. DiSalvo (2012) and Schlozman (2015) have shown that factional conflict shaped national party agendas in the past; factional conflict in our fifty-three WOSP primaries was having the same effect.

The overall picture emerging from our study is one in which groups and parties managing group interests seek the nomination of agents who will work for group agendas in Washington. We note, however, that the regularities that underpin this picture are from just one electoral cycle. More significantly, they have not been established through tests of pre-determined hypotheses, but merely suggested by inductive generalization over a mix of evidence.

The body of this chapter begins below with a description of our evidence. We then develop the theoretical framework that guides our interpretation of this data. In subsequent sections we analyze selected cases to show how group and party sponsorship of candidates organizes primary competition; we illustrate some forms that vetting and vouching networks take; we assess the frequency of anchoring across all fifty-three primaries, and acknowledge the limitations of the study. We conclude with remarks about the role of organized interests in party nominations.

THE PARTIES ON THE GROUND FIELD STUDY

This chapter is based on the Parties on the Ground field study at UCLA, a project that researched the fifty-three winnable open seat House primaries in the 2013–2014 electoral cycle. To define "winnable," we used Cook's Partisan Voting Index (PVI), along with the expectation that 2014 would be a good year for Republicans. Specifically, we counted a seat as winnable for Democrats if the PVI was Democratic or even. We counted a seat as winnable for Republicans if it was Republican, even, or up to D+4. As things worked out, our criteria excluded only one nomination that led to a general election victory (IA-1R).

Our cases included forty-one incumbent retirements, four of which counted as winnable for both parties, thus forty-five regular schedule nominations. We also included eight special primaries for seats that became vacant during the legislative session. None of the special election districts was competitive for both parties, giving a total of fifty-three.

We visited forty-three of the fifty-three winnable open seats from September 2013–July 2020, with most visits in 2014.[1] Visit length ranged from one to eight days, with some involving multiple trips. We did, out of district interviews in five cases and no interviews in five cases. This effort produced about 500 hours of recorded interviews with roughly 500 highly varied participants. Sources included candidates, campaign managers, donors, interest group leaders, party leaders, neighborhood activists, journalists, government officials, and local political scientists. We also used political blogs, newspapers and FEC reports.

In line with Bawn et al. (2012), one goal of PoG was to investigate group participation that had been overlooked in previous research. We did not, however, aim to test particular hypotheses. Aware that we ourselves could easily be guilty of overlooking critical elements of nominations, we sought through open-ended interviews to investigate whatever might be going on, depending on what our sources knew and were willing to talk about.

---

[1] Numerous UCLA undergraduates contributed to this research. We particularly thank Kat Bocanegra, Christine Kabayan, Christopher Leach, Caroline Leahy, Melissa Meisels, Axel Sarkissian, Christina Springer, Nico Studen, Karin Thrasher, and Angela Yip. Leach and Yip did interviews for one case and Springer for two. In addition, Spencer Hall of Vanderbilt University conducted one interview.

The evidence collected by this method is richly informative but also uneven. The schedule of primaries gave us more time in some districts than others. We had more success corralling high quality sources in some races than others. This unevenness creates the danger that our conclusions may be skewed toward races for which we got the fullest information. Moreover, even in our best understood races – those where many knowledgeable people spoke with us candidly and at length – we cannot claim to have a definitive interpretation of what happened. In several cases, a single interview changed our understanding of the race significantly, and we recognize that many interviews-that-didn't-happen might have had similar impact. More fundamentally, the primary environment is so uncertain at a deep level – in particular, so sensitive to which candidates enter – that it is unreasonable to try to identify "the" key factor in any particular race. The counterfactuals are too many and too complex. But we did turn up much evidence not observable by other means that sheds useful light on House primaries.

THEORETICAL BACKGROUND

What Do Groups Want?

Every student of Congressional politics knows that, on most important roll calls, nearly every Democrat and Republican votes with their own party and against the other. They also know that most House seats are safe for one party or the other. In the 114th Congress that we studied, only 17 out of 435 members were elected from districts that voted for the other party for president.

Why, then, should anyone besides the candidates themselves care about who wins congressional nominations? Won't representation be pretty much the same no matter who wins nomination?

For two reasons, the answer is no. The first follows from the nature of congressional work. Acts of Congress do far more than state policy; they amalgamate myriad detailed instructions on how public and private entities must behave. Even when legislative detail is non-controversial it may still be important, since poorly crafted laws may cause collateral damage to swaths of the economy or civil society. Other detail may be conflictual even among generally like-minded partisans. Blue collar employers, for example, might want different health policy details than would their white-collar counterparts.

Even in their first terms, MCs can exert significant influence over the high stakes details of national policy. They can sponsor bills, write special provisions of bills, broker private deals, put pressure on executive agencies, and much else (Chen, 2019, 29). As, moreover, Hall (1996) has observed, "Participation in Congress, for the most part, is not a matter of institutional design or authoritative delegation; for the most part, it is a matter of individual choice." This discretion is a standing invitation to groups to become involved in House primaries.

Factional Divisions

The second reason that group and party actors care who wins House nominations is that outcomes affect the balance of factional power within the party (DiSalvo, 2012; Schlozman, 2015). For example, an alliance of African Americans and unions – the so-called "black-blue coalition" – formed around 1940 and rapidly became a dominant force in the electoral politics of the Democratic Party outside the white South. The ensuing transformation of the Democratic party led the way to the civil rights acts of the 1960s and further party change thereafter (Schlozman, 2015; Schickler, 2016; Baylor, 2017). Similarly, religious conservatives, organized nationally through the Christian Coalition and locally through evangelical congregations, invaded Republican primaries in the 1980s and 1990s, working for candidates who were both pro-Life and pro-business rather than just pro-business (Baylor, 2017; Cohen, 2019). Their success helped transform the GOP from a mainly laissez-faire party to one committed to both social and economic conservatism.

Intraparty rivalries remain important today. We shall refer to groups that seek to maintain the existing party agenda and balance of factional power as "establishment" and those seeking to change them as "insurgents." Factions are, in effect, parties within the party, seeking either to defend or alter the party balance of power. Factions operate through a variety of means, most prominently national Super PACs. Important factional PACs on the Republican side in 2014 included Club for Growth, a Super PAC opposed to taxes and government regulation, and Eagle Forum, supporting traditional gender roles. While these groups sought to transform the GOP, others, such as the US Chamber of Commerce, defended the party status quo. Following a squabble between Tea Party and business Republicans over a federal government shutdown in 2013, the Chamber announced that it would challenge supporters of the shutdown in the upcoming primary cycle. *Time* reported that :

[T]he Chamber has cemented itself as the GOP Establishment's heaviest hitter in the fight to reclaim the party from Tea Party zealotry. It has forked over about $15 million to boost business-friendly candidates in 2014 [primaries], more than any other Republican group. And it has amassed an undefeated record in nearly a dozen races so far. (Altman, 2014)

Among Democrats, we observed several factional contests between an establishment union candidate and an insurgent EMILY's List candidate. EMILY's list was not concerned about ideology in the left-right sense, supporting candidates from the left, right, and center wings of the party. But it had a value-based factional goal: equalizing the male-female balance of power within the Democratic Party. Asked why this goal was important, a source explained:

A great example is [New York Senator] Kristen Gillibrand [who was supported by EMILY's List]. … This is someone who, as a woman has a unique voice on military sexual assault and will not tolerate it going through the military old boy's club. If she was a progressive man, I don't know if he would have stood up. In fact, we saw a lot of progressive men not stand up to the military on this.

Some scholars might theorize factional politics through the alternative lens of liberal-conservative ideology, viewing candidates as moderate or extreme rather than establishment or insurgent. There is warrant for this approach. Statistical scaling methods can assign groups such as Club for Growth and EMILY's List to reliable numerical positions on a Downsian left-right dimension (e.g., Bonica, 2014). These positions, moreover, generally seem reasonable to informed observers.

But left-right locations fail to capture the dynamics of House primaries. In a Downsian world, groups choose to support candidates based on their own position on the left-right continuum and their best estimate of the preferences of voters (see Aldrich, 2011). But this stylized dynamic was largely absent in our cases. Moreover, groups with similar left-right locations differed markedly in ways that had no connection to ideology but strongly affected their candidate choices. For example, Club for Growth and the Tea Party both supported candidates that might scale as strongly conservative, but Club's candidates would be pro-business and pro-immigration, whereas those of the Tea Party would be skeptical of business and opposed to immigration. On the Democratic side, EMILY's List and Sierra Club would both be seen as mainstream liberal. But the liberalism of the first centered on women's rights and that of the second on the environment, with neither group much concerned about other dimensions, much less, general ideological positioning. In these and other cases, factional groups are better understood in terms of particular policy demands rather than projected locations on a composite ideological dimension.

Another shortcoming of ideology as a tool for understanding House nominations is that it underplays key process elements: the willingness of a representative to prioritize one issue over others, to deploy effort and skill in the formulation of policy, and to attend to the implementation as well as the enactment of policy. As we will show, groups care about these elements and take them into account in their support decisions.

The deepest problem with viewing factional groups in terms of left-right ideology is that this dimension is endogenous to intraparty politics. Factional competition – e.g., the aforementioned rise of the blue-black coalition of the 1940s and the religious conservatives of the 1990s – continuously redefines the left-right dimension to include policy demands that were not previously part of it, thereby changing the content of left-right ideology. Ideology thus fails to provide a fixed yardstick for the analysis of intraparty conflict. In light of these concerns, we believe that House nominations can be more fruitfully studied in terms of factional rather than ideological conflict.

Anchoring a Champion

In their ideal world, every group would like to have its own MC – a legislative champion to look after its interests in Washington. But every district has many groups and can elect only one MC. The supply of legislative champions is another big constraint. To take an example that will come up below, every district has many pharmacists and perhaps some pharmacy supply companies, but how many have candidates who are qualified to advocate for pharmacy interests, want the job, and know how to win elections?

Still, every open seat has multiple politicians interested in it, including some who put themselves forward as group champions. Does it make political sense for groups to contribute to potential legislative champions?

The question is knottier than it may seem, so let's stick with a particular case, pharmacists. Pharmacists have professional associations, but their PACs are limited by law to contributions of only $5,000 each. The heavy lifting must therefore be done through contributions of individual pharmacists. According to Statista, there were 315,000 professional pharmacists in the USA in 2020, or about 720 per congressional district. If all 720 were to contribute $1,000 to a potential champion, it would amount to $720,000, which is roughly the total spending of the median winning candidate in our WOSP primaries. So yes, especially in a period in which a Republican Congress is expected to rewrite the Affordable Care Act and its many drug provisions, it could make sense for individual pharmacists to contribute heavily to – that is, anchor – the primary campaign of one of their own. And if this were so, it could make sense as well for pharmacist candidates to look to members of their group to support – that is, to anchor – their campaigns.

We don't claim that this brief analysis establishes the political rationality of group members supporting group candidates. Nor can we claim that existing scholarship, which focuses on ideology as the basis of representation in Congress, supports the idea. We aim only to provide a frame for one of the more notable patterns that has turned up in our data.

Party Organization

A serviceable definition of political party is that it is a coalition of interests and activists aiming to get control of government. The degree to which parties – that is, coalition members – organize in pursuit of this goal is highly variable. In textbook accounts of congressional primaries, there is little organization at all (Jacobson, 2013, 24). But recent research has reported cases in which coalition members work together in organized fashion. Most notably, Hassell (2017) has reported that the national congressional party committees influence Senate primaries by channeling the money of party-loyal donors to candidates they favor. Case studies by Schwartz (1990) and Fowler and McClure (1988) present compelling evidence of strong local organization in House primaries. Over a larger set of cases, Dominguez (2011) and Boatright (2014) likewise find evidence of organized party influence in House primaries, albeit weaker than in the previous two studies.

In our PoG field study, we observed House primaries that fit the textbook model: One group-backed candidate against another in a free-for-all melee (see MA-5 below). But we also observed cases of modern patronage parties that controlled their House primaries. Besides these formal party organizations, we found several cases of informal but decidedly party-like structures – "parties by other means" as Seth Masket (2004, 2011) has called them. These structures were so varied that one could almost say that each was unique, but they nonetheless functioned effectively in support of their candidates: A print shop owner who recruited candidates to mail campaigns that fed his business; a major national party fundraiser who, in retirement, led fundraising for his local party; a monthly poker game that endorsed, raised money and organized campaigns in local primaries. Masket has given a name, Informal Party Organization (IPO), to these groups and we shall adopt his usage. The defining feature of IPOs for us is that they involve coordinated candidate support by a range of party interests and actors, not simply one stakeholder group (e.g., unions).

What party organizations want in nominees is expected to be different than what individual groups want: Candidates committed to the preferences of the party coalition rather than of just one part of it and willing to cooperate and compromise with party leaders toward that end.

Finding a Champion: Principals and Agents in House Nominations

Identifying candidates that groups and parties can trust to represent them in Congress is no easy task. Some candidates have public records of past performance, but often in settings as opaque as the House of Representatives itself. Others have no public record at all. Candidates have no incentive to reveal past positions that might reflect poorly on them and little disincentive from misrepresenting their true views. In one Democratic primary, a candidate who had led conservative efforts to block progressive legislation in the state Assembly nonetheless called herself a "true American progressive" in her TV ads and went entirely unchallenged on this point in the campaign coverage of three local papers. Reliable candidate information at the pre-campaign stage at which most groups make their support decisions was even more difficult to come by.

In consequence, groups approach open congressional nominations with widespread uncertainty on two key dimensions: Which, if any, candidates are committed, in the sense of prioritizing the goals of potential supporters and deploying effort to pursue them? Which are competent to do so, capable of working effectively in Washington?

Principal-agent theory grew out of the desire to understand exactly this kind of dilemma. We use it here to understand how groups (principals) choose agents (candidates) to represent their interests in Congress.[2] In classic PA analysis, a business owner (principal) would like to hire an employee (agent) and the potential employee would like to take the job. But this mutually beneficial exchange of labor for wages may not take place if the principal cannot adequately monitor the agent's actions. A storeowner, for example, may not be able to directly observe whether the employee is helpful and polite to customers. The incentive for agents to underperform when their actions cannot be monitored is called "moral hazard." Moral hazard abounds in an opaque institution like the House of Representatives, with its hidden power centers, undisclosed deals, convoluted procedures, and scores of individuals contributing to each important bill.

Moral hazard can be offset by making agent compensation contingent on observables. The business owner, for example, might link employees' pay to sales revenue (Holmström, 1979). The ability of a principal to punish moral hazard ex post works to the advantage of both principals and agents by making the relationship sufficiently appealing ex ante.

In political contexts, however, principals have extremely limited options to offset moral hazard (Fearon, 1999). Groups cannot write enforceable contracts contingent on how politicians behave in office. Nor is it easy to "fire" individual MCs for poor performance. A group displeased by an MC's efforts can withhold future campaign contributions, or even support a challenger, but this may matter little to an MC protected by incumbency. Given this inability to influence or sanction politicians after they attain office, Bawn et al. (2012) have argued that groups do better supporting politicians at the nomination stage whom they know to be trustworthy, and the PoG project has focused on open seat nominations for exactly this reason.

In the same vein, PA theory argues that as moral hazard becomes harder to punish, principals and agents should concern themselves more with avoiding "adverse selection."[3] Adverse selection occurs when low quality agents are attracted to situations in which their shortcomings will not be punished. For example, jobs which shield employees from the consequences of being rude to customers may be particularly attractive to those prone to rudeness. The harmful effects of adverse selection are famously illustrated by George Akerlof's (1970) "market for lemons" example, in which the incentive to sell a bad used car (a "lemon") to an unsuspecting buyer destroys the market for good

---

[2] See Miller (2005) and Gailmard (2014) for overviews of principal-agent models and their use in political science, as well as Cameron and Gordon, Chapter 10, and Patty, Chapter 11, in this volume.

[3] Drutman (Chapter 13, this volume) argues that increasingly partisan elections have made it easier for organized interests to hold MC's accountability, relative to ordinary voters. We strongly agree that voters are in a worse position than groups to punish moral hazard by incumbents. But this does not undermine the argument that groups do better by focusing on selection.

used cars by scaring away buyers who cannot tell the difference. This same uncertainty can discourage qualified candidates from running, and motivated policy demanders from supporting them.

What, then, can groups do to avoid adverse selection? Adverse selection stems from incomplete information. A principal with good information about agent commitment and competence has no PA problem. Potential principals and agents who have previously worked together, know each other well, or are part of the same broad network, are thus greatly advantaged.

In the absence of direct experience, signaling by prospective agents and screening by prospective principals can mitigate adverse selection.

SIGNALING. Candidates provide plenty of information about themselves through websites, advertisements, and public appearance. But campaign messages rarely constitute effective signals of commitment or competence. The key feature of informative signaling is that it involves behaviors that a high-quality agent can take, and a low-quality agent cannot. This does not apply to campaign materials: low-quality candidates can say most of the same things high-quality ones can.

SCREENING. Groups seek reliable information about candidates by means we describe as vetting and vouching. By "reliable," we mean information that cannot be faked by a low-quality candidate. By "vetting," we mean generating reliable information about commitment to and competence in dealing with group agendas. Vetting takes many forms: close observation over a long time, working together on political projects, interviews, questionnaires, even hiring professional investigators. By "vouching," we mean avowals of support for which the endorser may be held accountable if the candidate underperforms.

Although no method is foolproof and good information can come from any direction, a vetter's experience working with the candidate on a political task may produce the most reliable information. Almost by definition, low quality candidates cannot fake good performance in a cooperative task. Close observation of candidates, and regular discussion with those who have dealt personally with them, may be almost as valuable.

In any given race, the number of people with this kind of information will likely be small, but they have a strong incentive to share it with like-minded others. Potential supporters who themselves lack personal experience with a candidate can get the next best thing if they have a relationship of trust with someone who does – that is, if they are part of a vouching network. Vetting and vouching networks thus have potential value to all who participate in House primaries. Network leaders use them to share candidate information with allies, thereby multiplying the benefits of vetting. Individuals in networks obtain reliable information about which candidates will best pursue their goals. And candidates who can credibly demonstrate commitment and competence to networks get that message out to large numbers of potential supporters.

Groups and candidates who can overcome the informational obstacles to principal-agent relationships will be systematically advantaged in House primaries. We turn now to a formal model highlighting the conditions necessary for a group to support a candidate, given uncertainty about commitment and competence.

THE DECISION TO PARTICIPATE.   When does a group (principal) support a candidate (agent) in a House primary? A natural way to think about this question is to compare the expected payoff from support to the costs, accounting for uncertainty about commitment and competence.

This is a complex decision, but patterns observed in our field research suggest reasonable simplifications. For our purposes, let g denote the probability that a candidate from the group's party wins the general election, p be the probability that the group's candidate wins the primary, and q the probability that the candidate is a competent and committed agent. Assume for convenience that these events are independent. Let V denote the payoff for the best outcome – a competent, committed agent elected to Congress. Let W denote the payoff if the agent is elected but fails to be competent or committed, and X the payoff if a different candidate from the group's party wins the general election. Finally, let Y be the payoff if the other party's candidate wins. The principal's expected payoff is thus

$$g\left[p\left(qV + (1 - q)W\right) + (1 - p)X\right] + (1 - g)Y. \qquad (5.1)$$

Restricting attention to districts that are safe for the dominant party – the typical House race – allows us to let $g = 1$. For now, we also assume that the principal's support decision only impacts the agent's probability of winning, it does not alter q. (We will relax this assumption shortly.)[4] We are thinking of X as the expected payoff when the general election is won by a generic politician from the group's own party. That is, X generally implies a reliable vote for the party's policy agenda, average (within-party) responsiveness to the group's concerns, average ability to understand relevant technical issues, average level of political efficacy. From this perspective, the difference between W and X blurs – both represent the value to the group of a non-champion co-partisan. We can thus further simplify by letting $W = X$.[5] These restrictions give the following formulation of a group's expected gain, S_C, from supporting a potential champion:

$$S_C = \Delta p q[V - X], \qquad (5.2)$$

where $\Delta p > 0$ denotes the difference the group's support makes in the candidate's probability of winning the primary.

---

[4] We also assume that the group's support does not affect X. This means that the group supporting its favorite candidate does not increase the chance of a truly terrible candidate winning the primary.

[5] In cases where a poor agent would be better than the likely alternative primary winner ($X < W$), there would be an additional incentive to support the candidate, even if their commitment and or competence was in question.

The question then is whether expected benefits S_C exceed the costs of support. With this in mind, consider each term on the right side of Equation 5.2. Most relevant is q, representing uncertainty about commitment and competence. The higher the probability that the candidate is a committed and competent agent, the greater the benefits of primary support.

Another component of S_C is $\Delta p = p_1 - p_0$, the impact of group support on the candidate's probability of winning the primary. This quantity is at its highest when p_0 is close to zero, corresponding to the case of an anchoring group.

The final component of S_C is $V - X$, the difference between a group champion and a generic co-partisan. Some groups, and perhaps most voters, care more about which party wins than about which person is nominated. When S_C is small because V and X are similar, there is no reason to participate in the nomination contest. And many groups do routinely stay out of nomination politics, waiting until after the primary to engage.

The set of groups who do participate in a given primary are thus the small subset for whom the difference between V and X is sufficiently large. Effectively excluded are groups with the resources and desire to support a champion, but are unable to find one among the set of candidates willing to run. Even with extensive group support, running for Congress demands significant time, money and personal effort. We encountered multiple cases of potential candidates who would have had high V for a powerful group, but were nonetheless unwilling to make the sacrifices necessary to run. Some groups actively recruit candidates, but many take a more passive role. Even those who do recruit sometimes come up short.

Middle ground exists, however, between supporting a champion and staying out of the primary completely. A group that finds itself without an obvious champion may decide to support an "ally" – to establish a relationship with a candidate to open a line of communication, to gain access to the politician's attention as needed, to (as a source in one race put it) increase the chance that one's phone calls are returned.

Although there is no obvious bright line between a champion and an ally, the distinction nonetheless merits attention. Champions are proactive on the principal's behalf; allies respond to what McCubbins and Schwartz (1984) called "fire alarms." For this reason, the commitment and competence necessary for a champion is much higher than for an ally, which in turn means that the pool of available champions is likely to be smaller than for allies.

With regard to allies, we must now consider cases where the candidate's effort on behalf of the group is contingent upon group support. That is, we need to allow for the possibility that the probability the candidate is a good agent depends on whether the group supports the candidate or not. Returning to Equation 5.1, allow p_1 and p_0 to represent the probabilities that the candidate wins the primary with and without the group's support, and q_1 and q_0 the probabilities that the candidate is a responsive ally with and without group support. The gain from supporting a potential ally is

$$S_A = (p_1 q_1 - p_0 q_0)[V - X]. \tag{5.3}$$

The value of an effective champion in office $(V - X)$ is higher than the corresponding value for an ally, and a given group may offer a lower level of support offered to an ally than a champion. But Equation 5.3 shows that the basic informational considerations are the same: Is the candidate competitive (p_1)? Are they sufficiently committed and competent to be an effective ally (q_1)?

The broader point here is that the set of groups who participate in any given primary is a small subset of all who might benefit from congressional champions and allies (those for whom $V - X$ is high). Even when potentially strong candidates exist (p_1 is high), uncertainty about the candidate's commitment and competence (low q) may torpedo the deal.

GROUPS, PARTIES, AND FACTIONS IN SELECTED PRIMARIES

This section presents descriptions of eight primaries chosen to illustrate the ideas sketched above. The first two – a Republican contest in Georgia and a Democratic one in Massachusetts – illustrate cases in which group interests dominated even though factional influence was present. In the next pair, two Republican contests in Alabama, factional conflict was at the forefront.

The remaining four cases illustrate different forms of party anchoring: A union-dominated local organization in New Jersey; a business-friendly local party in Pennsylvania; an effort by the national Democratic Party to manage the challenges of California's Top Two primary system; and a Democratic IPO in Michigan.

Group-Dominated Contests in Georgia and Massachusetts

Close observers identified State Senator Buddy Carter early on as the strongest contender for the open seat in GA-1, largely because of support from his occupational group, pharmacists. An observer explained:

You've got Obamacare, all the ... Medicare-Medicaid issues about payment for prescription drugs. You've got all the layers of regulatory paperwork that apply to all businesses, and so you've got a bunch of rich people out there who happen to be pharmacists who want one of theirs up there [in Congress].

A different source made the same point:

Everything inside a pharmacy is controlled by public policy. From how many technicians you can have in a pharmacy, to where you have to place certain drugs, how you're reimbursed, you know, it's all controlled by people who are elected.

But, the source lamented,

There are no pharmacists in Congress! Twenty-something doctors, a hundred something attorneys. You have two almond farmer ranchers. ... You know you've got two almond farmers who have more of a say as for what that legislation should look like than someone who deals with it on a daily basis.

Drawing on politics in the state legislature, where several pharmacists served, the source continued:

If there's something that deals with pharmacy and prescription drugs, then the legislators go to the five pharmacists and ask 'em "what does this do?" I would assume that the same thing would happen in DC, that you would have people wanting input from someone who actually knows what they're doing.

Based on FEC filings, Carter raised roughly $435,000 from pharmacy owners, PACs for pharmacy related businesses (e.g., drug manufacturers), and employees of pharmacy-related businesses. This support constituted 45% of all money raised by Carter, establishing him as serious contender and a credible target for support by other local benefit seekers.

The next strongest candidate was Bob Johnson, a physician who had not previously held elective office. He received support from several national conservative groups: Citizens United, Senate Conservatives Fund, Madison Project, and Club for Growth. Club for Growth's independent expenditure of $390,000 for Johnson constituted about a third of his total spending.

Like Carter, Johnson got strong support from members of his profession and associated PACs. By our calculation, contributions from medicine-related sources came to about $510,000, or 44% of all of Johnson's fund-raising. The third major candidate in this race, John McCallum, was a financial advisor who had served as an aide to Newt Gingrich. Our best-informed sources agreed in advance of the primary that Carter was the frontrunner but differed as to whether his strongest competitor was Johnson or McCallum. While Carter was slightly outspent by both Johnson and McCallum, he finished first in the primary with 36% of the vote. Johnson was second with 23%, followed by McCallum with 20.5%. In the ensuing runoff, Carter beat Johnson 54–46%.

Given his support from conservative groups, it is unsurprising that Johnson campaigned as a committed conservative. But so did Carter. In their advertisements both appeared in the white lab coats of their professions and both emphasized the standard Republican themes of opposition to taxes and Obamacare without taking any ideologically distinguishing position. The third candidate, McCallum, simply featured his family in both of his advertisements.

Johnson did signal extremism at one point by attacking security checks in airports, commenting at a candidate forum that "I'd rather see another terrorist attack, truly I would, than to give up my liberty as an American citizen." But he retracted the comment the next day, saying "I said something stupid." The episode got good play in the district's leading newspaper, but the district's second daily paper ran only the retraction and a third daily paper never mentioned the incident.

One might conjecture that Johnson's ideological support base was known to elite donors, prompting ideological moderates among them to support Carter. But when our sources discussed the broader fundraising strategies of candidates, they pointed to practical rather than ideological motives. For example, Carter and McCallum were seen as competing for support from the local business community, centered on agribusiness and the port of Savannah:

> Those businesses are in play for Buddy Carter and John McCallum... because they need a friend in Congress [PoG: what kind of things would be friendly?] Making sure that the guy wants to fight the EPA when they want to do stuff. Fighting the bureaucracy on their behalf when they want to expand or whatever the heck they want to do.

Here, as in many other races,[6] candidates who received business support may look "moderate" relative to candidates supported by ideological groups. But candidates do not bid for support from business by demonstrating moderation. Our source made this especially clear in his discussion of farmers, whose support would depend on who "will be the most pro-active for the industry."

> Farmers want day laborers, people allowed to get here easily. So you can't underestimate how important it is to know they're gonna have a guy [MC] who will stand up to Democrat or Republican administrations and say "you're not deporting our workers. We don't care what you have to say to the media or other Republicans, but these guys are gonna be here to pick the damn crops every time we need a crop picked."

Clearly no great display of moderation here!

In the end, Carter attracted the lion's share of the agriculture and other general business money in the race. As noted, he ended up raising close to half of his campaign funds from pharmacy-related interests. Like many group-backed candidates, Carter's campaign was anchored in a group that regarded him as a champion, thus making him viable in the eyes of a broader set of groups seeking allies.

Ideology was present in this race in the form of ideological PACs that played an anchoring role for Johnson. Yet Johnson did not run an ideological campaign and he got almost as much support from members of his occupational group as from the right wing PACs. Johnson was beaten by the candidate with deeper ties to the business and professional groups in the district.

---

[6] Chapter 12 (Powell et al.) in this volume also suggests that this kind of intervention may be common in DC.

Ideology played an even smaller role in most of the Democratic races we studied, including the special primary election held in October 2013 for the MA-5 district outside Boston. Our sources agreed that the main candidates were all "Massachusetts liberals" who would vote the liberal position on nearly every issue that came along. "I'm not sure there's any issues [in the election]," said a leading party insider.

Yet some five million dollars and tens of thousands of hours of volunteer time were spent in a hard-fought primary. Why so much effort if all candidates would vote the same in Congress?

A leader of one district group put it this way: "[Groups] want to know that they've got a candidate who's really going to carry their water … it's not so much how you vote on the bill at the end of the day, but how hard did you work to get that line item in the bill that is going to benefit [our group] in a significant way." Sometimes changes that are "imperceptible to the human eye … [can be] really important to a particular group." Another leader of an activist group put it more simply: "We look for champions – folks who will not only vote for us, but will be actively vocal about their support … and make efforts to encourage their colleagues to support."

Four of the five main candidates in the 5th district primary had an important commitment apart from their shared ideological liberalism, and group support related to that commitment. Much more than ideology, these commitments organized the race.

The early front runner and eventual winner was Katherine Clark. Her commitment was to women's issues. Prior to her service in the state legislature, she had been staff attorney for the state Office of Childcare Services, where she helped create a commission for primary education standards. NARAL and Planned Parenthood were key supporters in her state legislative races. Once elected, she sponsored a bill broadening the purview of restraining orders in domestic violence cases. In 2013, she was named Legislator of the Year by the Women's Bar Association. In the congressional primary, Clark's campaign made women's issues, especially equal pay, the main appeal, despite polls showing that voters were more concerned about economic issues. Clark won high profile endorsements from several women's groups, most notably EMILY's List. Indirect expenditure by EMILY's List nearly doubled Clark's funding for voter contact and communication in the final weeks of the campaign.

Runner-up Peter Koutoujian was the elected sheriff of the largest county in the district. His campaign was standard liberal fare, but Koutoujian's father was Armenian, giving him a strong connection to Armenian communities in the district and nationwide. The Armenian National Committee of America endorsed him, organized a phone bank, and helped him fundraise. An excerpt from an ANCA press release captures the attitude of many groups in House primaries:

"We have a chance to elect someone who has the same story we all have; who speaks not just as our friend, but as one of us," explained ANCA National Board Member Richard Sarajian at a weekend meeting of activists and supporters from throughout the Eastern United States. "I have one task for you. I want you to call every single friend, relative or other person that you know in Peter Koutoujian's district and get them out to vote."[7]

FEC filings show that about 37% of Koutoujian's individual campaign contributions came from persons having ethnically Armenian names.[8]

Third-place finisher Carl Sciortino claimed to be the "true progressive" in the race. But his campaign was most notable for a charming TV ad that featured a conversation between the openly gay candidate and his curmudgeonly but endearing Tea Party father. The ad went viral and marked him as the LGBTQ candidate in the race. Furthering this image, Sciortino married his partner ten days ahead of the primary. Sciortino was endorsed by the LGBTQ Victory Fund, which also helps explain how a member of the Massachusetts State Assembly got 47% of his individual contributions – by far the largest share of any candidate – from out of state.

Unlike other top candidates, the fourth-place finisher Will Brownsberger had no group associations, aside from a following he had cultivated for himself. Brownsberger presented himself as an iconoclastic truth teller who just wanted to get policy right.

Last among the main contenders was Karen Spilka. She carried union issues in the legislature, got many union endorsements and $7,500 from union PACs, and was viewed by some as labor's candidate in the primary. But if labor supported Spilka, it did not do so strongly. She remained in the legislature after losing the primary and labor may have aimed only to stay on her good side.

The campaign was fought through TV ads, mailers, and volunteer canvassers, with Clark the comfortable plurality winner. We offer no explanation for the electoral result except to observe that ideological appeals had little apparent importance.

Establishment vs. Insurgent in Alabama

Alabama had two high profile Republican contests in our study. The first was a special election held late in 2013, centered on the city of Mobile, the other a regular primary in Birmingham. In both, large multi-candidate primary fields resulted in runoffs between an establishment and an insurgent candidate. The establishment candidate won in Mobile and the insurgent in Birmingham. More important for our purposes is how group politics played out.

The establishment candidate in AL-1 (Mobile) was Bradley Byrne, a former Democrat who made his reputation as a tough-minded, pro-business reformer

---

[7] ANCA press release. www.anca.org/press_releases/press_releases.php?prid= 2325.

[8] This tally misses contributions from married Armenian women who had changed their names.

of the state community college system. The Alabama business community had supported Byrne for the Republican gubernatorial nomination in 2010, but he lost to a populist outsider. Following defeat, Byrne stayed involved with the Chamber of Commerce. "[Byrne] was always part of the Chamber of Commerce crowd," said one of our sources. "The corporate community knows Bradley Byrne, likes Bradley Byrne, that's been in place for years," said another.

The insurgent candidate, Dean Young, had been a campaign aide to Roy Moore, the controversial Chief Justice of the Alabama Supreme Court, and had roots in evangelical churches. Echoing remarks of several others, one source said that Dean

… was at every Christian conservative Bible study group that met on Wednesday night … a whole bunch of people who don't normally vote in a special election were there voting for Dean Young … If you're in a fire and brimstone congregation, you know Dean Young personally.

Beyond the large differences in their support coalitions, the two candidates presented radically different styles. Where Byrne described himself as a "work horse," Young told would-be supporters that, if he were elected, they should get

a big ole thing of popcorn and a big Super Gulp and lean back and turn on C-SPAN. Because I promise you, I will stand on the floor of the House and stand for the principles that we believe in that made this nation great.[9]

FEC records document the candidates' different support coalitions. Seventy-one corporate PACs contributed $205,000 to Byrne in the runoff; none gave to Young. There was significant overlap between contributors to Young and to Roy Moore in his recent election campaign for the state court.

The AL-1 special runoff took place in the shadow of a seventeen-day partial shutdown of the federal government that was instigated by the GOP's insurgent Tea Party MCs and resisted by its establishment wing. Pundits across the country saw the Byrne-Young contest as a test of strength between the two factions. "In Alabama election, a showdown between the GOP establishment and Tea Party" and "Establishment Republicans Declare War on Tea Party" read headlines in the *New York Times* (Robertson and Lipton, 2013) and *Time* magazine.

Despite this frame, policy differences between Byrne and Young were muted in the public campaign. Byrne, as noted, promised to be a work horse for the district. Young promised to be "the Ted Cruz Congressman," but spoke little about policy. When the candidates were asked in a public debate for their

---

[9] Isenstadt, Alex. "GOP Frets over Alabama Contender," *Politico*, November 3, 2014. Downloaded 11/19.

positions on the recent government shutdown, both gave short answers and moved on. "[T]he campaign isn't about policy – it's about style," said the *Daily Beast*.[10] "The contrast between the two is largely cosmetic," said *Mother Jones* (Murphy, 2013).

Byrne's spending advantage was enormous: about $865,000 in the runoff, compared to Young's $125,000. As for Young, MSNBC reported (Taylor, 2013),

While the GOP cavalry is riding in to protect Byrne, national Tea Party and conservative groups haven't shown up for Young – and he's clearly frustrated and puzzled by their absence.

"Where are y'all? Because we've got the classic battle taking place down here," Young said on Wednesday. "We've got the people; we just don't have the resources [Byrne has] with establishment groups .... That's very difficult to swallow."

Particularly disappointing to Young was that, despite his promise to be a "Ted Cruz congressman," one of Cruz's backers, the Stop Spending Now PAC, came into the race for Byrne (Kirby, 2013). Said its president:

It's a great talking point to say you'll be like Ted Cruz. But Ted Cruz is a very smart, a very thoughtful person. And we think Bradley Byrne is better on all of these points.[11]

Byrne won the runoff with 52.5%, so it is easy to imagine that Young would have won if he had received the hoped-for support from the GOP's conservative PACs. Their reluctance to accept Young as their agent thus emerges as the pivotal factor in this intraparty showdown. Young's commitment to the insurgent cause seems clear enough; what he lacked was commitment to legislative efficacy.

In the 6th Alabama primary a few months later, the GOP's establishment wing supported Paul DeMarco, a state legislator who epitomized candidate-centered political ambition. For years he had worked the district, including parts that did not overlap his state legislative district, meeting people, listening to them, and helping with their problems. Said the leader of a trade association that endorsed DeMarco:

[DeMarco] has really worked hard to get to know our folks. .... Making time to get out and meet with the board, spending time, getting to know their issues ... He does his homework.

---

[10] "Alabama's Republican Runoff Election May Predict the Party's Future," Ben Jacobs. Downloaded 11-2-19.

[11] "Dean Young vows to be 'Ted Cruz Congressman,' but pro-Cruz PAC backs Byrne," AL.Com, November 4, 2013. Downloaded 11-2-19.

Said another source of DeMarco:

He's a hustler, a grinder, smart guy. But always less ideological .... he's known as the guy who, if there's more than three people meeting in his district about anything, Paul's there ... When it was not campaign time, Paul was still out working the district. Always visible, always looking for ways to keep his name prominent.

Yet none of our sources spoke of DeMarco as a champion of business and several mentioned the downside of his political ambition. One observed that DeMarco "passed a lot of bills" but never championed a real cause:

It was much shallower than that ... It was never a bill that made one group mad. It was always, 'What can I pass that makes everybody happy?'
He was never somebody where, if it came down to being in the fox hole, he would be there with you.

The result was that business support for DeMarco was, several sources commented, consistent but tepid. DeMarco got business support, but his commitment from business was soft.

Among the insurgent candidates was Chad Mathis, a physician whose early entry to the race with Club for Growth support may have pressured the incumbent to retire. But Mathis turned out to be a poor campaigner and, despite strong funding, finished fourth in the primary. The strongest insurgent was Scott Beason, a state legislator who had sponsored a "take your guns to work" bill and an anti-immigration bill, both anathema to business. With this record, Beason raised even less money than Dean Young in the 1st district and ended up finishing third.

The insurgent conservative who did make the runoff was Gary Palmer. As a young man in the 1980s, Palmer founded a think tank for family policy, broadening later to include economic issues. By 2014, Palmer's Alabama Policy Institute (API) had a full-time staff of nine experts turning out reports touting free market solutions to a range of state problems. API was a respected policy advisor to the poorly staffed Alabama legislature, with Palmer himself lead fundraiser and policy wonk.

Palmer entered the race with an advantage that fellow insurgent Dean Young notably lacked, a stable of API donors from which he could raise $250,000 in the first two weeks of his candidacy, a feat that immediately established his viability as a serious candidate. One source commented that Palmer hardly needed to ask these donors for money; he only needed to tell them he was running. Palmer's business support was otherwise modest, but national conservative groups reacted much more favorably than they had to Young. Club for Growth, which had shunned Young in the primary, gave Palmer a second interview when he made the runoff and, after taking time to scrutinize his position on taxes, launched a $250,000 TV blitz against his opponent, DeMarco.

The GOP's establishment wing also reacted differently to Palmer's runoff campaign. One source said during the runoff:

Normally, when the Club for Growth gets in big behind a candidate, the [national] Chamber is coming in right behind to get behind somebody else ... I don't think that's going to happen [here].... I think they're going to say, 'we're fine with either of these guys.'

Another source offered a similar view:

There are corporate givers to the [Alabama] Policy Institute that are the mainstream corporate people in this country. ... It would not surprise me that if ... they're on the phone saying, "Stay out of this race. Gary will be just fine: he's a reasonable person, he's not Dean Young.... You all can live with the outcome of this race."

The national Chamber of Commerce, which had spent $200,000 on Byrne in AL-1, did indeed leave DeMarco to fend for himself in the AL-6. In contrast to Dean Young, whose fundraising lagged far behind Byrne's in both primary and runoff, insurgent Palmer actually raised more money than establishment DeMarco in his runoff. Palmer won the runoff with 64% of the vote.

The fates of the four candidates in these two runoffs illustrate our central point: Even where ideological concern is strong, principals want agents capable of promoting their particular goals. Both Young and Palmer were extremely conservative candidates, likely to be reliable insurgents within the House Republican caucus. But factional PACs gave Young the cold shoulder in a race they might have enabled him to win, while making big contributions to Palmer in a race that he was winning without them. The difference was likely due to the skills and commitments of the two candidates: Young seemed to care more about C-SPAN performances than political efficacy, whereas Palmer had two decades of experience as an expert advocate of the kind of free market policies favored by his principal PAC sponsor, Club for Growth. These races indicate that competition in House primaries is not denominated in general ideological location, but in the ability to work effectively inside the Washington Establishment for the agendas – whether particularistic or ideological – principals want. We now turn to four cases illustrating how different forms of party organization can anchor campaigns.

A Strong Democratic Party in New Jersey

The Democratic Party in NJ-1 consisted of three separate county party committees, each able to provide preferred ballot placement to its endorsee and to deploy hundreds of campaigners to knock doors. With these powers, the county committees essentially always carried the primary vote for their preferred candidates, which in 2014 was Donald Norcross for all three. Why Norcross? Because he had served for sixteen years as president of the Southern New

Jersey AFL-CIO Central Labor Council. He had spent much of his energy in this job building union representation in local offices, including Democratic County committees. In this situation, party and union support for Norcross were almost the same thing, and with both on his side Norcross was the easy winner.

The tight connection between parties and interests in this case was typical of other cases in which parties had strong institutional roles.

A Strong Republican Party in Pennsylvania

When the incumbent unexpectedly resigned from the historically Republican 6th Pennsylvania district, the *PoliticsPA* blog headlined that the primary was "wide open" and named five candidates who had expressed interest. But only three days later it reported that the field "is shrinking rapidly." Among those reconsidering was Patrick Collins, a party fundraiser and activist, who explained,

Over the past week I have had the chance to speak with many friends, colleagues, and community leaders … These conversations were terrific in highlighting to me both the potential benefits and hazards of running for the GOP nomination. After such discussions, it became clear to me that the Republican Party is coalescing around Ryan Costello as the preferred candidate for the nomination.[12]

An online comment suggested that Collins might be next in line for a party position, provided he didn't try to jump the pecking order. Ryan Costello was the chair of the Board of Commissioners of Chester County, the biggest of four counties in the district. When the Chester County Republican Party Committee met to interview candidates seeking its endorsement, Costello was the only one who showed up. He got the endorsement, remained unopposed through the primary, and was elected to Congress with 56% of the general election vote.

It is somewhat surprising that the primary for a Republican-leaning open seat drew only one candidate. What happened?

The committee's power appeared to rest on three foundations. The first is an army of some 400 campaign workers who go door-to-door for its endorsed candidates. Many of these workers are local government employees, contractors, and vendors whose livelihoods depend on GOP control of local offices. The second is business donors who are, as a source put it, "very loyal" to the committee. By this he appeared to mean that businesses donate to party-endorsed candidates and not to non-party candidates. The third foundation is that, while the 6th district includes parts of four counties, Chester is the largest, covering 42% of the district's population. "Other county chairs see that [our] candidate is going to win whether they put up somebody or not," said the party source.

---

[12] "PA-6: Republicans Rafferty and Collins Decide Against Run," PoliticsPA, January 20 2014.

So how did the Chester County GOP make its choice? As our source, who was a leading member of the Republican Committee, related it, he and Costello made the decision themselves. Both were interested in Congress, but after a slightly heated discussion – our source initially described it as a dustup, but then said this was too strong a word – they decided that Costello would run. With these two in agreement, "no one else was going to come in ... though there was a state Rep. who might have tried." When asked if business was influential in the endorsement process, the source said, "I guess the county Chamber is important, but I don't know how important." The source then asked a second individual, who had been listening to the interview, what he thought. "Most people stay out of the endorsement process and let us handle it," this person said. Left unmentioned in the interview but likely important in the story is that business is quite satisfied with the representation it gets from nominees of the Chester County Republican Party Committee.

National Party Intervention in a Top Two Primary

With a population 49.3% Hispanic, 9.9% black, and 7.4% Asian American, California's 31st district would seem to be safely Democratic. But in 2012, it elected conservative Republican Gary Miller. The 2012 election was California's first under the "top two" primary, whereby candidates from all parties appear on single ballot, with the top two advancing to the general election in November. In 2012, with the Democratic vote split among four candidates, Republicans finished first and second in the primary, and Miller went on to win the general election.

The Democratic Congressional Campaign Committee (DCCC) was mortified to lose a majority-minority district in this way, and it actively recruited Pete Aguilar, the strongest Democrat in 2012, to run again. Aguilar, the well-liked mayor of a small middle-class city, lacked views that might be problematic in the general election.

An activist from a local Democratic Club described an early DCCC-sponsored event to establish Aguilar as a frontrunner too strong to challenge:

It was a get-together including the unions and the clubs. ... This was real early in the process ... before anybody had declared ... It was to throw our support to [Aguilar]. [Neighboring congressman] Mark Takano was there and [congresswoman] Gloria Negrete McLeod. ... They were there to say, Yes, we support Pete, we encourage all of you to support Pete. We want to get out early so that we can discourage other candidates from running, so we can have a united party behind him and not run in to the same situation as in 2012 ... All of the presidents of the Democratic Clubs stood up and said, I'm behind Pete and I'm going to do this or that. And all the labor union representatives did the same thing. So the breakfast was really like kind of a rally, let's all get together and support this guy.

With the assistance of DCCC staff, Aguilar jumped to an early fundraising lead. But three other Democrats nonetheless entered the race. Then the

Republican incumbent resigned, creating an open seat, winnable for Democrats by our criteria. Three Republicans, none with electoral experience, also entered.

The strongest other Democrat was Eloise Gomez Reyes, a labor lawyer and community activist recruited by EMILY's List. "If EMILY's List had not spoken with me at the beginning of this campaign, I would not be in the race," Reyes told us.

With the help of EMILY's List, Reyes mounted a highly professional, $1.17 million campaign. Based on her activist background, Reyes herself was able to attract the support of some Latino organizations and leaders (Merl, 2014),[13] as well as progressive groups like Blue America PAC (Carmon, 2014).[14] In the last quarter of 2013, with incumbent Gary Miller still in the race, Reyes raised more money than he and Aguilar combined.

As the election approached, a repeat of 2012 seemed increasingly possible. A DCCC-commissioned poll showed Republicans in first and second place, followed by Aguilar and Reyes (Cahn, 2014).[15] Women Vote! (a PAC affiliated with EMILY's List) was spending on mailers supporting Reyes and against Aguilar. But the DCCC, watching closely, launched an attack on the second place Republican, knocking her down a notch and moving Aguilar up to second place in the primary balloting. Facing the top Republican in the November, Aguilar won 52 to 48%.

An observer from afar might view this race as an ideological battle. Aguilar was a mainstream Democrat, backed by unions, middle-class Democratic Clubs, and the national party establishment; Reyes was a progressive backed by assorted leftist groups. This view is not inaccurate, but it misses the real motivations. The DCCC was trying to unite its troops behind someone who could carry the district under difficult rules and, as is common in American politics, the troops were incorrigible. Asked why EMILY's List had risked losing the seat to the Republicans by recruiting Reyes, a knowledgeable source responded: "[EMILY's List's] mission is not for Democrats to control Congress. [Their] mission is to get to 50 percent of the Congressional Democratic caucus."

DCCC's support for Aguilar also fails to fit the Downsian model as neatly as the narrative so far might suggest. In contrast to the Alabama races, which were completely safe for Republicans, CA-31 was only D+5 and had elected a Republican in the last cycle. So while Aguilar did manage to win the general election, CA-31 is the kind of district in which Downsian logic implies that the party should back a genuine moderate. As it happens, there was a notable moderate Democrat in the race: Joe Baca, who had represented much of the

[13] www.latimes.com/local/political/la-me-pc-solis-reyes-20140224-story.html.
[14] www.msnbc.com/msnbc/the-underdog-becomes-the-favorite.
[15] www.rollcall.com/news/for-democrats-its-deja-vu-in-californias-31st-district.

district in Congress for six years prior to the redistricting. Baca was well-known for bringing federal money to the district, and his anti-gun control positions were popular with voters. Even his political enemies acknowledged that he was competent and hard-working. But his prior service in Congress had revealed him to be maverick, uninterested in cooperating with the party establishment. Worse, Baca had acquired a reputation for sexism that made him anathema to feminists in the party. Rather than follow Downsian logic pointing toward popular maverick Baca, the DCCC followed principal-agent logic favoring team-player Aguilar.

A Michigan IPO

Michigan's 14th district is 57% African American, 5% Hispanic, and over-whelmingly Democratic. It consists of the poorest sections of Detroit, a belt of middle class African American suburbs, and the state's richest suburb, Grosse Pointe. A dozen candidates considered running, four entered the primary, and two waged hard campaigns.

The main contender from Detroit was Hansen Clarke, who had served one term in Congress from a differently gerrymandered version of the district. Clarke finished third in the primary, but only five points behind the winner. This was notable because he entered the race at the last minute and, according to multiple sources, made little campaign effort. Clarke "just disappeared" from the campaign, said a supporter. "I don't think his heart was in it," said another source. Clarke's electoral strength was a carryover from previous office-holding. Two sources made the obvious point that Clarke probably could have won if he had run a stronger campaign. But it is not so easy for a politician from Detroit to mount a strong campaign. Another inner-city politician, State Senator Bert Johnson, started to campaign and wound up dropping out after raising only $100,000. Johnson had served seven years in the state legislature and held important leadership posts, but he could make little headway with donors in the more prosperous section of the district. Johnson was also handicapped by a prior campaign finance violation and an overhang of penalties from a previous race.

In the absence of a strong bid from Detroit, two candidates from suburban Oakland County, both African-American, finished first and second in the primary. One was Rudy Hobbs, a second-term member of the Michigan House. The other was Brenda Lawrence, a four-term mayor of Southfield, a largely African American suburb.

Hobbs had been an assistant party leader in the state Assembly, a staffer for a Democratic governor and lieutenant governor, a fundraiser for local party office holders, and the campaign manager for several campaigns. He won the support of the district's Democratic Party committee, 14 local political groups, most local office holders and most unions. Our sources mentioned five other capable Democrats who, despite ranking higher in seniority, tried but failed to get the party and union support that Hobbs got.

The key to Hobbs' impressive support, mentioned by every one of our eight sources, was a white Congressman from Grosse Pointe, Sandy Levin. Levin's brother, US Senator Carl Levin, was sometimes credited as well, but most sources named just Sandy. Sandy Levin had been state party chair and county party chair and had stayed involved in Detroit politics after becoming a member of Congress. Said a former Michigan state party chair: "Sandy has a lot of friends, a lot of relationships, a lot of ability to pull support." Moreover, said this source, Levin was "all in" for Hobbs – "financially, politically, personal time and care, staff attention." Another source said flatly that "Sandy Levin picked Rudy Hobbs to run." A third source: "The Levins sort of put out the word that 'Hey, this [Hobbs] is my guy." It was particularly galling to three sources that Hobbs "hadn't gone through any of the traditional chairs" – that is, hadn't come up through the party hierarchy – "no dues paid, no basis for his involvement in the race – except the Levin family."

Hobbs not only admitted but embraced Levin's support.

[Rudy] would talk about it openly "Hey, I came up through Sandy Levin. I understand the importance that we build, that we get a majority, that we're part of team."

Recalled another source:

Rudy came across as the establishment candidate, and that's the way he was running, "I'm the favorite of unions, I'm Sandy Levin's guy, and I've got the most money"

The basis of Levin's influence in this race was not entirely clear in our interviews. Levin's connections as former county and state party chair were probably important. Two sources made non-specific comments about money, which is a likely channel of influence for a leader hailing from Grosse Pointe. However he managed it, Levin exemplifies the conception of informal party leader.

The Levin/Hobbs team did not, however, win the primary. It had a formidable opponent in EMILY's List, whose candidate edged out Hobbs. Our sources attributed this to Emily's List taking over Brenda Lawrence's campaign with a canvassing operation that outshone the Levin/Hobbs effort.

These eight cases illustrate the variety of motives and organizational forms that underlie group and party anchoring of candidates' campaigns. In GA-1R and MA-5D we see how particularist policy demands can motivate such support. The two Alabama cases illustrate the importance of commitment and competence to groups driven by factional concerns that could be superficially understood as merely ideological. The New Jersey and Pennsylvania cases show how formal party institutions can serve group interests. In CA-31D, we see the national party organization defend the party establishment against a candidate backed by an insurgent group, and in MI-14D, we see a local IPO battling the same insurgent group. Taken together, they suggest that the role of groups and parties in House nominations is too important to ignore.

THE PRACTICE OF VETTING AND VOUCHING

We have proposed, first, that the groups and party organizations that anchor House primary campaigns want candidates who are committed to their agendas and competent to deal with them in Washington and, second, that they base their support decisions on reliable candidate information. We further argued that the best information comes from either direct working experience or close observation. Some group and party actors possess their own first-hand information about candidates, but most rely on what we have called "vetting and vouching networks" for their candidate information. Our evidence suggests that the benefits these networks offer to both candidates and stakeholders are significant enough to systematically shape the set of candidates who run, and, perhaps more importantly, the set of interests championed in the US House. In this section we describe some of the vetting and vouching practices that we observed, with particular attention to firsthand experience or observation of candidates by someone in the network.

Common Vetting

When members of a group or party can make informed decisions based on direct experience of a candidate over many years, we call it common vetting. Debbie Dingell's run in MI-12 makes a good example. From her 1981 marriage to then-incumbent John Dingell until the announcement of her campaign to succeed him 33 years later, she was never far from the political spotlight and always a force in her own right. She represented her state as Committee Woman to the national Democratic Party, her district to the Michigan state party, and her husband in the district. Along the way she chaired numerous political campaigns and was president of a political consulting firm. She served on many boards, commissions, and philanthropic bodies, including the Wayne State University Board of Trustees. All agreed, she was no shrinking violet. "She is one of the most aggressive, outspoken leaders behind the scenes in the party," said a source. Said another: "She's not someone who comes to a Democratic Party meeting and sits in the back of the room and nobody is going to notice. She's going to be front and center." The glamorous wife of a powerful congressman, she was covered on the society pages of local and national newspapers and was a regular TV commentator.

Dingell had some detractors, but after three decades as a leading political figure in the local, state, and national Democratic Party, few party stakeholders needed any additional vetting to know what they thought of her.

Another example of common vetting comes from the campaign of Reverend Jody Hice in the Georgia 10th district. A source told us:

This is probably one of the most important things I can tell you – that between the primary and the runoff and the general [the Hice campaign] did 289,000 doors and dials ... I just can't express to you how – that's a lot of voter contact! ... [that's] live doors and live dials, that's not robo calls, that's people talking to people.

So where did the person power for this labor-intensive campaign come from? Partly from Ten Commandments Georgia, an evangelical organization promoting the public display of important historical documents, including the biblical Ten Commandments. Hice had been "a leader" of that group "for several years," the source said. Another was the evangelical church at which Hice had been pastor. Hice resigned before beginning his campaign and did not recruit from the church, but he "just knew a lot of people [from the church] and those people came in and volunteered for him." A second source said, "It's a very close-knit community. ... it was very much like, 'we love Jody, so let's go do this'."

Hice had volunteer support from other groups as well, but the volunteers from Ten Commandments Georgia and his former congregation were obviously people with reliable first-hand information about the candidate they supported.

These two commonly vetted but otherwise quite different candidates were known to their core group supporters for years, if not decades. This level of deep familiarity between candidates and supporters was not typical. Most participants in most primaries had no personal experience working with or observing the candidate in close quarters. We turn now to what happens in this large number of quite different cases.

Insider Vetting

Many politicians do most of their work – sometimes nearly all of it – behind closed doors. This is particularly true of legislators, for whom working with a group means work with a handful of leaders – political directors, presidents, lobbyists, and well-connected members. The experience of these group leaders with politicians makes them gatekeepers, able to vouch for politicians who have served group interests, and to ignore or blacklist those who have not. Often these leaders need the approval of a board of directors to commit the group's resources or prestige, but the approval process varies from largely pro-forma to rigorous, depending on the group's prior experience with the candidate. We refer to this form of vetting as "insider vetting" and provide four examples below.

Our first example is based on an interview with the leader of an industry association in a southern state. "[This] industry is important enough that whoever wins will work fine," said the executive director of the association. "The reason we got into it is because [candidate] is, like, a member of the family

…. he has been a member of the association for a long time … and really no other candidate has those qualities."

The candidate was chair of the group's key committee in the state legislature so that "any legislation we [the group] have generally goes through that committee." The trade leader readily offered three examples of bills the candidate had helped to pass to create a "favorable environment" for the group's work: a limitation of lawsuits relating to the group's business, codification of trespass laws relating to industry interests, and a state bond issue for infrastructure projects helpful to the group. The candidate himself did not always formally sponsor them because "[we] prefer not to have committee chairs sponsor, so they can aid [bills] later as helpers." The candidate also offered general advice on the group's legislative wish list and "how best to craft a political strategy to achieve our objectives."

The trade group leader was quick with details throughout the interview. When asked how the group would help its candidate in the primary, the leader ticked off the number of voters in each county in the district and the fraction of these voters who were in four counties in which the group's business was concentrated.

Mark Takai's House campaign in HI-1 provides another straightforward example of insider vetting. Here, Takai is a Democrat rather than a Republican, and his group is a union rather than an industry.

Our sources described Takai as a serious-minded legislator who was not overly concerned about getting his name in the newspaper during his twenty-year stint in the state legislature. He had two main issues, one of which was public education from pre-K to University of Hawaii. By all accounts Takai worked closely with Hawaii's two teachers' unions on education issues and earned much gratitude for his effort.

"We could always rely on him," said one union source. "He always really, really supports our issues – always," said a second source, continuing that

He would take his time to call us, email us, text us … "what are you guys telling us, what do you folks want us to do, how do we get the votes, how are we going to get there. Let's help each other." That's the kind of person that we want [in Congress].

Takai's main opponent was Donna Kim, the president of the state Senate. The education unions had first-hand experience with her as well and it did not help her case:

It comes down very, very simply that he's helped us a helluva a lot more than she has as Senate president. He's helped us over the years on some of our major business and in fact we've found her quite aloof. … Mark is one of the guys we can always count on. … It's not just loyalty, we owe him.

All three sources readily enumerated projects on which they had worked with Takai: collective bargaining, a law evaluating teacher performance, state funding for pre-K, and funding for children of recent immigrants. The main benefit they hoped from Takai as Congressman seemed to be help securing greater federal funding for education programs.

Our third example of insider vetting has a quite different flavor. Three of the five candidates in the Democratic nomination in IA-1 were office holders with records of working closely with labor. Anesa Kajtazovic had based her state assembly campaign on the fire fighters' union in her home city of Waterloo; Monica Vernon had, as a member of the Cedar Rapids city council, helped local construction unions get federal contracts for flood repair; and Pat Murphy had, as Speaker of the state Assembly, worked closely with the SEIU and the AFL-CIO on their agendas. All three wanted the endorsement of the state AFL-CIO because it maintains a highly developed campaign organization and is the key to additional support from the national organization.

The danger to the state AFL-CIO in failing to make a firm choice among the three was that three union candidates in a five-candidate race could allow a non-union candidate to slip in. In this situation the state union's formal vetting procedure turned out to be critical. Each candidate appeared before the state convention to answer questions intended to test competence and commitment to union issues. The procedure was as follows:

We did a random drawing to determine the order of speaking. And they went into the room one at a time. None of their staff could go into the room to see how the other candidates responded. Everybody got treated exactly the same. Everybody got exactly the same questions, exactly the same time period. Our delegates had an opportunity to see these folks, see them on the same stage, asked the same questions, and measure their responses. So it was an apples-apples comparison …

We asked all five candidates the same three questions … Anesa [Kajtazovic] did what about what people thought she was going to do … She's young, she's articulate, but really hasn't been in a leadership role in the Iowa House, hasn't floor-managed bills and hasn't been in the press and stuff like that. … Dandekar, it wasn't good. Monica Vernon did a fair job. Obrien was good, and Murphy was lights out the best candidate.

Following this interrogation, a formal vote of convention delegates produced the two-thirds margin of support necessary to authorize state and national union support for eventual winner Murphy.

Our final case comes from the Republican primary in LA-6. Lane Grigsby, the head of a large maritime construction company in the district, was interested in the House candidacy of Garret Graves, a state administrator who had overseen several of Grigsby's business projects. Grigsby had known Graves since the latter's boyhood and thought well of him, but his company's executives felt Graves had made "blunders" in his work with the company. So Grigsby arranged a meeting, scheduled for the next day, for Graves to meet Grigsby's executives to discuss the alleged mistakes. Looking ahead to the meeting, Grigsby said:

I'm gonna tell you, everybody makes mistakes, everybody can't get things perfect. When you own your mistakes is when I like you. It's when you deny 'em, and you're absolutely assuming I'm stupid ... then you and I probably can't get along too well. So I'm interested to see what Garret says tomorrow.

The meeting, as Grigsby described it in a follow-on interview with us, went well.

[PoG] *What happened?*
[Grigsby] He gives his stump speech, and [the executives] ask questions
[PoG] *What were the questions about?*
[Grigsby] Issues that are interesting to them as individuals or us as a corporation ... further refinements of positions he might have had ... or about coastal recovery or programs for coastal recovery which he led first ... they were questions about issues he might have to vote on as a congressman.

The meeting lasted about an hour, with a third of the time spent on Graves' plan for winning the seat, a third spent on issues of national politics, such as abortion, and a third on particular maritime issues. On the most important of his supposed blunders, Graves admitted error, but said he had acted on incorrect information from subordinates whom he had subsequently fired.

We named the names and we named the instances and he [Graves] said, "egg all over my face, I listened to what staff was telling me, when you brought it back up I went and looked at it, absolutely we were wrong, that person has been terminated." ... And they [the executives] went back and checked up on his answers ... They came back later and said, "You know, he did fire that guy."

After Graves left, Grigsby said he would be supporting him and that others wishing to do so could leave checks on his secretary's desk. Grigsby recalled his comments to his executives as follows:

Hey, you know, your income stream is a function of how well we do as a business, my engagement in the community helps our business, I would ask you to make a personal sacrifice ...

Grigsby emphasized that his executives were free to follow his recommendation or not, as they saw fit. But many followed. His secretary collected about $100,000 in contributions to Graves, including some contributions from Grigsby's family.

Grigsby said also that he would relay his support for Graves to two leading electrical and mechanical contractors who regularly rely on his advice, and he said he would likely bring Graves before five PAC boards on which he has influence.

Vetting by National Groups

National organizations made PAC contributions in many of our WOSPs in amounts that affected the dynamics of competition. The groups included businesses, professional associations, politicians supporting other candidates of their party, and groups with ideological agendas. EMILY's List was the single most important of the national PACs, anchoring six campaigns with six-figure contributions and winning four of them. Club for Growth played a similar role in two races and Citizens United in one. In most of the rest, PACs played by rules that limit their contributions to $5,000, but some of these PACs cued members of their group to contribute at well. A number of the low-dollar PACs (FreedomWorks, Madison Project, the Progressive Change Campaign Committee) had clear ideological agendas and were perhaps the main access points of ideological influence in our cases.

With its focus on local interviews, the PoG field study developed limited understanding of the operations of national PACs. But from what we did see, vetting was as important to them as to other groups. Regarding the most active national group, EMILY's List, we heard numerous references to the national organization vetting candidates with local sources – and not just one local source but several. In another case, we asked a candidate how he had gained entry to an important national PAC at a stage of his career when he was a little-known local official. He replied that he knew the sources the national group used in his area and kept in touch with them. One local source recounted what she regarded as the humorous story of a candidate who flew to Washington to solicit contributions from PACs associated with her party, hired a hall for a fundraiser, and sent out invitations to PAC officers for the following week. The source laughed out loud at this. "You can't just invite [these people] and suddenly think they're going to show up," the source exclaimed. "[They] actually need to know you!" The standard procedure, they continued, is for the candidate to go to someone in her community who knows them and has personal connections to the PAC they're interested in. Once this person sends word that the candidate is okay, they can meet the PAC official for a private interview and, if all goes well, invite the official to a fundraiser a month or two later. Two personal relationships – one between candidate and local informant and another between local informant and PAC – were thus needed to get interviews and then contributions. Overall, candidates needed a local reference to establish their commitment to group concern and then an interview to demonstrate their competence in dealing with them.

Even high-level local players may require introduction, as indicated by a Minnesota insider who was asked how much of candidates' fundraising is based on "cold calls":

[Source] Well, none of it would be cold, ever. When you say cold, do you mean just call somebody out of the blue?
[PoG: Yeah.]
[Source] That would be never. There would have to be some kind of relationship from somebody, some referral or something. You would never just say, oh this guy's an executive at US Bank, call him. You would just never do that … There's no percentage in cold calls, probably a lower percentage than selling siding.

No doubt there is exaggeration in this response, but considerable truth as well.

PAC contributions are limited by law to $5,000, but they can be followed by emails and newsletters to group members from whom the candidate can then raise much larger amounts of money – but only by dint of strenuous effort. Many candidates have a fundraising director who will generate the phone numbers and organize the candidate's call schedule. One candidate described the follow-up process on endorsements as follows:

> I just methodically ... did what every candidate does. ... as I would get [endorsements], I would look up everyone who had donated to that PAC [group] and call them and say "Listen, you know I have got money from your board, but I'm hoping you'll give to me personally." I was in call time pretty much five days a week.

This candidate, a Democrat, had special success with younger members of the organizations that endorsed them. "[T]here is a whole other universe of [group members] out there" who are not well represented by their professional association and "who were just ecstatic to have a Democratic [group member] to donate to. Many of these people had never donated before to another candidate."

Most of the endorsements we observed in our study were made by professional or business organizations, but candidates endorsed by ideological organizations followed up in a similar way. For example self-proclaimed "liberal lion" Daylin Leach, a Democrat running in PA-13, was a vanguard supporter of dozens of progressive causes in the state legislature, from same sex marriage to marijuana legalization to banning the sale of shark fins. Leach successfully sought the endorsements of left-wing groups like Daily Kos, MoveOn, and Progressive Change Coalition. He also hit up niche groups, such as advocates of animal rights. Just as in the previous example, he phoned members of the groups that endorsed him, touted the endorsements, and asked for help. "There may not be a lot of people who care deeply about animal rights or medicinal marijuana," as a source told us, "but there are enough rich people in Colorado and Michigan and California who care that you can get ten to twenty $2,500 donations for each of these issues." Leach spent months of his campaign making calls to these people and in so doing raised more than a million dollars.

Personal Networks

The networks described so far can reach hundreds or even thousands of contributors. We turn now to personal networks that may typically involve between five and twenty-five people. Though small, they are often aggregated into larger and quite consequential entities and many candidates rely on them as backbones of their campaigns. In this section we describe two cases in which political party fundraisers used personal networks for their work.

Paul Dickson, described to us as the leading GOP fundraiser in northern Louisiana at the time of our study in 2014, spoke on the record. Dickson raises campaign funds through a network of sub-leaders who solicit funds from their professional acquaintances. As Dickson described his network, it consisted of about twenty self-interested professional groups, each with its own pecking order. To raise campaign funds, he cultivated the natural leaders of these groups – people, he said, who will act as a "bell cow" for the others by allowing their names to be used in invitations to fundraisers.

To build his network, Dickson identified natural leaders in the local media and sought them out at social events.

I will walk up to anybody at a cocktail party and start up a conversation … and it'll often turn to politics. And I'll say, "I sure would like to talk to you some time when we got a race going," and [he'll say] "sure, call me" – I got 'em! [Dickson raps his desk] …. Put his name on the invitation [to the fundraiser] and the others will come ….

In the race we studied, a group of state leaders arranged for the 5th district incumbent to resign (to take a state job) and for Neil Riser, a member of the GOP leadership in the state house, to succeed him in a special election. As part of the leadership team in the state legislature, Riser was well-known to the party leaders who supported his candidacy.

Dickson, who described himself as a party soldier, was not part of the group that chose Riser but was asked by a party leader to help with fundraising. He replied that he would first need to talk to Riser, whom he knew only slightly, to be sure of his qualifications. After interviewing Riser, Dickson agreed to fundraise for him.

Dickson said that when he fundraises for presidential candidates, the "bell cows" and their group followers are concerned about national issues. But, consistent with our general argument in this chapter, their concerns in lower level office like Congress are more concrete:

Everybody is motivated by what's going to promote your own well-being. The doctors are going to be motivated by medical issues and health care issues. Oil and gas owners are gonna be motivated by both environmental and taxation issues. Business leaders are going to be affected by taxation and regulatory issues, particularly labor issues. When people are talking about shelling out money, it's a business decision for them usually, or a professional decision … Anybody that gives a large sum of money is looking at it that way.

In order to be credible with such people, Dickson follows news about the policies that concern them, which takes him hours each day away from his business. He said that he himself does not contact officials whom he has assisted into office for help on political problems, either his own or those of his group leaders. "I'm just supporting the people [candidates] I think who will do good and then I'm out of it."

Our second example of party fundraising is, like Dickson, one of the leading party fundraisers in his area, but his method was quite different.

You might be the kind of person who would hold a dinner party for someone?
[Source:] Yes, if I liked them and thought they were gonna be a good candidate.
[PoG: Would you need to meet them first?]
[Source:] Oh yeah! You don't want to be recommending somebody to your friends who you don't know anything about! You check 'em out, you find out what their record is, you meet 'em, you get to know 'em. Then you say to your friends, I checked this guy out, or this gal out. Usually with fundraisers, they make the commitment that they're gonna write a check before they come to the dinner and they've never met the person. They really rely on the host.

In this case, the fundraiser not only knew the candidate but had previously worked with him on a civic improvement project. He was so pleased with the result that he called the candidate to offer support before the candidate could call him. Besides his own dinner event, this fundraiser persuaded a friend, who did not previously know the candidate, to meet him and, if satisfied by the qualities of the candidate, sponsor his own fundraiser. All this amounted to "a huge risk, because I used all my political capital to get everybody I knew to back [my candidate]. Because I believed that he would be effective as a congressman. Good, honest, and effective." The two dinner events together may have raised $40,000.

ANCHORING

Previous sections have sketched examples of campaigns in which groups or parties provided substantial support to winning candidates. But how representative are the examples? To address this question, we define a unit of campaign support and assess how many winners of our fifty-three WOSP primaries acquired that level of support from a single group or party. This exercise will necessarily be subjective, but still, we hope, an improvement on argument by example.

Our conceptual unit is the minimum amount of support necessary for a candidate to be viable, by which we mean having a reasonable chance of winning the primary. We refer to campaigns receiving this level of support as anchored in the group or party that supplied it.

We propose that any of the following is sufficient to endow a candidate with political viability.

- **Coordinated support.** Groups and parties that coordinate behind a common candidate may deter other candidates from running, thereby conveying viability on their own candidate. An example is the DCCC's effort to establish the candidacy of Pete Aguilar in CA-31.

- **Monetary support.** The median winner of a contested WOSP spent $715,000. In light of this figure and our subjective sense of the evidence, we take a single group or party contribution of $250,000 as conferring viability.
- **Volunteer support.** Volunteer phone bankers and door knockers can be campaign mainstays. We could not directly observe and measure their activity, but when, as with the Hice campaign, a credible source told us that volunteers had been critical to a campaign, we counted them as an anchor.
- **Expertise.** We also counted expert staff assistance to campaigns from groups as partial contributions to anchoring.

Except for coordinated support that clears all but one candidate, none of these amounts can fully underwrite a campaign. But any one of them – or combination of them, such as money and volunteers from one source – can establish a candidate as sufficiently viable to attract additional support from allies and benefit seekers.

Evaluating all fifty-three WOSPs by these general criteria, we judge that forty winners were anchored in a group or party and that an additional three winners probably were, for a combined rate of 81% anchoring. This figure breaks down as 47% group anchored and 34% anchored in a local, national or informal party. There were also six non-anchored winners, as follows: two self-financing millionaires, two candidates who had previously held statewide office, and two veteran state legislators who beat neophyte candidates. The remaining four cases were unclassifiable due to lack of evidence.

The cases of possible anchoring in a volunteer group are the most difficult to classify. It is typically easy to see that volunteers have been important but hard to tell how important. Two of our three "probable" anchor classifications and three of four unclassified cases center on judging the importance of volunteer campaign efforts. Our research is continuing and may change some results.

An Online Appendix to this paper presents case summaries containing the information on which each of the 53 anchoring classifications is based. The appendix also has further discussion of the classification system itself.[16]

We do not have a numerical estimate of the percent of WOSP losers who lacked anchors, but it is likely high. One should not, however, assume that these anchorless losers were necessarily weak candidates or otherwise undeserving of support. As a veteran state legislator with an outstanding record of group service lamented:

It's weird because you run for office time after time [in general elections], and then you run in a primary and suddenly good friends of yours who have always been helpful to you are with someone else … it's sort of emotionally jarring at first … for all the candidates … because we all had disappointments in terms of people we thought would be naturally for us who weren't …

---

[16] www.pog.polisci.ucla.edu.

Such cases are, we believe, common in House primaries. So also are accomplished politicians who would like to run for Congress but stay on the sidelines because they anticipate the same fate. These disappointed candidates and might-have-been candidates, and the vetting and vouching decisions that lie behind them, are part of the reason we view groups and parties as the key players in House nominations.

LIMITATIONS

Our argument has important limitations. One is that it consists mainly of cases selected to illustrate specific ideas, rather than chosen at random. This limitation is due to thin information in many of our cases. For example, even though we have many reports of business groups interrogating candidates, we have only one that goes into the detail of Grigsby et al. in LA-6. We would like to know how often such grilling occurred, but lack the evidence.

A second limitation follows from the nature of exploratory study. Because we had not fully crystallized our ideas at the time of our field work, we failed to elicit information that might have more clearly supported or refuted the ideas we ended up with. For example, we asked few questions about experience-based vetting because we were not alert to that idea until our interviewing was complete. Likewise with group anchoring and volunteer campaigners.

A third important limitation of our study is that it is timebound. Did the dynamics of open seat House primaries look the same in a year like 2010, the height of the Tea Party uprising in the Republican Party, as it did in our 2014 study? Did dynamics look the same in 2022, with former President Trump making endorsements in many races? Does the recent rise of Justice Democrats analogous to the insurgent Republicans that we saw in 2014 signal the emergence of a more militantly factional – perhaps even ideological – politics in Democratic nominations? We obviously do not know.

CONCLUSIONS

We have argued that most winners of WOSP primaries in 2013–2014 anchored their campaigns in the support of a group or party, that sponsoring anchors were typically seeking agents for group agendas, and that most anchors probably performed due diligence to assure the competence and commitment of candidates to group agendas.

These findings have not been established through tests of pre-determined hypotheses, but rather have been induced from a messy mix of evidence. Further research is therefore needed before they can be accepted. This research might take the form of field study like ours, but it might also involve quantitative tests of hypotheses derived from our work.

If supported in future research, our findings have potentially large implications. Most obvious is that congressional politics is – at its base and perhaps in higher reaches as well – more multi-dimensional than polarized voting in Congress makes it seem. Closely related is the possibility that the agendas of interest and values groups may rival or surpass ideology as drivers of congressional politics.

In raising these implications, we are mindful that House primaries are only one part of a much larger system of congressional politics and perhaps not the most important part. One can imagine that the hoops aspiring candidates jump through to win House nominations recede into the distant background once politicians enter Congress and face its demands. Yet if we evaluate the responsiveness of MCs mainly in terms of the roll-call votes they cast – even when we do it carefully, as in the work of Clinton et al. and Canes-Wrone and Kistner, Chapters 2 and 6 in this volume – we risk missing much of the impact of groups, missing how they can shape the detailed content of bills through the selection of the particular politicians who write the bills. We also risk missing the intraparty factional competition that determines which particular issues, and whose interests, form each side's agenda in a polarized party system.

The question of who most influences House nominations is thus central to who is represented in Congress. Primary voters are formally sovereign in nominations, but often appear to pay too little attention to make effective use of it. The result is a huge opportunity for organized interests to take up the slack.

PART II

THE MEDIA AND THE INFORMATIONAL
ENVIRONMENT

6

Local Newspapers and Ideological Accountability in US House Elections

Brandice Canes-Wrone and Michael R. Kistner

Classic perspectives of congressional representation and accountability hold that the policy and ideological positions of candidates affect their electoral performance. Harking back to Mayhew (1974) and Fenno (1978), generations of students have learned that position-taking is a critical component of the electoral connection between members and voters. Scholarship that builds on these foundations to study legislators' behavior in-office similarly assumes candidates' stances influence voters' choices (e.g., Arnold, 1990; Grimmer, 2013). As Arnold (1990, 14) notes, "citizens choose among congressional candidates by evaluating both the candidates' policy positions and their connections with policy effects." Jacobson and Carson (2019, 192) provide survey evidence for this claim, finding that "issues now have a formidable direct as well as indirect connection to the congressional vote."

Yet a spate of recent evidence points to a decline in the extent to which candidate position-taking matters come election day. In fact, several papers argue that party-based voting has eclipsed candidate-based accountability in recent decades (e.g., Bonica and Cox, 2018; Utych, 2019). Some scholarship pushes back on this claim, at least partially. For instance, Canes-Wrone and Kistner (2022) find that the observed decline in candidate accountability has been driven by changes in how challengers' ideology corresponds to their electoral performance, with incumbent accountability not necessarily decreasing. Consistent with this result, Clinton, Sances, and Sullivan (Chapter 2, this volume) provides evidence that on high salience issues, constituents evaluate incumbents less favorably if they vote out of step with the district. Likewise, in Chapter 9, Lee describes the efforts of incumbents to avoid alienating constituents when crafting major legislation. All of these pieces allow, however, that Downs's (1957) candidate-based model, in which voters choose between partisan opponents' ideological stances, may not operate as it did in the 1980s and 1990s.

Alongside this evidence on candidate accountability is a plethora of research that documents massive developments in local news. The number of local papers, staffing at those remaining, and associated coverage of local representatives have all plummeted (e.g., Napoli et al., 2017; Peterson, 2021b). Correspondingly, Huber and Tucker (Chapter 8, this volume) describe how circulation is now half of what it was in 1990. Given that local newspapers have historically served as voters' primary source of information on congressional candidates (e.g., Arnold, 2004; Snyder and Strömberg, 2010), these developments carry potentially important political consequences. For instance, Hayes and Lawless (2018) show that as coverage has weakened, citizens' political knowledge has undergone an associated decline. Yet existing research on the relationship among local media, candidate positions, and electoral outcomes arrives at inconsistent conclusions, and no scholarship examines how this relationship has changed since the onset of the internet age (Cohen, Noel, and Zaller, 2004; Bawn et al., 2012; Hall, 2015, 2019).

The following chapter considers these questions with new analyses. The data on the local media, which are from Snyder and Strömberg (2010) and Peterson (2021a), begin in 1990 and extend through 2014, thereby encompassing the aforementioned developments in local news. These data measure the congruence of the local newspaper market with the geographic boundaries of the congressional district, a factor that earlier studies establish offers exogenous variation in the amount of coverage a House candidate receives. Additionally, the specifications include ones with district and year fixed effects, and therefore identify the impact of the local newspaper market through within-district change.

In evaluating the changing effect of candidate positioning on electoral outcomes, we make use of contribution-based measures that capture both incumbent and challenger ideology (Bonica, 2016, 2018). Recent work identifies important differences in the way voters respond to the positions held by incumbents and challengers (Peskowitz, 2019; Canes-Wrone and Kistner, 2022), providing an empirical justification for considering separate effects for each type of candidate. There are also important theoretical reasons for including challenger positioning in a study of accountability. First, the extent to which challenger positions affect voters' choices may influence incumbents' in-office behavior. The possibility of a challenger more in-step with a district's preferences may be enough to prevent an incumbent from voting out-of-step with their district, but only if the incumbent believes voters recognize and respond to challenger positioning. Second, an electorate ignorant of challenger positions may replace an out-of-step incumbent with an even more out-of-step challenger, a possibility that undermines congruent representation. Further complicating this matter is that local news developments may not have had equal impacts on incumbents and challengers, a point reiterated by Huber and Tucker in Chapter 8, this volume. It is therefore necessary to consider how the changing media environment has affected each type of candidate in order to understand how electoral accountability operates.

The analysis produces three major findings. First, for the aggregate time period, media congruence strengthens the link between candidates' ideological positions and electoral outcomes. Voters reward ideological moderation more as the local newspaper market provides greater coverage of House candidates. This relationship is particularly robust for challengers. Second, in the absence of congruence with local newspapers, voters punish incumbents but not challengers for ideological extremism; in other words, when media congruence is low, challengers face no electoral penalty for extremism or reward for moderation. Finally, and consistent with work that suggests local newspapers have become less important to voters' knowledge about candidates over time (Peterson, 2021a), the effects of media congruence on candidate accountability are no longer as strong as they were in the 1990s.

LITERATURE OVERVIEW

Historically, the local media have provided the foundation for congressional accountability. Relative to the national media, local outlets are much more likely to report on the policy positions, actions, and background of congressional members and their opponents. As Arnold (2004, 2) notes,

The so-called national press – the networks, newsmagazines, and national newspapers – could not possibly cover the individual activities of every senator and representative ... The typical representative does not appear even once a year in Newsweek, USA Today, or on the CBS evening news.

By comparison, in a representative sample of local newspapers, Arnold finds they carried an average of fourteen articles a month on individual representatives in the 103rd Congress (1993–1994). Likewise, he observes that local papers are the source most likely to provide information about a representative's primary and general election opponents (Arnold, 1990, 8). This evidence is consistent with more recent work by Hayes and Lawless (2015), who show that coverage of US House races is lower in districts served by large circulation outlets, such as national newspapers, than in districts served by lower circulation ones.

Among the variety of local media, newspapers have traditionally been the primary source of citizen knowledge on local and regional affairs. Mondak (1995a, 525) highlights that this is not due to some "mystical capacity" of the print media but instead because "the local newspaper ... is often the only medium to provide adequate coverage" of local House races and other regional political matters. Mondak's insight comports with Snyder and Strömberg (2010), who demonstrate that congruence between the local newspaper market and congressional district boundaries is positively associated with voters' knowledge about their representative, while a comparable measure for the local television market is not. Notably, the importance of local newspapers goes beyond direct readership; research establishes they influence the content of other local media and conversations readers have with their families and friends (e.g., Arnold, 2004). In the language of Cameron and Gordon's work (Chapter 10, this volume), local newspapers serve as a sentinel for voters.

Since the advent of the internet, the number and capacity of newspapers have plunged (e.g., Napoli et al., 2017; Peterson, 2021b). Indeed, newsroom staffs have been cut by 47% since 2004 (Center, 2019; Huber and Tucker, Chapter 8, this volume). Peterson (2021b) shows that a typical staffing decrease is associated with 300–500 fewer politics articles written per year. Likewise, comparing coverage in 2010 and 2014, Hayes and Lawless (2018) find that in 2014 newspapers carried fewer politics stories in the weeks before the election, including fewer that covered both candidates. Consistent with this decline, daily news circulation has dropped in half since 1990 (Center, 2019; Huber and Tucker, Chapter 8, this volume). Members have made efforts to fill the void through press releases, which often serve as the primary source of information for resource-deprived outlets (e.g., Grimmer, 2013). This type of downstream consequence highlights how local news developments may have affected challengers and incumbents differently, especially given incumbents' publicity and fundraising advantages (e.g., Prior, 2006; Fouirnaies and Hall, 2014).[1] Overall, McChesney and Nichols (2011, 3) characterize the situation for candidate accountability as a "crisis," noting that "our nation faces the absurd and untenable prospect of what James Madison characterized as impossible: to be a self-governing constitutional republic without a functioning news media."

In the wake of these developments, political scientists have investigated the extent to which the decline of local newspapers is associated with diminished voter knowledge of congressional candidates. For example, Hayes and Lawless (2018) show that as the quantity and substance of local newspaper articles covering congressional elections decreased, respondents became less able to place the Democratic candidate to the left of the Republican one, to express a vote intention, or rate the incumbent. Likewise, Peterson (2021a) extends the Snyder and Strömberg (2010) measure of local newspaper congruence to assess whether since 2006 such congruence has a similar, or even any, impact on voter knowledge of congressional candidates.

A few pieces directly examine the relationship among incumbents' ideological positions, electoral performance, and local media markets, but these studies produce divergent findings. In a conference paper, Cohen, Noel, and Zaller (2004) develop a measure of congruence between local television markets as defined by Nielsen and congressional district boundaries for the years 1972–2000. With this measure, they show that media congruence strengthens the association between a member's likelihood of winning reelection and their roll-call record as captured by the Poole and Rosenthal (1991) DW-NOMINATE

---

[1] Correspondingly, some research suggests that fragmentation of television markets aids incumbents due to challengers' greater difficulty in obtaining publicity (e.g., Levy and Squire, 2000).

scores.[2] One limitation of Cohen, Noel, and Zaller (2004) is that it does not analyze the role of challenger positions. Moreover, because the data extend only through 2000, right as the decline in local news is taking off (Center, 2019), the analysis cannot speak to how the internet age has affected the impact of local media. More recently, Bawn et al. (2012) evaluate the relationship among television market congruence, incumbents' policy positions, and electoral performance through 2010 and find that for the elections as a group, there is no significant relationship; only for an atypical election such as the 1994 Republican takeover is an effect observed.

Furthermore, the results in Hall (2015, 2019), which involve the Snyder and Strömberg measure of local newspaper congruence for 1991–2002, do not provide a clear answer on whether the local media play a role in candidate accountability. Hall's (2015) examination of general elections uncovers an effect that is not at all significant at conventional levels, potentially due to the small sample size ($N = 114$) necessitated by his regression discontinuity design. Yet Hall (2019) analyzes the impact of media congruence on primary elections and finds that in the least congruent districts, challenger extremism is actually rewarded. Additionally, in the most congruent districts, there is no significant punishment for extremism in primaries.

Other research offers evidence that indirectly bears on the topic. For instance, scholarship suggests media congruence is associated with less partisan voting (Peterson, 2017). Similarly, existing work connects the reduction in split-ticket voting with newspaper closures (Darr, Hitt, and Dunaway, 2018) and expanded access to broadband internet (Trussler, 2020). None of these studies, however, examine whether the local media environment affects candidates' accountability for their policy positions.

The question of whether such a relationship exists is not only important in terms of understanding the consequences of media developments, but also because it potentially sheds light on how and why candidate accountability has changed over time. As mentioned in the introduction, several pieces suggest that ideological extremism is no longer punished by voters. For instance, Bonica and Cox (2018) assess whether a candidate-based Downsian model of accountability better explains congressional election outcomes than a party-based one. Using finite mixture models that separately examine the pre- and post-1994 periods, the authors find that prior to 1994, the candidate-based model better explains the data while post-1994, the party-based model does. Similarly, Utych (2019) presents evidence that the association between candidate ideological extremism and electoral performance has decreased between 1980 and 2012. In Utych's case, however, he finds a gradual decline and the effect does not

---

[2] Also, the authors show that candidates are better able to win in a less ideologically friendly district when the local media market is stronger. This analysis, which makes use of the authors' own television congruence measure as well as Arnold's (2004) data on local newspaper coverage, does not incorporate candidate positions, however.

disappear until the 2000s. Each of these studies groups together incumbents and challengers, leaving open the possibility that one type of candidate is driving the effects.

This limitation is highlighted by the results of research that separates challengers from incumbents or examines only the latter. For instance, Tausanovitch and Warshaw (2018) show that the level of incumbent accountability in the 2000s is similar to the level Canes-Wrone, Brady, and Cogan (2002) find for earlier decades. Similarly, Canes-Wrone and Kistner (2022) establish that if the impact of ideological extremism is allowed to vary between incumbents and challengers, then the original methods and measures of Bonica and Cox (2018) show that incumbent accountability has not declined even though challengers no longer pay the electoral price they once did for ideological extremism.

All the above-described observational analyses are complemented by a growing experimental literature that randomizes the positions of candidates and their communications. Interestingly, this literature has produced conflicting results, with some work suggesting candidates' positions do not affect voter evaluations (e.g., Broockman and Butler, 2017) and other work suggesting that they do on salient issues (e.g., Mummolo, Peterson, and Westwood, 2021). These experiments, although not focused on the local media market, highlight the need to investigate more thoroughly the conditions under which candidates are held accountable for their positions.

Finally, this chapter relates to various studies that argue congressional elections are increasingly nationalized. These works do not analyze the impact of candidates' positions per se but contend that the forces driving electoral outcomes have become less candidate-specific. For example, Jacobson (2015) shows that the incumbency advantage has decreased in association with the growth in party-line and president-centered voting over the past several decades. Hopkins (2018) not only concurs, but also advances the decline in local news as one of the causes. Similar arguments regarding the nationalization of congressional voting appear in Fiorina (2016) and Caughey, Dunham, and Warshaw (2018), among others.

In summary, various literatures indicate that candidate accountability has changed over time and point to the possibility that developments in local media may be a factor. However, the evidence on the role of the local media is conflicting, does not separate out challenger positions, and does not examine how any such relationship has changed in the internet age. In the following, we investigate these issues, focusing on the role of the local newspaper market.

EMPIRICAL STRATEGY

We analyze twenty-five years of House elections spanning 1990–2014. Across the tests, the general empirical model is based on the approach adopted in previous work on whether candidates with more extreme policy positions pay a price for these views at the ballot box (e.g., Canes-Wrone, Brady, and Cogan, 2002; Erikson and Wright, 2017; Bonica and Cox, 2018; Carson and Williamson, 2018). In particular, a candidate's vote share is regressed on candidate ideology, holding constant the ideology of the district and other factors believed to influence electoral outcomes.[3] Because of our interest in local newspaper coverage, we examine how this coverage conditions any impact of candidate ideology. As later discussed, the use of the newspaper congruence variable developed by Snyder and Strömberg (2010) enables exogenous identification of the effect of local newspapers. In particular, while coverage itself may be endogenous to campaigns and congressional member activity, congruence between newspaper coverage and district boundaries has been shown to be exogenous to such factors (Snyder and Strömberg, 2010; Peterson, 2017).

Variables and Measurement

The dependent variable is *Democratic Candidate Vote Share*, the Democratic candidate's share of the two-party vote. The key independent variables are *Incumbent Ideology* and *Challenger Ideology* as measured by the Bonica (2016, 2018) scores that are based on the contribution decisions of campaign donors. Higher scores reflect more conservative positions. We present results with two types of these scores, each offering different advantages. The Bonica (2016) CFscores are estimated using an unsupervised method that considers donation patterns but no in-office behavior of winning candidates. These scores have been employed previously to analyze candidate accountability (e.g., Bonica and Cox, 2018; Utych, 2019). One critique advanced by Tausanovitch and Warshaw (2017) is that although the CFscores reliably distinguish Republican from Democratic legislators, they are less successful at distinguishing among same-party members.[4] To address this issue, Bonica (2018) uses supervised machine learning to map the campaign donation patterns onto an existing measure of legislative voting, specifically the widely utilized DW-NOMINATE scores (Poole and Rosenthal, 1991); the resulting measures are therefore referred to as DW-DIME scores (e.g., Hall and Thompson, 2018). Although the DW-DIME scores are more predictive of winners' roll-call voting, they are available only through 2012 and even in these years require a greater number

---

3 Earlier analyses of this question typically do not include interactions between district and candidate ideology, perhaps because research suggests elites of both parties are ideologically extreme relative to the general electorate and even same-party voters (e.g., Bafumi and Herron, 2010; Fiorina, Abrams, and Pope, 2010). We follow this lead. Moreover, as described subsequently, the main specifications already include two-way interaction terms involving media congruence and some involve three-way interaction terms.

4 Similarly, Hill and Huber (2017) find that the CFscores better distinguish between than among partisan affiliates.

of contributors than the CFscores, which extend throughout the entire time series.[5] Therefore, we conduct the analyses with each measure.

As noted above, for both types, a higher score reflects a more conservative candidate. Accordingly, under the assumption that the Democratic candidate is to the left of the Republican, a higher level of conservatism should be associated with a lower vote share for Democratic and Republican candidates alike, regardless of whether they are incumbents or challengers.[6] We do not constrain the weight of the challenger and incumbent ideology estimates to be equal, such as, for instance, taking the midpoint between them, given that research suggests voters know more about incumbents' than challengers' positions (e.g., Woon and Pope, 2008; Peskowitz, 2019). We have also analyzed the data substituting for the incumbent estimates the DW-NOMINATE scores (Poole and Rosenthal, 1991; Lewis et al., 2018), and the results are substantively similar. Full descriptive statistics on the ideology scores and other variables are given in Appendix Table 6.A.1.

To capture the level of news coverage associated with the local newspaper market, we use the Snyder and Strömberg (2010) measure developed for this purpose. Snyder and Strömberg (2010, 361) estimate the congruence of a newspaper market to a congressional district based on the market share of each newspaper within the counties of the district and the proportion of the papers' readers who live within it. The key assumption underlying the measure, which the authors verify empirically, is that a newspaper is more likely to write articles about a representative the higher is the proportion of the readership that lives in the district. Formally, for each paper m sold within a district d and county c:

$$Media\ Congruence_{cd} = \sum_{m=1}^{M} Market\ Share_{mc} Reader\ Share_{md}. \qquad (6.1)$$

Note that by definition, market share sums to 1 for all papers M within a county c.

With this measure, a district covered by only one paper that has a low percentage of its readers within the district, perhaps a national paper, would have low media congruence. By comparison, a district with two papers, each of which has a high proportion of their readers within the district, would have high media congruence. As Appendix Table 6.A.1 shows, the variable ranges from 0.002, reflecting almost no congruence between newspaper coverage

---

[5] Even with the CFscores, to ensure that differences in accountability between challengers and incumbents are not due to measurement error resulting from a small number of donors, we exclude all races featuring a major party candidate receiving contributions from ten or fewer unique donors, following Bonica (2018).

[6] The assumption that the Democratic candidate is to the left of the Republican candidate holds in all but 8 of the observations. Excluding these 8 observations does not alter the results.

and the geographic boundaries of the district, to 1.000, reflecting perfect overlap. Snyder and Strömberg (2010) calculate the variable for 1991–2002, and Peterson (2021a) extends it through the 2014 elections. Each of these studies provides evidence that the measure is exogenous to factors affecting vote share such as the members' actions and campaign activity.

The empirical analysis includes interactions between media congruence and the incumbent and challenger ideology estimates, in addition to the main effect of media congruence. We have no expectation regarding the main effect, as it should not necessarily favor Democratic versus Republican candidates. However, if media congruence increases the impact of ideological extremism on electoral outcomes, then the coefficients on the interaction terms should be positive. Likewise, if media congruence is important to only challengers or incumbents, then just that interaction term would have a (significant) positive sign.

The control variables are standard ones including district ideology, campaign spending, challenger quality, freshmen, party, and (in tests that do not include year effects) factors that vary by year (e.g., Canes-Wrone, Brady, and Cogan, 2002; Erikson and Wright, 2017; Bonica and Cox, 2018). *District Ideology* is based on the two-party presidential vote for the Democratic presidential candidate, as in Jacobson (2015).[7] Other control variables also follow established measurement practices. Candidate spending reflects the difference between the log of the Democratic candidate's spending and the log of the Republican candidate's spending and is accordingly labeled *Difference in Logged Spending*. Quality challengers are ones with political experience (Jacobson and Kernell, 1983; Jacobson, 1989), and freshmen are members serving their first term (Canes-Wrone, Brady, and Cogan, 2002). Because the effects of the quality challengers and freshmen variables on the Democratic vote share will vary by party, separate indicators are included for Democrats and Republicans. For instance, *Democratic Quality Challenger* equals 1 if the challenger is a politically experienced Democrat and 0 otherwise, and *Republican Quality Challenger* equals 1 if the challenger is a politically experienced Republican and 0 otherwise. Additionally, the control *Democratic Incumbent* is included to account for the personal vote, as any personal vote would cause Democratic vote share to be higher for Democratic incumbents (e.g., Han and Brady, 2007; Jacobson, 2015).

Finally, we account for factors that vary by year. In the baseline specification, following Bonica and Cox (2018), these variables include an indicator for

---

7 It is worth emphasizing that the specification does not assume district ideology and candidate positions are estimated jointly on the same scale, as previous research has identified substantial challenges with jointly scaling candidates and voters (Hill and Huber, 2019). Consequently the analyses do not directly examine the effect of the distance between a district and a candidate's ideal point but instead the average effect of candidate extremity across all district types, holding constant district ideology.

midterm elections, the presidential approval rate from the last Gallup poll prior to the election, and the percentage change in gross domestic product (GDP) per capita between the third quarter of the election year and prior third quarter. Each of these controls is included as a main effect as well as interacted with whether a Democratic president holds office, to allow the impact to vary between the in- and out-party. As noted earlier, some specifications replace these factors with a set of year effects. For instance, the models with district fixed effects include the year effects so that all factors specific to an election, in addition to all factors specific to a particular district, are held constant.

Specifications and Methods

The analysis centers on three types of specifications. First, at the outset, we examine a straightforward Ordinary Least Squares (OLS) model with the observations pooled across time. The results from this model provide a baseline and direct comparison to earlier studies. Formally, the OLS specification for district i in year t is:

$$Democratic\ Candidate\ Vote\ Share_{it} = \alpha_{it} + \beta_1 Incumbent\ Ideology_{it}$$
$$+ \beta_2 Challenger\ Ideology_{it} + \beta_3 Incumbent\ Ideology_{it} \times Media\ Congruence_{it}$$
$$+ \beta_4 Challenger\ Ideology_{it} \times Media\ Congruence_{it} + \beta_5 Media\ Congruence_{it}$$
$$+ \beta_6 District\ Ideology_{it} + \beta_7 Democratic\ Incumbent_{it}$$
$$+ \lambda Additional\ Controls_{it} + \varepsilon_{it}. \tag{6.2}$$

The expectation is that β_3 and β_4 will be positive, given that media congruence should increase the effect of ideology on vote share.

Second, we employ district-specific fixed effects. Because the boundaries shift each decade due to redistricting, these are "district by decade" effects. The identification accordingly derives from how media congruence varies within a decade in a given district. Also in the fixed effects analysis, we omit controls such as spending or challenger quality that may be considered "post-treatment," or subsequent to a candidate adopting positions (Caughey and Warshaw, 2019).[8] Formally, we estimate:

$$Democratic\ Candidate\ Vote\ Share_{it} = \alpha_{it} + \beta_1 Incumbent\ Ideology_{it}$$
$$+ \beta_2 Challenger\ Ideology_{it} + \beta_3 Incumbent\ Ideology_{it} \times Media\ Congruence_{it}$$
$$+ \beta_4 Challenger\ Ideology_{it} \times Media\ Congruence_{it} + \beta_5 Media\ Congruence_{it}$$
$$+ \beta_6 District\ Ideology_{it} + \beta_7 Democratic\ Incumbent_{it} + \gamma_i + \eta_t + \varepsilon_{it}, \tag{6.3}$$

where γ_i are the district effects and η_t the year effects. This specification provides the most plausibly causal estimate of the impact of media congruence. By holding the district and year constant, the analysis reduces bias from

---

[8] Including these controls, however, does not alter the findings.

factors that may cause some districts to have both high media congruence and higher candidate accountability. Similarly, the omission of post-treatment variables reduces bias from potential endogeneity among factors that media congruence may influence, such as candidate spending or the emergence of quality challengers.

The third type of specification examines how the impact of the media has changed over time. As noted earlier, Peterson (2021a) finds that since 2006, the relationship between citizen knowledge of candidates and media congruence is only one-third to one-half the magnitude of that uncovered in Snyder and Strömberg (2010). We accordingly analyze separate effects for the pre- and post-2005 periods. Specifically, for each of the effects involving incumbent ideology, challenger ideology, and media congruence, we estimate a pre- and post-2005 effect (of course including as well the main effect of the post-2005 indicator). Because the motivating interest is to compare the entire pre- and post-2005 time periods, not simply a few years within a redistricting cycle, this analysis builds off the specification of Equation 6.2.[9]

RESULTS

Table 6.1 presents the baseline results. Recall that for both the DW-DIME and CFscores, the expectation is that the effects of the interaction terms with media congruence will be positive.

Table 6.1 largely confirms these expectations. For the DW-DIME scores, shown in Column 1, media congruence significantly strengthens the association between candidate ideology and electoral outcomes for incumbents and challengers. With the CFscores, in Column 2, these coefficients are again positive although only significant at conventional levels for challengers. The greater precision of the observed effects when using the DW-DIME scores is not surprising given that they require a larger number of donors and are designed to be predictors of roll-call votes, which are the types of policy positions on which the local media report (e.g., Arnold, 2004; Snyder and Strömberg, 2010).

Interestingly, there does not appear to be a substantial difference in the impact of media congruence for incumbents versus challengers. Across each measure of ideology, the magnitudes of the interaction effects are statistically similar for the two types of candidates. At the same time, the main effects of candidate ideology, which reflect the context where media congruence is zero, significantly differ between the candidate types. Incumbents suffer an extremism penalty (and conversely, benefit from moderation) even when congruence is at its lowest level. By comparison, there is no significant relationship between

---

[9] Note that a district fixed effects specification of the pre- and post-2005 eras would only compare the effects for the 2002 and 2004 elections versus the 2006–2010 ones given that the pre- and post-2005 eras do not vary within a district in the other decades. If we limit the analysis in this way, the results are qualitatively similar.

TABLE 6.1 *Media congruence and electoral accountability*

	Dependent Variable: Dem. Cand. Vote Share			
	DW-DIME (1)	CFscore (2)	DW-DIME (3)	CFscore (4)
Incumbent Ideology	6.907	2.348		
× Media Congruence	(3.374)	(1.403)		
Challenger Ideology	8.092	2.197		
× Media Congruence	(3.139)	(1.064)		
Incumbent Ideology	6.906	3.983	8.330	4.477
	(1.210)	(0.508)	(1.054)	(0.407)
Challenger Ideology	0.730	−1.020	2.309	−0.616
	(1.129)	(0.322)	(0.986)	(0.275)
Media Congruence	−0.381	0.315		
	(0.687)	(0.595)		
District Ideology	55.768	51.602	55.389	51.378
	(2.097)	(1.604)	(2.076)	(1.594)
Dem. Incumbent	16.509	19.679	16.627	19.834
	(1.300)	(0.910)	(1.293)	(0.902)
Difference in Logged Spending	2.215	2.188	2.227	2.187
	(0.131)	(0.113)	(0.131)	(0.113)
Democratic Freshman	−0.927	−0.368	−1.002	−0.415
	(0.535)	(0.451)	(0.533)	(0.450)
Republican Freshman	1.515	1.215	1.519	1.217
	(0.382)	(0.359)	(0.383)	(0.359)
Democratic Quality Challenger	0.837	0.869	0.788	0.859
	(0.391)	(0.356)	(0.393)	(0.357)
Republican Quality Challenger	−1.971	−1.839	−1.969	−1.814
	(0.487)	(0.423)	(0.487)	(0.423)
Election Year Control Variables	✓	✓	✓	✓
Observations	1,728	2,164	1,728	2,164
Adjusted R^2	0.856	0.865	0.856	0.865

Note: Robust standard errors shown in parentheses.

the main effect of the challenger's DW-DIME score and vote share, and a negative one with the CFscores. The relative strength of the base incumbent ideology effect is consistent with the fact that incumbents have additional means of reaching out to voters, such as through the franking privilege and electronic communications managed by staff (e.g., Hassell and Monson, 2016; Straus and Glassman, 2016).

To better visualize how the local media market conditions the impact of candidate ideology on vote share, Figure 6.1 depicts the effect of incumbent and challenger ideology across the entire range of possible media congruence values using the DW-DIME scores. The figure presents the effect of a one unit

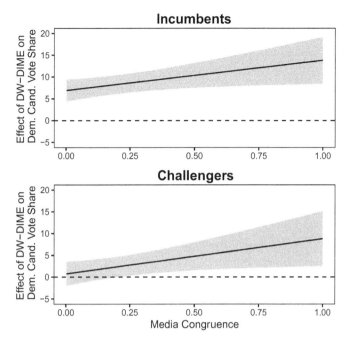

FIGURE 6.1 Ideology and vote share by media congruence

Shaded area indicates 95% confidence intervals for marginal effect of DW-DIME score on Dem. Vote Share for given media congruence level.

change in DW-DIME score, equivalent to slightly more than a two standard deviation shift in the underlying variable.

The top panel of Figure 6.1 shows that with no media congruence, a positive shift in an incumbent's DW-DIME score of one is predicted to increase the Democratic vote share by 6.9 percentage points. Likewise, a standard deviation increase in the DW-DIME variable (0.4) would produce a positive vote share shift of 2.8 percentage points. By comparison when media congruence is at its mean of 0.22, the effect on vote share of a one-point DW-DIME shift becomes 8.4 percentage points, and that of a one standard deviation shift 3.4 percentage points. By a 0.5 level of media congruence, these effects increase to 10.4 and 4.2 percentage points, respectively.

In comparison, as the bottom panel of Figure 6.1 shows, the overall impact of challenger ideology is lower even though the conditioning effect of media congruence is similarly high. Although there is not a significant association between challenger ideology and vote share when there is no media congruence, by the mean level of congruence of 0.22 the association becomes statistically significant. At this level, a one-point increase in the challenger's DW-DIME score is associated with a 2.5 percentage point increase in Democratic vote share (and a standard deviation increase in the DW-DIME score is associated with a one percentage point increase). At media congruence of 0.5, this effect grows to approximately 5 percentage points. Notably, while the 95% confidence intervals for the candidate estimates do overlap at higher levels of congruence, a two-tailed F-test for a difference in marginal effects suggests that the estimates are significantly different even when congruence is at its maximum (p-value = 0.01, two-tailed).

Returning to Table 6.1, Columns 3 and 4 provide a reference for the results on the main ideology effects in the first two columns. In particular, in the right-hand side of the table, the specifications exclude the media congruence variables and therefore estimate the average effects of incumbent and challenger ideology across all ranges of media congruence. Notably, the overall differences between incumbents and challengers are significant at conventional levels. These results demonstrate that the estimated difference between the main effects in Columns 1 and 2 are not merely a function of how media congruence is specified in these models.

Across all columns in the table, the candidate-specific controls present no surprises. District ideology, incumbency, challenger quality, freshman status, and candidate spending are each associated with vote share in the predicted way. The main effect of media congruence is not significant, which was also expected. Overall, Table 6.1 shows that even after controlling for standard determinants of vote share, media congruence has a substantial effect on the relationship between candidate positions and electoral outcomes.[10]

Of course, it is possible that there are factors specific to the districts or years that are not among the standard controls, and these factors could be positively correlated with media congruence. Moreover, some of the controls are arguably post-treatment in that they could be a function of candidate position-taking, thus leading to bias in the previously displayed results.[11] To address these issues, Table 6.2 presents analysis that both includes election and district fixed effects and excludes post-treatment factors.

Columns 1 and 2 describe the estimates for the DW-DIME scores, first with just the election year fixed effects and then adding the district fixed effects. Similarly, Columns 3 and 4 describe these findings for the CFscores.

Consistent with the findings from Table 6.1, the estimates on the interaction terms between media congruence and the DW-DIME scores are significant at conventional levels in both Columns 1 and 2. Even with the district

---

[10] An interesting question is whether this effect may be associated with the competitiveness of the district. On the one hand, media congruence may only matter if the race is competitive. On the other hand, prior research suggests political advertising is concentrated in competitive districts (e.g., Schaffner, 2006b), potentially substituting for a lack of local newspaper congruence. Initial analysis of our data points to the latter. Future research may benefit from a thorough investigation of how media effects and district competitiveness relate to each other.

[11] Future research may wish to endogenize these factors in an analysis of media congruence and candidate accountability.

TABLE 6.2 *Fixed effects specifications*

| | Dependent Variable: Dem. Cand. Vote Share | | | |
| | DW-DIME | | CFscore | |
	(1)	(2)	(3)	(4)
Incumbent Ideology	7.000	15.867	2.270	2.978
× Media Congruence	(3.339)	(5.498)	(1.386)	(2.340)
Challenger Ideology	8.036	17.105	2.144	3.712
× Media Congruence	(3.102)	(4.862)	(1.036)	(1.919)
Incumbent Ideology	6.804	7.944	4.288	5.010
	(1.212)	(3.608)	(0.509)	(1.495)
Challenger Ideology	0.500	2.445	−0.816	−0.400
	(1.116)	(1.803)	(0.312)	(0.576)
Media Congruence	−0.473	−5.224	0.171	−5.779
	(0.686)	(2.776)	(0.580)	(2.564)
District Ideology	55.423	50.848	52.500	45.761
	(2.114)	(6.650)	(1.607)	(5.853)
Dem. Incumbent	16.761	13.007	20.287	18.881
	(1.284)	(2.495)	(0.899)	(2.498)
Difference in Logged Spending	2.228		2.101	
	(0.132)		(0.114)	
Democratic Freshman	−0.946		−0.412	
	(0.537)		(0.454)	
Republican Freshman	1.529		1.284	
	(0.385)		(0.351)	
Democratic Quality Challenger	0.869		0.908	
	(0.393)		(0.348)	
Republican Quality Challenger	−1.991		−1.842	
	(0.482)		(0.414)	
Election Year Fixed Effects	✓	✓	✓	✓
District Fixed Effects		✓		✓
Observations	1,728	1,728	2,164	2,164
Adjusted R^2	0.856	0.670	0.871	0.740

Note: Robust standard errors shown in parentheses.

fixed effects, changes in media congruence have a significant impact on the relationship between a candidate's ideological positioning and vote share. In fact, for both incumbents and challengers, the estimated size of the coefficient is approximately double that of the specifications without the district effects.[12] Given that the district fixed effects specification provides the most plausibly

---

[12] These larger magnitudes are not due simply to excluding the post-treatment variables. With them, the coefficient on the interaction between media congruence and challenger ideology is 14.3 and that for incumbent ideology is 11.9 (each significant at $p < 0.05$, two-tailed).

causal estimate, these results offer strong support for the claim that the local media market shapes candidate accountability.

In the analyses with the CFscores, the results of which are presented in Columns 3 and 4, the estimated effects of the interaction between media congruence and challenger ideology are again significant. Also, again the magnitudes are higher with the district fixed effects. These findings provide further evidence that the impact of challenger positions is conditioned by the local media. For incumbents, the results are not as robust although still suggestive of an effect. More specifically, the coefficients on the interactions with media congruence are positive but not significant and, as with the DW-DIME scores, higher when the district fixed effects are included.

Notably, in all of the analyses in Table 6.2, at the base level of zero media congruence, incumbent positions have a significantly larger effect on electoral outcomes than challenger positions do. Indeed, as in Table 6.1, without a local newspaper market, ideological moderation on the part of a challenger does not significantly improve their electoral chances. In three of the four specifications, the base effect of challenger ideology is not at all significant, and in the one it is (for the CFscores with year effects but no district effects), the impact is even negative. Only as media congruence increases beyond the lowest levels does ideological extremity harm challengers in the voting booth. For instance, in Column 2, with the DW-DIME scores and district fixed effects, the impact of challenger positions becomes significant once media congruence reaches a level of 0.04.

In summary, Tables 6.1 and 6.2 suggest that local media markets play an important role in determining the extent to which voters will punish candidates' ideological extremism and reward moderation. Using a measure that captures how well local newspapers are expected to cover the district's candidates, the evidence supports the contention that when coverage is high, voters will evaluate candidates based on their policy positions, not simply party affiliation. For challengers, at the lowest levels of local media congruence, there is no relationship between their ideological positioning and electoral performance; however, as congruence increases, the association becomes significantly positive. For incumbents, even with no media congruence, ideological accountability remains. Yet at the same time, most specifications indicate the local media market increases the level of incumbent accountability.

The question remains, however, as to whether these effects are constant across time or instead diminish with the expansion of the internet as a source of news. Table 6.3 addresses this question.

Recall that Peterson (2021a) finds a lower, but still significant, effect of media congruence on voter knowledge about candidates beginning in 2006. The key results in Table 6.3 accordingly involve the three-way interactions among media congruence, the ideology scores, and the post-2005 period. These estimates reflect any differences in the effect of media congruence on candidate accountability since 2006.

TABLE 6.3 *Media congruence and accountability across time*

	Dependent variable: Dem. Cand. Vote Share			
	DW-DIME (1)	CFscore (2)	DW-DIME (3)	CFscore (4)
Incumbent Ideology × Media Congruence × Post-2005	−4.444 (6.630)	−1.640 (2.732)		
Challenger Ideology × Media Congruence × Post-2005	−10.298 (6.000)	−4.090 (2.014)		
Incumbent Ideology × Post-2005	−0.969 (1.819)	0.213 (0.788)	−1.654 (1.312)	−0.051 (0.580)
Challenger Ideology × Post-2005	−2.327 (1.714)	−0.362 (0.583)	−4.306 (1.232)	−1.180 (0.427)
Incumbent Ideology × Media Congruence	9.682 (4.768)	2.881 (1.957)		
Challenger Ideology × Media Congruence	13.224 (4.264)	4.129 (1.393)		
Incumbent Ideology	6.675 (1.470)	3.585 (0.669)	8.530 (1.258)	4.129 (0.541)
Challenger Ideology	1.805 (1.292)	−0.313 (0.484)	4.346 (1.123)	0.509 (0.425)
Post-2005	2.945 (1.035)	2.848 (0.594)	2.697 (1.035)	2.638 (0.566)
Media Congruence	−1.718 (1.329)	−1.062 (1.176)		
Media Congruence × Post-2005	0.289 (0.914)	0.516 (0.865)		
Candidate Controls	✓	✓	✓	✓
Election Year Controls	✓	✓	✓	✓
Observations	1,728	2,164	1,728	2,164
Adjusted R^2	0.858	0.868	0.857	0.867

Note: Robust standard errors shown in parentheses.

For each measure of candidate ideology, the coefficients on this interaction term for challengers are negative and at least marginally significant ($p < 0.05$, one-tailed). Furthermore, the magnitudes suggest that the role of media congruence declines substantially. The relevant comparison is to the two-way interaction term between challenger ideology and media congruence, which reflects the pre-2005 impact. With either measure of challenger ideology, the post-2005 effect takes away more than two-thirds of the impact for the earlier period.

The coefficients on the interactions for incumbents are also negative but not significant at conventional levels. The magnitudes are also smaller than for incumbents, both in absolute value and relative to the analogous pre-2006 effect for same-candidate type. However, the differences between the three-way interactions for challengers and incumbents are not significant. Thus, although the results point to a possibility that the changes in the local media have not affected incumbents to the same degree as challengers, any such distinction is merely suggestive.

Table 6.3 also indicates that at the lowest levels of media congruence, there is no evidence that the effects of candidate ideology have changed over time. In particular, in Columns 1 and 2, the two-way interactions between the post-2005 indicator and ideology scores are not significant at any conventional level, and the effect of this interaction for the incumbent CFscore is even positive. These findings suggest that it is in the districts with a higher newspaper presence in which a decline in the relationship between candidate ideology and vote share has occurred. Correspondingly, if all variables involving media congruence are excluded from the analysis, so that the conditioning effect of the local media market is not taken into account, there is evidence of an over-time decline in the impact of challenger ideology. Columns 3 and 4 present these findings, which comport with Canes-Wrone and Kistner's (2022) finding of a decrease in the impact of challenger ideological extremism since 1980.

None of the other results in Table 6.3 offer any surprises. As already noted, the two-way interactions between media congruence and candidate ideology reflect the impact of this factor in the pre-2006 elections. Like earlier analyses, media congruence significantly increases the effect of challenger ideology and although the estimates on incumbents are not significant for one of the ideology measures, the coefficients are consistently positive. Also as before, with no media congruence, incumbent extremism has a significantly higher impact on electoral outcomes than challenger extremism does.[13]

In summary, Table 6.3 indicates that the impact of the local media on ideological accountability has decreased over time, particularly for challengers. Alongside the reductions in local newspaper staffing and coverage, challengers now receive fewer rewards for ideological moderation and are punished less for ideological extremity. Although the results are not as large or statistically significant for incumbents, here too there is suggestive evidence that the role of the local media has declined. Together, these findings imply that the developments in local news may be contributing to fewer incentives for elected politicians to represent their constituents' policy positions.

---

[13] A potential concern is that challenger ideology may be measured less precisely due to challengers having fewer donors and that therefore measurement error could produce the observed differences between challengers and incumbents. In addition to following Bonica and Cox (2018) in excluding races in which a candidate had fewer than ten donors, we have conducted robustness checks with higher donor thresholds. When a 25-donor threshold is adopted for the analysis in Table 6.3, the difference between the main effects of challenger and incumbent ideology is significant with either the CFscores or DW-DIME scores. Even with a 100-donor threshold, this difference remains significant for the CFscores and qualitatively similar for the DW-DIME scores.

CONCLUSION

This chapter has examined whether and how ideological accountability in congressional races is shaped by the local media market. To ensure that the media context is exogenous to candidates and their electoral districts, we have used data on the congruence between the local newspaper market and congressional district boundaries. Three main findings emerge. First, on the whole, as media congruence increases, candidate positions have a larger effect on electoral outcomes; voters punish candidate extremism more heavily, and likewise, offer higher rewards for ideological moderation. This finding is consistent with the work of Cameron and Gordon in Chapter 10, this volume, which argues that the media is a prototypical sentinel and that its decline has potentially serious consequences for democratic accountability. Second, our analysis reveals that when media congruence is low, only incumbent positions affect electoral outcomes. In other words, in the absence of media congruence, challenger extremism is not punished by voters. Third, the effects of media congruence have decreased since 2006 for challengers, and there is suggestive evidence of a decline for incumbents. This last finding aligns with research that indicates local newspaper markets no longer have the same impact on voter knowledge that they did prior to the internet age (e.g., Hayes and Lawless, 2018; Peterson, 2021a).

These findings provoke a series of normative and empirical questions regarding the relationship among the local media, candidate positions, and electoral accountability. One such question is whether voters ought to consider challenger positions when deciding whom to support. Unlike incumbents, who have taken actions in office, challenger positions may be nothing more than cheap talk. If incentivizing such cheap talk is undesirable, then neither the negligible effect of challenger ideology when media congruence is low, nor the declining importance of media congruence across time, should be of concern.

There are several reasons to believe a relationship between challenger positions and electoral outcomes is desirable, however. As discussed earlier, if voters assume challengers simply share the views of their national parties, incumbents may have fewer incentives to be responsive to voter preferences; in a district where the position of the opposing party is far from the pivotal voter, an incumbent could take relatively extreme positions and face no electoral consequence. Second, research suggests congressional campaign appeals are not cheap talk but instead have a "lasting legacy" on the members' behavior once in office (Sulkin, 2011). Finally, many challengers have held prior political office and therefore already have an established record on certain policies.

A second question raised by the findings is how to think about the role of local newspapers in an internet age. As described in this and Huber and Tucker's work in Chapter 8, this volume, the number of such papers has declined, and among those that still exist, the capacity for political reporting is dramatically lower than what it was a few decades ago (e.g., Napoli et al., 2017; Peterson, 2017). Yet traditionally local newspapers have been the best source of coverage for local officials, including House candidates (e.g., Arnold, 2004; Cohen, Noel, and Zaller, 2004; Snyder and Strömberg, 2010), and no clear replacement has emerged. Initial investigation of internet sources finds that they offer less news than traditional print publications (Hindman, 2011; Gavazza, Nardotto, and Valletti, 2019). Still, given the increasing displacement of print by the internet, future research would benefit from the development of a measure that incorporates district internet usage of local sources (a point also made in Huber and Tucker's work in Chapter 8). Correspondingly, the reductions in local newspapers may have amplified the role of local television news, which has been shown to affect electoral outcomes (e.g., Dunaway, 2008; Martin and McCrain, 2019). Here too, however, trends toward greater consolidation of stations by corporations focused on national politics makes this alternative unlikely to offset the decline of local newspapers; indeed, Martin and McCrain (2019) find that conglomeration buy-outs have decreased the television news coverage of local politics.

This chapter also suggests several other topics for future scholarship. For instance, as a field we know little about the ways in which the local media influence the emergence of quality challengers. Thomsen (2019) finds that challengers have become more likely to drop out of primary races over time, with politically experienced candidates being even more likely than inexperienced ones to do so. Whether developments in local news are a causal factor in this development is worth investigating. Separately, the field would benefit from studying other factors that may be directly contributing to changes in candidate accountability. Such developments include the decline of competitive and cross-pressured districts (Han and Brady, 2007) and new fundraising practices (Barber, 2016; Gooch and Huber, 2020).

The results also potentially relate to the rise in elite-level polarization. Although Prior (2013) suggests that polarization is not due to voters opting into news sources that reinforce existing ideological biases, he also finds it is associated with substantial segments of the public opting out of news altogether. Correspondingly, Peskowitz (2019) offers evidence of a positive association between a member's ability to signal distinct positions from their party and the incumbency advantage, and the decline in local news has coincided with a weakening of the incumbency advantage (Jacobson, 2015). This chapter provides a foundation for developing subsequent analyses on whether the developments in local media have contributed to elite-level polarization indirectly, such as by reducing members' incentives to take positions favored by their districts.

6.A APPENDIX: DESCRIPTIVE STATISTICS

TABLE 6.A.1 *Descriptive statistics*

Variable Name	Mean	Std. Deviation	Minimum	Maximum
Democratic Candidate Vote Share	50.366	14.338	3.030	93.939
Incumbent DW-DIME	0.029	0.412	−0.766	0.983
Challenger DW-DIME	0.068	0.420	−0.597	0.983
Incumbent CFscore	0.062	0.807	−1.556	1.471
Challenger CFscore	−0.005	1.108	−4.878	2.595
Congruence	0.221	0.223	0.002	1.000
District Ideology	0.521	0.115	0.208	0.939
Democratic Incumbent	0.506	0.500	0	1
Difference in Logged Spending	−0.053	1.918	−6.954	5.569
Democratic Freshman	0.089	0.284	0	1
Republican Freshman	0.112	0.316	0	1
Democratic Quality Challenger	0.134	0.340	0	1
Republican Quality Challenger	0.134	0.341	0	1
Democratic President	0.625	0.484	0	1
Presidential Approval	−1.674	20.458	−45	35
Midterm	0.494	0.500	0	1
GDP Growth	2.634	1.988	−2.810	5.000

Note: Descriptive statistics shown are for data through 2014, with the exception of DW-DIME, which extends through 2012.

7

Inequality, or Invisibility and Inaccuracy? How Local Newspapers Cover the Occupational Backgrounds of Congressional Incumbents and Challengers

Nicholas Carnes

How often do journalists cover the economic backgrounds of politicians? When they do, are their stories thorough and accurate, or brief, incomplete, and slanted? Would a citizen who reads the local newspaper every day learn very much about the economic backgrounds of the people who represent her?

Research on how the media cover other aspects of politicians' personal backgrounds has often reached alarming conclusions. Schaffner and Gadson's (2004, 604) study of how local journalists cover Black members of Congress argues that "local television news stations may be partially responsible for the prevailing stereotype of African-American House members who are narrowly focused on race-oriented issues." Conroy et al.'s (2015, 573) analysis of news coverage of vice-presidential candidates over two decades finds "sex inequalities in coverage tone, type, and hard sexism (overtly gendered insults)."

To date, however, there hasn't been analogous research on how the media cover the economic backgrounds of politicians, that is, how journalists report on things like how wealthy politicians are, how much formal education they have, and what kinds of occupations they had before holding office. Scholars occasionally point to individual examples of journalists neglecting or distorting candidates' economic backgrounds, but political scientists have never systematically studied how the media cover the economic backgrounds of politicians.

There are good reasons to wonder how journalists cover this topic. Scholars have found, for instance, that leaders from different occupations tend to bring different perspectives to public office, with consequences for everything from roll-call voting and bill introductions to agenda control and public policy

I am grateful to Donald Pepka and Kendrik Icenhower for research assistance; to Bill Adair, Jay Hamilton, and Jason Wright for feedback; to the anonymous reviewers for detailed comments; and to workshop participants at Princeton University.

(e.g., Carnes, 2018; Kirkland, 2019; Witko and Friedman, 2008), even decades after politicians take office (Carnes, 2013, ch. 2). And the economic makeup of political institutions in the United States is profoundly lopsided. Millionaires comprise around 3% of the public but majorities of every Congress since the 1980s (Eggers and Klašnja, 2019). In contrast, working-class occupations – manual labor, service industry, and clerical jobs – make up most of the labor force, but people with significant experience in working-class jobs have never made up more than 3% of Congress (Carnes, 2018; Chinoy and Ma, 2019).

When citizens have access to information about the economic backgrounds of politicians, they seem to care, suggesting that this information is somehow relevant to the evaluations that are at the heart of political accountability. A growing body of experimental research argues that voters make inferences about candidates based on things like their wealth and past jobs (e.g., Carnes, 2018; but see Nakanishi, Cooper, and Kassarjian, 1974),[1] just as they do with other candidate traits.[2] Voters seem keen to interpret candidates' occupational histories as markers of issue expertise; they see candidates who were teachers, for instance, as better at handling problems related to education (Coffé and Theiss-Morse, 2016; McDermott, 2005).[3] One recent study found that when voters learned that President Trump inherited tremendous wealth, they saw Trump as less adept and empathetic (McDonald, Karol, and Mason, 2019).

But do the media regularly provide the public with this kind of information about the economic backgrounds of politicians? Whereas voters can usually pick up on many of the consequential characteristics of a politician – like race and gender – from just a photograph, campaign ad, or even a name, a leader's economic background is a *less visible* characteristic unless journalists, campaigns, or interest groups bring it to the forefront (McDonald, Karol, and Mason, 2019).[4] For voters to be informed, news outlets would need to provide a steady stream of stories throughout the cycle of campaigning and governing that allude to politicians' economic backgrounds. Do they?

This study reports the first exploratory analysis of how local newspapers cover the economic backgrounds of members of Congress and their general election challengers. I focus primarily on newspaper coverage of members' and challengers' occupational backgrounds, the economic background characteristic that seems to best predict legislators' conduct in office (Carnes, 2013). (I also report secondary analyses of how newspapers cover members' and challengers' education and wealth.)

---

[1] Class-related media can also influence voters' general views (Kane and Newman, 2019).
[2] E.g., see Dolan (2004) and McConnaughy et al. (2010). For a useful review, see McDonald, Karol, and Mason (2019).
[3] Some studies even treat occupational backgrounds as proxies for the quality of candidates (Roberts and Roberds, 2002) and potential candidates (Lawless and Fox, 2005).
[4] One notable exception is California, which lists candidates' self-reported occupations on the ballot.

My research is organized around three empirical questions: How often do local newspapers cover the occupational backgrounds of members and candidates for Congress? When they cover occupational backgrounds, how accurate are they – specifically, how often do they omit certain occupations? And regardless of whether and how thoroughly newspapers cover members' and challengers' occupations, do newspapers report differently on politicians from historically underrepresented working-class occupations?

As a first cut at these questions, I analyzed over 1,200 stories written about a sample of thirty-two members of the 110th House of Representatives – the seven who have extensive experience in working-class jobs and a random sample of twenty-five other members – and their major-party opponents – twenty-eight of the thirty-two faced such challengers – during the ten weeks prior to the 2010 election (or the last election the member ran in, if he or she did not run in 2010). I focused on local newspapers because national media outlets rarely cover the vast majority of congressional elections (Arnold, 2004, 3) and because citizens consequently get far more news about their own House races from local news (Hayes and Lawless, 2016). And I focused on a small, exploratory sample (just thirty-two members and twenty-eight challengers) as opposed to a larger automated data collection process because the traits I studied were hypothesized to be absent or easy to miss, and in the broader hope of developing a grounded understanding of media coverage of politicians' economic backgrounds that could inform future large-scale projects. Of course, as Canes-Wrone and Kistner note in Chapter 6 of this volume, the media environment has become more complex in the last two decades, and as Huber and Tucker note in Chapter 8 of this volume, future research may do well to simultaneously analyze print news, cable television, online news, and other media. In this analysis, I start with local newspapers, but obviously future work would do well to consider other media outlets.

Although past work on how journalists cover women and politicians of color might lead us to suspect economic biases in the media, I find no evidence of coverage inequalities in this study. When it comes to members' and challengers' occupational backgrounds, inequality is not the issue, but rather invisibility and inaccuracy. Many newspapers in my sample never reported on the occupational backgrounds of members of Congress or their challengers (or, for that matter, their education or wealth) in the ten weeks prior to the election, and the little information other newspapers provided was often shallow and incomplete; many of the occupations listed in congressional almanacs do not appear in newspaper coverage, and the occupations that appear in the news mostly seem to track the stylized occupational histories members and candidates present on their own websites. This seemed to be especially true for incumbents; whereas challengers' occupational backgrounds might make the news (perhaps simply because they are new to politics), local papers almost never mention incumbents' occupational backgrounds.

Of course, these findings are not necessarily out of step with existing normative models of media coverage, which argue that citizens mostly need information about politicians' views and choices on the important issues of the day. This study suggests, however, that regardless of whether the media provide the information citizens need to hold politicians accountable for their issue positions, the news still routinely leaves out information about politicians' economic backgrounds that voters deem relevant to their choices. This in turn suggests that perhaps political scientists' ideals about news coverage should be broadened to acknowledge that voters deserve to know not just what politicians do and say, but who they are.

INEQUALITY, INVISIBILITY, AND INACCURACY

To date, most research on how the media cover politicians from different demographic backgrounds has focused on questions about coverage inequality, that is, whether journalists somehow differ in how they report on politicians from social groups that have historically been underrepresented in public office. The first wave of research in this literature focused on gender and race and argued that *coverage inequalities* were routine: women[5] and people of color[6] in politics receive less prominent coverage and less favorable, more stereotypical coverage. Although recent studies have begun to challenge these conclusions, (e.g., Hayes and Lawless, 2016; McIlwain, 2011), the case is far from closed, and first-wave research on coverage inequality looms large in the literature.

It seems highly plausible that the media might cover politicians differently based on their economic backgrounds. Candidates with experience in historically underrepresented working-class jobs might be ignored, or exoticized, or disparaged.

However, coverage inequalities aren't the only issues scholars should consider when they study the role of politicians' economic backgrounds in the news. Unlike more-visible traits like race and gender, economic backgrounds can easily be overlooked or distorted, raising the possibility that those traits might not just trigger coverage inequalities, but might also be invisible or inaccurate in the news. If journalists don't explicitly state a politician's economic background, their audience might not know what it is. If they don't interrogate what they hear about a politician's economic background, they might spread misleading information.

It is difficult to say up front exactly how much coverage it takes to educate the public about the economic background of a given leader, of course. Discussing his Burglar Alarm news standard, Zaller's (2003, 125) clearest quantitative measure of sufficient coverage was a reference to members running

---

5 See, e.g., Kahn (1994); Conroy et al. (2015).
6 See, for instance, Caliendo and McIlwain (2006); Gershon (2012); Lucas (2017); and Terkildsen and Damore (1999).

for re-election in tight races who received "twice-a-day coverage ..., probably prominently displayed and spread over both candidates." This is a high bar, and information presented less often may still reach the public. But it probably stands to reason that if a media outlet doesn't mention a leader's economic background fairly prominently – at least once every few stories about the leader, or once every few days during a campaign – there is a good chance that that information will be invisible to most citizens.

If we care about how the news covers politicians' economic backgrounds, we cannot simply focus on coverage inequality; we should also be concerned about inaccuracy and invisibility, that is, how well and how often journalists report on politicians' economic backgrounds in the first place. There are at least a few reasons for hope. Reporters have ample space to provide detailed and accurate information about politicians: cable news stations have twenty-four hours a day to devote to politics, online news outlets have limitless bandwidth, and even local newspapers have the space to cover politicians regularly and prominently (Arnold, 2004, ch. 2). Reporters also have easy access to information about the economic backgrounds of politicians, which is readily available on campaign websites, in biographical almanacs, and in financial disclosure statements.

However, there is one paramount reason to be concerned about invisibility and inaccuracy in news coverage of politicians' economic backgrounds: static biographical facts aren't usually news. Journalists don't have strong incentives to rehash biographical information (e.g., Hamilton, 2004), and they often have to make tough choices about how to spend their limited time and resources (especially as many local newspapers – big and small – face declining readerships and tough financial constraints). The morning newspaper isn't an encyclopedia.

Of course, there are a few situations in which the logic of news might drive journalists to cover the economic backgrounds of politicians. Journalists might report economic and other biographical information *when politicians first run for a given office.* A new entrant into the political arena is herself newsworthy, and journalists might report on a new candidate's economic background as part of the larger process of introducing her to the community she hopes to represent. Journalists might also mention politicians' economic backgrounds *when they think doing so will provide some useful context* for some newsworthy issue. Or, related, journalists might report on politicians' economic backgrounds *when people in and around government talk about them in connection to newsworthy issues.* Politicians sometimes highlight their economic backgrounds to help explain their positions on relevant issues (e.g., as a farmer, I understand the importance of agricultural subsidies), claim credit for favorable policy outcomes (e.g., as a farmer, I was proud to vote for these important new subsidies), or advertise their positive qualities (as a farmer, I know the value of hard work). Likewise, observers sometimes comment on a politician's economic background when it is relevant to a controversy or scandal, like a politician who is accused of hiding wealth in off-shore bank accounts or doing something unethical in a previous job. When people in and around government attempt to use a politician's economic background to bolster a story – or when it is central to the story – journalists are likely to cover it.

LOCAL NEWSPAPER COVERAGE OF MEMBERS OF CONGRESS

As an exploratory first cut at understanding media coverage of politicians' economic backgrounds, I studied how local newspapers covered a sample of members of the 110th Congress and their major-party general election challengers. Congress was ideal for this study because members are more numerous and economically diverse than presidents (thereby providing more examples of politicians from the working class for my tests of coverage inequalities) and higher-profile than state or local leaders (which should help rule out invisibility and inaccuracy that occur simply because the leader isn't politically influential). I focused on the 110th Congress (2007–2008) because in 2010 I compiled detailed occupational histories for each member who served during that term from congressional almanacs (data that are useful as a benchmark for determining how thorough newspaper accounts are) and because in 2010 I also recorded how each member in the sample described their occupational history on their official website (data that are useful for assessing the extent to which newspaper accounts overlap with members' own narratives about their economic backgrounds). As for the medium, I studied local newspaper coverage because local papers are numerous and consequential (as Hayes and Lawless [2016, 60] note, citizens are "more than four times as likely to get information about the House race in their district from a local newspaper than a national one") and because local newspapers are archived online in easy-to-use databases (unlike local television and radio coverage).

Following early efforts to develop a grounded understanding of media coverage of members of Congress (e.g., Arnold, 2004; for a more detailed history, see Huber and Tucker in Chapter 8 of this volume), I selected a relatively small sample of members and articles. This approach was especially useful for studying occupational information, which can be easy to miss in rapid or automated analyses. Of course, the obvious downside is that I cannot make the broad and confident statistical generalizations that have been possible in more recent large-scale studies of media coverage of Congress (e.g., Hayes and Lawless, 2016). As a first pass at an empirical question about a trait that may well be invisible in the news, however, it seemed fitting to begin with a careful reading of a smaller sample and to leave larger-scale data collection and analysis to future studies.

To ensure that I had as many members as possible from historically under-represented economic backgrounds (to increase the odds of detecting any coverage biases that might exist), I started by identifying every member of the

110th House who spent at least one third of his or her pre-congressional career doing working-class jobs. (There were seven in all.) Then, following Arnold's (2004, first dataset) approach in his pioneering study of local news coverage of members of Congress, I randomly selected twenty-five additional members of the 110th House. I then identified the major-party challengers who ran against the members in question in the 2010 general election (or if they did not run then, the most recent general election the member ran in).

My analysis focused on the ten weeks leading up to election day, a period that usually includes both the bulk of campaign-related coverage and a steady stream of non-campaign coverage (Arnold, 2004). For each member, I searched *Newsbank* for the newspaper that ran the most stories about them in the ten weeks prior to the 2010 election (or the last prior election they ran in). After identifying the newspaper that wrote the most stories that mentioned each member, if any member's top newspaper produced fewer than twenty search results, I included results from the next largest newspaper (repeating until I exceeded twenty raw search results).

I collected stories that mentioned the member's name, removed duplicate and irrelevant stories, and coded each story with the help of a research assistant. My coding process recorded any information about the member's occupational background, education, and wealth (to test my invisibility and inaccuracy hypotheses) as well as the issues each story discussed in connection with the member and any positive or negative comments it reported about the member (to test the traditional coverage inequality hypothesis).

Using this bank of stories, I then recorded any references to the member's major party challenger in the general election, in the hopes of increasing the number of cases available for study (and to test one of the corollaries of the invisibility hypothesis, namely, that journalists are more likely to cover the economic backgrounds of new candidates than incumbent politicians). By using articles that mentioned incumbents to study challengers as well, I essentially assumed that every story that mentioned a congressional challenger would also mention the incumbent they were running against. This assumption seemed reasonable; for a handful of cases, I tried to locate stories that mentioned challengers but not the incumbents they were challenging in the ten weeks prior to election day, but didn't find any.

There were twenty-eight challengers; four of the thirty-two members did not face a challenger from the other major party in the general election in question. For these twenty-eight challengers, I coded references to their occupations (and educations and wealth) in the same way that I did for incumbents, and I used the Internet Archive's Wayback Machine to find and code archived copies of the challenger's campaign website during that race. Unfortunately, the congressional almanacs I compiled to create detailed "true" occupational histories for incumbents do not include information about challengers, and there is no analogous challenger database to my knowledge. As such, I could test my invisibility and inequality hypotheses on challengers, but not my inaccuracy hypothesis (although I could at least compare the information in the news to the information challengers presented on their own websites).

The twenty-five members I randomly drew at the start of my data collection process were generally representative of the 110th House. They were 48% Republican (the entire chamber was 46% Republican), they had served in the House for twelve years on average (the chamber average was twelve), and 8% of them were chairs or ranking members of committees or subcommittees (compared to 9% in the entire chamber). Not surprisingly, my non-random sample of seven working-class members was far less representative; they were 14% Republican, they had served nine years on average, and 14% of them had committee leadership positions.

Overall, the media seemed to cover these thirty-two members at similar rates to what past research has found. In total, I collected 1,222 stories (articles, opinion pieces, letters to the editor, and other pieces), or about 3.8 stories per member per week. Reassuringly, this figure was similar to the coverage rates reported in other recent studies (Arnold, 2004; Hayes and Lawless, 2016).

Table 7.1 briefly summarizes my dataset. Of the thirty-two members of the 110th Congress I studied, twenty-one campaigned for re-election in 2010, seven last ran in 2008, and four last ran in 2006 (but due to a coding error, data were collected for 2006 for one member, Dennis Moore, although he ran again in 2008). For six members, I studied multiple newspapers because no one newspaper produced at least twenty results when I searched for the member's name during the relevant timeframe. And even when my search results exceeded twenty articles, the process of eliminating duplicates and irrelevant results sometimes left fewer than twenty relevant pieces. (In my analyses of coverage inequality below, I take this feature of the dataset into account.) With these data, we can investigate the issues of invisibility, inaccuracy, and inequality in coverage of candidates from working-class occupations.

INVISIBILITY

First, how often do local papers cover the economic – and, specifically, the occupational – backgrounds of members of Congress and their challengers? Are they covered often enough that a citizen who reads the news fairly regularly could be expected to encounter that information? Occupational backgrounds are less visible characteristics unless campaigns and journalists bring them to light. How often do they make the news?

For members of Congress, the answer, at least in my dataset, was almost never. Of the 1,222 articles I compiled, just 44 (3.6%) mentioned any of the occupations the member held prior to serving in Congress, including military service and work in other levels or branches of government. For sixteen of the thirty-two members – around half of my sample – the newspapers that covered the member most often didn't run a single article that mentioned

TABLE 7.1 *Members, challengers, and newspapers*

Name	% Career in Wrk-class Jobs	Major Party Challenger	Inc. Vote Margin (%)	Party	State	Dist.	Elec. Studied	Top Newspaper(s)	# of articles
Brady, Robert A	37	None	100	D	PA	1	2010	Phil. Inquirer, Erie Times-News, Bucks County Courier Times, Times Leader	10
Carson, Julia	57	Eric Dickerson	54	D	IN	7	2006	Post-Tribune, Jour. Gazette, Evansville Courier & Press, News-Sentinel	7
Lynch, Stephen F	67	Vernon Harrison	68	D	MA	9	2010	The Enterprise	19
Michaud, Mike	62	Jason J. Levesque	55	D	ME	2	2010	Bangor Daily News	82
Napolitano, Grace	78	Robert Vaughn	73	D	CA	38	2010	San Gabriel Valley Tribune, Whittier Daily News, La Opinion, Fresno Bee,	15
Sanchez, Linda	38	Larry Andre	63	D	CA	39	2010	Long Beach Press-Telegram, Whittier Daily News	20
Davis, Jo Ann	41	Shawn M. O'Donnell	63	R	VA	1	2006	Free Lance-Star	69
Bachmann, Michele	0	Tarryl Clark	52	R	MN	6	2010	St. Paul Pioneer Press	49
Bachus, Spencer	0	None	100	R	AL	6	2010	Birmingham News	20
Boustany, Charles	0	None	100	R	LA	7	2010	Advocate	12
Brady, Kevin	0	Kent Hargett	80	R	TX	8	2010	Beaumont Enterprise	18
Feeney, Tom	0	Suzanne Kosmas	41	R	FL	24	2008	Orlando Sentinel	62
Johnson, Sam	0	John Lingenfelder	66	R	TX	3	2010	Dallas Morning News	12
LaHood, Ray	0	Steve Waterworth	67	R	IL	18	2006	Peoria Journal Star	81
Lucas, Frank D	0	Frankie Robbins	78	R	OK	3	2010	Oklahoman	20
Peterson, John E	0	Donald L Hilliard	70	R	PA	5	2006	Centre Daily Times	10
Rogers, Hal	0	Jim Holbert	77	R	KY	5	2010	Lexington Herald-Leader	22
Thornberry, Mac	0	None	87	R	TX	13	2010	Wichita Falls Times Record News	37

Note: Shaded rows are incumbents who spent at least 30% of their pre-congressional careers in working-class jobs.

TABLE 7.1 *(continued)*

Name	% Career in Wrk-class Jobs	Major Party Challenger	Inc. Vote Margin (%)	Party	State	Dist.	Elec. Studied	Top Newspaper(s)	# of articles
Walden, Greg	0	Joyce B. Segers	74	R	OR	2	2010	Bulletin	34
Berkley, Shelley	0	Kenneth A. Wegner	61	D	NV	1	2010	Las Vegas Review-Journal	40
Boyda, Nancy	0	Lynn Jenkins	46	D	KS	2	2008	Topeka Capital-Journal	75
Cohen, Stephen	0	Charlotte Bergmann	74	D	TN	9	2010	Commercial Appeal	68
Costello, Jerry	0	Teri Newman	60	D	IL	12	2010	Belleville News-Democrat	52
Emanuel, Rahm	0	Tom Hanson	73	D	IL	5	2008	Chicago Sun-Times, Daily Herald	17
Hooley, Darlene	0	Mike Erickson	54	D	OR	5	2006	Oregonian	35
Lampson, Nick	0	Pete Olson	45	D	TX	22	2008	Houston Chronicle	45
Mahoney, Tim	0	Tom Rooney	39	D	FL	16	2008	St. Lucie News Tribune	105
Moore, Dennis	0	Chuck Aher	56	D	KS	3	2006	Kansas City Star	48
Pelosi, Nancy	0	John Dennis	80	D	CA	8	2010	San Francisco Chronicle	53
Rangel, Charles	0	Michel J. Faulkner	80	D	NY	15	2010	New York Daily News	25
Scott, David	0	Mike Crane	69	D	GA	13	2010	Atlanta Journal-Constitution	11
Wasserman Schultz, D	0	Karen Harrington	60	D	FL	20	2010	Sun Sentinel	49

their occupational background during the ten weeks prior to election day. Information about members' educational backgrounds and wealth was even scarcer. Just seven (0.6%) of the 1,222 articles mentioned member education, and just six (0.5%) mentioned member wealth.

The story was somewhat different for challengers. I hypothesized that biographical information about new candidates might be more newsworthy than background facts about incumbents, and indeed it seemed to be. Of the 1,143 articles written about members facing major-party general election challengers, 120 (10.5%) mentioned the challenger's occupation at least once. Education and wealth information was still rare, however; just thirteen articles (1.1%) mentioned a challenger's educational background, and just three (0.2%) mentioned wealth (even in vague terms like "he made his fortune as an entrepreneur"). Even so, consistent with the idea that a politician's occupational background is more newsworthy the first time he or she runs, in a sample of stories selected because they mentioned members of Congress, a reader was around three times more likely to hear about a challenger's occupational history than a member's.

Table 7.2 lists the numbers of distinct paragraphs that referenced each member's and challenger's occupation, along with the total article counts for each member (from Table 7.1). For all but two of the thirty-two members, the newspapers that covered them most often mentioned their occupational history in fewer than five paragraphs during the ten weeks leading up to election day, that is, in less than one paragraph every other week.

Challengers' occupations were covered more often, but the rates were still generally low; fifteen of the twenty-eight challengers' occupations were mentioned in fewer than five paragraphs in the ten weeks leading up to election day. No paper covered members' or challengers' occupational backgrounds in more than two paragraphs per day on average (a slightly relaxed version of the standard Zaller described as clearly above the bar for sufficient coverage of a race), and only one politician's occupation appeared in even two paragraphs per week.[7] Only two members' and eight challengers' occupations were mentioned in more than two paragraphs per *month* in the run up to election day. The occupations of half of the members and five of the challengers in this sample were completely invisible in the ten weeks leading up to the election, and for most other members and challengers, coverage of their occupations was sufficiently sporadic to raise doubts about whether the information was really visible to all but the most vigilant newspaper readers.[8]

Consistent with the idea that economic background information isn't newsworthy in itself, when newspapers mentioned members' occupational backgrounds, they often did so because the occupations related to some other newsworthy issue. Table 7.3 briefly summarizes the context of each paragraph that referenced a member's or challenger's occupational history. Across these 1,222 campaign-season articles, there were just twenty purely biographical references to members' occupations (in just fifteen articles, around 1.2% of the sample) and just twenty-six purely biographical references to challengers' occupations (in just twenty articles, around 1.6% of the sample), that is, references that were part of a biographical narrative about the member or challenger or a breakout box that listed biographical facts. The other references to members' occupations were either brief asides or references to ongoing

---

7 Rep. Nancy Boyda's challenger, State Treasurer Lynn Jenkins, was involved in a scandal related to her work as Treasurer, so her occupation was mentioned in fifty-two paragraphs – an average of five per week. This was undoubtedly a case of a politician's occupation being discussed to provide context for a newsworthy issue, although reporters also sometimes mentioned her occupation as an aside.

8 The same was true for incumbents when I focused only on close races (those where the incumbent received less than 55% of the vote). Challengers' occupations were covered at higher rates than incumbents' in non-close races (an average of 4.14 paragraphs) and even higher rates still in close races (15.43 paragraphs).

TABLE 7.2 *Coverage of occupational backgrounds is rare*

Name	Occupation Paragraphs	Articles	Para. / Article	Challenger Occ. Para.	Para. / Article
Bachus, Spencer	0	20	0	n/a	n/a
Boustany, Charles W Jr	0	12	0	n/a	n/a
Brady, Kevin	0	18	0	n/a	n/a
Brady, Robert A	0	10	0	0	0
Carson, Julia	0	7	0	0	0
Costello, Jerry F	0	52	0	0	0
Emanuel, Rahm	0	17	0	1	0.06
Johnson, Sam	0	12	0	1	0.08
Lampson, Nick	0	45	0	12	0.27
Lucas, Frank D	0	20	0	0	0
Napolitano, Grace	0	15	0	0	0
Pelosi, Nancy	0	53	0	2	0.04
Peterson, John E	0	10	0	6	0.6
Rangel, Charles B	0	25	0	6	0.24
Rogers, Hal	0	22	0	6	0.27
Scott, David	0	37	0	2	0.05
Boyda, Nancy E	1	75	0.01	52	0.69
Feeney, Tom	1	62	0.02	15	0.24
Lynch, Stephen F	1	19	0.05	3	0.16
Berkley, Shelley	2	40	0.05	1	0.03
Cohen, Stephen Ira	2	68	0.03	1	0.02
Wasserman Schultz, D.	2	11	0.18	11	1
Bachmann, Michele	3	49	0.06	2	0.04
LaHood, Ray	3	81	0.04	3	0.04
Michaud, Mike	3	82	0.04	17	0.21
Walden, Greg	3	49	0.06	6	0.12
Hooley, Darlene	4	35	0.11	12	0.34
Mahoney, Tim	4	105	0.04	15	0.14
Sánchez, Linda	4	20	0.2	9	0.45
Thornberry, Mac	4	34	0.12	n/a	n/a
Davis, Jo Ann	7	69	0.1	2	0
Moore, Dennis	10	48	0.21	10	0.19

Note: Shaded rows are incumbents who spent at least 30% of their pre-congressional careers in working-class jobs.

newsworthy issues like re-election campaigns and policy positions. (Paragraphs referencing members' occupations could be coded to more than one issue-related category, so the counts in Table 7.3 do not sum to the same totals as the counts in Table 7.2.) In the articles I collected, journalists rarely talked about members' or challengers' occupational backgrounds for their own sake – they more often mentioned them in connection to newsworthy issues.

Challengers differed from incumbents in two notable ways in Table 7.3. As Table 7.2 also illustrated, challengers' occupations were more likely to be mentioned. Second, challengers' occupations were far more likely to be

TABLE 7.3 *The context in which stories mentioned members' and challengers' occupations*

Context	Incumber para.	Challenger para.
Issue-related references		
Explaining an issue position	8	9
Supporting a positive evaluation	6	21
Supporting a negative evaluation	0	19
In a quote or paraphrase	4	25
Explaining qualifications	3	0
Refuting an issue position	2	0
Accusation of corruption	1	4
Elaborating a quotation	1	2
Biographical references		
Bio sketch	10	19
Breakout box	10	6
Other references		
Aside	12	97
Other	3	2
Total	60	204

mentioned in brief asides – about half of the paragraphs that referenced challengers' occupations were coded as such. The most common (representing 30 paragraphs) was Rep. Nancy Boyda's challenger, the sitting Kansas State Treasurer, who was often referred to using language like "State Treasurer Lynn Jenkins" or "Lynn Jenkins, the State Treasurer" when first introduced in the article. Many other challengers were referred to in a similar fashion; journalists often introduced challengers in articles by saying things like, "Erickson, a Lake Oswego entrepreneur, positions himself as an outsider ...," "Olson, a former Senate aide and Navy pilot, said repeatedly ...," and "Former state legislator Suzanne Kosmas easily beat fellow Democrat Clint Curtis. . . ." Journalists routinely inserted a bit of biographical information about challengers into sentences where that detail was unrelated to the main topic of the sentence.

Of course, all of this was a drop in the bucket relative to the other kinds of content in the stories I analyzed. Figure 7.1 plots the numbers of stories that mentioned each incumbent in my sample, the numbers of stories and paragraphs that mentioned the incumbent in connection to some issue (which I defined as a public problem, an action taken by the incumbent, or an action taken by the government; unfortunately I did not code parallel information about challengers), the numbers of stories and paragraphs that included a negative or positive evaluation of the incumbent (specifically, an evaluation of their position on an issue, the likely effects of a proposal, a trait the

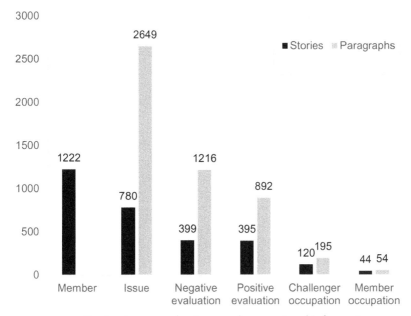

FIGURE 7.1 Stories, issues, evaluations, and occupational information

member had, or the member's involvement in a scandal), and the numbers of stories and paragraphs that mentioned a challenger's or an incumbent's occupational background. Viewed this way, issues and evaluations clearly dwarf occupational information in local news coverage of members of Congress. For every paragraph that referenced a member's occupation, there were sixteen paragraphs that referenced a positive evaluation of the member, twenty-two that referenced a negative evaluation, and forty-nine that referenced an issue.

Simply put, politicians' occupational backgrounds usually aren't news. In this sample, local papers focused on the issues of the day, they covered evaluations of members, but they only rarely mentioned what members or challengers did for a living, or other information about their economic backgrounds. If we wanted citizens to know about the occupational backgrounds of their members of Congress or the candidates running against them, we would want newspapers to provide a steady stream of relevant information. Most do not. Even to local news enthusiasts, the occupational backgrounds of their members of Congress and congressional challengers could easily be invisible.

INACCURACY

Moreover, even a vigilant daily newspaper reader – one who catches every reference to what her member of Congress does for a living – still might not have a very complete picture of the occupational backgrounds of incumbents and challengers.

When politicians campaign and govern, they inevitably spin their economic backgrounds, playing up information that they want constituents to focus on and downplaying facts that they don't. Newspapers could, of course, cut through the spin by presenting complete and detailed occupational histories. As the previous section noted, however, newspapers rarely cover politicians' occupational backgrounds in the first place. And if economic backgrounds aren't newsworthy, when journalists occasionally cover them, it is difficult to imagine that they would spend a great deal of time fact-checking.

Indeed, in practice, the limited occupational information in my sample of news articles was often far from thorough. Of the fifty-four paragraphs that referenced members' occupations, most (32, or 59%) didn't include any information about when or for how long the member had worked in her prior occupations.[9] For challengers, the number was actually smaller; of the 195 paragraphs that referenced challengers' occupations, just fourteen (7%) mentioned dates or durations.

For many incumbents, moreover, journalists only told part of the story about their occupational histories. To find out how complete journalists' coverage was, I compared the occupations reported for each House member in my sample of newspaper articles to the occupations they listed on their congressional web-sites and to the occupations listed in four prominent congressional almanacs.[10] (No such almanacs exist for challengers, unfortunately, so I simply compared coverage of their occupations in newspapers to coverage of their occupations on their campaign websites.) Did the news provide complete occupational histories – or at least occupational histories that were more complete than what members themselves provided? Did local papers simply report members' own self-styled versions of their work histories or omit past occupations altogether? (Or, in the case of challengers, were newspapers at least *as complete* as candidates' campaign websites?)

Figure 7.2 plots the distributions of the numbers of occupations listed for incumbent House members in almanacs, websites, and newspapers. For example, the almanacs I compiled listed between one and eight past occupations for each of the thirty-two members; the gray bars in the upper left panel report the numbers of members who had one occupation listed (three members), two occupations listed (two members), and so on, up to eight occupations (two members). In Figure 7.2, the top two panels use my entire sample of thirty-two members, and the bottom panels focus only on members who had *any* occupational information listed in newspaper articles. The leftmost panels

---

[9] Moreover, seven occupations were so vague that it was difficult to classify them.
[10] Working with a team of research assistants, I gathered detailed information about each legislator's occupational background from *The Congressional Biographical Directory*, Congressional Quarterly's online *Politics in America* almanac, Lexis-Nexis Congressional, the National Journal's online *Almanac of American Politics*, and candidate websites (sometimes archived using the Internet Archive's "Wayback Machine").

Full sample (32 members)

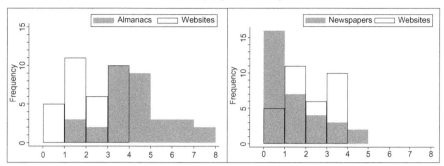

Members with at least one occupation mentioned in the news (16 members)

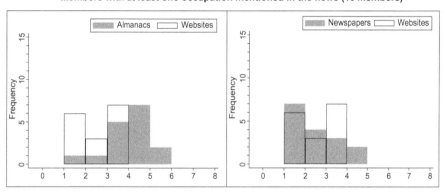

FIGURE 7.2 Histograms of member occupation counts, by source

compare the occupational information in almanacs (gray) to the information members listed on their websites (white), and the rightmost panels compare websites (again white) to newspapers (gray).

Collectively, the four congressional almanacs listed an average of 3.8 distinct occupations for each of the thirty-two members in my samples (top left panel, gray bars), including service in the military and work in other levels and branches of government (being a state legislator and a city council member would count as two separate occupations). Not surprisingly, members were more selective in what they reported on their congressional websites; the typical member listed just 1.8 occupations in the biography section of her website (top left panel, white bars; the difference in means was significant at $p < 0.001$ in a t-test). Newspapers reported even less, an average of just 1.0 past occupation (top right panel, gray bars), a value that was statistically distinct from the averages for almanacs ($p < 0.001$) and websites ($p < 0.01$).[11]

---

[11] These patterns were essentially unchanged when I limited my analysis to the seven members in close races (i.e., <55% of the vote): almanacs included 3.9 occupations on average, websites listed 2.0 occupations on average, and newspapers included 1.3 occupations on average.

Local papers' performance on this measure was partly driven by the fact that many newspapers didn't report any occupational information during the ten weeks leading up to the election (as the previous section noted). Even among the sixteen members whose occupations were mentioned in the local news at least once, however, newspapers mentioned an average of 2.1 occupations (bottom right panel, gray bars), still slightly less than what those sixteen members shared on their websites (bottom right panel, white bars), which listed 2.5 occupations on average ($p < 0.56$), and significantly less than the 3.6 occupations listed for the average member in almanacs ($p < 0.001$; bottom left panel, gray bars). That is, even the newspapers that provided information about members' occupations did not provide any more information than members themselves.

For challengers, I could only study the differences between websites and newspaper coverage. For this group, local papers actually presented fewer occupations than candidates themselves. On their websites, the twenty-eight House challengers in this sample reported 3.6 distinct occupations, on average. In contrast, news stories mentioned just 1.7 on average ($p < 0.01$) – readers who never missed a word of the coverage of these congressional challengers might still miss about half of the occupational information available about them. Both estimates were higher than for incumbents (and the differences between challengers and incumbents were at least marginally significant; $p < 0.01$ for websites and $p < 0.10$ for newspapers); relative to incumbents, challengers provide more detailed occupational histories on their campaign sites, and newspapers listed more of their past occupations, consistent with the idea that challengers' biographies are more newsworthy (in the eyes of both journalists and campaigns). But, as with incumbents, for challengers, the occupational information in the papers was often incomplete.

With the almanac data on incumbents, we can also ask whether members downplayed any particular types of occupations, especially those associated with affluence. Figure 7.3 plots the odds that any one of the 121 occupations recorded in almanacs for the thirty-two incumbents would appear on the member's website and in the news coverage of the member. In the figure, I have grouped occupations using a simple coding scheme that I have used elsewhere and that predicts differences in floor voting and bill introductions (e.g., Carnes, 2013; 2018).

The most pronounced pattern in Figure 7.3 is that members and newspapers alike only occasionally mentioned members' past government experience (top pair of bars); two thirds of members' jobs in government were not mentioned on websites or in newspapers during campaign season. Moreover, consistent with the idea that members downplay economic privileges and play up hardships, members only mentioned jobs as business owners or executives on their websites about half of the time, but members mentioned working-class occupations about 80% of the time. There were too few cases in each occupation category in Figure 7.3 to distinguish these rates statistically, but the patterns in the data

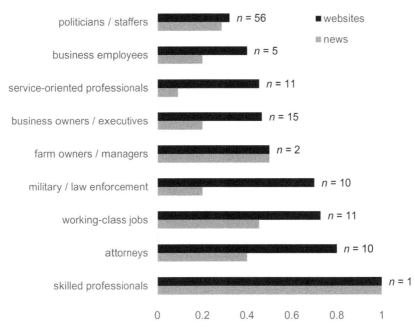

FIGURE 7.3 Probability that a past job appeared on a member website or in the news, by type of job

were generally consistent with the idea that members strategically downplay some occupations and play up others. As for local newspapers (gray bars), however, there were no obvious patterns in the types of occupations that were more and less likely to be covered. Most kinds of jobs in Figure 7.3 had a 20–40% chance of appearing in the local paper.

What seemed to predict whether a given job was mentioned in the paper wasn't the *type* of job, but *whether the job appeared on the member's website*. If a given almanac occupation wasn't listed on a member's website, there was only an 11% chance that it was listed in a newspaper article. In contrast, if a member's website listed an occupation, there was a 47% chance that it was mentioned in the news (and this difference was significant at $p < 0.001$). For the most part, what readers saw in the papers looked like a random sample of what members themselves chose to highlight about their occupational backgrounds.

Overall, these data are consistent with the idea that journalists don't usually consider occupational information newsworthy and don't typically report on it thoroughly. For half of my sample, newspapers were silent about incumbent House members' occupational histories, and in the other half, more than 60% of the time, a reader who caught every reference to a member's occupation in the local newspaper still wouldn't have the entire story. Although newspapers are more likely to cover challenger occupations, there were still gaps in that information as well.

EQUALITY

If journalists don't devote much energy to covering politicians' economic backgrounds, it may be that they simply don't care all that much, that is, that they have something of a blind spot when it comes to politicians' economic backgrounds. However, from the standpoint of traditional academic concerns about coverage inequality, that might be a good thing. Scholars often worry that journalists give politicians from historically underrepresented social groups (like women or politicians of color) different levels of coverage – either ignoring them because they seem less credible or exoticizing them because they seem different – and that the coverage they get might be more negative or somehow reinforce stereotypes about the underrepresented group. But if journalists really don't pay all that much attention to politicians' economic backgrounds, the processes that give rise to the invisibility and inaccuracy documented in the previous sections may have a surprising side-effect: coverage *equality*.

The newspaper data I analyzed suggested that members of Congress and challengers with significant experience in working-class jobs were covered at about the same rates as white-collar candidates. My research design produced slightly fewer articles for the average working-class incumbent in my sample (31.7) than the average white-collar incumbent (40.0), but the difference was not statistically significant ($p < 0.46$), and it wasn't any different when I adjusted the data to account for members for whom I had to search multiple newspapers to get twenty search results. (Taking out the backup papers, the averages were 29.3 and 39.4, and a t-test produced a non-significant $p < 0.39$). For challengers, the number of articles that mentioned candidates with any known experience in working-class jobs (13.8) was nearly identical to the number that mentioned candidates with no known experience in working-class jobs (14.3).

Moreover, the not-statistically-significant ten-article difference between white-collar and working-class incumbents seemed modest compared to other differences in coverage. Figure 7.4 plots the numbers of articles that I collected for each incumbent against the share of each incumbent's career spent in working-class jobs (left panel) and the vote margin each incumbent earned in the general election (right panel). Members from working-class backgrounds are denoted with "w"s and those from white-collar backgrounds are denoted with dollar signs. Coverage rates seemed to have a great deal more to do with whether a member was at risk of losing her re-election bid – the traditional horse race – than her economic background. A member who spent 40% of her career in a working-class job was covered in about six more articles over ten weeks (about one every other week) than a member who spent 70% of her career in a working-class job. A member who lost with 40% of the vote

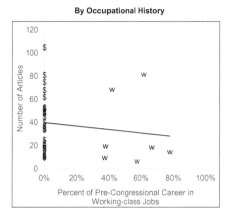

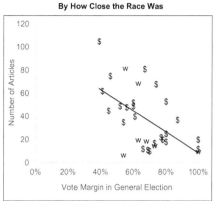

FIGURE 7.4 Coverage didn't seem to depend on class

was covered in 28 more articles (almost three per week) than a member who won with 70% of the vote (and a challenger was covered in twenty-three more articles). Even if incumbents from working-class backgrounds are covered at slightly lower rates, the social class gaps in coverage in this sample were substantively small by the standards of newspaper coverage.[12]

When it came to how members *were evaluated* in the news, moreover, the trends non-significantly *favored* working-class incumbents. (Unfortunately, for this analysis, I do not have comparable data on challengers.) For each of the 1,222 articles I collected, I recorded whether each paragraph included a negative and/or positive evaluation of the member. I defined an evaluation as (1) a statement (made by anyone) that a proposal or action associated with the member has done or will do good or bad things, (2) a favorable or unfavorable statement about the member's traits or personal characteristics, (3) a favorable or unfavorable statement about the member's position on an issue, (4) or any reference to a scandal involving the member (all references to scandals were counted as negative).

On average, the articles about incumbents from working-class backgrounds contained more paragraphs with positive evaluations (37.3 across the ten weeks, vs. 25.2 for white-collar members; $p < 0.344$) and fewer paragraphs with negative evaluations (20.9, vs 42.8 for white-collar members; $p < 0.438$), although the differences were not statistically significant. If anything, in these data, reporters were biased *in favor of* leaders from the working class.[13]

I also didn't find evidence of anti-worker biases in the volume of issue-related content associated with each member. As I read each article, I coded

[12] When I regressed coverage rates on a larger set of district-level characteristics, the differences between workers and professionals were even smaller.
[13] I also found no evidence of explicit social class slights or stereotypes in any of my 1,222 articles. I attempted to code these occurrences, but found none.

paragraphs that mentioned the member in connection with any issue, which I defined as a public problem, an action taken by the government, or an action taken by the member. In my sample, local newspaper readers were exposed to roughly the same volume of issue-related content about members from working-class backgrounds (75.7 paragraphs across ten weeks) and members from white-collar backgrounds (84.8 paragraphs across ten weeks; difference non-significant at $p < 0.809$).

Whereas past research on race and gender has found troubling evidence of coverage inequalities, my analysis did not produce any compelling evidence that journalists reported differently on the incumbents in the 110th House of Representatives or their challengers based whether they came from working-class jobs. (When I re-ran the analyses in this section dividing the sample by race and gender, I also failed to find any statistically significant differences.) Members and challengers from the working class were covered in about as many articles as those from white-collar jobs; members from the working class were mentioned in about as many issue-related paragraphs and were mentioned in about as many paragraphs with positive and negative evaluation statements. There were differences, but they were substantively small, not statistically significant, and not consistently in the same direction (members who were workers were a little less likely to appear in stories or issue-related paragraphs, but a little more likely to be evaluated favorably and a little less likely to be evaluated negatively). Overall, I didn't find that journalists exoticized politicians from the working class or shut them out, and I didn't find that journalists praised or punished them excessively.

THE PRESS AND POLITICAL REPRESENTATION

When political scientists have developed normative frameworks for evaluating the news – when they've discussed what journalists *should* report about politicians – they haven't typically assigned much importance to economic background information. But perhaps they should. Politicians regularly make decisions about scores of economic issues, and when they do, their own economic backgrounds seem to influence their choices. The kinds of jobs politicians had before they held office can affect the problems they focus on and the expertise they bring with them. A politician's economic background can also drive her to behave in a self-interested manner; if politicians vote to protect the industries they worked in or the tax brackets they belong to, citizens can only see that self-interested behavior for what it is if they know what the politicians did for a living or how wealthy they are.

And citizens seem to *want* to know these kinds of details. The week of this writing, a Democratic presidential candidate made headlines by bowing to pressure to release his tax returns, which revealed him to be far wealthier than many supporters realized, and a Republican president ordered the Director of the Treasury to withhold the president's tax returns from Congress. Although information about the economic backgrounds of politicians is usually not essential to issue-based notions of political accountability, citizens often see it as essential to other important normative ideals like fairness, transparency, and representation.

Even so, local journalists have to make tough choices – they have limited time, energy, and resources to devote to their work – and they usually don't have strong incentives to cover politicians' economic backgrounds, except perhaps when candidates first run, when journalists wish to provide contextual information, or when people in and around politics link a politician's economic background to a newsworthy issue. These things rarely occur in practice, at least in the local newspapers where citizens often get their news about members of Congress. Although past research on media and candidate demographics might lead us to worry that journalists are somehow biased against working-class candidates, it seems that journalists rarely think politicians' occupational backgrounds are newsworthy, especially after leaders have held office for some time.

Of course, this study has several important limitations. By design, it trades breadth for depth, focusing on a close reading of the media coverage of thirty-two members and twenty-eight challengers from the 2006, 2008, and 2010 election cycles; follow-up studies using larger samples could ultimately support different conclusions. This study also cannot test the possibility that citizens get information about politicians' economic backgrounds from other sources, like interest groups, campaign ads, or coverage in other media like television and the internet. This is an important next step; as Canes-Wrone and Kistner discuss in more detail in Chapter 6 of this volume, citizens increasingly get information from sources besides local newspapers.

Overall, however, this first-cut analysis suggests that local newspapers are not good sources of information about the economic backgrounds of politicians. This finding does not seem to be confined to any particular type of local context. The list of lawmakers whose occupations were never mentioned in the articles I compiled included legislators covered by large newspapers (Rep. Charles Rangel was most often covered in the *New York Daily News*, which today has a daily readership of around 200,000) and by the small papers that others in this volume (Canes-Wrone and Kistner, Chapter 6, Huber and Tucker, Chapter 8) note are regularly in danger of closing for good (Rep. John Peterson was most often covered in the State College, PA, *Centre Daily Times*, which has a daily readership of around 23,000). I do not have readership or budget data for many newspapers in the sample during the early 2000s, but the simple correlations between the population size of the cities each paper was located in and the number of paragraphs that referenced an incumbent or challenger's occupation (from Table 7.2) were small, negative (suggesting that in larger cities, occupations were covered less often), and not statistically significant. In big and small media markets alike, local newspapers rarely tell readers much about the occupational backgrounds of congressional candidates and incumbents.

And that may, in turn, have more significant effects that are worthy of future research. In a 2016 survey, the average respondent estimated that more than a quarter of members of Congress come from working-class jobs (Carnes and Lupu, 2019); in reality, fewer than 3% do. This may well be a downstream consequence of the pressure journalists face to focus on current events and not biographical facts.

If the media cover the economic backgrounds of politicians at the low rates that this study reports, this phenomenon could also have an even more profound effect on the scope of the American political imagination. Citizens who never read about politicians' economic backgrounds might not just be unaware of where their representatives come from, they might not think to ask.

8

Congressional Accountability in the Contemporary Media Environment: Arguments, Data, and Methods

Gregory A. Huber and Patrick Tucker

A key question of representation is whether citizens (as voters or potential voters) can select or incentivize elected officials to represent their preferences through the tool of elections. In most theoretical accounts of this accountability relationship, effective governance requires that voters are either informed or potentially informed about legislator behavior. While the exact information on which voters rely to make decisions may vary – from information about a specific legislator's policy or valence at one extreme to information about the macro-economy or general party performance at the other – information provides citizens with their ability to match their votes to incumbent behaviors, allowing effective selection or appropriate electoral sanctioning.

Understanding citizens' informational environment is therefore at the heart of understanding the nature of accountability for members of Congress (MCs) in the United States, and for the study of electoral accountability more generally. The key source of this informational environment is likely the mass media because it subsidizes an otherwise inefficiently costly individual search for relevant information. Past scholarship on what citizens know about elected members of Congress has highlighted how, during the mid to late twentieth century, local newspapers were a key source of voter knowledge because they were one of the few mediums to cover individual MCs in great detail.

The most exhaustive studies of the content of newspaper coverage of MCs, including Vinson (2003) and Arnold (2004), described coverage at the tail end of the period of local newspaper dominance, before the internet, rise in national newspapers, and expansion of cable television upset this media landscape. The declining reach and profitability of local newspapers have reduced access to local newspapers and potentially altered the content of those that remain. Moreover, these changes for local papers have occurred alongside an expansion of national newspapers (and access to those papers through the internet), a large increase in cable television availability and the extensive media choices that accompany it, and the rise of the internet (including social media and mass-streaming video services).

In light of these changes, this chapter has three goals. First, it discusses the theoretical relationship between media coverage of MCs and accountability. Second, we review prior research on newspaper coverage of MCs, as well as coverage of MCs by other media. This structured review of prior work devotes the most space to newspaper coverage of MCs, including canonical work on the content of this coverage. Finally, in light of this empirical lacuna, we propose an agenda for a unified cross-media data collection project on citizens' political informational environments vis-à-vis Congress. We note that because of the nature of the data to be collected, this sort of research both requires new computational and data-intensive infrastructure and is unlikely to be feasible as a retrospective activity. We conclude our discussion by providing a summary of what previous literature identifies as necessary for citizens to hold their MCs accountable and what data have been collected to measure those accountability mechanisms as well as areas for further research.

THEORETICAL OVERVIEW, MEDIA AND ACCOUNTABILITY

Before discussing prior empirical research on media coverage of legislators, we discuss the theoretical linkage between both actual media coverage, and the potential for that coverage, and legislator accountability. This overview helps to understand the key role of the media in shaping democratic accountability, as well as theoretical uncertainty about how changes in the volume and content of media coverage may affect the dynamic relationship between citizens and elected members of Congress. In the simplest form, in this accountability relationship the voter may use her vote to select an incumbent (from a set of candidates) or to incentivize desired legislator behavior. The media serve as a (potential) conduit for information about an incumbent and (potential) challengers. While we focus on general election voting here, voting in primary elections also gives citizens the opportunity to shape the slate of candidates (and potentially incumbent behavior), both in open seat races and in challenging incumbents.

Broadly speaking, coverage can focus on two different dimensions of legislator performance: policy and valence (e.g., Eulau and Karps, 1977). Policy is usually thought of as ideological conflict, analogous to candidate positions in a simple spatial model of voting (e.g., Downs, 1957; Jessee, 2012). Valence is non-ideological policy issues and non-policy content. For example, valence may include pork delivered to a district, constituency service, non-ideologically related candidate traits (e.g., honesty or intelligence) or symbolic behaviors that signal a shared identity with constituents (e.g., Mayhew, 1974; Fenno, 1977).

Additionally, coverage can be thought of as systematic or episodic (Arnold, 2004). Systematic coverage, mostly relevant for incumbent legislators, is any regular flow of information about a candidate. Such coverage may provide information about policy or may communicate (positive) valence. Episodic coverage, by contrast, is driven by events – either those that arise haphazardly (e.g., important legislation in Congress) or regularly (most obviously, elections). Incumbent legislators may play an important role in shaping the nature of systematic coverage through their press teams and personal brands that set expectations and perceptions for the local media (Hess, 1991; Cook, 1988). Episodic coverage, however, likely arises for reasons beyond the control of a particular incumbent.

If incumbents (and challengers) were not strategic, analyzing the relationship between the degree of media coverage of individual MCs and accountability would be somewhat straightforward. Systematic media coverage of incumbents would be expected to induce greater knowledge of their ideological positions vis-à-vis challengers, and provide information about their valence. Challengers, by contrast, would in general have more uncertainty associated with their evaluations along both of these dimensions. Absent surprising revelations about ideologically incongruent or low valence incumbents, one would expect that past winners are on average of higher quality (both better positions and valence) than non-winners (e.g., Jacobson, 1989). A more robust media environment would therefore tend to reinforce the advantage for high (valence) quality and moderate (ideologically aligned with their district) incumbents. In contrast, more robust episodic coverage of campaigns could allow unknown challengers to communicate their positions and valence, potentially offsetting some of the advantages that accrue to incumbents from more systematic coverage.

If incumbents are strategic, the expected effects of media availability are potentially much more complicated, however. For example, one might believe that incumbents can choose how they appear ideologically or their degree of investment in valence (e.g., district service, see for example Grimmer, 2013). In this case, incumbents might strategically moderate to avoid being challenged (potentially improving citizen welfare) or invest in valence to overcome ideological incongruence in the voter's candidate choice (which could arise even if voters value policy more if they desire to avoid uncertainty). In the latter case, the fact that incumbents are better known than challengers could potentially lead them to be selected even if voters would prefer, if fully informed, a more ideologically congruent challenger.

Implicit in the preceding discussion is an assumption about how voters decide in the absence of robust information about incumbents. One simple assumption, as discussed elsewhere in this volume by Canes-Wrone and Kistner, is that absent legislator-specific information, voters turn to heuristics such as party (or incumbent-president popularity) to make decisions (e.g., Snyder and Ting, 2002). In that case, the key value of media coverage of specific legislators is to potentially allow legislators to attract votes apart from the performance of the national parties and politicians (Grimmer, 2013; Grimmer, Westwood, and Messing, 2015).

With this assumption in mind, it is useful to highlight that the nature of political coverage of legislators is also important, and not just the levels. While member-specific coverage may encourage legislators to invest in district-matching policy positions and valence activities, if that coverage is replaced by coverage emphasizing national-level party dynamics and policy conflict the implications for strategic legislator behavior are less clear. One possibility, however, is that national-focused coverage encourages legislators to worry about coverage of their party vis-à-vis coverage of them as individual legislators. Setting aside changes in legislator behavior, with less coverage of locally focused stories, voters could rely more heavily on party heuristics when voting.

Moreover, lower levels of legislator-specific coverage (or even simple increases in nationally oriented coverage) could lead to reinforcing changes in legislator behavior. Knowing that voters care more about the national parties' performance, incumbents might spend less time concentrating on the non-policy dimension of representation, leading to a decline in constituency service and valence promotion more generally. Additionally, legislators who believe their electoral fortunes are tied to the overall favorability of their party vis-à-vis the opposition might engage in more party-based behavior, including partisan agenda control and voting as a partisan block. Doing so would allow the party to maintain an appearance of partisan unity while portraying the opposition party as ideologically extreme (Groseclose and McCarty, 2001; Cox and McCubbins, 2005). Cumulatively, legislator behavior focused on national-level party performance could in turn further contribute to the nationalization of US elections (Hopkins, 2018) and party-based conflict beyond that induced directly by changes in voter knowledge.

This theoretical account presupposes that national party performance supplants legislator-specific knowledge as information about locally elected MCs declines. There are two other plausible theoretical possibilities to consider, however. First, it may be that when less information about individual legislator performance is available that voter engagement simply declines. Second, for similar reasons, it may be that a decline in coverage enhances the power of political outsiders who already have name recognition and positive valence evaluations apart from any career in politics. That is, unconventional candidates may be more viable when incumbents are unable to communicate their performance, particularly for voters who are less concerned with national-level programmatic conflicts.

In light of these theoretical possibilities, the first key empirical question is to understand what information was previously available to citizens before major shifts in the media landscape and how that environment may have changed in the period since prior empirical research was conducted. Identifying appropriate tools for characterizing empirically the news environment is essential for answering this question. Second, in light of any changes in the nature of coverage of MCs, researchers must understand how those changes have altered the incentives and behaviors of incumbent legislators (and candidates for office). As the media environment changes, MCs may modify their legislative actions in ways that depart from the predictions provided by prior accounts. Depending on how legislators adapt, this may have implications for the legislator's behavior in office. A final and related question is to understand what drives and who consumes the content of coverage of MCs in this changing environment. Researchers need to investigate how the proliferation of new outlets and the decline of others potentially gives MCs a new ability to shape how they are covered but perhaps also vastly reduces their ability to reach most citizens. At the most basic level, what is the content of such coverage and what are the effects of that coverage, through consumption by ordinary citizens, on their political knowledge, attitudes, and choices?

PRIOR EMPIRICAL RESEARCH ON MEDIA COVERAGE

Prior Large-Scale Content Analyses

Undertaking comprehensive analysis of how local media cover MCs is a daunting task. A lack of comprehensive access to digital versions of local newspaper stories (and television or radio broadcast transcripts) severely limits researchers' abilities to measure the frequency and content of the local press's coverage of incumbent legislators and candidates for those offices. Nonetheless, three prior pieces of work stand out for their large-scale efforts to collect and analyze local media coverage of individual MCs. (We set aside a somewhat larger set of work that simply counts the frequency with which members are mentioned, see below.)

Hess (1991) was one of the first researchers to track coverage of MCs on local television broadcasts. While not exhaustive, Hess gathered news transcripts and logs from thirty-three stations that filed news broadcasts from Capitol Hill between 1979 and 1985. Hess followed this analysis by gathering local evening news broadcasts tapes from September 1987 through April 1988 for fifty-seven local television stations in thirty-five American cities varying in size. He then counted the frequency with which stories covered local Senate and House members as well as whether the coverage had a national or local focus. Hess found that House members received significantly less coverage than senators in local newscasts. When House members received coverage, it was frequently due to their position in party leadership or their plans to run for higher office.

Vinson (2003) chose eight media markets to analyze coverage of local congresspersons during four-week periods between September 1993 and January 1994. Markets were chosen to ensure variation in size, market-district congruence, partisan balance, and incumbent legislator gender. In each market she selected "one daily newspaper, one early and one late evening local television newscast, and at least one weekly newspaper" to collect content

(Vinson, 2003, 12). Vinson found that district-media market congruence was positively associated with the frequency of coverage for an individual MC, while electoral vulnerability was negatively associated with coverage. District-market congruence was also positively correlated with the likelihood that a story about an MC would be favorable. Stories on incumbents from local television were less likely to be unfavorable and more likely to be ambiguous in their tone relative to newspapers.

Arnold (2004) focused exclusively on newspaper reporting. He first chose twenty-five local newspapers and randomly selected one representative to analyze in each newspaper's media market. The twenty-five newspapers were chosen from the eighty-eight newspapers that were electronically available on Dow Jones News Service or Lexis-Nexis for all stories from January 1993 through Election Day 1994. Arnold also collected a second data set that matched six of the newspapers with another newspaper in the same media market. Finally, he created a third data set with sixty-seven local newspapers available on Lexis-Nexis or Dow Jones News Service (of which the original twenty-five were included) and matched the newspapers with the ninety-one legislators they covered from 1993 through November 1994. In each sample Arnold counted the frequency with which members were covered, and in the first two he also coded the tone and content of this coverage. In these analyses, Arnold found wide variation in the coverage given to MCs. Those legislators who represented districts more congruent with the media market received more coverage. Coverage increased during elections and those incumbents involved in more competitive challenges were likely to receive more frequent coverage. While local newspapers were likely to provide some information on roll calls taken by incumbents, they varied greatly in providing analysis of such votes.

These studies provide an essential foundation for understanding how media covered legislators and how legislators interacted with the press to achieve their goals. Cumulatively, these three studies provide two snapshots of local newspaper coverage and two snapshots of local television. Yet, print media's reach and the overall media landscape have changed enormously in the nearly twenty-five years since these data were collected. Contemporary coverage, as well as conclusions about how the press affects the nature of accountability in light of that coverage, should therefore be reexamined. In the following sections, we therefore review prior empirical research on newspaper and other medium coverage of MCs. We also discuss prior work that may be relevant for understanding how the decline in coverage and the changing nature of the press may have influenced the incentives and behaviors of members of Congress.

Newspapers

NEWSPAPER COVERAGE OF MEMBERS OF CONGRESS. Newspapers were a major force in covering political affairs during the second half of the twentieth century, even while competing with radio and television broadcasters. But by the early 2000s, newspapers faced new challenges from changes in ownership, declining circulation, and the rise of the internet as a competitor (Peterson, 2021b). In 1993 more than 50% of Americans reported that newspapers were one of their major sources for news about national and international events.[1] By 2018, the percent of Americans identifying a print newspaper as a major source of information was 16%, behind television news, internet websites, radio, and social media.[2] As Figure 8.1 demonstrates, Pew estimates that the weekly and Sunday circulation of daily newspapers has declined by 50% over the past thirty years. Still, newspapers have served an important position in providing information to citizens. Consequently, political scientists have studied the nature of newspaper coverage and the ways in which their coverage may have altered the accountability relationship between citizens and elected MCs.

For instance, a newspaper's resources and media market structure influence how the local press covers politics. Those newspapers that face a local competitor may report local stories more frequently than those newspapers that hold dominance in a market (Lacy, 1987). This local competition, however, is essentially an artifact of a bygone era. With only a few exceptions, cities with multiple daily newspapers no longer exist. Even before the rise of the internet, the rise in one-newspaper cities was clear (Rosse, 1980).

Competition from national news sources, however, may be associated with changes in how individual members are covered. When there is greater competition from a national news outlet, such as the *New York Times*, local newspapers lose circulation. But circulation is typically associated with greater revenue, and it is that revenue that provides resources for original reporting on local issues. Papers with greater circulation generate more coverage of local representatives (Dunaway, 2008). But greater circulation does not always translate into more coverage of MCs. Studying 405 races in the 2010 US House elections, Hayes and Lawless (2015) found that greater circulation was negatively related to the number of stories about a campaign and fewer number of issues addressed. This is likely because newspapers with larger circulations are typically in markets that cover more congressional districts, necessarily increasing the number of races to cover. The arrival of a major national competitor could also force local press to adjust their coverage to retain readership. A study of the expansion of the daily circulation of *The New York Times* found that national press penetration significantly altered how the local press competed: local papers responded by devoting less coverage to national and international stories and more coverage to local stories (George and Waldfogel, 2006). We are not aware of a study that examines how the *Times* influenced coverage of MCs specifically, however.

[1] www.pewresearch.org/wp-content/uploads/sites/8/2017/05/State-of-the-News-Media-Report-2004-FINAL.pdf.
[2] www.pewresearch.org/fact-tank/2018/12/10/social-media-outpaces-print-newspapers-in-the-u-s-as-a-news-source/.

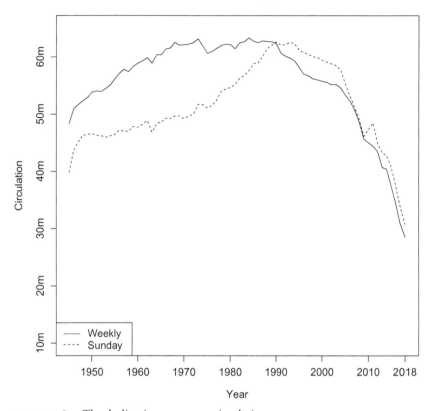

FIGURE 8.1 *The decline in newspaper circulation*

The solid line represents the Monday–Friday average of weekday circulation for US newspapers that report their circulation numbers to the Alliance for Audited Media. The dashed line represents the average Sunday circulation for newspapers that report their circulation to AAM. Data for 2015–2018 are estimated by Pew Research Center and AAM. See Barthel, Michael. 2019. "5 Key Takeaways about the State of News Media in 2018," available at www.pewresearch.org/fact-tank/2019/07/23/key-takeaways-state-of-the-news-media-2018/.

The extent to which a newspaper's market and a district align geographically also influences how members are covered (this is the idea of congruence, introduced above). For example, a congressional district, such as those in most major metropolitan areas, may be one of many in a newspaper's audience market. Newspapers in this context may have more resources than those in smaller areas, but their ability to cover each member is still limited. For this reason, the overall per-member coverage may decrease since the local daily newspaper cannot give extensive and frequent coverage to a legislator who is of interest to only a small portion of a paper's readership. In light of this incentive, an important innovation in Arnold (2004) was to account for the fact that coverage of members may appear in regional/area-specific editions of larger papers, rather than being published in all editions of the newspaper. Empirically, if a district constitutes only a small part of a media market, the local paper tended to give less coverage to that district's representative (e.g., Schaffner and Sellers, 2003). During campaigns these more congruent district-market dyads are likely to provide more coverage of candidates' issue platforms (Hall and Lim, 2018). In Chapter 6 of this volume, Canes-Wrone and Kistner find that higher congruence between district and media market appears to improve the ability of voters to associate their incumbents with ideological positions, but that the relationship between accountability and district-market congruence has decreased in recent decades.

Traditionally, many local newspapers employed a full-time reporter in Washington, DC who reported not only on national politics, but also provided direct coverage of the local media market's Senate and House members. Local newspapers have continued to decrease their presence in Washington, with a 2016 Pew study finding that twenty-one states did not have a newspaper with a permanent correspondent on Capitol Hill.[3] The decline in the number of DC-based reporters could lead to a drop in the frequency of coverage, but this question is currently unresolved; indeed, newspapers with Washington reporters are not associated with higher rates of coverage of local representatives (Fogarty, 2008). At the same time, the decline in reporters and staffers is not limited to ones in DC. As Figure 8.2 demonstrates, the number of employees in local press has declined sharply over the past decade.

The ownership structure of a newspaper has also been found to influence the frequency and content of their coverage of MCs. A publicly traded media corporation is assumed to be primarily concerned with maximizing its profits, while an independent, privately owned newspaper may be driven by the ideological preferences of its owner (Hamilton, 2004). Publicly owned corporations may devote fewer resources to covering local politics because that content is expensive to produce compared to relying on wire services. While Gentzkow and Shapiro (2006) find no evidence that ownership of newspapers is associated with a slant in their coverage, others find that corporately owned newspapers provide less substance when reporting, including on policy issues (Arnold, 2004; Dunaway, 2008).

Ownership structure also plays an important part in how members of Congress are covered. As one might expect, the heavier focus on local issues from independently owned newspapers is associated with greater coverage of the local MC, while corporately owned papers are likely to write fewer stories about the relevant House member (Schaffner and Sellers, 2003). Newspapers owned by national chains are growing at a rapid pace in the current media marketplace. Following the recession of 2009, hundreds of local papers were purchased by corporate interests.[4] Many of these newspapers ceased operations entirely, but those that remain are now part of national chains with centralized

---

[3] www.pewresearch.org/fact-tank/2016/01/07/in-21-states-local-newspapers-lack-a-dedicated-reporter-keeping-tabs-on-congress/.

[4] www.usnewsdeserts.com/reports/rise-new-media-baron/.

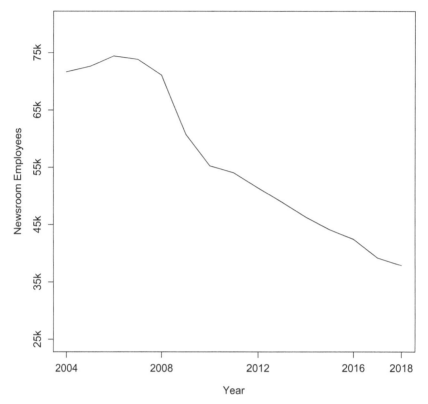

FIGURE 8.2 The decline in newspaper employment

The solid line represents the number of newsroom employees as designated by the Occupational Employment Statistics Survey. Newsroom employees are identified as news analysts, reporters, journalists, editors, photographers, camera operators, and editors. News industries include newspapers, radio broadcasters, television broadcasters, cable programmers, and other information services. Source: Grieco, Elizabeth. 2020. "10 Charts About America's Newsrooms," available at www.pewresearch.org/fact-tank/2020/04/28/10-charts-about-americas-newsrooms/, *supplemented with earlier data from Pew.*

content production. With fewer locally owned papers, less local news coverage is likely to follow.

Legislator characteristics, rather than structural characteristics of the district or the newspaper market, also explain how legislators are covered. There is little evidence that newspapers discriminate ideologically in which MCs receive coverage (Arnold, 2004). This is consistent with other work that found that, on the whole, pre-internet coverage of MCs was relatively fact-based and neutral in its presentation (Tidmarch and Pitney, 1985). While legislators on a given side of the aisle are not necessarily expected to receive more coverage, incumbents' ideological orientation may still influence their likelihood of being covered. Cook (1986) found that at the national level, the more extreme a member of the 95th Congress was, the more likely they were to be covered by *the New York Times*. While it is less clear whether local newspapers cover ideologically extreme MCs more than moderates, Fogarty (2008) found that MCs who were out of step with their constituents were more likely to receive coverage.

Legislators can also influence the amount of coverage they get. Taking controversial votes (Fogarty, 2013) is one strategy to attract press coverage, although that coverage might be negative. Legislators can also make use of their press release system to receive more coverage from the local print media. Those who release more press releases are more likely to receive coverage in newspapers (Gershon, 2012).

THE EFFECTS OF NEWSPAPER COVERAGE ON LEGISLATOR ACCOUNTABILITY. Newspapers provide legislators with resources to promote their achievements, but they also provide citizens with a means to hold legislators accountable for their actions. The press therefore plays an invaluable role in informing the electorate about elite behavior. Content analyses of newspaper coverage find large variation in the frequency and type of information provided about incumbent MCs. This variation in coverage, if it is an essential source of information, should be associated with differences in perceptions of legislators.

The most common content analysis of members of Congress focuses on the frequency with which local papers provide coverage to local MCs. On its face this activity may seem quite perfunctory, but it could also have substantive effects with respect to accountability. Without regular monitoring of their actions, legislators who are covered less often may be less concerned with how the constituents evaluate their performance. Thus, important dimensions of representation may go neglected. Almost uniformly, more newspaper coverage is associated with more knowledge of the MCs (e.g., Goldenberg and Traugott, 1987). For example, leveraging a newspaper strike in Pittsburgh, Mondak (1995b) demonstrated that a decline in access to campaign coverage was not associated with less information about national news, but it was associated with less information about local news. Those affected by the strike were less likely to express opinions about the candidates for Congress in the 1992 election (Mondak, 1995a). In a more comprehensive study, Snyder and Strömberg (2010) conducted a content analysis of 161 newspapers in 385 districts from 1991 to 2002. They demonstrated that respondents to the ANES who lived in districts with more congruent papers were more likely to identify as having read about the legislator in the newspaper and more likely to identify the representative on an ideological scale. They also showed that those who represent areas with less coverage on average were likely to allocate fewer resources to constituency service and secured fewer appropriations for their district.

More newspaper coverage and the resulting increase in citizen knowledge may improve a constituent's image of the legislator. Incumbents typically maintain a substantive advantage in their name recognition over the course of the campaign and survey respondents are more likely to report hearing from the incumbent (Cook, 1988). By producing more stories about the incumbent, it is possible that newspapers assist in cultivating positive impressions of candidate valance. Schaffner (2006a) demonstrates that more local newspaper stories were positively associated with perceptions of the incumbent being "in touch" with the constituency. Relatedly, more newspaper stories were also positively associated with voting for the incumbent, especially when the incumbent's party was not the same as the voter's partisan identification. The causal mechanism here is unclear. More coverage could be associated with increasing the incumbency advantage through name recognition alone. It could also be the case that an increase of coverage is associated with differences in perceptions of the incumbent's attributes, promoting a more favorable personal brand. Further research is required to investigate this question.

Stepping back, changes to the media landscape may have decreased constituents' abilities to hold legislators accountable. As newspapers lose resources, devoting fewer reporters to covering local politics and members of Congress, or as more newspapers close, citizens could come to understand much less about incumbent behavior. Fewer reporters could bring about less reporting and critical analysis of incumbent behavior. If legislator press releases fill this reporting void, incumbents could enjoy greater incumbency advantages (e.g., Grimmer, 2013). The rapid consolidation of newspapers in the internet era may be associated with changes in the relationship between MCs and the media. Darr, Hitt, and Dunaway (2018) explore the closure of local papers and find that voters in those areas served by dailies that closed were less likely to engage in split-ticket voting.

The implication of this finding, relevant for the general theoretical discussion of accountability that opened this chapter, is that while MCs may be able to dictate coverage through press releases in this new era, they may be hindered in their ability to build personal brands through print media as they once did. Rather, the lack of substantive reporting at the local level could lead voters to rely more on nationally oriented outlets and become more sensitive to party brands. In this way, a lack of local news coverage could exacerbate polarization and the nationalization of politics at lower levels.

Finally, in a pair of papers, Hayes and Lawless (2015, 2018) investigate the political engagement effects of newspaper closures. They find that as coverage of local races in certain areas decreased, citizens were less likely to be engaged in congressional politics. In those areas that witnessed closure of newspapers and an overall decrease in the number of stories about MCs between 2010 and 2014, constituents were less likely to declare an intention to vote and were less likely to correctly identify the partisanship of their local MCs.

Television

TELEVISION COVERAGE OF CONGRESS AND PUBLIC AFFAIRS.   Television as an important medium developed in the United States beginning in the late 1940s.

By 1954, 50% of American households had television sets, and by 1962 90% of Americans had access to broadcast TV.[5] While there are rich histories of the national news coverage provided by the dominant networks, we have much less information about the nature of local news coverage. In part, this likely reflects the fact that local programming was not systematically recorded or transcribed, making archives of coverage difficult to obtain, although certain new technologies may have diminished this concern.

In theory, local television provides MCs with an opportunity to reach an audience that extends beyond those who read daily newspapers. House members and senators can provide interviews, appear at local events, and seek coverage of their legislative votes, accomplishments, and outreach. Unfortunately, systematic analysis of the coverage of MCs on local news is quite rare. Research to date about local television coverage (Hess, 1991; Vinson, 2003) reaches the conclusion that local stations largely eschew coverage of MCs, although this conclusion rests on a relatively modest number of samples of coverage taken during short discrete intervals.

Most of what is known regarding MCs and their television coverage is limited to national news broadcasts. In part, this may reflect data availability, as written transcripts and video recordings of national coverage are more readily available (e.g., The Vanderbilt Television News Archive, tvnews.vanderbilt.edu). The primary research question is typically which MCs were most likely to receive airtime. Network news is motivated by increasing ratings and, consequently, providing coverage of stories that will be most appealing to a wide audience. Unsurprisingly, therefore, networks provide coverage of those legislators who might be of greatest interest to a national audience. Content analyses reveal that MCs in leadership positions and those with presidential prospects are the most likely to receive coverage (e.g., Cook, 1986; Squire, 1988). Networks may also be motivated to cover partisan conflict to increase their ratings: broadcasts provide more discussion of ideologically extreme MCs (Cook, 1986). Maltzman and Sigelman (1996) found that those who are ideologically extreme were the most likely to participate in one- and five-minute speeches that were broadcast on C-SPAN, a non-profit government cable TV channel. They also found that members from marginal districts were more likely to make such speeches, which may be a gateway to local TV coverage.

Although the audience for network TV national news has decreased, television remains the leading medium through which Americans get their information about national and international affairs.[6] Local news, while also decreasing

[5] www.tvhistory.tv/facts-stats.htm.
[6] www.pewresearch.org/fact-tank/2018/12/10/social-media-outpaces-print-newspapers-in-the-u-s-as-a-news-source/.

in its overall audience size, still serves as a key source of information about local affairs.[7]

TELEVISION AND ACCOUNTABILITY.   The consequences of appearing on television are not always clear. Prior (2006) provides perhaps the most thorough investigation of television's effect on voters' relationships with their incumbent MC. Examining the expansion of local television in the late 1950s and early 1960s, he finds that citizens who lived in regions served by more local television stations had higher levels of knowledge about their incumbent MC. Data in the aggregate suggested that more television stations in a district increased incumbent MCs' vote shares. In this case, the introduction of a local television station likely included treatment with both national TV news and, later, the emergence of local news.

Given the factors that explain national coverage and the clear lack of knowledge about what factors explain local coverage (and that no systematic records of that coverage exist), it is perhaps not surprising that the relationship between TV coverage and incumbent electoral performance is inconclusive. Niven and Zilber (1998) found no association between appearances on national television broadcasts and electoral margins in the 1980s, but they found a significant negative relationship in the 1990s, although it was unclear if the relationship is causal. Levy and Squire (2000) found that congruence between market and district improved incumbent name recognition in addition to making it easier for challengers to become known to voters. More recently, Moskowitz (2021) used data from ninety-nine local television stations broadcasting in 2016 and showed that respondents to the 2012 and 2016 CCES who lived in more state-congruent media markets were more likely to engage in split ticket voting, suggesting coverage reduced the link between an individual's partisanship and their vote for these offices.

An open question is whether the nature of local TV coverage has changed over time with consolidation in the ownership of local news stations. Martin and McCrain (2019) used a data set gathered from TVEyes, a company that records and transcribes local television news coverage, to classify and measure local television news broadcasts of national affairs for each metropolitan media market. They investigated the effects of local affiliates being purchased by a national media conglomerate, Sinclair Broadcasting, on coverage. They find that stations with national ownership focused more on national rather than local news and that the overall bias of the coverage became more conservative.

There is not a large literature on how other changes in the media environment have affected the nature of local TV news coverage of politics. On the one hand, the decline in local newspapers means that another key source of local political coverage has declined, potentially encouraging local TV to step up coverage for market reasons. But local newspaper coverage may be a source

---

[7] www.pewresearch.org/fact-tank/2018/01/05/fewer-americans-rely-on-tv-news-what-type-they-watch-varies-by-who-they-are/.

of local TV content. Additionally, how the emergence of the internet and cable TV have affected the market incentives for local TV news coverage has not been thoroughly explored.

Moving beyond local television coverage, the expansion of cable (non-broadcast) television has also had important consequences for the information available to citizens. Partially this has operated by changing the incentives for local stations to cover local and national politics, but this may be a second-order concern relative to the fact that national all-news stations have become the dominant source of political news for many interested viewers. The importance of the historical big three networks in their coverage of events, and their ability to dominate content, has declined substantially. This may in turn reduce local news viewership, because these broadcasts abut one another. Others have noted that those citizens who desire to avoid news altogether can now do so more easily. Additionally, the way in which national all-news networks cover TV has both substantially increased the amount of information citizens could, if they were interested, glean about national events and raised the possibility of more nationally focused, and perhaps ideologically slanted, coverage.

This concern about biased coverage is perhaps best exemplified by the ascendance of Fox News as a permanent fixture in American politics and the media. While the network provides an outlet for conservative voices and may be consumed by relatively few Americans, relative to local newscasts during their peaks, research suggests it has a significant effect on the behavior of MCs. For example, Clinton and Enamorado (2014) demonstrate that those MCs who represented districts serviced by Fox News in its earliest days of availability were less supportive of the Clinton administration. While this review focuses on Fox News, MSNBC may serve a similar roll on the left, and even CNN is perceived as moderately left of center. Critically, because these networks focus on national events (like Fox) they are less concerned with coverage of individual members in their districts and instead focus on narratives about national legislation and conflicts. As such, they may make it harder for legislators to depart from partisan stereotypes/brands This is part a broader pattern of nationalization in which local differences are subordinated relative to national concerns (Hopkins, 2018), perhaps exacerbated here by the focus on national conflict between the programmatic parties.

Nonetheless, despite this extensive literature on the role of television, it remains the case that we have little direct measurement of the frequency or nature of coverage that MCs attract on local media outlets. Our best evidence about the importance of local TV is largely indirect, focused on state-level offices, or from pre-internet periods. One possibility is to exploit private sector products that record local TV coverage, such as TVEyes data on local news coverage, to directly code both the frequency and nature of coverage of MCs both outside of and during campaign season to understand the volume and content of that coverage and, in light of that coverage, what strategies voters are likely to be able to use in choosing among candidates. Unfortunately, we are unaware of any means for obtaining systematic information about local TV coverage in earlier eras to describe changes that have taken place or correlate the nature of coverage with legislator behavior.

Social Media and New Internet Mediums

The way in which the emergence of the internet has disrupted the print news market is well understood. The internet has reduced the demand for advertising, which has either moved online or the retailers that previously advertised have disappeared altogether. But less well understood is how the internet has altered the nature of coverage in existing media outlets as those outlets have embraced the internet as a media delivery outlet. Additionally, the rise of social media supplements the traditional tools of member outreach for communicating with constituents, perhaps by bypassing traditional media outlets altogether.

Not by coincidence, the decline in the consumption of print and television news has coincided with a rise in the consumption of news through various internet mediums. The growth of internet outlets has provided more (national) news options, as well as more entertainment sources, and both may explain the decline in the consumption of the local press. While the direct effect of this market shift on the local coverage of local MCs is less clear, recent research suggests incumbents now have a harder time crafting a positive personal brand and that the personal incumbency advantage is also dwindling. For example, Trussler (2020) demonstrated that split-ticket voting decreased in those Congressional districts in which broadband internet access was first made available, suggesting that greater access to the internet was associated with greater partisan voting in House races, that is, the nationalization of congressional politics. This finding is largely consistent with that of Darr, Hitt, and Dunaway (2018) who showed that diminished access to local press correlated with a decline in split-ticket voting.

Turning to how MCs have used the emergence of the internet to promote their own agenda, the use of Twitter, Facebook, and other social media platforms are not well understood. Twitter's user base is small and elite-driven, whereas Facebook is an obvious market for campaign communications. Less is known about how members use Facebook apart from advertising to either disseminate news/information or to recruit and harness potential voters and donors. Moreover, the key role of Facebook as a news delivery service that may be a conduit for voters to learn about their MC is less well understood. In part this reflects the new emergence of the medium, but also the fact that even relative to local broadcast TV, data gathering is extremely difficult. Each Facebook user's experience, their relevant informational environment, may be different, but it is extremely difficult to observe or measure that environment because Facebook is a private company and does not make that data readily available (or, perhaps, even archive it) (but see Guess, Nyhan, and Reifler, 2019).

If Facebook is an important source of news about an individual MC, it is unfortunate that it is proving so difficult to study it systematically.

One possible way forward for assessing citizens' information environments and their effects on attitudes and political knowledge may be found in the work of Barbera et al. (n.d.). These researchers monitored the websites visited by a sample of American survey panelists, scraping the text of the pages they visited and the social media posts they encountered. Simultaneously, they repeatedly administered surveys to these individuals about their political attitudes and issue priorities. This approach, while it does not deal with the thorny selection question of why citizens opt into different media diets, does allow researchers to accurately categorize the information environment citizens encounter and the correlation between any possible changes in political attitudes and changes in news consumption. Applying this sort of approach to simply classify the nature of the information citizens encounter about MCs, both on average and by respondent characteristics (e.g., degree of political engagement), would be extremely valuable. Such an approach is also amenable to pairing with field experimental interventions that would allow understanding the causal effects of (induced) shifts in media content on citizen attitudes.

CONTEMPORARY MEDIA COVERAGE OF MEMBERS OF CONGRESS: THE NEED FOR A UNIFIED APPROACH

The preceding review shows that despite a rich body of prior scholarship, there is still a great deal that we do not know about contemporary media coverage of MCs and the implications of that coverage for political accountability. Most centrally, we simply have an insufficient understanding of the nature and content of contemporary media coverage of MCs, including coverage that extends beyond traditional mass media outlets like local newspapers and local television affiliates (although see Carnes' analysis in Chapter 7). In light of this lack of systematic data on what citizens could learn, we propose an agenda for a unified cross-media data collection effort on coverage of MCs. While such a collective enterprise would be a large undertaking, we believe that advances in data availability, data collection tools (e.g., computer-assisted and automated content search), and data coding would make previously very difficult or impossible work feasible on a large and continuing basis.

Our argument is that rather than continuing a medium-by-medium approach that characterizes most prior work, researchers should undertake an across-medium approach that focuses on the district-legislator dyad as a unit of analysis. In this approach, researchers would first pre-specify a set of relevant information sources – most obviously local newspapers (including local editions of more national or regional papers), local television stations, radio (if feasible), social media outlets including Twitter and Facebook, and internet news coverage more generally. Second, they would undertake to collect all coverage of the local MC, and perhaps Congress more generally, in those outlets. Here we believe the key hurdle is both specifying those outlets and identifying ways to gain access to their content, which we discuss in greater detail below. Finally, using computer-assisted coding, we believe these data should be processed to create a "story"-level summary of the nature of coverage, perhaps including direct (textual or visual) extracts of that coverage where feasible. These data could then be merged with other information about legislators, including, for example, the Wesleyan Advertising Project record of broadcast campaign advertisements (although, notably, that project does not include advertising on mediums other than television).

We first briefly highlight what these data would allow researchers to do. First, and most centrally, these data would allow scholars to fully characterize the total information environment, both in its frequency of coverage and in the substance of its coverage, for MCs. As of now, there is simply a great deal we do not know about, for example, whether MCs are locally newsworthy, whether that coverage is framed in terms of national party conflict, whether the frequency and tone is dynamic for a given MC, etc.

Second, it would allow researchers to understand how features of local media markets, including the absence of local newspapers in many markets, shape the overall information environment. As we note above, hypotheses about the effects of the decline of local newspapers on information abound, but we lack systematic data about, for example, whether places that once had a local paper have seen coverage of MCs diminish or if local TV and other sources have taken up that role. Similarly, it would enable researchers to understand how legislators behave in light of the local media environment. As more locations become market-incongruent, because of a lack of local newspapers, legislators may have turned to online outreach to both shape remaining coverage and compensate for the overall decline in print news. The cheap, quick, and targeted use of tactics such as electronic newsletters (Cormack, 2016) could signal a shift in the importance of newspapers and television, which also give MCs editorial control over their publicity that does not always exist in television and newspapers (Gershon, 2012).

Despite this promise, there are nonetheless several open questions, potential hurdles, and limitations of this approach. A key open question is about scope, and in particular what media should be collected. In part, this depends on how one conceives of media, and whether it should be confined to originally produced content distributed through broadcast mass media. Our view is that the traditional idea of media as encompassing only the original transmission/publication of material on television/radio or in a newspaper is unlikely to capture the relevant information environment. But, once one expands the idea of media, where does it stop? A useful demarcation is probably to account for the scope of dissemination, but measuring that is likely a challenge. Additionally, it may be relevant to consider what people would encounter if they were to affirmatively search for news about an MC.

Turning to hurdles, we see three concerns. The first is about how to effectively capture local newspaper and television coverage, particularly given that relatively few papers are fully archived online and no such archive exists for television. A necessary first step is therefore to understand what newspapers have their content archived in existing databases (e.g., Factiva, Lexis/Nexis, etc.) or can be archived/searched in real time. One possible path forward that has yet to be fully exploited by researchers is Media Cloud. Media Cloud collects and archives news stories from several print and online publications, allowing researchers to empirically investigate the frequency, sources, and context of news coverage for a given topic. While the available archives cover only the past decade and it is not fully clear which content are included from all outlets, the site's greatest advantage is available data on sources that have been almost entirely neglected by congressional researchers and cannot otherwise be gathered retrospectively. For example, Media Cloud provides comprehensive tracking information on popular blogs, as well as the websites for some local television news affiliates. For television, a private sector company offers some hope. TVEyes collects closed captioning data for local newscasts, but the data are not archived for past periods. We know of no such resource for radio, and it is unclear how to gather other non-traditional local news coverage.

The second concern is how to access online content that is available, or (re)distributed, via private social media platforms. For some platforms, such as Twitter, public APIs are readily available. At the other extreme, private email dissemination or private chat software will remain unavailable. But for other platforms, most notably Facebook and other public chat forums (e.g., Reddit, DailyKos, 4Chan, etc.), there is a question of access and availability. In terms of substantive importance, Facebook is likely the biggest challenge. Because it is a private company with proprietary content control, we know comparatively little about how it shapes news that is presented to users and the variation in that user experience. One possibility is to employ a strategy where private users are solicited and compensated for providing access to their news experience, but those are generally bigger hurdles than one would encounter in retrieving newspaper content.

The final hurdle is about human subjects and privacy concerns. Private users typically post their social media and chat forum content in publicly accessible venues. Yet, the collection of those public posts (which may be identified) may constitute human subjects data. Whether one must, or should, obtain consent in that setting is unclear.

In terms of limitations, we see two key drawbacks to the project we propose. First, it is not possible to conduct this research retrospectively, and so key questions about how the media environment have changed, either globally or on a market-by-market basis, are beyond the scope of this project. However, going forward, if these data were collected regularly, it would be feasible to examine these sorts of dynamics. Second, we are proposing to gather information about available content, but we have not proposed a method to gather exposure to that content. This is of course also a limitation of prior related work, but for those interested in understanding citizens' effective, rather than potential, information environment, understanding actual consumption of knowledge is key. To overcome this drawback, it could prove useful to adopt a forward-looking strategy, such as those research strategies proposed by Barbera et al. (n.d.) and Munger et al. (2020). This approach is not without concerns, such as the representativeness of a sample that allows for tracking. Nor does it deal with the problem of tracking exposure to non-internet new sources, or measuring the information individuals consume on devices other than those enrolled in the tracking program. Nonetheless, the key innovation in that work is to think seriously about measuring actual news consumption.

Finally, this research would examine the content of media coverage, but it would not reveal how MCs interact with media and shape that coverage. Work by Cook (1988), who interviewed and surveyed MCs and their press teams, revealed that both television and newspapers were highly valued for promotion of the incumbent's brand. We do not fully understand how MCs understand the current media environment, nor their efforts to shape its content (but see Grimmer 2013).

CONCLUSION

This chapter discusses the ways in which local media, particularly print media, have served as a source of citizen information about MCs. In Table 8.1 we provide a brief summary of research on the relationship between legislative accountability and local press by type of media, known available data sets to understand this relationship, as well as areas that have yet to be fully explored. Prior research provides important historical information about the volume and nature of coverage, as well as district-, member-, and other sources of variation in coverage. It suggests that a robust local press, as well as geographic and commercial context, can influence the ways in which citizens hold their representatives accountable. At the same time, the overwhelming majority of that work predates the massive changes that have occurred in the media landscape over the past few decades. As local media continues to change, researchers ought to consider new approaches to studying the relationship between Congress and the press, including identifying new data sources and innovative ways to measure consumers' information diets.

If previous accounts of the interrelationship between media and the accountability of MCs have been outstripped by technological and commercial change, it is necessary to reconsider what we know about media and its coverage of incumbent MCs. In light of these clear changes to the media landscape, we presented three key empirical questions. First, we asked what the information landscape was before vast shifts and how it has changed since those shifts. We have shown that the literature provides some information about how MCs were covered prior to these major changes, but that even that knowledge is

TABLE 8.1 *MCs and media accountability: existing data and opportunities*

	What Is Needed for Accountability	Available Data	What Literature Covers	New Opportunities
Print Media	• Newspaper presence in a media market	• Internet databases (e.g., Lexis, Factiva)	Market structures such as geography, corporate ownership, and partisan composition drive local press coverage.	• Exploiting the decline in the media environment
	• Resources for coverage	• Newspaper websites		• Identifying what types of local press arise where print media disappears.
	• Congruence between newspaper audience and district constituency	• Circulation data		
	• Competitive environment	• Newspaper closure data		
Television	• Congruence between television audience and district constituency	• Internet archive of broadcasts	Market structures such as geography, corporate ownership, and partisan composition drive local press coverage.	• Investigating the nationalization and ideological tone of local television
	• Competitive environment	• Television transcripts		• Content analysis of local news broadcasts
	• Incentivized ownership	• Databases such as the Vanderbilt Television News Archive		• Visual classification of coverage
	• Resources for coverage	• Third Party Vendors		
Internet	• Less clear	• Tweets and Facebook Posts	MCs use internet websites and social media to provide unfiltered positive coverage of activities.	• Tracking consumers' news diets
		• Campaign and Official Press Releases		• Panels tracking views of MCs and Congress
		• Online sites for local press	Consumers can structure their information environment to fit their preferences.	• Identifying the effects of mis-information
		• Blogs and internet only news sites		

limited. Research does suggests that the decline of local print media, along with the consolidation of media production, has been associated with a decline in the coverage of local politics. Second, we asked what effects these changes may have on the incentives for incumbent MCs. The findings from Darr, Hitt, and Dunaway (2018) and Trussler (2020) would seem to suggest that on average media changes have led to greater nationalization of politics at the district level. Incumbents may be less able to build a personal brand because fewer local media outlets cover their activities. As such, the incentives to be a partisan may increase. But such an account presumes that this is not due to changes in the types of individuals who currently seek office and has not considered the possibility that MCs can adopt different strategies to build their personal brand through non-traditional media outlets. Finally, we asked who drives and who consumes coverage. This question is hard to answer, both historically and contemporaneously, because comprehensively measuring what is available and what is consumed are difficult tasks. Yet, technology provides more opportunities to answer these questions. Tracking citizens' online diets (Barbera et al., n.d.), as well as massive scraping and archiving endeavors across several media, such as Media Cloud, may provide an opportunity to answer these questions.

PART III

POLICYMAKING, INFORMATION PROVISION,
AND ACCOUNTABILITY

9

Coalition Leadership in the Polarized Congress

Frances E. Lee

This chapter examines the processes of coalition building in the party-polarized Congress. Given the increased ideological homogeneity of legislative parties today, it seems reasonable to expect that intra-party coalition building will be simpler and more straightforward in the contemporary Congress than it was during eras when the parties were less internally cohesive. But is this the case? Can today's more cohesive parties easily coalesce to enact their agenda priorities, at least when they possess unified control of government? Examining each of the major legislative drives of the 115th Congress (2017–2018) – tax reform and the repeal and replacement of Obamacare – I find that the answer is no. Both of these legislative drives were heavy lifts, even though neither required bipartisan support to succeed. Despite strenuous efforts, coalition leaders failed outright on one of these efforts and had to significantly scale back their ambitions on the other.

In his seminal book, *Logic of Congressional Action*, Arnold (1990) described the complex maneuvers coalition leaders of the 1980s deployed to secure support from reelection-oriented members. According to Arnold's account, leaders build coalitions for their policy proposals in two primary ways. First, they modify the allocation of costs and benefits across constituencies so as to increase the incidence and salience of benefits and to reduce the incidence

I thank SoRelle Wyckoff Gaynor for excellent research assistance. For comments on earlier drafts, I thank Jim Curry, David Karol, Emery Lee, Eric Schickler, and Keith Whittington. I am also grateful to the University of Maryland and the Library of Congress's John W. Kluge Center for research support.

and salience of costs. Second, they use procedures to obscure lawmakers' responsibility for imposing costs and to clarify legislators' responsibility for providing benefits.

This chapter asks whether coalition leaders in the party-polarized Congress need to have recourse to such devices. Today's legislative process is far more streamlined and centralized in party leadership, particularly on high profile initiatives (Sinclair, 2016). Committees are regularly overruled or bypassed (Bendix, 2016; Curry and Lee, 2020b). Floor processes are tightly regulated (Harbridge, 2015; Smith, 2014; Tiefer, 2016). Rank-and-file members often have little time even to review legislative language before they vote (Curry, 2015). Under these conditions, transaction costs would seemingly be lower and coalition building should be more straightforward.

Looking outside the institution, members' political incentives also align more closely with their parties. Measures of incumbency advantage have fallen to levels not seen since the 1950s (Jacobson, 2015, 2021). Few members represent constituencies that lean toward the opposing party. Split-ticket voting has sharply declined (Fiorina, 2016). As Drutman in Chapter 13 in this volume observes, fewer members today worry about a general election challenger. Taken together, contemporary members have much less electoral motivation to buck their parties compared to members in the second half of the twentieth century (Mayhew, 1974). In such a context, members may not perceive many conflicts between their individual and partisan interests. A closer political alignment between individual members and their parties should thus render intraparty coalition building less onerous.

In such a changed context, do congressional leaders continue to employ the elaborate coalition-building efforts necessary in the less party-polarized Congress of the 1980s (Arnold, 1990)? Examining the major legislative drives of the 115th Congress (2017–2018), I find that the answer is yes. Contemporary coalition leaders still need to show considerable flexibility to build support for legislation, even when they only seek to build coalitions from within one political party. Even with unified government and no need to persuade members of the opposing party, coalition leaders found that they could not assume that sufficient support would be forthcoming. This was the case even though no Republican members expressed opposition to either legislative effort in principle. Republicans, moreover, believed that success on these efforts was critical to their party's continued majority control (Green and Deatherage, 2018). Despite all these favorable conditions, coalition leaders had to substantially modify their proposals to make them more attractive to members. In so doing, they employed the same policy and procedural techniques that had been used in less polarized congresses to assemble more ideologically heterogeneous coalitions. Throughout the process, there was considerable uncertainty as to the final outcome of their efforts. In the end, Republicans failed to pass their first legislative priority (ACA repeal) and had to limit the scope of their second priority (tax reform).

Navigating Policy and Political Trade-offs

Much work on coalition building in Congress begins by assuming that legislators seek to maximize their policy preferences. Spatial theories generally turn on an assumption that members make decisions by voting for the alternative more proximate to their ideal point along an underlying continuum structuring national policy disputes (e.g., Krehbiel, 1998; McCarty, Poole, and Rosenthal, 2006). Divide-the-dollars models likewise assume that members make decisions on the basis of straightforward calculations of policy benefits for their constituencies (e.g., Ansolabehere, Snyder, and Ting, 2003; Baron and Ferejohn, 1989).

Although such models shed important light on congressional policymaking, coalition leaders often confront a more complex environment in which members must navigate trade-offs between politics and policy or among different features of a policy. First, members must consider their electoral interests. What members want to achieve in policy terms may not necessarily be popular with constituents. Polling revealed that the Republican efforts to pass tax reform[1] and Obamacare repeal and replacement[2] both fell well short of majority approval. Electoral considerations may trade off against members' policy preferences.

Second, members frequently confront trade-offs in which outcomes on one policy dimension entail undesired outcomes on another dimension. Tax reform, for example, can yield efficiencies for the economy as a whole, but closing loopholes and abolishing tax breaks inevitably entails reductions in benefits for particular constituencies. Obamacare repeal and replacement may simultaneously make health insurance premiums less expensive for healthy people but more expensive for people with health problems. Rather than calculating a policy's distance from an ideal point, members must instead assess differential policy effects across diverse interests.

Coalition leaders can sometimes achieve their desired outcomes by uncovering ways to reduce such trade-offs. Coalition leaders know that members weighing policy choices will "estimate[e] the electoral consequences of being associated" with each alternative (Arnold, 1990, 8). As such, members' choices will turn not just on the content of policy itself but on how "being associated" with it will affect their electoral prospects. Coalition leaders can win support not just by moving policy toward pivotal members' ideal points, but instead by structuring policies or packaging them procedurally so as to affect members'

[1] John Sides, "Here's the Incredibly Unpopular GOP Tax Reform Plan: In One Graph," Monkey Cage, *Washington Post*, November 18, 2017, www.washingtonpost.com/news/monkey-cage/wp/2017/11/18/heres-the-incredibly-unpopular-gop-tax-reform-plan-in-one-graph/.

[2] Christopher Warshaw and David Broockman, "G.O.P. Senators Might Not Realize It, but Not One State Supports the Republican Health Bill," The Upshot, NYTimes.com, June 14, 2017, www.nytimes.com/2017/06/14/upshot/gop-senators-might-not-realize-it-but-not-one-state-supports-the-ahca.html.

association with outcomes, meaning constituents' ability to perceive that costs were imposed or that members were responsible for imposing them.

As a consequence, coalition leaders can build support by manipulating a policy's "traceability." A "traceable" policy effect is one where "a citizen can plausibly trace an observed effect first back to a governmental action and then back to a representative's individual contribution" (Arnold, 1990, 47). Members may be willing to support unpopular policies if their political responsibility for enacting those policies can be attenuated. Perceptions – not just the realities – of public policy affect members' preferences.

Empirical Work on Coalition Building

Outside of formal theory, there is relatively little work in political science aside from *Logic of Congressional Action* that even attempts to generalize about the coalition-building process in Congress. There is a large literature analyzing which members engage in more legislative entrepreneurship (Bernhard and Sulkin, 2018; Burden, 2007; Schiller, 1995; Wawro, 2000) and with what effect (Anderson, Box-Steffensmeier, and Sinclair-Chapman, 2003; Volden and Wiseman, 2014). But scholars need to investigate not just who becomes a coalition leader, but how coalition leaders go about their work. Such questions have seen limited systematic analysis (for exceptions, see Evans 2004; Curry and Lee 2020a, 85–122).

Do coalition leaders in today's much more centralized, partisan Congress still employ the tactics that coalition leaders used to build support in the Congress of the 1980s? To answer these questions, this chapter closely examines each of 2017s major legislative drives. If leaders have an easier task building coalitions in the party-polarized Congress, we should be able to see the effects on the cases examined here. Republicans' efforts to repeal Obamacare and reduce taxes were exercises in one-party coalition building. Via budget reconciliation, Republicans could enact these policies without any support from Democrats. Republicans had long waged campaigns on these issues, and there was no principled intraparty dissent about the broad policy goals involved. Leaders employed centralized processes to develop the legislation. All negotiation was internal to the majority party and, in most cases, conducted behind closed doors. In summary, the only task for coalition leaders was to hold their party together.

The chapter proceeds by first identifying each of the major political chal-lenges coalition leaders faced and then analyzes how they attempted to address those challenges. Following Arnold (1990), the chapter examines whether and how leaders adjusted (1) the allocation of costs under the proposed policy and (2) the extent to which costs would be traceable back to legislators' decisions. Even though Republicans wanted to enact tax reform and Obamacare repeal as a matter of both shared ideology and partisan interest, they nevertheless faced difficult policy and political trade-offs. I find that despite many other changes in congressional processes and electoral politics, coalition leaders still build legislative support through the same policy and procedural accommodations that were employed in congresses of the 1980s.

COALITIONAL POLITICS OF OBAMACARE REPEAL

Launched in the first week of the 115th Congress, the effort to repeal Obamacare was the top agenda priority for the new unified Republican government elected in 2016. Less than two weeks into the new congress, the House and Senate passed a concurrent resolution (S. Con. Res. 3) to permit Obamacare repeal via the budget reconciliation process, thus allowing Republicans to enact legislation without bipartisan support. This was not an untested approach. Republicans had employed reconciliation procedures in 2015 to pass an Obamacare repeal (H.R. 3762), which was subsequently vetoed by President Obama.

Political Challenges for Obamacare Repeal

In considering the costs of ACA repeal, coalition leaders confronted an array of constituencies that benefited from the policy status quo or feared change. Repeal would directly impact individuals who received health insurance via the state exchanges established under the ACA or from the ACA's Medicaid expansion. As of 2017, more than 12 million people obtained their health insurance on the Obamacare state exchanges[3] and an additional 12.7 million had been enrolled in Medicaid expansion programs.[4] Such individuals packed into town hall meetings of Republican members over the summer of 2017 to protest repeal.[5] Over the course of the debate, news headlines would trumpet each Congressional Budget Office estimate of the number of people who would lose insurance under proposed legislation. "Can't sugarcoat it. Doesn't look good," said Sen. Bill Cassidy (R-LA) after one such estimate.[6] These concerns were reflected in public polling. As early as January 27, a poll showed that 56% of adults were "extremely" or "very" concerned that many would lose health insurance if the ACA were repealed.[7]

---

[3] Marketplace Enrollment, 2014–2019, Kaiser Family Foundation, www.kff.org/health-reform/state-indicator/marketplace-enrollment.

[4] Medicaid Expansion Enrollment, Kaiser Family Foundation, www.kff.org/health-reform/state-indicator/medicaid-expansion-enrollment.

[5] See, for example, Joshua Stewart and Teri Figueroa, "Issa, Hunter Face Raucous Anti-Trump Crowds at Town Hall Meetings," *The San Diego Union-Tribune*, March 11, 2017.

[6] Kyle Cheney, Burgess Everett, and Rachel Bade, "GOP Scrambles After Scorching Health Bill Appraisal," *Politico*, March 13, 2017.

[7] NBC News, "Americans Fear They'll Lose Coverage with Obamacare Repeal: Poll," January 27, 2017, www.nbcnews.com/health/health-care/americans-fear-they-ll-lose-coverage-obamacare-repeal-poll-n713356.

Organized groups and interests across the health care sector also opposed ACA repeal, including hospitals, physicians, and insurers as well as patient advocacy organizations, such as the American Heart Association and the March of Dimes. "A bill that's completely opposed by the whole health care establishment is very, very difficult to pass," said John Rother, AARP's long-time top lobbyist.[8] When the ACA was developed in 2009–2010, President Obama and congressional Democrats carefully cultivated support from health insurance companies, doctors' groups, hospitals, and the pharmaceutical industry. These groups and organizations feared that ACA repeal would harm their interests. Characterizing the political landscape, *Politico* reported, "Just about every major health care group opposes President Donald Trump's health care overhaul."[9] House Energy and Commerce Committee Chair Greg Walden (R-OR) said, "There's a pretty big medical-industrial complex in America. And when you touch it, I've discovered, it touches back."[10]

Third, the states that had expanded Medicaid under the ACA were concerned about the future status of those insured under the program. Of course, Democrats representing states that expanded Medicaid wielded limited influence with congressional Republicans who neither expected nor sought to win their support. But sixteen Republican governors and twenty-one Republican senators represented states that had expanded Medicaid.[11] Even before President Trump was inaugurated, nearly a dozen of these governors went to Capitol Hill to express their concerns about repealing the Medicaid expansion.[12] Republican senators from Medicaid-expansion states – 40% of the Senate Republican conference – echoed these concerns. In early March, four Republican senators – a number sufficient to deny Republicans a legislative majority – wrote a letter to Majority Leader Mitch McConnell (R-KY) objecting that the legislation being considered "does not provide stability and certainty for individuals and families in Medicaid expansion programs."[13]

---

[8] Adam Cancryn, Sarah Karlin-Smith, and Paul Demko, "Deep-Pocketed Health Care Lobbies Line up Against Trump," *Politico,* May 5, 2017.

[9] Ibid. See also Juliet Eilperin and Mike DeBonis, "Doctors, Hospitals, and Insurers Oppose Republican Health Plan," *Washington Post,* March 8, 2017 and "Checks and Balance: Health Care Insiders Are Outside Looking In," CQ *Magazine,* July 10, 2017, http://library .cqpress.com/cqweekly/weeklyreport115-000005137342.

[10] Juliet Eilperin and Mike DeBonis, "Doctors, Hospitals, and Insurers Oppose Republican Health Plan," *Washington Post,* March 8, 2017.

[11] Rachana Pradhan, "GOP Governors Fight Their Own Party on Obamacare," *Politico,* January 13, 2017.

[12] Caitlin Huey-Burns and James Arkin, "GOP Governors Worried about Obamacare Repeal," *Real Clear Politics,* January 20, 2017, www.realclearpolitics.com/articles/2017/ 01/20/gop_governors_worried_about_obamacare_repeal.html.

[13] Press release, "Capito, GOP Senators Say House Health Care Draft Lacks Key Protections For Medicaid Expansion Population," March, 6, 2017, www.capito.senate.gov/news/ press-releases/capito-gop-senators-say-house-health-care-draft-lacks -key-protections-for-medicaid-expansion-population. The four signatories to the letter were: Senators Shelley Moore Capito (R-WV), Rob Portman (R-OH), Cory Gardner (R-CO), and Lisa Murkowski (R-AK).

A fourth challenge for ACA repeal was the relative lack of groups advocating for it. Groups supporting repeal were largely confined to organizations formed to push an ideological or partisan agenda. The American Action Network – an advocacy group with close ties to House Republican leaders – ran a multi-million dollar ad campaign in support.[14] But most of the conservative groups active in the debate demanded stricter adherence to ideological principles and thereby limited coalition-leaders' flexibility. Republican coalition leaders received more criticism than support from these groups. Heritage Action actively opposed the House leadership's first attempt to repeal and replace Obamacare because of its insufficient conservatism.[15] Likewise, the Club for Growth opposed the legislation assembled by Senate Republican leaders as not "real repeal."[16] Few organizations, and certainly no large-scale interest-group coalitions, advocated for ACA repeal on the basis of concrete policy benefits the legislation would provide. Coalition leaders pushing ACA repeal had few allies among organized interest groups.

Adjusting Costs in Obamacare Repeal

Throughout 2017, coalition leaders worked frantically to address rank-and-file Republican members' concerns about the costs Obamacare repeal would entail. Their first major policy concession was that it would be necessary to replace some or most of the benefits of Obamacare at the same time as it was repealed. This concession had not been necessary in 2015 to pass the sure-to-be-vetoed repeal, but in 2017 members demanded a replacement package.

At the start of the 115th Congress, the plan was to repeal Obamacare immediately and then work on a replacement.[17] Repeal would come first, followed by replacement much later in 2017.[18] Another early idea was "repeal and delay," in which the ACA would be repealed but the effective date of implementation would be delayed until 2019 or 2020 to allow time for a replacement.[19] As anxiety began to mount about the policy uncertainties involved, leaders floated a more accelerated replacement timeline in which only a month would elapse between repeal and replacement.[20]

[14] Rachel Bade, "GOP-Aligned Group Launches Obamacare Ad Blitz," *Politico*, January 25, 2017.
[15] Heritage Action, "'No' on American Health Care Act (H.R. 1628)," March 23, 2017, http://heritageaction.com/key-votes/no-american-health-care-act-h-r-1628/.
[16] Club for Growth, "Senate Bill Is Not Obamacare Repeal," June 27, 2017, www.clubforgrowth.org/club-for-growth-senate-bill-is-not-obamacare-repeal/.
[17] Jennifer Haberkorn and Burgess Everett, "GOP Airs Obamacare Divisions in Pence Meeting," *Politico*, January 4, 2017.
[18] Robert Pear, "Republicans Four-Step Plan for Dismantling the Care Act," *New York Times*, January 5, 2017, A1.
[19] Joseph Antos and James C. Capretta, "The Problems with 'Repeal and Delay,'" *Health Affairs*, January 3, 2017.
[20] Jake Sherman, Anna Palmer, and Daniel Lippman, "About that Memo-The New GOP Obamacare Plan," Playbook, *Politico*, January 11, 2017.

Republican senators of varying ideological stripes, however, refused to accept any time gap at all between repeal and replace. Libertarian Sen. Rand Paul (R-KY) urged Republicans to vote on a replacement plan at the same time as they passed a repeal bill. He was followed a day later by the conservative Sen. Tom Cotton (R-AR), then by the more centrist Sen. Bob Corker (R-TN).[21] Republicans feared the political consequences of "wreaking havoc on the health care system and causing people to lose their coverage without any assurance that they have a superior – or any – plan of their own."[22] Republicans were hearing "apocalyptic" scenarios from hospital and health plan leaders if they repealed Obamacare without a replacement.[23]

By late January, Republican coalition leaders had agreed to repeal and replace simultaneously. They then sought to craft a replacement that would address concerns about lost coverage both for those purchasing health insurance in state ACA markets as well as those covered by the Medicaid expansion. Republican leaders' plans would replace the ACA's subsidies for purchasing health insurance with refundable tax credits, with the Senate setting eligibility at higher income levels than the House. Likewise, Republican leaders' plans would phase-in the cuts for Medicaid expansion states gradually over a four- or eight-year period. In other words, coalition leaders designed modifications to soften the blow of repeal.

These modifications, however, failed to assuage members' worries. Republican resolve wavered every time the CBO released an estimate of the millions of people who would lose insurance as a result of the proposals. "GOP Scrambles After Scorching Health Bill Appraisal," read one headline.[24] "CBO Score Sure to Add to McConnell's Headaches," read another.[25] According to CBO estimates, out-of-pocket costs for purchasing health insurance would also increase substantially, particularly for older people.[26]

At the same time, coalition leaders' policy modifications softening the impact of ACA repeal undercut support for the proposed legislation among conservatives. Conservative organizations, including Heritage Action, the Club for Growth, and the Charles and David Koch-funded Freedom Partners, all opposed both the refundable tax credits and the gradual phase-out of the Medicaid expansion.[27] In other words, the accommodations coalition leaders

[21] Burgess Everett, "GOP Resistance Grows to Obamacare Repeal without Replacement," *Politico*, January 7, 2017.

[22] Everett, "GOP Resistance."

[23] Paul Demko and Adam Cancryn, "Obamacare Repeal's Doomsday Scenario," *Politico*, January 9, 2017.

[24] Cheney, Everett, and Bade, "GOP Scrambles."

[25] Adam Cancryn and Dan Diamond, "CBO Score Sure to Add to McConnell's Headaches," *Politico*, June 26, 2017.

[26] Congressional Budget Office, "H.R. 1628, Better Care Reconciliation Act of 2017: Cost Estimate," June 26, 2017, www.cbo.gov/publication/52849.

[27] Michele Hackman, "Conservative Groups Jeopardize GOP Plan to Repeal Affordable Care Act," *Wall Street Journal*, March 5, 2017.

adopted to cultivate support from undecided members repelled long-time advocates of ACA repeal. Conservative groups denounced the replacement plans as "Obamacare-lite."[28] House Freedom Caucus Chairman Mark Meadows (R-NC), Republican Study Committee Chairman Mark Walker (R-NC), Sen. Mike Lee (R-UT), and Sen. Ted Cruz (R-TX) all objected to the creation of a new entitlement program providing refundable tax credits for the purchase of health insurance.[29] Conservative commentators termed Republican leaders' proposals "Swampcare"[30] or "RINOCARE,"[31] referencing the derisive acronym, "Republicans in Name Only." Based on such objections, twenty-eight of the House Freedom Caucus's approximately three dozen members withheld their support from House leaders' first Obamacare repeal and replacement package, forcing Speaker Ryan to pull the bill from the floor on March 24.[32]

After their first effort to repeal the ACA had failed, House Republicans regrouped with a second initiative, this one negotiated directly between Freedom Caucus chair Meadows and Rep. Tom MacArthur (R-NJ), co-chair of the centrist Republican Tuesday Group. Meadows and MacArthur struck a deal on an amendment that would permit states to opt out of the ACA's insurance regulations, such as requirements to cover maternity care, ban denial of coverage based on preexisting conditions, and cap consumers' annual out-of-pocket spending. Not surprisingly, these modifications proved controversial, given that polls consistently found the ACA's insurance regulations to be its most popular feature.[33] But the MacArthur-Meadows amendment induced the Freedom Caucus to come on board.[34] The legislation successfully cleared the House (217-213) on May 5, with twenty Republicans – mostly from districts that had been carried by presidential candidate Hillary Clinton – voting against.[35]

The passage of the House bill did not signal the emergence of a broader Republican consensus. Weeks before the House passed its bill, Sen. Lamar Alexander (R-TN), chair of the Senate Health, Education, Labor and Pensions committee, had announced, "We're writing a Senate bill and not passing the

[28] Jake Sherman, Anna Palmer, and Daniel Lippman, "The Inside Scoop: Obamacare Replacement Politics," Playbook, *Politico*, March 7, 2017.
[29] Burgess Everett and Rachel Bade, "GOP Conservatives Oppose Leaked Obamacare Plan," *Politico*, February 27, 2017.
[30] Erick Erickson, "Swampcare: The Great Betrayal," RealClearPolitics, May 10, 2017, www.real clearpolitics.com/articles/2017/03/10/swampcare_the_great_betrayal_ 133307.html.
[31] Mark R. Levin, Twitter post, March 7, 2017, 4:39AM, https://twitter.com/mark levinshow/status/839093091449589760.
[32] Rachel Bade, Josh Dawsey, and Jennifer Haberkorn, "How a Secret Freedom Caucus Pact Brought Down Obamacare Repeal," *Politico*, March 26, 2017.
[33] Steven Shepard, "Poll: Voters Resist Pre-Existing Condition Opt-Out," *Politico*, March 3, 2017.
[34] Rachel Bade and Kyle Cheney, "Tuesday Group Leader under Fire over Health Care Deal," *Politico*, March 3, 2017.
[35] House roll-call vote 256, May 4, 2017.

House bill."[36] When they passed their American Health Care Act (H.R. 1628), House members thus knew that they were not voting on a finished product. They expected the legislation to see very substantial revision if not a complete reworking in the Senate. Rep. Joe Barton (R-TX) acknowledged as much during floor debate: "Vote for this bill. Let's send it to the other body and continue to work to improve it."[37] Kicking Obamacare repeal and replace to the Senate would allow House Republicans to move on to other priorities while forcing the Senate to absorb blame for any failure.

When the action moved to the Senate, coalition leaders struggled to reconcile the same competing demands that had bedeviled House Republicans. Coalition leaders had not found a satisfactory resolution to the Medicaid expansion issue. Republicans from states where Medicaid had been expanded wanted the benefits continued, while Republicans from states that had not expanded Medicaid resented their states' lower per capita funding under the slow phase-outs being proposed. Even Sen. Jerry Moran (R-KS), former Republican campaign committee chairman, began to express reservations.[38]

When Senators Moran and Lee formally declared their opposition, Majority Leader McConnell announced, "It is now apparent that the effort to repeal and replace the failure of Obamacare will not be successful."[39] The leadership-negotiated Better Care Reconciliation Act would go on to fail in the Senate by a vote of 43–57, far short of a chamber majority.[40]

Senate Republican leaders mounted their last effort at assembling a majority coalition by modifying the policy once more in late July. Rather than adjusting the bill to accommodate conservative demands, as House Republicans had done with the MacArthur-Meadows amendment, Senate leaders pursued a lowest common denominator approach in what became known inelegantly as "skinny repeal."

Skinny repeal – properly the Health Care Freedom Act (HCFA) – was a very modest measure that imposed almost no costs. The HCFA would repeal none of the Affordable Care Act's major provisions. It would maintain the ACA's subsidies to purchase insurance, its Medicaid expansion, and its regulations on insurance companies.[41] Rather than imposing costs, skinny repeal aimed exclusively to distribute benefits to various groups. HCFA would end the ACA's individual and employer mandate to purchase health insurance, increase tax-free contributions to health savings accounts, and suspend the medical device

---

[36] Burgess Everett and Jennifer Haberkorn, "Senate GOP Rejects House Obamacare Bill," *Politico*, March 5, 2017.

[37] *Congressional Record*, March 24, 2017, H2416.

[38] Thomas Kaplan, "Unlikely Holdout Underscores Challenge for Senate Health Bill," *New York Times*, July 6, 2017, A14.

[39] Richard Cowan and Yasmeen Abutaleb, "U.S. Republicans Divided after Second Healthcare Bill Collapses," *Reuters*, July 17, 2017.

[40] Senate roll-call vote 177, July 27, 2017.

[41] Henry J. Kaiser Family Foundation, "Compare Proposals to Replace the Affordable Care Act," www.kff.org/interactive/proposals-to-replace-the-affordable-care-act/.

tax for three years. The only constituency that would have absorbed any direct costs was Planned Parenthood, for which Medicaid funding would be prohibited for one year.

In other words, skinny repeal would not take away anyone's Medicaid, lift any of the ACA's coverage requirements for "essential health benefits," or rescind any subsidies used to purchase health insurance. But even though coalition leaders had drastically scaled back their ambitions, skinny repeal was still rejected 49-51 when Sen. John McCain (R-AZ), newly returned from cancer treatment, cast the decisive vote in opposition.[42]

Regulating Traceability in Repealing Obamacare

As they endeavored to repeal and replace the ACA, coalition leaders also sought to regulate the policy's "traceability," meaning constituents' ability to perceive legislators' responsibility for policy changes (Arnold, 1990, 47). Coalition leaders employed a panoply of procedural tactics to reduce traceability. Secrecy was a vital tool. Legislation was negotiated behind closed doors rather than in open committee, so that interested outsiders could not ascertain which members supported or opposed what provisions. Throughout the process, legislative language was tightly held, with few members in either chamber having access to the text being developed (Curry, 2017). No committees in either House or Senate held hearings on their chamber's bills before unveiling their legislation. House Republicans kept health care lobbyists at arms-length by holding abbreviated committee mark-ups.[43] The Senate did not conduct committee mark-ups.[44]

Breakneck speed in moving the legislation also inhibited groups from mobilizing to object to particular provisions. Legislative text was available for only a very short time before votes were taken. Within 48 hours of the American Health Care Act's release, the two House committees of jurisdiction had conducted and concluded simultaneous mark-ups and reported the legislation to the House floor.[45] House floor debate was confined to two days. Senate floor debate was limited to parts of three days.

A second means of reducing traceability is to "eliminate[e] identifiable governmental actions" (Arnold, 1990, 102), meaning to reduce the number of actions that can pinpoint lawmakers as responsible for imposing costs. One way of accomplishing this goal is to take votes only on omnibus legislation

---

[42] Senate roll-call vote 179, July 28, 2017.

[43] Adam Cancryn, Sarah Karlin-Smith, and Paul Demko, "Deep-Pocketed Health Care Lobbies Line Up against Trump," *Politico*, May 3, 2017.

[44] Audrey Carlsen and Haeyoun Park, "Which Party Was More Secretive in Working on Its Health Care Plan?" *New York Times*, July 10, 2017, www.nytimes.com/interactive/2017/07/10/us/republican-health-care-process.html.

[45] Robert Pear, "Law Took Months to Craft; Repeal May Be Much Swifter," *New York Times*, March 8, 2017, A14.

without opportunities for amendments. The House's bill was considered under a rule permitting no amendments (H. Res. 308). The rule also self-executed changes to the legislation pursuant to the Meadows-MacArthur agreement, such that members never had to go on the record in support of its controversial provisions. Similarly, only a handful of votes were taken in the Senate.

A third means of limiting traceability is to "weaken or break the traceability chain" (Arnold, 1990, 104). Long transition periods make it harder for voters to blame lawmakers because the effect is so remote in time from the cause. Coalition leaders seeking to repeal and replace the ACA repeatedly proposed lengthy transition periods so that the cuts lawmakers voted for would go into effect only gradually. The Medicaid expansion phase-outs in both the House and Senate leadership bills would have reduced benefits over a period from four to eight years. The MacArthur-Meadows amendment would not have directly deregulated health insurers; it would instead have permitted states to do so on their own responsibility. On this same model, a final, last-ditch effort at repeal-and-replace led by Senators Lindsey Graham (R-SC) and Bill Cassidy (R-LA) would have packaged funds for Obamacare subsidies and the Medicaid funding into block grants to states. These block grants would gradually decline in value, with by far the largest cuts scheduled to go into effect all at once nine years in the future between 2026 and 2027.[46] The block grant structure would have transferred the responsibility for imposing specific health care program cuts onto states. The long phase-in combined with the states' increased authority would have greatly attenuated the traceability chain for Congress.

Outcome of the ACA Repeal Drive

In the end, all of these efforts at adjusting costs and limiting traceability failed to produce successful legislation. Nevertheless, it is clear that these policy modifications and procedural tactics were the principal resources available to coalition leaders as they sought to marshal support. Coalition leaders attempted to lessen the costs of repealing Obamacare by (1) ensuring that repeal would not happen at all if a partial replacement for many of Obamacare's benefits was not immediately implemented, (2) replacing ACA subsidies with new refundable federal tax credits to purchase health insurance, and (3) maintaining the Medicaid expansion and decreasing it only gradually. In addition, coalition leaders limited traceability by restricting debate, holding few recorded votes, and utilizing policy phase-ins lengthening the time span between the government action and the observable consequences.

Obamacare repeal fits nicely Arnold's concept of the *"politically infeasible policy,"* meaning legislation that "would impose large and direct early-order costs on … constituents" (Arnold, 1990, 73). Even with the modifications

---

[46] Kim Soffen, "There's One Obamacare Repeal Bill Left Standing. Here's What's in It," *Washington Post*, September 25, 2017.

to reduce and delay costs and to make it harder for constituents to identify the lawmakers responsible for imposing them, repealing Obamacare would result in constituents losing health insurance coverage and, in many cases, paying more for it. On the other side of the ledger, the political benefits for repealing and replacing the ACA were quite limited. There were few organized groups who stood to gain anything tangible. Health insurance companies did not support the effort, even when the House bill would have lifted the ACA's regulations of the industry. Not even conservative advocacy groups were pleased with the replacement plans.

In the end, the primary political benefit Republicans could have won from repealing and replacing Obamacare would have been the ability to claim collective credit for delivering on a party campaign promise. Their failure is consistent with the (Arnold, 1990, 64) generalization that members of Congress "invariably" prioritize making themselves look good over making their parties look good. In short, members still perceive conflicts between their individual and partisan interests and act accordingly.

COALITIONAL POLITICS OF THE TCJA

The second major legislative drive of 2017 focused on tax cuts and tax reform. Coalition leaders aimed to make US businesses more internationally competitive by reducing corporate tax rates and moving toward a territorial tax system that would exempt from federal taxation income earned by US corporations overseas. Reformers also wanted to lower individual taxes, simplify tax filing, and reduce economic distortions created by tax expenditures.

This effort got underway in October after the final collapse of the health care initiative with the failure of Graham-Cassidy in late September.[47] On October 26, Congress passed a second budget resolution unlocking the use of reconciliation for tax legislation (H. Con. Res. 71), thereby ensuring that Senate Democrats could not stop the effort via filibuster. The resulting Tax Cuts and Jobs Act[48] was passed on December 2. Mirroring the analysis above, I will begin by identifying the key challenges coalition leaders faced in building majorities for the legislation. Then, I will examine how coalition leaders made the package more attractive by (1) adjusting the distribution of costs and (2) manipulating traceability.

Political Challenges for the TCJA

Reducing taxes is undoubtedly an easier proposition than cutting health care benefits. Even so, there was no preexisting majority for tax reform at the start

---

[47] Jennifer Haberkorn, Burgess Everett, and Seung Min Kim, "Inside the Life and Death of Graham-Cassidy," *Politico Magazine*, September 27, 2017.
[48] Pub. L. 115–97.

of the 115th Congress. The big challenges stemmed from coalition leaders' ambition to enact long-term tax reforms on the model of 1986,[49] not temporary rate reductions on the model of the Bush tax cuts of 2001.[50] "The notion that tax is easier than health is not borne out by the facts," said a Senate Republican aide in March.[51]

Two related challenges emerged for coalition leaders as they launched the TCJA legislative effort. First, permanent tax reform would require tax increases to offset the cost of tax cuts. Under the Byrd rule, legislation passed via reconciliation cannot increase the deficit outside of the time frame covered by the budget.[52] Coalition leaders in 2017 did not want to enact temporary changes that, like the 2001 Bush tax cuts, would expire at the end of the budget window. Per Congressional Budget Act rules, permanent tax reductions would need to be "paid for." Second, a vast array of organized interests feared being made worse off by policy change (see Patashnik, 2008, 35–54). As soon as Republicans kicked off the tax reform drive, journalists began to report on the "scramble among lobbyists and interest groups desperate to preserve prized tax breaks."[53] Longstanding tax expenditures would potentially be targeted for reduction or elimination, including the deductions for state and local taxes, 401(k) retirement contributions, charitable contributions, home mortgage interest, and the tax exclusion for employer-sponsored health benefits. Broad revision of the corporate tax code also threatened an array of business tax breaks, such as the carried interest loophole, as well as the deductions for interest, net operating losses, entertainment, and employee fringe benefits. All the organized interests adversely affected would work to preserve the status quo, an enterprise at which lobbying tends to excel (Baumgartner et al., 2009, 216–254).

Adjusting Costs in Tax Reform

Coalition leaders aimed to reduce the corporate income tax rate from a statutory top marginal rate of 35% to a flat rate of 20% and to cut and simplify individual income taxes.[54] Given Budget Act rules and fiscal realities, making these changes on a permanent basis would require revenue enhancements elsewhere. The proposed offsets caused the most legislative controversy.

---

[49] Tax Reform Act of 1985 (Pub.L. 99–514).

[50] Economic Growth and Tax Relief Reconciliation Act of 2001 (Pub. L. 107–16).

[51] Richard Rubin, "Republicans' Tax Overhaul Likely to Face Its Own Slings and Arrows," *Wall Street Journal*, March 26, 2017.

[52] Congressional Budget Act, Section 313(b)(1).

[53] Jim Tankersley, Thomas Kaplan, and Kenneth P. Vogel, "Lobbyists Rush in to Save Breaks As Pace Quickens on an Overhaul," *New York Times*, November 4, 2017, A14.

[54] See the Report of the Tax Reform Task Force, "A Better Way: Our Vision for a Confident America," June 24, 2016.

As they worked to build the necessary majorities, coalition leaders spent much of their time searching for new revenue sources acceptable to members. Overall, this process steadily eliminated alternatives for offsetting the rate cuts. In the end, they were left with too few revenue enhancements to enact permanent reforms to the individual tax code. Coalition leaders would have to settle for permanent changes only to corporate taxes. Because corporate taxes constitute a vastly smaller component of federal revenue (9%) than individual income taxes (48%), coalition leaders did not face the same challenges in identifying offsets for corporate tax rate reductions.[55] Furthermore, few corporations actually paid the top statutory tax rate of 35%, making a 20% target less of a tax cut than it might appear.[56] Coalition leaders thus did not have to identify as much compensating revenue to achieve the corporate tax reductions they sought. But it would prove too difficult for them to cover the cost of their rate reductions for individual taxpayers.

To compensate for lower tax rates, Speaker Ryan and Ways and Means Chairman Kevin Brady (R-TX) proposed a new "border adjustment" tax (BAT),[57] a destination-based cash flow tax that would exempt exported goods from taxation while subjecting imported goods sold in the United States to the tax.[58] The proposed tax was projected to raise $1 trillion in revenue over ten years. As such, it was the largest single source of new revenue considered. House leaders initially saw the BAT as vital for their success.[59]

The BAT, however, spawned large-scale pushback both on K Street and from conservative advocacy organizations. As early as February, more than 100 businesses and trade associations had assembled a coalition to oppose the BAT.[60] The Koch brothers-backed Americans for Prosperity (AFP), wrote to

---

[55] Office of Management and Budget, Historical Tables, "Table 2.2: Percentage Composition of Receipts by Source: 1934–2024," www.whitehouse.gov/omb/historical-tables/.

[56] According to GAO estimates for 2002–2012, the effective tax rate for large corporations was 14%. See Government Accountability Office, "Corporate Income Tax: Most Large Profitable U.S. Corporations Paid Tax but Effective Tax Rates Differed Significantly from the Statutory Rate," Report to the Ranking Member, Committee on the Budget, U.S. Senate, GAO-16-363, March 2016, www.gao.gov/assets/680/675844.pdf.

[57] Richard Rubin and Peter Nicholas, "Donald Trump Warns on House Republican Tax Plan," *Wall Street Journal*, January 17, 2017.

[58] For a discussion, see Alan J. Auerbach, "Demystifying the Destination-Based Cash-Flow Tax," Brookings papers on Economic Activity, Fall 2017, www.brookings.edu/wp-content/uploads/2018/02/auerbachtextfa17bpea.pdf.

[59] See Anna Palmer, Jake Sherman, and Daniel Lipman, "White House in Crisis," Playbook, *Politico*, February 2, 2017, www.politico.com/tipsheets/playbook/2017/02/white-house-in-crisis-netanyahu-visit-comes-as-us-backs-away-from-two-state-solution-doubts-grow-on-obamacare-repeal-ivanka-has-dinner-at-masseria-roger-stone-matt-boyle-at-the-palm-218745.

[60] "Our Mission," Keep America Affordable, https://keepamericaaffordable.com/our-mission/.

Chairman Brady voicing strong opposition.[61] The National Retail Federation and the AFP ran ads mocking the idea.[62]

As this advocacy campaign gained traction, Speaker Ryan attended a Senate Republican Policy Committee luncheon to sell the BAT idea. His presentation did not go well. "Some ideas are so stupid only an intellectual could believe them," said Sen. Tom Cotton (R-AR) of the proposal.[63] Two days later, Sen. Graham said on *Face the Nation*, "the House is talking about a tax plan that won't get ten votes in the Senate."[64] House Republicans persisted with the idea, however, and took new hope when President Trump remarked during a late February interview that the plan "could lead to a lot more jobs in the United States."[65] But in April, Majority Leader McConnell told a group of CEOs that the BAT tax would be "dead on arrival" in the Senate.[66] Nevertheless, Speaker Ryan and Chairman Brady were still arguing for the BAT in late May.[67]

Over time, it became clear that there would not be sufficient Republican consensus to make the BAT part of the package. BAT seems to have been taken off the table by midsummer.[68] But once the BAT was dead, it was not clear that Republicans would be able to offset the rate cuts. As late as September, the *Washington Post* reported that "after months of negotiations, the thorniest disagreement remains in view: how to pay for the giant tax cuts."[69] Tax reform "is always difficult, because it means what do you cut?" said Senate Finance Committee Chairman Orrin G. Hatch (R-UT). "Everything on the books has a constituency."[70]

After dropping the BAT, coalition leaders began to consider eliminating more tax deductions, but they kept running into road blocks. President Trump

[61] Brent Gardner, Chief Government Affairs Officer, Americans for Prosperity, Letter to House Ways and Means Chairman Kevin Brady, January 27, 2017, https://americansfor prosperity.org/wp-content/uploads/2017/01/AFP-LoO-Border-Adjustments 1-1.pdf.

[62] National Retail Federation, "B.A.T. Is a BAD Tax," YouTube, February 27, 2017, www.youtube.com/watch?v=23SXAYWZHc8; Nicholas Confessore and Alan Rappeport, "Divide in G.O.P. Now Threatens Trump Tax Plan," *New York Times*, April 2, 2017, A1.

[63] Rachel Bade, Burgess Everett, and Eliana Johnson, "Ryan Struggles to Sell Tax Reform Plan to Fellow Republicans," *Politico*, February 16, 2017.

[64] Transcript, Sen. Lindsey Graham on Face the Nation, CBS News, February 19, 2017, www.cbsnews.com/news/face-the-nation-transcript-february-19-2017-priebus-graham-nunes-cummings/.

[65] Steve Holland, "Exclusive: Trump Says Republican Border Tax Could Boost U.S. Jobs," Reuters, February 23, 2017, www.reuters.com/article/us-usa-trump-tax-exclusive-idUSKBN1622J5.

[66] Ibid.

[67] U.S. House of Representatives, Committee on Ways and Means, "Increasing U.S. Competitiveness and Preventing American Jobs from Moving Overseas," Communications Document for May 23, 2017 Tax Hearing, www.politico.com/f/?id=0000015c-31c0-d476-abdf-7df235b70002.

[68] The BAT would not be in the bill House Ways and Means reported to the floor on November 15.

[69] Damien Paletta, Sean Sullivan, and Kelsey Snell, "Trump's Push for Tax Cuts Is Coming Up against a Familiar Challenge: Divided GOP," *Washington Post*, September 12, 2017.

[70] Ibid.

promised that the legislation would not affect benefits for 401(k) retirement plans.[71] Republicans briefly considered limiting the tax exclusion for employer-sponsored health insurance – the most costly tax expenditure – but soon dropped the idea.[72] Treasury Secretary Steve Mnuchin promised that tax reform would retain deductions for mortgage interest and charitable contributions.[73] President Trump favored ending the carried interest loophole that benefited hedge-fund managers, but that idea was also dropped before the first version of the tax bill cleared the House.[74]

As they searched for offsets, the tax breaks most vulnerable to elimination were those that disproportionately benefited Democratic-leaning states and districts, especially the deduction for state and local taxes (SALT). The SALT deduction was of relatively greater value in high-tax jurisdictions, which tended to elect Democrats to Congress. Targeting the SALT deduction became "the only big revenue-raising provision with anything close to Republican consensus."[75]

Even on SALT, there was resistance from within the GOP. Republican members from New York, New Jersey, and California repeatedly pressed party leaders to relent.[76] High-tax states elected few Republicans to the Senate, leaving the SALT deduction with little defense in that chamber.[77] But New York, New Jersey, and California contributed twenty-one members to the House Republican majority, a bloc nearly sufficient to defeat the bill. Eventually Ways and Means chair Brady agreed to preserve a reduced SALT deduction for property taxes.[78]

Another highly sensitive issue was the mortgage-interest deduction. Mnuchin had indicated that the administration wanted to keep it.[79] But as one of the most costly tax expenditures, coalition leaders continued to eye the mortgage-interest deduction for reductions. With housing costs highest in Democratic-leaning major metropolitan areas, reducing this tax break would fall harder

[71] Damian Paletta and Mike DeBonis, "Trump's Promises Narrow GOP's Options," *Washington Post*, October 23, 2017.

[72] Richard Rubin, GOP Bid to Rewrite Tax Code Falters," *Wall Street Journal*, May 30, 2017, A1.

[73] Anna Palmer, "Playbook Interview: Treasury Secretary Steven Mnuchin," *Politico*, April 24, 2017.

[74] The House, Senate, and final version of the TCJA limited the carried interest loophole to assets that were held for three years instead of one, a change that would have little effect on beneficiaries of the loophole. On the impact of the change, see Allan Sloan, "The Carried-Interest 'Reform' Is a Sham," *Washington Post*, December 1, 2017.

[75] Rubin.

[76] Brian Faler, "6 Obstacles to the GOP's Tax Plans," *Politico*, October 26, 2017.

[77] The nine states with the highest income taxes (CA, HI, OR, MN, IA, NJ, VT, NY, WI) elected only three Republican senators; meanwhile the seven states (WY, WA, TX, SD, NV, FL, AK) with no state income tax elected ten Republican senators.

[78] Ben Brody, "House Tax Writer Gives Ground on a State and Local Tax Break," *Bloomberg*, October 28, 2017, www.bloomberg.com/news/articles/2017-10-28/ryan-s-tax-bill-loses-home-builder-support-before-it-s-released.

[79] Palmer, "Playbook Interview."

on Democratic constituencies than on Republican constituencies.[80] But this
tax expenditure had powerful defenders in the National Association of Home
Builders and the National Association of Realtors, groups with a presence
in every congressional district.[81] Camped out in front of a district office of
House Majority Leader Kevin McCarthy, a leader of a Bakersfield realtor group
pointed out: "We don't consider ourselves to be Republicans or Democrats.
We are the Realtor Party."[82] As with the SALT deduction, jurisdictions with
high housing costs had better Republican representation in the House than
the Senate. Coalition leaders considered a range of other tax deductions for
elimination or reduction, though the deductions for SALT and mortgage interest
remained by far the two biggest tax expenditures seriously targeted.

Coalition leaders eventually resolved their party's internal difficulties, and
Congress enacted the TCJA.[83] Table 9.1 displays the most significant revenue
enhancements that appeared in either the House or Senate bills, along with
the outcome reached in the final version of the legislation. In the end, the
TCJA did not reduce the number of tax expenditures in either the corporate or
individual code.[84] The only two major deductions for individual taxpayers that
were limited were those for SALT and mortgage interest. The TCJA capped the
previously unlimited SALT deduction at $10,000 for property taxes only and
lowered the limit on deducting new mortgage and home equity loan interest
from a principal of $1 million to $750,000.[85] As shown in the first column of
Table 9.1, few ideas for rescinding deductions survived even as far as the first
bill to pass the House. Like the BAT, most ideas for cutting tax deductions
got eliminated before the first draft of the legislation saw the light of day.
Of the few deductions the House bill targeted beyond those for SALT and
mortgage interest, the Senate in the end accepted only the temporary repeal
of the deduction for moving expenses.

Because they could not secure sufficient offsets for their rate reductions,
coalition leaders had to concede that the changes to individual taxes would
expire at the end of the ten-year budget window. Even in the corporate tax
code, finding offsets was sufficiently difficult that it became necessary to accept

[80] Ronald Brownstein, "The Big Blue Losers in the GOP Tax Plans," *The Atlantic*, November 23, 2017, www.theatlantic.com/politics/archive/2017/11/the-big-blue-losers-in-the-gop-tax-plans/546665/.
[81] Julie Bykowicz, "U.S. News: Realtors Launch Blitz to Save Popular Deductions," *Wall Street Journal*, November 2, 2017, A4.
[82] Conor Dougherty and Ben Casselman, "Real Estate Industry Mobilizes to Shield Homeowners' Tax Breaks," *New York Times*, November 23, 2017, B3.
[83] The original House bill cleared on November 16 by a vote of 227-205 with no Democratic support and thirteen Republicans in opposition (12 from NJ, NY, and CA). The Senate bill passed on December 2 by a vote of 51-49, with only Sen. Corker in opposition. The conference report then cleared both chambers on December 20. The final legislation passed the House by a vote of 224-189 (with 12 Republicans voting no) and the Senate by a party-line vote of 51-48.
[84] Robert Bellafiore, "Tax Expenditure before and after the Tax Cuts and Jobs Act," Tax Foundation, Fiscal Fact, No. 627, December 2018.
[85] Interest on home mortgage or home equity debt incurred on or before December 15, 2017 remains deductible up to the maximum principal of $1 million.

TABLE 9.1 *Revenue enhancements in House, Senate, and final versions of the Tax Cuts and Jobs Act of 2017*

	House	Senate	Final
Individual Taxes			
SALT deduction	Limited to property taxes and capped at $10,000	Same as House except for expiration after 12/31/25	Same as Senate
Mortgage interest	Eliminated deductions for second home; capped deductible mortgage debt at $500,000	Repeals deduction for home equity debt only, expires after 12/31/25	Reduced limit on deductible mortgage-interest debt to $750,000; keeps deduction for second homes, expires after 12/31/25
Moving expenses	Eliminated	Eliminated, reinstated after 12/31/25	Same as Senate
Medical expenses	Eliminated	Retained and expanded	Same as Senate
Personal casualty / property loss	Eliminated	Retained	Same as Senate
Capital gains home sales	Limited in various ways	Limited less than in House bill	Current law retained
Dependent Care Flex Accounts	Repealed after 12/31/22	Retained	Same as Senate
Student loan interest	Eliminated	Retained	Same as Senate
New inflation measure	Chained CPI for adjusting tax brackets	Same as House	Same as House
Corporate Taxes			
Net interest deductions	Caps net interest deduction at 30% of earnings before interest, taxes, depreciation, and amortization (EBITDA)	Caps net interest deduction at 30% of earnings before interest and taxes (EBIT)	Caps net interest deduction at 30% of earnings before interest, taxes, depreciation, and amortization (EBITDA) for four years, and 30% earnings before interest and taxes (EBIT) thereafter

TABLE 9.1 *(continued)*

	House	Senate	Final
Net operating loss (NOL) deduction	Limited to 90% of current year taxable income, with carryovers permitted.	Limited to 90% of taxable income, declining to 80% of taxable income after 12/31/22.	Follows Senate, except deduction is limited to 80% after 12/31/17.
Entertainment and fringe benefits	Prohibited for entertainment, parking, athletic facilities and on-premises food	Same as House, but would allow deductions for on-premises food and athletic memberships	Same as Senate
International tax rules	Modified territorial system with base erosion provisions with 10% international minimum tax and 20% excise tax on some transactions	Modified territorial system with anti-abuse rules – new 17.5 tax on intangible income, 10% excise tax on some transactions	Follows Senate, except tax on intangible income ranges from 10.5% to 13.125%, rising after 12/31/25; tax on base erosion reduced to 5% of intangible income for one year, rising to 10% through 2025 then to 12.5% afterwards

a flat corporate tax rate of 21% in the final legislation, rather than the 20% rate coalition leaders initially sought and the 15% rate demanded by President Trump.

Regulating Traceability in Tax Reform

As they sought to reform the tax code, coalition leaders engaged in a variety of tactics to affect constituents' ability to perceive legislators' responsibility for policy changes. The procedural maneuvers executed during the TCJA debate mirror those used during the ACA repeal drive. Coalition leaders sought to reduce traceability for the costs imposed.

As with the ACA, secrecy was maintained by keeping the text of legislation closely held. Initial drafts were developed in private meetings of the "Big Six" principals, meaning Treasury Secretary Mnuchin, National Economic Council Director Gary Cohn, Speaker Ryan, Senate Majority Leader McConnell, Senate Finance Chairman Hatch, and Ways and Means Chair Brady. Even as these leaders began to coalesce on a framework, they declined to release draft language.[86] Secrecy protected members from pressure from organized interests seeking to ascertain who supported and opposed particular provisions. Through the summer, Senate Finance and House Ways and Means hearings were kept to general topics, such as "How Tax Reform Will Grow Our Economy," without making available legislative text. Even in late October, members of the tax panels were still waiting to see a draft bill. In the lead-up to the release of Brady's chairman's mark, staffers to Ways and Means members expressed anxiety about preparing their bosses for the coming "onslaught" of lobbyists once the bill was finally released.[87]

Coalition leaders' next step was to get the legislation across the finish line as quickly as possible with as few recorded votes as possible. Committee action was perfunctory. House Ways and Means held four days of markup and Senate Finance held three days. The House went from introduction to bill passage in two weeks; the Senate received the bill from the House on November 16 and passed its version by December 2. The conference committee process was concluded in both chambers by December 20. Such an accelerated process, wrote the *Wall Street Journal*'s Richard Rubin, is "close to financial-crisis speed."[88]

As with the ACA, identifiable governmental actions were kept to a minimum. Tax reform was considered as a single omnibus bill. No separate votes were taken on unpopular aspects of the legislation. The legislation (H.R. 1) was considered under a closed rule in the House of Representatives (H. Res. 619). In the Senate, roll-call votes were taken on only ten amendments, all offered by Democrats.

Finally, coalition leaders made it difficult for constituents to hold legislators accountable for revenue enhancements by gradually phasing them in over years. The TCJA included a provision shifting to the "chained consumer price index" measure of inflation for adjusting tax brackets. This indicator increases more slowly than the Bureau of Labor Statistics' consumer price index, so that tax brackets adjust upward more slowly. According to Joint Committee on Taxation estimates, this change would raise tax revenue by only $800 million in 2018, but in 2027 would yield an additional $31.5 billion.[89] Unlike the TCJA's other changes to the individual code, this change to the adjustment of tax brackets was permanent, not set to expire in 2025. As shown in the right-hand column of Table 9.1, the revenue enhancements in the corporate code tended to exhibit a phase-in structure, as well.

[86] Bernie Becker and Aaron Lorenzo, "The Next Big Bill That Could Be Written in Secret," *Politico*, June 23, 2017.

[87] Aaron Lorenzo and Seung Min Kim, "GOP Tax Bill Shrouded in Secrecy," *Politico*, October 28, 2017.

[88] Richard Rubin, "GOP Plan for a Speedy Tax Overhaul Faces Uncertain Road," *Wall Street Journal*, October 29, 2017.

[89] Joint Committee on Taxation, "Estimated Budget Effects of the Conference Agreement for H.R. 1, the 'Tax Cuts and Jobs Act,'" JCX-67-17, December 18, 2017, www.jct.gov/publications.html?func=startdown&id=5053.

Taken together, coalition leaders employed the full range of procedural maneuvers to make it easier for lawmakers to vote for the revenue enhancements in the TCJA. It is actually rather remarkable that Congress went to such lengths to obscure traceability for the relatively few tax increases embedded in the TCJA. After all, increases were quite modest in size, and they occurred in the context of legislation that reduced taxes overall by $1.5 trillion!

Outcome of the Tax Reform Drive

The TCJA was a significant legislative accomplishment. It reworked corporate taxation wholesale on a permanent basis. In addition, it reduced taxes for individuals for ten years, with especially large tax cuts for businesses incorporated as pass-through entities (such as sole proprietorships and partnerships) previously taxed at individual rates. The TCJA also simplified tax filing for individuals by raising the standard deduction. The TCJA included several other top Republican party priorities. It opened the Arctic National Wildlife Refuge to oil and natural gas drilling. In addition, it abolished the Affordable Care Act's individual mandate. Republicans were clearly elated by their success.

A look back at the coalitional politics of the TCJA shows that coalition leaders had to make many policy adjustments in order to build their majorities. As with the ACA repeal drive, coalition leaders also employed an array of procedural maneuvers to make it easier for members to support the legislation. Considering that nearly the same set of procedural maneuvers were employed during both the tax reform and ACA repeal drives, the divergent outcomes on the two efforts suggest that policy substance likely made the critical difference. While the ACA repeal effort fit Arnold's (1990, 73) concept of the "*politically infeasible policy*" as legislation that "would impose large and direct early-order costs," the TCJA more closely aligns with his concept of the "*politically attractive policy*" as legislation that "delivers perceptible benefits for which legislators can then claim credit" (Arnold, 1990, 75).

What TCJA reveals is that not even politically attractive policies are easy to pass. Even though about 65% of taxpayers would receive a tax cut under the TCJA and only 6% would see an increase,[90] coalition leaders still had to show a lot of policy flexibility and procedural heavy-handedness to build the bicameral majorities necessary.

[90] Tax Policy Center, Urban Institute and Brookings Institution, "T18-0026 – The Tax Cuts and Jobs Act (TCJA): All Provisions and Individual Income Tax Provisions; Tax Units with a Tax Increase or Tax Cut, by Expanded Cash Income Level," February 2018, www.taxpolicycenter.org/model-estimates/individual-income-tax-provisions-tax-cuts-and-jobs-act-tcja-february-2018/t18-0026.

CONTINUITIES IN THE POLITICS OF CONGRESSIONAL COALITION-BUILDING

The major legislative drives of 2017 – Obamacare repeal and tax reform – reveal that the underlying political logic of congressional action has not fundamentally changed. No question, formal legislative processes have changed tremendously since the 1980s. But the task of coalition building itself remains challenging, and leaders employ the same policy and procedural maneuvers used by leaders of earlier eras.

The cases examined here repeatedly show contemporary coalition-builders struggling to come up with adjustments to accommodate recalcitrant members, very much like the coalition leaders of the 1980s. Coalition leaders had to design packages that could attract reelection-minded lawmakers. This meant imposing as few costs as possible on constituents. To even get their ACA repeal drive underway, coalition leaders had to immediately promise to replace many of the benefits constituents were receiving under Obamacare. To move forward on the TCJA, coalition leaders had to drop their proposed border adjustment tax (BAT), their only idea for a substantial source of new revenue.

Once they assembled their packages, coalition leaders then pursued procedural strategies designed to give lawmakers as much distance from any painful policy impacts as possible. They limited traceability by keeping legislative text far from lobbyists' eyes, moving legislation through Congress at top speed, holding few recorded votes, and gradually phasing-in the costs imposed such that years would elapse before their full effect would be felt.

In short, despite the tremendous increases in congressional party cohesion since the 1980s, coalition building remains a very difficult enterprise. If rising partisanship, centralization of power in top leaders, and other transformations of the legislative process had altered the logic of congressional action, changes should have been apparent in the cases examined here. Tax reform and ACA repeal were issues on which most Republicans had campaigned and on which nearly all Republicans agreed, at least in principle. Success on both efforts was widely viewed as central to Republicans' case for retaining their majorities. Using budget reconciliation to circumvent the Senate filibuster, Republicans did not need to win any support from Democrats.

Tracing the history of these legislative drives reveals deep continuities in the challenges congressional coalition builders face and the tools they use to address those challenges. Throughout each of these legislative drives there was uncertainty about coalition leaders' eventual success. In the process, they had to scale back their ambitions. In the case of the ACA, scaling back eventually resulted in Senate leaders' comically weak "skinny repeal" proposal that would not have repealed any of the ACA's major provisions. In the case of the TCJA, coalition leaders were never able to identify sufficient new revenue sources to offset their rate reductions. Under Budget Act rules they were thus unable to accomplish the permanent tax reforms they sought. Most of the tax expenditures coalition leaders considered for elimination were dropped over the course of the debate. The sum total of tax expenditures in the code increased slightly.

Members were clearly reluctant to court electoral risk by running afoul of their constituents' interests and policy preferences. In other chapters, this volume reveals that members are right to worry. Clinton, Sances, and Sullivan, in Chapter 2, show that constituents still consider more than just their member's party and evaluate their representatives' issue stances. Likewise, Canes-Wrone and Kistner, in Chapter 6, point to the continued, albeit attenuated, capacity for local news to hold incumbents accountable for their positions. Even if issue-based accountability is diminished relative to the past, contemporary members anticipate the need to defend their positions to constituents.

Finally, coalition leaders' enormous difficulty inducing members to support benefit cuts or impose costs underscores that Congress as an institution remains acutely sensitive to preference intensity. Coalition leaders backed down repeatedly during these legislative drives, even from relatively modest benefit cuts. They also employed every available technique to limit constituents' ability to perceive members' responsibility for any unpopular policy changes. Even so, leaders struggled to build majorities and failed altogether on one of the party's top priority agenda items. On the one hand, these sensitivities testify to Congress's capacities as a representative assembly. On the other hand, they raise serious questions about the institution's ability to tackle policy problems involving difficult trade-offs, particularly under conditions where one party would bear undiluted responsibility.

10

Fire Alarms and Democratic Accountability

Charles M. Cameron and Sanford C. Gordon

A pernicious obstacle to electoral accountability is the problem of asymmetric information: how many voters have the knowledge to assess whether a given action by an incumbent actually improved their welfare, all things considered? A lack of transparency about actions and the obscurity between means and ends can further render nominal accountability moot in practice.

In the face of prohibitive information costs, a simple intuition is the following: *mechanisms that lower informational costs for voters ought to enhance electoral accountability.* Unfortunately, recent theoretical advances show that this intuition can be wrong. For example, when politicians' actions are readily observable but their consequences delayed or obscure, politicians may have incentives to "pander" – that is, to take popular actions even when they know the ultimate consequences may prove ineffectual or even harmful to voters (Canes-Wrone, Herron, and Shotts, 2001; Maskin and Tirole, 2004; Fox and Van Weelden, 2012). Some opacity concerning a politician's actions, accordingly, may actually improve the lot of voters.

Nonetheless, the sense remains strong that if voters had access to mechanisms that lower their information costs – at least for the "right" kind of information – then democratic accountability might be enhanced, to the benefit of voters. What might those mechanisms be?

One important cost-lowering mechanism is *fire alarms*. In the context of accountability between an agent and a principal, a "fire alarm" connotes a readily perceived, reliable notice about bad agent performance that – critically – comes free or nearly free to the principal herself. In an electoral setting, a fire alarm consists of such a notice to voters about the performance of an incumbent. Might fire alarms snatch electoral accountability from the jaws of information costs? That is our subject in this chapter.

The idea of fire alarms gained currency from a celebrated analysis of congressional oversight of the bureaucracy (McCubbins and Schwartz, 1984).

McCubbins and Schwartz note that administrative procedures provide opportunities for private interests to relay information to Congress about bureaucratic noncompliance with legislative preferences. Relying on third parties – whom we will refer to generically as *sentinels* – is more efficient for Congress, they argue, than undertaking costly, active "police patrol" oversight. Moreover, anticipation of the fire alarm may deter bureaucratic deviation from congressional desires. It seems plausible, then, that accountability can prevail so long as some actor has incentives to bear the informational costs for the principal.

But what happens when the sentinel is biased? Prendergast's (2003) game-theoretic analysis of service-providing bureaucracies analyzes a strategic situation closely related to the one discussed by McCubbins and Schwartz, but in which the sentinel is not neutral in the signals it sends to a bureaucrat's political bosses. A bureaucrat's client only complains when a service or benefit is wrongly denied but not when one is wrongly granted. Prendergast explores how this asymmetry affects the behavior of bureaucrats, and how their political principals may respond. More generally, Patty (Chapter 11, this volume) notes that fire alarm oversight might amplify the influence of biased interests.

Political scientists have explored the logic of fire-alarm oversight in other settings. A notable one is Supreme Court oversight of decisions in the US Courts of Appeals. Cross and Tiller (1998), for example, note that a dissenting vote on an appeals panel can serve as a fire alarm for the higher court. But Beim, Hirsch, and Kastellec (2014) note that sentinels with extreme preferences may sound alarms too frequently and be ignored as a consequence.

The logic of fire alarm oversight would seem to extend naturally to an electoral context. Here, the seminal analysis was offered by Arnold (1993), who noted that fire alarms arise in the principal-agent relationship between voters and elected officials. He argued that political activists may have, and electoral challengers certainly do have, strong incentives to sound an alarm in the event of legislative malfeasance or error. It is the threat of fire alarms, in this view, that might motivate compliance with the preferences of inattentive citizens.

As in the bureaucratic and judicial examples, careful attention to sentinels' incentives is essential in mapping out the promise and perils of fire alarms for democratic accountability. We aim to open this black box.[1] We show that the consequences of electoral fire alarms for voters depend critically on four factors: (1) whether information provided by sentinels is verifiable (at sufficiently low cost) to voters; (2) the *relative* rates at which different policy choices generate verifiable information about their consequences; (3) whether the sentinel is *neutral* (and passes along all available information); a *challenger* (who simply wants to publicize bad news for the incumbent) or an *interested party* (who wants to publicize favorable news when it concerns a favored policy,

---

[1] A related examination appears in Ashworth and Shotts (2011). Gordon and Huber (2007) contains an informal theoretical discussion of the challenger as fire alarm.

and bad news when it concerns a hated one); and (4) whether incumbents can offset bad news via credit-claiming. We then offer an application of some of the insights from our analysis to the politics of criminal justice.

SENTINELS AND THE THEORY OF POLITICAL AGENCY

The Voter and the Official

Our analysis of sentinels in the next section draws heavily on recent theoretical advances in the theory of political agency (see Ashworth, 2012 and Gailmard, 2014 for a review), which have tended to abstract away from the multiplicity of legislators, focusing instead on the relationship between a single elected official (the incumbent) and an electorate (often abstractly signified by a single, representative voter) that must decide periodically whether to retain her. The point of this stark abstraction is not to deny the importance of the institutional and behavioral richness of legislatures, but rather to hold fixed one set of relationships in the political environment in order to focus on and gain insight about another.

In the starkest models coming out of this tradition, there are just two players: the incumbent official and the (representative) voter. (A third player, the challenger, is often treated as a passive alternative.) Below, we will consider situations in which challengers are active players in their own right. An archetypal game consists of two periods: in the first, an incumbent takes some action, which has some consequences for the voter; then, the voter may observe something – perhaps the action, perhaps the consequences (which one, as we will see, matters *a lot*) – and decides whether to retain the incumbent or replace her with a challenger. In the second period, the incumbent (or her replacement) again takes an action. This simple approach introduces a motivation for voters to prefer candidates they anticipate will act on their behalf after the election.[2] The elected official cares about holding office (for intrinsic or instrumental reasons). Voters casts ballots based on what they observe in the first period, but with an eye toward what will happen (or is likely to happen) in the second.[3]

The vast majority of recent research in this tradition takes the heterogeneity of politicians as a starting point. In this view, elections are an institutional mechanism for differentiating "bad types" of politicians from good ones; the politician's actions (if observed) or their consequences (if observed) may provide useful information that facilitate the selection mechanism. What makes an official "good" or "bad" depends on the context. For example, a good politician may be one with preferences or values that are *congruent* with those

---

[2] Many models "roll up" second period behavior and payoffs into first period payoffs and dispense with an explicit second period – our approach below.

[3] See Patashnik et al. (Chapter 3, this volume) for a discussion of potential biases in how voters evaluate information about incumbent performance.

TABLE 10.1 *Archetypal informational environments in the political theory of agency*

Actions	Outcomes/Consequences	
	Observable	Not Observable
Observable	Full Transparency (FT)	Non-Transparent Consequences (NC)
Not Observable	Non-Transparent Actions (NA)	No Transparency (NT)

of the voters (e.g., Morelli and Weelden, 2013; Wolton, 2019; Snyder and Ting, 2003). Is an official the sort of person who would faithfully represent voter interests in office *even in the absence of electoral pressures to do so?* As Bawn et. al. note in Chapter 5 in this volume, sussing this out is a fundamental concern of organized interests weighing in on candidate selection in congressional elections.

Good or bad could could also denote the politician's skill or expertise – does the official know what she's doing? Here, accountability models often employ a convenient device: state-contingent preferences with private signals. In this approach, which we employ below, the voter wants the official to take an action appropriate to an imperfectly observed state of the world. A good example is counterterrorism: the policies we want our leaders to adopt in this area are highly contingent on whether the threat of a terror attack is imminent.

If politicians want to be reelected, then they will want to be perceived by the voters as good types. Whether this leads those politicians to take actions that further voter interests requires us to consider what the voter can observe about an incumbent, and what inferences she can draw on the basis of what she has observed. An important distinction is between *actions* and *consequences*. Table 10.1 displays a two-by-two contingency table arraying actions (observed or not observed) and consequences (observed or not observed). The result is four archetypal information environments. These are named following a taxonomy due to Fox and Van Weelden (2012) (which resembles a similar one from Wilson, 1989).

Under full transparency (FT), the voter can see both the incumbent's actions and the resulting consequences. This situation would seem most favorable for the voter, both in terms of selecting good types and inducing the incumbent to act in the voter's best interests. However, when actions translate into outcomes probabilistically, voters may still face a tricky inference problem – perhaps the official took an action that gave the best chances for the outcome preferred by the voter, but things went south by chance.

At the opposite extreme, under no transparency (NT) the voter can see neither actions nor consequences. Clearly, this is the situation most ripe for incentive and selection problems. As a practical matter, this environment is probably the most relevant baseline for most voters most of the time with respect to most policy making.

An interesting environment is non-transparent action (NA) where the voter can observe outcomes but not actions. In our example, suppose the voter observes no terror attack. Was this because a secret counterterrorism operation was successful, or because there was no imminent threat to begin with? The NA case is applicable to retrospective voting with respect to economic performance: many factors affect unemployment, inflation, growth, and trade, perhaps more strongly than most actions a president can take. But if the economy is somewhat more likely to do better when the president takes the right actions and somewhat more likely to do worse when he takes the wrong ones, rewarding the president for strong economy's performance may be sensible on the part of the voter if it bodes well for future performance.

Another well-studied environment is non-transparent consequences (NC). Here, the voter can observe the politician's action but not the consequences of the action (at least in time for the election). This situation can lead to pandering, in which the politician takes a visible, popular action even though the politician may know full well that it isn't the smart choice (Canes-Wrone, Herron, and Shotts, 2001; Maskin and Tirole, 2004). Suppose, for example, an incumbent knows an attack is not imminent, but voters believe it is. That politician may implement costly but unnecessary policies to cater to the public's fear.

Sentinels as Third-Party Information Providers

A sentinel is a player who sees and reports (1) the politician's action, (2) the consequences of her action, or (3) the state of the world (when there are state-contingent preferences) at the time the incumbent took her action. A truthful report about these matters, if believed, has the effect of *moving the voter from one information environment to another*. So, using Table 10.1, a believable report about the official's action may shift the voter from NT to NC (e.g., "The President raised tariffs" or "The President abused his power"), for instance.

We consider how the introduction of a sentinel might affect accountability under different circumstances, and then evaluate the consequences for voter welfare. But before doing that, we need to answer two preliminary questions: what incentives motivate different sentinels to make reports, and what factors make sentinel reports credible for the voter? To get traction here, we distinguish three kinds of sentinels: *neutral conduits*, *interested parties* (or *activists*), and *challengers*.

A neutral conduit provides a handy analytic benchmark. Such a sentinel simply would report all available information it has at its disposal and cover up nothing. And it is disinterested – it has no stake in the information itself or what the voter does with it. Neutral conduits approximate one ideal for the press, and for scientific experts. A strong intuition is that neutral conduits, if they exist, will be very valuable to the voter.

In contrast, an interested party or activist has a definite stake in a particular policy that it may hold *irrespective of the actual state of the world*, and potentially even irrespective of the identity of the incumbent officeholder. Suppose, for example, that the voter has state contingent preferences about infrastructure expenditures: "If our national infrastructure is run down, then I favor a big infrastructure plan even if taxes have to go up. But if our national infrastructure is in basically decent shape, then I favor no plan and low taxes." Whereas a neutral conduit would relay any available information to the voter about the state of the world, a concrete manufacturer or association of civil engineers, favoring large infrastructure investments irrespective of the actual state of the world might not. Rather, we would anticipate that these parties will seldom pass on good news about the state of infrastructure if it might result in a smaller government investment. The civil engineers' trade association will always give our bridges, roads, and airports a failing grade (e.g., Society for Civil Engineers, 2017). This means that silence from an interested party may actually connote good news, and that announcements of the failing state of infrastructure should be taken with a hefty grain of salt unless accompanied by *hard information* that the voter can independently verify (Milgrom, 2008).

Challengers are distinct from both neutral conduits and interested parties. The key feature for challengers is that they are in conflict with the incumbent: only one of the two contenders can win the election. Therefore, any information that hurts (helps) the incumbent is good (bad) for the challenger. Consider the infrastructure example again, and assume that reports from the challenger are nearly costlessly verifiable. Suppose the incumbent has correctly matched the state, supporting the infrastructure plan if it was needed and opposing it if it was not. The challenger will not want to point this out to voters, as doing so will make the incumbent look skillful. The challenger will therefore remain silent. However, if the incumbent failed to correctly match the state, the challenger will delight in pointing out the incumbent's blunder and apparent incompetence. The challenger's motives are distinct from those of the interested party or activist because challengers are happy to make any report about the state of world, so long as it hurts the incumbent; and stay silent, regardless of the information available to them, when that information would help the incumbent.

A MODEL

Preliminaries

To explore how the introduction of a sentinel can affect democratic performance, we describe a highly stylized model with state contingent preferences and hidden information of varying kinds. We begin with two players, an incumbent (she) and a voter (they), and then add a third: the sentinel (he).

There is a state of the world, ω, which can take on values of 0 or 1. Both states are equally likely, and this is common knowledge. An incumbent can be described by her "type," t_i, which can be either low (L) or high (H). The incumbent initially knows her own type, but the voter has some uncertainty about the incumbent. Specifically, from the voter's perspective at the beginning of the game, the prior probability the incumbent is type H is given by α_i, and the probability that the incumbent is type L is $1 - \alpha_i$. The voter has a corresponding belief about the challenger's type, α_c. Both α_i and α_c lie between zero and one.

The incumbent receives a signal θ about the state of the world, which can take on values of either 0 or 1. The signal is correlated with the state of the world ω, but the quality of the signal depends on the incumbent's type. Specifically, high-type incumbents receive perfect signals about the state of the world ($\Pr(\theta = \omega | t_i = H) = 1$). In other words, if the state of the world is 1, a high-quality incumbent will know it's 1 for sure; if 0, she will know it's 0. Low-type incumbents, by contrast, receive imperfect signals. Specifically, their signals are correct with probability q (i.e., $\Pr(\theta = 1 | \omega = 1, t_i = L) = \Pr(\theta = 0 | \omega = 0, t_i = L) = q$), where q lies between $\frac{1}{2}$ and 1. We will often refer to q as the *quality* of the low-type incumbent's signal.

The incumbent must take a policy action $a \in \{0, 1\}$. In other words, she must choose between two policy actions, though one can interpret $a = 0$ as "do nothing" or "retain the status quo." The incumbent's action translates into consequences for voters in a simple way: if the incumbent's action matches the state, then the result is good for the voters. But if the incumbent fails to state-match, the result is bad for the voters. These payoffs are encapsulated in the following utility function:

$$u_v(a, \omega) = \begin{cases} 1 \text{ if } a = \omega \\ 0 \text{ otherwise.} \end{cases}$$

In the interest of simplicity, let $\tilde{\alpha}_i(\mathcal{I})$ denote the posterior probability the voter assigns to the incumbent being high quality given information $\mathcal{I}$. We assume the probability the voter retains the incumbent is equal to $F(\tilde{\alpha}_i(\mathcal{I}) - \alpha_c)$, where $F(\cdot)$ is a strictly increasing function on the closed interval between zero and one, with $F(-\alpha_c) = 0$ and $F(1 - \alpha_c) = 1$. This formulation is intended to capture the idea that if the voters know for certain that the incumbent is low (high) quality, they will definitely elect the challenger (incumbent). Given lingering uncertainty, the incumbent benefits from voters' positive impressions of her quality, but other (stochastic) features of the political environment, as well as her impression of the challenger, may also affect the ultimate selection. The key element in this formulation is the voter's posterior beliefs about the incumbent, which we assume are arrived at via Bayes' Rule wherever possible given available information.

We assume the incumbent wishes to maximize the probability she retains office. So, the incumbent (or her ally) will seek to maximize $\tilde{\alpha}_i(\mathcal{I})$, whereas an opponent (possibly a challenger, but also potentially a non-aligned media outlet) will seek to minimize it. The zero-sum nature of the competition between the incumbent and the challenger is a key point.

In the absence of a sentinel, the incumbent faces an essentially decision-theoretic problem, though one strongly shaped by the voter's rational updating of beliefs. The addition of a sentinel then creates a game between him and the incumbent.

As discussed above, both incentive/sanctioning effects and politician selection effects are critical components of a theory of democratic accountability. Our model allows us to study both. A critical question we ask is the following: *can "virtuous behavior" by the incumbent benefiting the voter be sustained in equilibrium?*[4] In the context of our model, an incumbent who behaves virtuously is simply one who follows her signal – doing so maximizes the voter's *ex ante* expected welfare for the period, irrespective of the incumbent's type.

Another critical component in the theory of democratic accountability concerns how much voters learn about the incumbent's quality, thus permitting them to make more informed choices at election time. So the issue is, in equilibrium do voters learn much about the incumbent's type? While our simple model has only one period, the probabilistic vote function effectively captures a more complicated, multi-period model in which voters enjoy downstream benefits from having a high-type incumbent in office. These benefits are more likely to accrue to voters, *ceteris paribus*, when they have better information about the incumbent's type, as it will permit them to make fewer errors in determining whether the incumbent or challenger is the better choice.

We now turn to the four information environments from Table 10.1 *in the absence of a sentinel.*

NT (NO TRANSPARENCY). If the voter can observe neither the incumbent's action a nor whether it was correct (i.e., whether $a = \omega$), there is nothing that the incumbent can do to alter the voter's beliefs. The voter will then reelect with probability $F(\alpha_i - \alpha_c)$. Note that because the incumbent's electoral fortunes are unaffected by her policy choice, any policy choice in any incumbent information set is an equilibrium. Of course, this includes "doing the right thing" by following the signal. We can easily break this indifference by giving the incumbent some infinitesimal benefit from pursuing the voter's interests. In that case, behaving virtuously is the unique equilibrium. But voters still won't learn about the incumbent's type from that behavior.

NC (NON-TRANSPARENT CONSEQUENCES). This is almost as simple as the NT baseline. Suppose that in equilibrium, both low- and high-quality incumbents behave virtuously. Because we have deliberately set up the model so that both states of the world are equally likely, and so that the accuracy of the incumbent's information is independent of the state, the voter will be just as likely to observe $a = 0$ as $a = 1$. Hence, the policy will provide no new information about the incumbent's type. And given this, the incumbent has no incentive to deviate

---

4 This does not necessarily imply or require that virtuous behavior be the unique equilibrium.

TABLE 10.2 *Summary of baseline cases absent a sentinel*

Actions	Outcomes/Consequences	
	Observable	Not Observable
Observable	FT: virtuous equilibrium unique, some updating	NC: virtuous equilibrium possible, no updating
Not Observable	NA: virtuous equilibrium unique, some updating	NT: virtuous equilibrium possible, no updating

from virtuous behavior – just like in the case in which the voter observes neither the policy action nor the outcome.[5]

NA (NON-TRANSPARENT ACTIONS). In this informational environment, the voter learns whether the incumbent was right or wrong in their policy choice, even though she cannot observe incumbent actions. Now suppose both types of incumbent behave virtuously. High-quality incumbents will always choose the correct policy, and low-quality incumbents will choose the correct policy more often than not. The voter, upon learning that the wrong policy was chosen, will know with certainty that the incumbent is low quality ($\tilde{\alpha}_i(a \neq \omega) = 0$), thus decreasing the probability the incumbent is retained. If, by contrast, the voter learns that the correct policy was chosen, then the voter will know that it was chosen either by the high-quality incumbent or by a low-quality incumbent who received a signal that turned out to be correct. The voter's posterior belief on the incumbent will then (by Bayes' Rule) be equal to, $\tilde{\alpha}_i(a = \omega) = \frac{\alpha_i}{\alpha_i+(1-\alpha_i)q}$, which is strictly greater than α_i, thus increasing the probability the incumbent is retained. Given the foregoing, the low-quality incumbent has every incentive to get the policy right.

FT (FULL TRANSPARENCY). Given the setup of the model, the logic is identical to the previous case.

We summarize the no-sentinel baselines in Table 10.2, which mirrors Table 10.1. It is worth noting, in terms of motivating virtuous actions, our simplifying assumptions bias the model in favor of the incumbent doing right by the voter. This allows a clear baseline from which to consider whether the strategic game between the incumbent and the sentinel actually improves voter welfare.

Introducing the Sentinel

Our sentinel-free analysis demonstrates how access to verifiable information about the outcome can enhance accountability, both by strengthening the incentives for the incumbent to behave virtuously, and by enhancing the ability

---

[5] Note that this virtuous behavior is sustainable because of our deliberate choice to make both states of the world equally likely, eliminating an incentive to pander.

of voters to select good types. We also see the limitations of informational environments in which the voter can observe the incumbent's action but not the consequences of the choice.

With these considerations in mind, consider the following permutation of the model. Suppose we are in a world in which absent any fire alarm, the voter observes neither the policy nor the outcome (the NT environment). A third party, whom we call the sentinel, s, receives some information that he may pass on to the voter. Specifically, if the incumbent chooses policy action $a = 1$, the sentinel receives evidence that the policy was either right (if $\omega = 1$) or wrong (if $\omega = 0$) with probability π_1; with probability $1 - \pi_1$, the sentinel receives no such information. Likewise, if the incumbent chooses policy action $a = 0$, the sentinel receives evidence that the policy was either right or wrong with probability π_0, and with probability $1 - \pi_0$ receives no such information. Note that π_1 need not equal π_0.[6]

There are now several things to consider. First, consider the sentinel's preferences (neutral party, challenger, or interested party), as discussed above. Obviously, in a world of self-interested political actors, we would have strong reason to believe that the sentinel is unlikely to be a neutral conduit. Nonetheless, as noted above, a neutral and honest sentinel is a useful benchmark against which to compare the challenger and interested-party sentinels.

Next, consider the nature of the evidence the sentinel may pass on to the voter. Two extreme cases are the following:

- The information may be *cheap talk*, in the sense that there is nothing to validate the veracity of the information other than the voter's belief that the sender is being honest; or
- the information may be *hard*, in the sense that it will be taken as fact by a voter presented with it. (For example, the message may be costlessly verifiable or falsifiable.)

Of course, many other kinds of evidence are possible. Information may be verifiable at cost, or verifiable at cost with some probability, for example. To convey the intuition as expeditiously as possible, we will consider only the more stark examples above.

The Cheap Talk Fire Alarm

Our first step in demonstrating the contingency of the purported democracy-enhancing properties of fire alarms is to consider them when evidence is cheap talk. For informative communication between the sentinel and the voter to be possible, the latter must take the former's word as given.

---

[6] This setup resembles the "asymmetric resolution" extension explored by Canes-Wrone, Herron, and Shotts (2001). For a discussion of the political implications of asymmetric resolution for coalition politics, see Lee (Chapter 9, this volume). For a related discussion concerning incumbent evaluation rules, see Egan and Prior (Chapter 4, this volume).

NEUTRAL SENTINELS WITH CHEAP TALK.   By construction, this actor is the perfect agent for the voter. An equilibrium exists in which the sentinel neutrally and honestly conveys information to the voter (when he has it) and the voter believes the sentinel and acts accordingly.

Moreover, consider the incentive effects of the neutral sentinel on the reelection-minded incumbent. Recall that high-quality incumbents can always choose the policy that is correct from the voter's perspective. Suppose she does so. Then the sentinel will either have good news to pass on to the voter (the policy was correct), or no news. By contrast, the low-quality incumbent may err, generating bad news that the sentinel will dutifully, and credibly, pass on. Bad news perfectly reveals that the incumbent is a low-type. Clearly, then, low-quality incumbents have an incentive to minimize the probability of bad news. They do this by behaving virtuously.

If we understand "fire alarms" to be signals purporting malfeasance (bad news), then in the presence of a neutral sentinel, there is an equilibrium in which cheap talk fire alarms (1) are taken seriously by voters; (2) strengthen the incentives of the incumbent to behave virtuously; and (3) help voters make more informed choices come election time. Note that this intuition would be preserved even if the only evidence available to the neutral sentinel were evidence of bad news – that is, the original conception of fire alarms. Incumbents would still be motivated to minimize the probability of bad news, which they accomplish by behaving virtuously. This situation seems to confirm Arnold's optimism about fire alarms in an electoral context.

CHALLENGER SENTINELS WITH CHEAP TALK.   Of course, in politics, neutral conduits may be hard to come by. As noted previously, the sentinel is much more likely to be a self-interested actor like a challenger or activist, whose interests may not perfectly align with those of the voter. It turns out that if talk is cheap, there exists *no informative equilibrium* in which the voter takes statements by the sentinel as credible.

It's easy to see why. If the sentinel is a challenger, his objective is to damage the incumbent's reputation. Now suppose, again, that high-quality incumbents always choose the policy that matches the state of the world. Irrespective of the information actually received by the sentinel, he will always have an incentive to try to convince the voter that he received information about incumbent performance and that it was bad – that is, that the policy chosen did not match the state. But because this motivation persists regardless of the truth, the voter *will learn nothing* from his utterances. Not all is lost, however: the incumbent will still weakly prefer to pursue the policy expected to most benefit the voter, just as she did in the case with no sentinel.

INTERESTED-PARTY SENTINELS WITH CHEAP TALK.   Sometimes the sentinel is an activist or advocacy group. Are things better when the sentinel is an interested party? Not really. Unlike the voter (and the challenger), the activist does not care about the occupant of the office, and is happy as long as a favored policy is pursued. Consequently, there exists no equilibrium in which his utterances are informative: no matter the state, he always has an incentive to talk up the favored policy or bash the disfavored one. But again, the incumbent will continue to at least weakly prefer to do right by the voter.

The upshot of the foregoing is that if information is cheap talk, the possibility that fire alarms will improve the voter's lot compared to a counterfactual world with no fire alarms is contingent on very strong (and probably unrealistic) assumptions about the preferences of the sentinel pulling the alarm.

Fire Alarms with Hard Evidence

We now suppose information is hard rather than cheap talk. In other words, we consider a setting in which, if the sentinel has "good" or "bad" news to transmit and does so that voters will accept it at face value. But of course, the sentinel is not required to share news, so we will also need to consider what voters will believe if they receive *no* news. No news admits two possibilities: either the sentinel had no information to transmit; or, the sentinel had information but suppressed it.

NEUTRAL SENTINELS WITH HARD INFORMATION.   In this stark informational environment, consider first the neutral-conduit sentinel. Moving from a cheap talk to hard information environment does not change the sentinel's incentives: he will still report information available to him, and now, the evidence will be even firmer than it was in a situation where it was already accepted at face value. Voters will have access to all available information, facilitating their goal of selecting the best available officeholder. And incumbents, for their part, will have strong incentives to behave virtuously, as doing so maximizes their probability of reelection.

CHALLENGER SENTINELS WITH HARD INFORMATION.   In a world where high-quality incumbents always choose the correct policy, the challenger has a clear incentive to report all bad news regarding the incumbent's choice to the voter, because the voter will infer from verifiable bad news that the incumbent is a low type, thus enhancing the challenger's electoral prospects. Just as bad news undermines the incumbent's reputation in the eyes of the voter, so too does good news enhance it; hence, the challenger will suppress any good news he has at his disposal. High-type incumbents will clearly prefer selecting the correct policy: doing so guarantees that no news will be conveyed to the voter, whereas deviating and choosing the wrong policy will result in a lottery between the electoral consequences of no news and bad news. No news is better.

But now consider the problem from the perspective of the *low*-quality incumbent: she has an incentive to minimize the likelihood of bad news. But given the special incentives of the challenger, this may mean *departing* from virtuous behavior, at least under some conditions.

Specifically, suppose $\pi_1 > \pi_0$, so that the challenger is more likely to receive hard information to pass on to voters when the incumbent has chosen $a = 1$ (depart from the status quo) than when she has chosen $a = 0$ (maintain the status quo). If the incumbent is a low type, and receives a signal of $\theta = 0$, she has two reasons to follow her signal and choose the corresponding action of $a = 0$, to the benefit of the voter: the choice is more likely to be correct, and if it is incorrect, it is less likely to yield bad evidence for the challenger to transmit to voters.

If the incumbent is low quality and receives a signal of $\theta = 1$, however, she faces a trade-off given the threat of the fire alarm: if she chooses $a = 1$, she is more likely to be correct, but if she is incorrect, the challenger will "have the goods" on her with relatively high probability. If, on the other hand, she chooses $a = 0$, she is less likely to be correct, but if she chose incorrectly, it is less likely that the challenger will actually receive the bad news to pass on to the voters. It turns out that given a signal $\theta = 1$, the low-quality incumbent will take the non-virtuous action that *hurts* the voter in expectation ($a = 0$) if and only if

$$\frac{\pi_1}{\pi_0} > \frac{q}{1 - q}.$$

In other words, if the risk of bad news associated with choosing the policy that is correct in expectation is sufficiently great relative to the low-quality incumbent's expertise, the low-quality incumbent will choose the policy more likely to be *wrong*.

The upshot of the foregoing analysis is that the presence of the sentinel may distort the incentives of some (low-type) incumbents relative to a world with no sentinel. Note, however, that the effect of the sentinel's presence on the voter's overall well-being is ambiguous. This is because relative to the baseline with no sentinel, voters can update their beliefs about the incumbent's type: those beliefs will be revised downward (to zero, in fact) given the provision of bad news; and they will be revised upward given the provision of no news. Hence, our partially-informed voter is more likely to get a high-type incumbent in office after the election than she would have been in the absence of the challenger sentinel. The incentive and selection effects from the presence of a challenger sentinel are in tension, making overall welfare effects ambiguous.

INTERESTED-PARTY SENTINELS WITH HARD INFORMATION. Next, suppose the sentinel is an interested party – say an activist or advocacy group – and in particular, one who cares only that the incumbent selects the policy action $a = 0$, irrespective of the state of the world. The group is indifferent with respect to the occupant of the office, and can craft a fire alarm strategy that maximizes the incumbent's incentive to choose $a = 0$, even when she receives the signal suggesting she ought to take the opposite course ($\theta = 1$). That strategy is to report available good news if and only if the incumbent turns out to have correctly chosen the action $a = 0$; and report available bad news if and only if the incumbent turns out to have incorrectly chosen $a = 1$. Given this sentinel strategy, a high-quality incumbent who always follows her signal need never fear bad news – from her perspective, no news is the worst possible outcome. And so, the voter could again infer from bad news that the incumbent was low quality with certainty.

Now consider the game from the perspective of the low-quality incumbent. She will, of course, prefer to follow her signal given $\theta = 0$ – doing so maximizes the odds that the voter will receive good news about her performance. The interesting question concerns what she will do when $\theta = 1$, which could place her at odds with the interested-party sentinel. Suppose she behaved virtuously in that circumstance and chose $a = 1$. Then with probability $(1 - q)\pi_1$, she would be wrong, and the advocacy group would learn about it and publicize the bad news to the voter, driving the incumbent's reputation $\tilde{a}_i$ down to zero. With complementary probability $(1-(1-q)\pi_1)$, the voter would receive no news. But recall that from the voter's perspective, receiving no news is also consistent with the incumbent being high quality. Clearly, the low-quality incumbent would prefer no news to bad news.

Given this preference, the low-quality incumbent can improve her lot by deviating from virtuous behavior by choosing policy $a = 0$ when her signal is $\theta = 1$. With probability $(1 - q)\pi_0$, this was actually the right move and the advocacy group will have good news to convey to the voter about the incumbent's correct choice. With complementary probability, there will either be no news to report, or bad news that the interested-party sentinel will suppress – hence, no news from the perspective of the voter. But a lottery between good news and no news is clearly better from the low-quality incumbent's perspective than a lottery between bad news and no news. Hence, virtuous behavior by the low-quality incumbent given $\theta = 1$ cannot be part of an equilibrium. Given reasonable restrictions on beliefs off the path of play (namely, if we assume the voter will infer the incumbent is low quality given bad news), we can establish the converse: the low-quality incumbent's disregarding the signal $\theta = 1$ *is* consistent with equilibrium play. As in the case of the challenger sentinel, the activist sentinel induces incumbents sometimes to do the wrong thing from the voter's perspective. Note that unlike in the case of the challenger sentinel, this will be the case irrespective of the underlying parameters.

Despite the bias in reporting from an interested-party sentinel, voters will, on occasion, have access to hard information about the incumbent's performance (although, in equilibrium, the voter will never receive any bad news due to the distortion in the low-quality incumbent's behavior). Accordingly, the voter's selection problem will be mitigated relative to a baseline in which the voter has no access to information about policy or performance. As in the case with the challenger sentinel, however, there is again a trade-off from the voter's perspective between the selection benefits and the incentives for some incumbents to do the wrong thing, some of the time.

Can Incumbent Credit-Claiming Mitigate Biased Fire Alarms?

A natural question to ask is whether extending the model to permit the incumbent to transmit good news to the voter about their performance (e.g., Mayhew, 1974) might mitigate some of the distortions associated with biased sentinels that we described in the previous section. We restrict our attention in this section to the hard information environment (there can be no credible communication between incumbent and voter if talk is cheap), and assume for simplicity that if there is information to pass on to the voters, it will be in the possession of both the incumbent and the sentinel. To the extent that "the truth will out" given a neutral sentinel, the information conveyed to the voter via credit-claiming will be redundant. Accordingly we would anticipate no changes to the welfare of the voter – either through the selection or incentive channels – given the presence of a credit-claiming incumbent and neutral sentinel.

Consider, next, the case of the challenger sentinel. Recall that the challenger transmits information to the voter if and only if it is bad news for the incumbent. By the same logic, the incumbent will only transmit information to the voter if it is good news. So with the addition of a credit-claiming incumbent and a detractor challenger, *all available evidence will ultimately be passed on to the voter*: good news by the incumbent, and bad news by the challenger. But then, from the perspective of the voter, we are in a rosy world equivalent to one with the neutral sentinel.

The question of whether credit-claiming by the incumbent can mitigate the biased information coming from an interested-party sentinel is more subtle. To be sure, when we allow for credit-claiming with hard information, more information can potentially reach the voter. Specifically, suppose a low-type incumbent were to choose the policy disfavored by an activist. In the absence of credit-claiming, the voter would only observe no news or bad news. Add a credit-claiming incumbent and now good news is also a possibility. More information will be revealed than before, and the downside electoral risk of crossing the interested-party sentinel will be muted.

Suppose, by contrast, the incumbent chooses the policy the activist wants despite receiving the signal suggesting the contrary action. Now, both the incumbent and the activist have a mutual interest in suppressing any bad news about that policy. Implicitly, the incumbent colludes with the interested party against the voters.

The downside risk of bad news to the low-quality incumbent may thus continue to motivate her to insure against its adverse consequences by selecting the policy favored by the interested-party sentinel, even if she believes it is the wrong policy. However, this downside risk is offset to some extent by the potential upside: credit-claiming if she chooses the policy the advocacy group dislikes and it turns out to have been the right choice ("standing up to the special interests").

Given the foregoing analysis, introducing hard information credit-claiming doesn't bring us quite back to a situation equivalent to that of the neutral sentinel, as it did in the case of the challenger sentinel. In supplementary analysis (see Appendix), we demonstrate the existence of conditions under which virtuous behavior cannot be sustained in equilibrium, even given the

TABLE 10.3 *The conditional effects of third-party sentinels on democratic accountability*

	Cheap Talk		Hard Information		Hard Info + CC	
Sentinel Type	Revelation	Distortion	Revelation	Distortion	Revelation	Distortion
Neutral	Full	None	Full	None	Full	None
Challenger	None	None	Partial	Sometimes	Full	None
Interested Party	None	None	Partial	Always	Partial	Sometimes

Credit-claiming abbreviated as CC. Full revelation means full revelation of available evidence.

otherwise ameliorating effects of credit-claiming. In other words, the distorting effects of a biased sentinel cannot be fully eliminated when the sentinel is an interested party.

Summary

Table 10.3 summarizes the implications of our simple model. With respect to electoral selection, introducing a sentinel cannot hurt (no revelation), and may possibly help (partial or full revelation) a voter distinguish high- and low-quality candidates for office. Some sentinels will strategically withhold information in pursuit of their own interests, but voters can adjust for this if they understand the sentinel's motives. This serves as a partial confirmation of the conventional understanding of fire alarms as beneficial to a principal in principal-agent relationships.

Regarding the incentive component of democratic accountability, however, our conclusions are less sanguine. Whereas the presence of sentinels won't distort the incentives of the incumbent if sentinel communications are cheap talk, the presence of a sentinel may indeed distort incentives when sentinels can present hard information to voters. Distortions take the form of an incumbent choosing a policy not because it is best *ex ante*, but because it minimizes the probability of bad headlines. Allowing the incumbent a channel to publicize her positive accomplishments (using hard information) can eliminate the distortion when the sentinel is a challenger, but not necessarily if he is an interested party.

EXAMPLE: THE INFORMATIONAL ENVIRONMENT OF CRIMINAL JUSTICE POLICY

In this section, we argue that a change in the information available to a sentinel – the media – helped drive a change in the political incentives involving criminal justice policy in the early twenty-first century.[7] While we did not

[7] For discussions of the media and political incentives, see, especially, the review essay by Huber and Tucker (Chapter 8) and the analysis of media congruence and democratic accountability of Canes-Wrone and Kistner (Chapter 6), both in this volume.

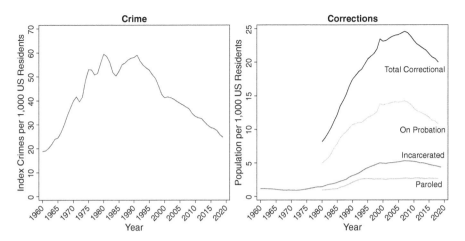

FIGURE 10.1 Crime and correctional supervision in the United States, 1960–2020

Crime rate data derived from FBI Uniform Crime Reporting Statistics (www.bjs.gov/ ucrdata/abouttheucr.cfm). Correctional Data (1980–2019) from Bureau of Justice Statistics, Key Statistics (https://bjs.ojp.gov/data/key-statistics), with earlier data from "Prisoners 1925–1981", a BJS Bulletin (www.bjs.gov/content/pub/pdf/p2581 .pdf).

explicitly consider the media in our analysis of sentinels above, they are clearly *the* major conduit through which information is passed. And critically, news outlets are heavily incentivized by the profit motive to prioritize sensational stories (as captured by the cynical cliché, "If it bleeds it leads").

Figure 10.1 displays historical crime and corrections data. The years 1960– 1990 saw a huge increase in crime in the United States, rising from an index crime rate of somewhat less than 20 incidents per 1,000 US residents to nearly 60 from the early-1960s to late 1980s. The policy response is hinted at in the correctional statistics displayed in the right panel: starting in the mid- to late-1970s, a dramatic increase in the fraction of US citizens under some form of correctional supervision. The burden of incarceration has fallen disproportionately on communities of color.

The twenty-year period from 1990 to 2010, however, was characterized by the odd juxtaposition of a marked decline in crime with the enactment, at the local, state, and national levels, of ever-more punitive criminal justice policies. Famously, the 1994 Crime Bill passed with bipartisan support (including the support of a majority of the Congressional Black Caucus, although Weaver (2007) notes serious reservations). At the state level, provisions such as truth-in-sentencing laws, mandatory minimums, the abolition or severe curtailment of parole, and sentencing enhancements for repeat offenders, all contributed to the sharp increase in the proportion of American citizens in the correctional system. This proportion, around 8 individuals per 1,000 in 1980, peaked at nearly 25 per 1,000 in 2007 (more recent data, from 2018, put the figure at around 20 per 1,000).

Coincident with the rise in incarceration was an increased willingness at the local level to employ policing practices such as stop, question, and frisk and militarized police tactics such as SWAT deployment and warrantless, no-knock raids (Mummolo, 2018). The antecedents of these developments are numerous, including asset forfeiture laws and the reliance of localities on fines and fees as sources of revenue (Goldstein, Sances, and You, 2018), which create high-powered incentives to police aggressively, particularly in disadvantaged communities of color (United States Department of Justice, 2015). Federal law and agency policies also contributed: the 1994 Crime bill provided funds for hiring 100,000 new police officers. The drug war, combined with the cheap availability of surplus military hardware, contributed to militarization (Balko, 2013). And the Justice Department's Equitable Sharing program (suspended under the Obama administration but reinstituted under President Trump) allocated a portion of assets seized by federal law enforcement to state and local agencies.

Our model illuminates some of the *political* incentives for public officials to support such tough-on-crime policies, and how those incentives may have shifted in the past decade. A key lesson from our analysis is that elected officials may make policy decisions that deviate from the welfare of their citizens in order to minimize the risk that a sentinel will have bad news to pass on to voters. This risk is determined in the model by the sentinel's incentives, and also by the fact that policy choices differ in the probability with which they generate verifiable news (as summarized by the ratio of the parameters π_1 and π_0).

Now suppose, using the language of our model, that $a = 0$ denotes a lenient policy and $a = 1$ a punitive one. Historically, sensational news about crime has meant stories about crime victimization, neighborhood blight, and recidivism, and *not* stories about the social costs of incarceration or aggressive policing. In other words, π_0 was far larger than π_1. In the presence of a sentinel incentivized to publicize bad news, public officials – be they mayors, legislators, or elected prosecutors or judges – all had electoral incentives to push for more punitive policies to avoid the political risk of a harmful headline.

Over the last decade, we have gradually seen an apparent loosening of these incentives: progressive prosecutors have been elected in places like St. Louis, Philadelphia, San Francisco, and Durham. Large majorities of Americans favor reform of the US criminal justice system. With bipartisan support, Congress passed, and President Trump signed into law, the First Step Act of 2018, which contained a host of sentencing and prison reform provisions. And Civil asset forfeiture reform has support from both sides of the aisle among lawmakers.

What changed? While a number of factors are clearly at play, one is a massive increase in the availability of hard information about the downsides of punitive criminal justice policy. Clearly, it has been increasingly difficult to ignore the effects of mass incarceration on communities of color. But technology has also played a significant role of bringing sustained attention to the adverse consequences of incarceration and aggressive policing, beyond those communities. A critical development is the ubiquity of cell phone cameras, which has brought instances of police-initiated violence into the public eye in an unprecedented way. In the language of the model, π_0 may have remained relatively fixed, but π_1 has increased dramatically. Accordingly, officials have reason to fear the political consequences of both kinds of "bad news," which alleviates the political pressure on policymakers toward ever greater levels of punitiveness.

CONCLUSION

Political observers have long worried about the performance of electorates composed largely of ill-informed citizens. Many scholars have pointed hopefully to elites as an imperfect solution: by providing cues, for example, elites might help citizens act *as if* they were truly informed. In this chapter, we examined a related but distinct role for elites: as knowledgeable third party "sentinels" that can sound "fire alarms" about incumbent performance. We have considered how such fire alarms can enhance or, alternatively, undermine electoral accountability. Four considerations play fundamental roles:

First, *sentinel bias* is critical. We have distinguished neutral conduits, challengers, and interested parties. Neutral conduits face no incentive to withhold or distort information, but may represent more an ideal than a reality. Zero-sum electoral competition implies that challengers happily provide bad news about incumbent performance while suppressing good news. Interested parties – firms, organized groups, or activists – prioritize their own interests, which may not coincide with those of voters.

Second, *verifiability* matters. Voters will lean toward heavily discounting unverifiable fire alarms from challengers who hope to tarnish the incumbent's reputation or by interested parties who transparently wish to boost a favored policy.

Third, and relatedly, *different policy choices may be more or less likely to generate verifiable information* that elites can (selectively) pass along to voters. This can create incentives for incumbents to tack toward policy choices that are unlikely to generate bad headlines should they go south.

Fourth, *credit claiming by incumbents* may yield an additional source of valuable information to voters. If the sentinel is a challenger, verifiable incumbent credit claiming may help voters get a more complete picture. But low-quality incumbents may collude with interested party sentinels to suppress bad news about policies those actors like.

Our analysis demonstrates how the presence or absence of these factors may lead incumbents to pursue actions *detrimental to their constituents*. An incumbent might be willing to risk an uncertain but probably well-considered policy if a veil of secrecy shields her should matters go awry. But the presence of a biased sentinel eager to deliver bad news may induce undue caution. A biased sentinel thus creates an inherent trade-off: while it may create a richer informational environment, which helps voters weed out poor-quality incumbents; its presence may distort an incumbent's incentives, which hurts them. As shown in the case study of policing, fire alarms provide no easy panacea for an ill-informed electorate.

10.A APPENDIX: FORMAL RESULTS AND PROOFS

The solution concept is Weak Perfect Bayesian Equilibrium. In each version of the game, Let N be the probability the incumbent is reelected given no news, and G be the corresponding probability given good news. (From the text, the probability of reelection given bad news is zero.)

Proposition 10.A.1 (Challengers and Hard Information) *In the presence of a challenger sentinel, given signal $\theta = 1$ a low-quality incumbent will choose $a = 0$ if and only if $\frac{\pi_1}{\pi_0} > \frac{q}{1-q}$.*

Proof From Bayes' Rule and the definition of $F(\cdot)$ in the text, $0 < N < 1$. Then given the incentives to publicize hard information described in the text,

$$E[u_i(a = 1|\theta = 1)] = qN + (1 - q)(1 - \pi_1)N$$
$$E[u_i(a = 0|\theta = 1)] = (1 - q)N + q(1 - \pi_0)N.$$

Comparing these two quantities yields the inequality in the proposition. □

Proposition 10.A.2 (Interested Parties and Hard Information) *Suppose there is an interested party sentinel. Then a low-quality incumbent will always choose $a = 0$, irrespective of θ.*

Proof From Bayes' Rule and the definition of $F(\cdot)$ in the text, $0 < N < G < 1$. Suppose $\theta = 0$. Then choosing $a = 0$ maximizes the probability the voter receives good news, while eliminating the possibility the voter receives bad news. Suppose $\theta = 1$. Then given the incentives to publicize hard information described in the text,

$$E[u_i(a = 1|\theta = 1)] = qN + (1 - q)(1 - \pi_1)N$$
$$E[u_i(a = 0|\theta = 1)] = (1 - q)(\pi_0 G + (1 - \pi_0)N) + qN.$$

Comparing these two quantities, the low-type incumbent will choose $a = 0$ given $\theta = 1$ if and only if $\pi_1 N + \pi_0(G - N) > 0$, which always holds. □

Proposition 10.A.3 (Challengers, Credit-Claiming, and Hard Information) *Suppose there is a challenger sentinel but incumbents can claim credit. Then all incumbents choose $a = 0$ given $\theta = 0$ and $a = 1$ given $\theta = 1$.*

Proof See text. $\qquad\qquad\qquad\qquad\qquad\qquad\qquad\qquad\qquad\qquad\qquad$ □

Proposition 10.A.4 (Interested Parties, Credit-Claiming, and Hard Information) *Suppose there is an interested party sentinel but incumbents can claim credit. Then given signal $\theta = 1$, a low-quality incumbent will choose $a = 0$ if and only if $(\pi_1 - (1 - q)\pi_0)N > (q\pi_1 - (1 - q)\pi_0)G$.*

Proof From Bayes' Rule and the definition of $F(\cdot)$ in the text, $0 < N < G < 1$. Given the incentives to publicize hard information described in the text,

$$E[u_i(a = 1|\theta = 1)] = q(\pi_1 G + (1 - \pi_1)N) + (1 - q)(1 - \pi_1)N$$
$$E[u_i(a = 0|\theta = 1)] = qN + (1 - q)(\pi_0 G + (1 - \pi_0)N).$$

Comparing these quantities yields the inequality given in the proposition. □

11

Achieving Accountability: Aligning Institutions and Behavior

John W. Patty

Decades of scholarship have noted and explored the challenges of designing efficient institutions for democratic policy choice and implementation. My immediate goal in this chapter is to consider how some empirical features of how people evaluate alternatives and make choices interact with institutional details in organizational decision-making settings. The more general goal is to expand our positive understanding of how to structure the relationships between – and responsibilities of – elected and unelected officials in order to promote policies that serve the public interest. A simpler way to describe this is that I hope the chapter provides some new insights into how to achieve *political accountability*.

While the theoretical literature on institutional design and the empirical literatures on individual choice and belief formation are each well-developed and active, there has been much less study to date of their intersection. For multiple reasons, direct observation of the effects of institutional design on accountability is deeply challenging. Instead, much of the current work focuses on determinants of how individuals assess either performance or responsibility (or both) when attempting to hold agents accountable (for example, see Chapter 3 by Patashnik, Tucker, and Gerber and Chapter 4 by Egan and Prior in this volume). For example, Landa and Duell (2015) provide some laboratory evidence that social identity affects the behaviors of both principals and agents. Nielsen and Moynihan (2017) provide evidence of partisan differences and, more strongly, of the "leadership attribution heuristic" or *correspondence bias*, which describe a general tendency of individuals to overestimate the role of individual-level factors (such as competence or ability), as opposed to situational ones (such as circumstances or chance), in determining the outcome of stochastic processes.

Accountability Challenges in Policy-Making

To what extent are citizens able to control their government in a representative system? This is – or should be – one of the central questions in political science, one that should occupy the combined talents of democratic theorists and institutional specialists. (Arnold, 1990, 265)

Accountability is a contested notion. In line with Cameron and Gordon's Chapter 10 in this volume, I define it within the setting of a *principal-agent relationship*, consisting simply of a relationship between two individuals: the "principal" and the "agent." The agent is someone who is faced with making some decisions that will affect the principal. The principal is allowed to offer some reward to (or threaten some punishment of) the agent based on how the agent's choice affects the principal. When these rewards and punishments are such that the agent finds it in his or her interest to make the choice that maximizes the principal's welfare, then full accountability has been achieved. When the rewards and punishments are such that the agent's choice is independent of the principal's welfare, then zero accountability has been achieved. Of course, in many settings, the best that one can achieve is somewhere in between. Despite its relative simplicity, this framework helps isolate two fundamental challenges to accountability.

As described by Cameron and Gordon (Chapter 10, this volume), the two challenges are (1) *moral hazard*, which describes the challenge of making sure that an agent makes the choice that the principal wants even though the principal may not be able to observe the agent's choice, and (2) *adverse selection*, which emerges when the agent has private information that the principal cares about but that the agent may want to hide from the principal. While both are fundamental to achieving accountability, I focus in this chapter on adverse selection.[1]

Adverse Selection in Policy-Making

Adverse selection is ubiquitous in policy-making, and particularly in technical and ideologically contested policy settings, such as many regulatory realms. Most notably, adverse selection emerges in these areas because of uncertainty about which policy is best. A current high profile example of such a situation is climate change: to what degree do human activities affect global temperatures and weather patterns? The adverse selection "problem" in this case is based on divergence of economic and political interests. The biases induced by such differences can hinder information transmission.

---

[1] This choice is presentational only – it does not reflect a judgment that adverse selection is more important than moral hazard in achieving accountability. Indeed, the methods to "solve" adverse selection (even if only partially) often exacerbate the challenges caused by moral hazard, and vice-versa. Unfortunately, space precludes me from considering this bigger issue in depth in this chapter.

In practice, overcoming adverse selection in policy-making is difficult for several reasons. First, some commonly employed mechanisms for monitoring policy-making, such as "fire alarm" oversight (McCubbins and Schwartz, 1984) simultaneously leverage and amplify the potential impact of biased interests. Second, a key justification for bureaucratic autonomy is the expertise possessed by bureaucrats themselves (e.g., Gailmard and Patty, 2012b; Miller and Whitford, 2016). In this vein, eliminating adverse selection requires that Congress possess equivalent expertise. Given that this is often difficult to achieve, adverse selection problems are common in policy-making. Short of endowing the principal with the agent's information directly, overcoming adverse selection requires aligning the agent's incentives with the principal's. I now turn to the question of how such incentives can be induced.

Incentivizing Good Choices

Theoretically, achieving accountability through institutional design requires that the institution possess both *selective rewards* and *diagnostic information*. Without selective rewards, or "carrots and sticks," the institution has no inducements to alter the agent's individual incentives. Similarly, without diagnostic information about the agent's choices, it is impossible to use selective rewards to align the agent's incentives with the goals of the organization.

SELECTIVE REWARDS. The New Public Management movement has prompted some government agencies to design and use tangible selective reward systems such as explicit material incentive schemes, short-term contracts, and/or outsourcing selected internal tasks to the private sector. That said, selective rewards need not be material in nature in order to be effective in motivating individuals. For example, a large literature documents how social rewards such as praise and intrinsic rewards such as pride can provide sufficient motivation to overcome agency problems (e.g., Paarlberg and Lavigna, 2010; Patty and Penn, 2020).

From a behavioral perspective there are at least three challenges to properly designing selective rewards in public agencies. First, aligning rewards with the agency's goals can be very difficult. Second, such rewards can undermine salutary intrinsic behavioral incentives (such as *esprit de corps* and organizational identity) through both selection and crowding out effects (e.g., Moynihan, 2008). Third, if the rewards are awarded on a discretionary basis, credibility issues may arise. Specifically, agents may be uncertain whether the principal will actually reward and/or punish different choices the team members may make. Such uncertainty can reduce the rewards' effect on the agent's decision-making (e.g., Fearon, 1999).

The proper design of selective rewards to mitigate these challenges varies across policy settings. However, one general rule of thumb is a "Goldilocks principle": the rewards need to be large enough to alter the agents' decisions, but without being so large that the agents consider nothing else when making their choices. In other words, the principal seeks to create a mix of intrinsic and extrinsic incentives that is "just right."

DIAGNOSTIC INFORMATION.   Rewards can alter individuals' incentives with respect to their decisions only to the degree that the rewards can respond to these decisions. This responsiveness requires *diagnostic information*: institutional structure determines how such information is generated, recorded, and reported. A key insight from principal-agent theory is that the agent must be aware of how the diagnostic information is both generated and translated into rewards. The various ways of doing these things represent various forms of *transparency*. "Pure" transparency requires that rewards are reliably responsive to individual choices *and* that members are aware of this.

Generating strongly diagnostic information requires that institutions be well-understood by the individuals working within them. Such an understanding often requires understanding not only how one's own choices will be rewarded by the institution, but also how *other* members understand and respond to these aspects of the institution. By their nature and origins, "bureaucratic" institutions have an inherent advantage with respect to generating strongly diagnostic information in complicated policy settings. That is, an institution that generates *effective* diagnostic information will tend to accord to Weber's description of bureaucratic institutions (Weber, 1946, 956–1005).

BALANCING INFORMATION AND REWARDS.   From a theoretical standpoint, incentives and information have complementary effects in a principal-agent situation by changing the agent's incentives with respect to all of his or her possible choices. From a behavioral standpoint, the specific features of institutional design additionally shape decision-making by altering how the individual perceives his or her incentives, which alternatives he or she evaluates, and how he or she compares the alternatives. More simply, institutional design can affect the agent's decision-making *process* by altering how the agent perceives and evaluates his or her various choices. In this chapter, I focus on one such empirical feature of decision-making, known as *bracketing*.

Bracketing and Decision-Making

Bracketing refers to how individuals contrast and compare alternatives when making choices (see Read, Loewenstein, and Rabin, 1999; Thaler, 1985). In this section, I apply the bracketing framework to the question of how to design incentives to achieve accountability in policy-making. The relationship is bidirectional: the effects of bracketing on individual decision-making has implications for how to design institutions, and institutional design affects how individuals bracket their decisions. Taking both of these directions into account is key to designing institutions that achieve political accountability. Before diving into that relationship, however, I describe the different types, and effects, of bracketing.

Broad versus Narrow Bracketing

Bracketing is an intuitive notion: a decision-maker's "brackets" represent how he or she groups his or her choices when comparing them to make a choice. A decision-maker compares any potential choice only with the other choices within the same bracket. Thus, bracketing simplifies decision-making for the decision-maker (though not always without cost).

One example of bracketing in modern public decision-making in the United States is provided by the judicial practice of deciding "one case at a time" (Sunstein, 2001). Similarly, legislative and executive decision-making is frequently explicitly carried out in ways that "bracket" in the sense of constraining choices to a subset of the feasible options.

FORMS AND TYPES OF BRACKETING. Unsurprisingly, individuals bracket choices in different ways. In what follows, I discuss two common forms of bracketing: *categorical bracketing*, in which the decision-maker separately compares "apples to apples" and "oranges to oranges," and *temporal bracketing*, in which the decision-maker separately considers "short-term" and "long-term" impacts of their choices. Regardless of the nature of the bracketing, a simple and ubiquitous distinction between two brackets are their *breadths*. For simplicity, I discuss these breadths in terms of being *narrow* or *broad*.

When a decision-maker considers only a few choices at a time, he or she is using a *narrow bracket* and, conversely, he or she is using a *broad bracket* when he or she considers many, or all, of the choices at the same time (e.g., Arnold, 1979, 20–26). The breadth of a decision-maker's bracket can have both subtle and dramatic effects on his or her decision-making.

The Effects of Bracketing on Decision-Making

Read, Loewenstein, and Rabin (1999) describe four types of bracketing effects. Here I focus on two of them, which they refer to as *adding-up effects* and *emergent properties*.[2]

ADDING-UP EFFECTS. Adding-up effects describes how the breadth of a decision-maker's brackets can affect how he or she "adds up" the costs and/or benefits of multiple decisions. An essential ingredient of bracketing is a form of forgetfulness: when evaluating and choosing from the options in one bracket, the decision-maker both neglects to consider both the implications of his or her current choice on his or her future choices and, perhaps, the implication of his or her earlier choice(s) from other brackets.[3]

Adding-up effects frequently emerge from bracketing decisions that are, taken individually, "small stakes," in the sense that the welfare implications of

[2] Read, Loewenstein, and Rabin (1999) also describe *taste change* and *trade-offs* effects of bracketing.
[3] Of course, reality is complicated: it is not necessary that the decision-maker *always* ignore the implications of choices in one bracket for his or her choices from other brackets.

any single decision are insufficient to warrant in-depth, costly consideration. Everyday examples of such choices include going to the dentist, smoking a cigarette, and wearing one's seat belt on a short trip to the market. Looking to public policy choices, there are many examples of low stakes, everyday decisions such as whether to grant a continuance in a trial, renew a broadcast license, or waive a procedural requirement.

EMERGENT PROPERTIES. Emergent properties of bracketing typically flow from other behavioral biases in the decision-maker's decision-making that are sensitive to the size of the set of alternatives under consideration. A few examples of such biases include *trade-off contrast* and *extremeness aversion*, *tastes for diversity*, *preferences over streams of outcomes*, and *perceptions of risk*. The emergent properties of bracketing complement its adding-up effects. Both families of effects are consistent with forgetfulness or myopia, and broader bracketing can ameliorate these effects.

Two Types of Bracketing: Categorical and Temporal

Below, I describe categorical and temporal bracketing. I choose these two categories because they seem particularly relevant for political accountability. Categorical bracketing is a natural result of delegating to agents with specialized jurisdictions, as is common in many modern governments. Temporal bracketing is similarly a natural result of periodic review and budgeting, a characteristic of many "standing" delegations of authority to government agencies.

CATEGORICAL BRACKETING. Categorical bracketing occurs when an individual must make several decisions at the same time but considers the decisions separately. For example, suppose a government agency must choose both a maximum price, p, and minimum quality, q, that a regulated firm may offer for some good. If the regulator uses a broad bracket to make his or her decision, then he or she compares all price-quality pairs at once. In public policy, an agency might first compare some potential price levels with each other, and then compare the potential quality levels with each other, thereby producing a "price-quality" threshold pair.

Categorical bracketing is commonplace across branches of government. One (very high profile) example of such decision-making (during the Cuban Missile Crisis) is described by Allison (1969).[4] More generally, the potential for such bracketing is illustrated with a few quick examples.

- **Categorical Bracketing in Legislative Policy-Making.** From a legislative perspective, most standing committees of the US House of Representatives have variously defined substantive jurisdictions, and these jurisdictional lines are relevant and, accordingly, contested. This bracketing facilitates the

---

4 Specifically, his Models II ("organizational process") and III ("bureaucratic politics") are each characterized by categorical bracketing.

processing of legislative businesses in many circumstances but increase the complexity of processing business that straddles more than one committee's jurisdiction (Adler and Wilkerson, 2008). Similarly, legislatures sometimes create special committees with explicit (even if sometimes waived) limitations on the options they may consider, such as conference committees and ad hoc extra-legislative committees such as the Base Realignment and Closure Commission (the choice set of which is, by statute, determined by the Department of Defense and subject to an up-or-down vote in each chamber of Congress). Finally, on a day-to-day basis party leaders attempt to structure the processing of legislative business so as to both constrain and protect their members (see Lee's contribution, Chapter 9, in this volume).

- **Categorical Bracketing in Judicial Policy-Making.** With relatively few exceptions, the jurisdiction of all US Federal Courts is governed by various Congressional statutes. These jurisdictions are shaped both by overarching statutes creating ancillary (Article I and Article III) courts and by more narrowly written provisions peppered through various statutes delineating the rights and obligations of those seeking judicial redress.

- **Categorical Bracketing in Bureaucratic Policy-Making.** In 1983, in *Motor Vehicle Manufacturers Association* v. *State Farm Mutual Automobile Insurance Company*,[5] the Supreme Court unanimously ruled that the National Highway Transportation Safety Administration's rescission of a passive restraint rule was "arbitrary and capricious" under the Administrative Procedure Act.[6] The Court clarified the categorical nature of congressional delegation by distinguishing between "relevant factors" that are required to be part of the agency's decision-making process and those that "Congress has not intended [the agency] to consider."[7] Indeed, this decision followed an explicit Congressional statutory rejection and prohibition (Public Law 93–492, October 27, 1974) of a similar regulation by the Department of Transportation in 1974. The statute also limited the National Highway Transportation Safety Administration's choices of restraint system in other substantive ways (Rugaber, 1974). Along the same lines, Congress explicitly precluded the Food and Drug Administration (FDA) and Environmental Protection Agency (EPA) from approving any food additive, color additive, or cosmetic that is a known carcinogen. This has been interpreted by courts as precluding the consideration of issues such as cost when evaluating a carcinogenic additive or cosmetic (Pierce Jr., 2009; Merrill, 1978).

BRACKETING AND ELIMINATION BY ASPECTS Categorical bracketing in decision-making has several similarities to Amos Tversky's *elimination by aspects* (EBA) heuristic (Tversky, 1972; Patty, 2007). EBA involves no bracketing of choices, per se, but rather a bracketing of how the various characteristics of the potential choices are used to produce a choice. Under EBA,

---

[5] 463 U.S. 29 (1983).   [6] 60 Stat. 237 (1946).   [7] 60 Stat. 237 (1946), 42–43.

for example, a decision-maker might compare all options on the basis of cost first, eliminate those that are too costly, then compare the remaining choices on the basis of some other desiderata, such as quality, eliminating those that do not offer the highest quality, and continue with other characteristics until a single alternative remains. The outcome of this incremental process of comparison is in general sensitive to the order in which the decision-maker applies the various "aspects" to whittle down the choice set, just as the decisions produced by bracketing will tend to be sensitive to the decision-maker's brackets.

TEMPORAL BRACKETING. Temporal bracketing revolves around the degree to which the decision-maker considers the future impacts of his or her current choices. For example, consider the situation faced by a police officer who observes a motorist who appears intoxicated but has just arrived home. Nobody immediately benefits from the officer arresting the motorist at this point in time, but it does entail paperwork for the officer. Thus a simple, narrowly bracketed choice calculus suggests that the best response is to let the motorist go in his or her house and sleep it off. However, a broader bracket – one that took into account either the future behavior of the motorist or the overall social impact of repeatedly making this decision (or both) – would be more likely to recognize that the aggregate, across-time benefits from arresting the motorist.

A narrow temporal bracketing necessarily promotes myopic decision-making but also may yield benefits when information is costly to acquire, the decision-maker is making choices within a "strategic environment" involving other actors, and/or when the principal is attempting to mitigate adverse selection in a delegation setting. From a public policy perspective, institutionally induced temporal bracketing is commonplace. As with categorical bracketing, I provide a few examples of settings in which temporal bracketing might emerge.

- **Temporal Bracketing in Legislative Policy-Making.** A large proportion of elected officials desire, and seek, reelection. Pursuit of this may induce elected officials to focus more on short-term costs and benefits of their policy choices than would be the case if they held their office for life (or, perhaps, if they were prohibited from seeking reelection due to term limits). Less obviously, legislators often determine the frequency with which a statute needs to be reviewed and/or reauthorized (a prominent example is the "farm bill," which is supposed to be reauthorized every five years).

- **Temporal Bracketing in Judicial Policy-Making.** Courts are sometimes subject to temporal bracketing through statutory provisions such as statutes of limitation. In common-law systems, courts face the prospect of their current decision raising future questions, sometimes inducing a desire to engage in temporal bracketing (Beim, Clark, and Patty, 2017). This behavior is arguably reflected in the Supreme Court's tendency to make policy "one case at a time" (e.g., Sunstein, 2001; Clark and Patty, 2021).

• **Temporal Bracketing in Bureaucratic Policy-Making.** Bureaucratic agencies typically confront numerous institutional features that promote temporal bracketing. For example, in the United States Federal government, in addition to the annual appropriations process or sunset provisions in authorizing statutes, permanent legislation sometimes prescribes reporting and/or rulemaking schedules. An important current example of this is the Safe Drinking Water Act (SDWA).[8] The SDWA requires the EPA to publish a contaminant candidate list (CCL) every five years (subject to notice and comment) and then determine which of these, if any, should be subject to new (or altered) regulations.

Bracketing and Institutional Design

With the broad strokes of bracketing described, I turn to some speculative thoughts about how bracketing interacts with institutional design features to affect policy decisions by and within an agency. As stated above, it is important to remember that this interaction is bidirectional: how agents bracket their decisions alters the effects of diagnostic information and selective rewards on their ultimate choices and, conversely, the choice of diagnostic information and selective rewards can affect how agents bracket their decisions.

How Bracketing Might Affect the Impact of Selective Incentives

An individual's bracketing shapes how he or she perceives and responds to his or her incentives (both extrinsic and intrinsic). This can alter the impact of selective rewards on decision-making. For example, if an individual makes his or her choices on a daily basis, then an annually awarded incentive, such as a rebate on one's income tax, will tend to have little effect on his or her decision-making. Consider the classic example of (daily) temporal bracketing by New York City taxi drivers identified in Camerer et al. (1997). When a taxi driver received an unexpected large tip, he or she was much more likely to stop driving for the rest of the day – even though the occurrence of a large tip should not decrease the driver's estimate of his or her hourly earnings driving the rest of the day. Using a bracketing broader than "one day at a time" makes clearer that the windfall of a large tip should not affect the driver's decision about whether to keep driving or not – the narrow bracket ultimately lowers the taxi driver's annual income. Furthermore, when using a narrow temporal bracket, the taxi driver is unlikely to think about this.

In order for a public policy intervention to affect choices that tend to be made within narrow brackets, individuals must be able to identify the change in their incentives by comparing the choices that are within his or her framing of the decision. Consider designing financial incentives for (1) brushing one's

---

[8] Pub.L. 93–523, December 16, 1975, as amended by Pub.L. 104–182, August 6, 1996.

teeth or (2) installing energy efficient windows in one's home. Brushing one's teeth any one time is a small stakes decision made everyday (and – hopefully – multiple times a day). Therefore, it is likely to be viewed in a narrow frame in the sense that immediate costs and benefits will loom much larger than more long-term concerns such as a tax credit for an annual clean dental bill of health. On the other hand, the decision about which windows to install in one's home is probably made using a broader temporal frame. After all, the price difference between windows is much larger than the net benefit of brushing one's teeth one time, and the decision to buy the home in the first place probably involved considering a long stream of future costs and benefits. Accordingly, a tax credit for choosing the energy efficient windows will be more likely to factor into the decision.

How Bracketing Might Affect the Impact of Diagnostic Information

As described above, the use of diagnostic information to award selective rewards can affect decision-making only to the degree that the agent considers the informational effect of his or her choices. Accordingly, if the choices "within the agent's bracket" do not differ much in terms of their informational impact, the effect of diagnostic information, and accordingly selective rewards, on the agent's decision will be mitigated. Thus, agents with narrow brackets will tend to be less sensitive to changes in how their choices are measured.

For example, narrow temporal bracketing will mitigate the impact of periodic measurement on the agent's decision-making, providing a rationale for frequent assessment. This comes at a cost, though – not only is assessment directly costly, factors that can be measured on a frequent basis will tend to be less strongly correlated with either the agent's choices or the goals of the organization (or both). Such evaluation/accountability mechanisms may tend to be perceived by members of the organization as inefficient "red tape."

How Selective Rewards Might Affect Bracketing

An explicit reward scheme can affect how individuals make comparisons in several ways. The most obvious effect is to make alternatives more easily comparable. For example, *taboo* represents a very strong version of bracketing: a taboo choice is effectively never evaluated. Selective rewards can change taboo, as potentially demonstrated by the "Israeli day care study" by Gneezy and Rustichini (2000). In that study, the imposition of a fine for being late to pick up one's child from day care led to an *increase* in the number of parents who were late. One explanation for this is hinted at by the title of the article, "a fine is a price": by providing an explicit selective reward for being on time, the incentive system legitimated evaluating the purposeful choice to be late.

As discussed above, if the timing of a selective reward extends beyond an agent's temporal bracket, then it is unlikely to influence the agent's decision-making. However, the timing of selective rewards can also affect the agent's temporal bracketing. For example, there is evidence that giving rewards in a piecemeal fashion "along the way" toward an ultimate goal can induce narrow bracketing (Stracke, Kerschbamer, and Sunde, 2017). This indicates a trade-off suggesting that selective rewards ought to be awarded with moderate frequency – often enough to fall within the decision-maker's temporal bracket, but not so frequent so as to further narrow the temporal bracket.

How Diagnostic Information Might Affect Bracketing

The design of diagnostic information can be thought of coarsely as assigning different weights to an agent's various tasks in the creation of a measure of performance. The degree to which various decisions have similar weights in the evaluation scheme can affect how an agent brackets his or her choices. There is evidence that this type of bracketing – which has similarities to the psychological notion of framing – can lead to decisions that appear ignorant of the fungibility of monetary or temporal resources. Similarly, diagnostic information shapes how individuals set goals for themselves and goal-setting can affect both individual motivation and risk attitudes.

The effect of diagnostic information on bracketing will depend on whether the agent expects to observe the information. Diagnostic information is a performance evaluation and accordingly can become a goal in and of itself. In other words, diagnostic information can induce an apparently intrinsic motivation by some agents to "perform well" as measured by the measure itself, independent of the selective rewards tied to the measure. The desirability effect is further complicated by the comparison of relative versus absolute measures of performance: relative comparisons can encourage team members to undermine each other's efforts (Miller and Hamblin, 1963), but can also provide stronger incentives for effort exertion.

Bracketing and Accountability

As my very preliminary musings in the previous sections hopefully indicate, there is much to learn about how institutions and choice bracketing interact in the real world. One thing seems clear, however: the interaction is almost certainly bidirectional – the effectiveness of incentives is conditioned by how individuals' choice brackets and, simultaneously, the details of an incentive scheme may affect how individuals working within the scheme bracket their choices.[9] Keeping this possibility in mind is particularly important when designing incentive schemes, particularly when the existing incentive scheme

---

[9] On this point the chapters by Clinton, Sances, and Sullivan and Carpenter and Libgober (Chapters 2 and 14 in this volume, respectively) illustrate how the impacts of bracketing by external actors such as voters and lobbyists might affect policymakers' brackets.

is deemed to be "failing" (see below). In such situations, it is important to investigate not only the intrinsic incentives of the agents, but also how they structure their decision-making. With this noted, I now focus a bit more narrowly on how *oversight* interacts with bracketing.

Congressional Oversight and Bureaucratic Bracketing

Many have worried that Members of Congress do not have sufficiently strong individual incentives to spend the time and effort required to collect information and use that information to hold federal agencies to account for those agencies' policy choices and outcomes. While the empirical question of the degree to which Members of Congress actually carry out oversight is still open (McGrath, 2013), it is important to note at least in passing that, in order for a legislator to reliably make proper decisions regarding how much effort he or she should put into oversight requires that the legislator have a very broad choice bracketing. To the degree that Members take a narrower view of bureaucratic decisions – for example, by using a "what have you done for me lately?" heuristic, oversight induces a bias toward short-term reactionary behavior by policy-makers (e.g., Arnold, 1979).

Similarly, if Members of Congress or bureaucrats take a particular policy program or goal as given and then evaluate options relative to it, they are adopting a narrower bracketing of the choices subsequently considered. The example of the Model Cities program (Arnold, 1979; 1981) is illustrative in two ways. First, the Model Cities program – like many other federal aid programs – was based upon application: in order to be included in the program, a city must complete a fairly extensive application process. Second, the number of Model Cities was fixed (150 total, 75 per year over two years). Of course, these two features shaped the bracketing of choices regarding the applications within the Department of Housing and Urban Development. The decision-makers' reaction to this bracketing in view of the program's budgetary uncertainty, clear expression of Congressional interest in the program, and concomitant Congressional oversight was accordingly unsurprising: the program provided detailed information about *all* of the applications and a description of how its decisions were (supposedly) structured.

The Model Cities example illustrates that the proper structuring of oversight should keep in mind both the agency's preexisting bracketing *and how the oversight structure will affect the agency's bracketing in the future*. For example, from a temporal bracketing standpoint, if an agency is subject to regular budgetary review and revision and/or the managers of the agency are subject to regular turnover, its decision-making will tend to bracket choices in ways that mirror these schedules. Similarly, from a categorical bracketing perspective, agencies subject to periodic oversight may have an incentive to bracket their decisions in line with their expectations regarding how their performance will be evaluated.

An intriguing aspect of bracketing from a positive theoretic standpoint is that a changing how an agent brackets his or her choices has impacts that extend beyond the incentives of the agent, per se. This is because bracketing alters how the agent makes comparisons between alternatives. These potential impacts of bracketing might be described as "pathological" in the sense that the nature of an agent's bracketing often goes unnoticed. In this way, bracketing can open up space for a "second kind of regret." While theories of "rational" choice are consistent with a decision-maker wishing that he or she had known something that was unknown at the time he or she made a decision. When a decision-maker adopts a narrow bracket, he or she may regret that he or she had not even thought about one or more relevant factors. This suggests an importance of *ex post* Congressional oversight beyond serving as a "stick" to punish unfaithful or lazy bureaucrats. For example, reviews following policy failures can be viewed as attempts to consider the decision-making processes – which are partly the result of the bracketing(s) used within the agency during the decisions leading up to the failure.

Structure, Process, and Bracketing

The possible interactions between oversight and how agents bracket their decisions have important implications for the design of policy-making procedures. Below, I briefly consider the implications of bracketing for three properties of oversight institutions: distinguishing between *ex ante* and *ex post* controls, centralization of decision-making authority, and task specialization.

EX ANTE VS EX POST CONTROLS.   Scholars have explored and debated the differences between *ex ante* controls, such as notice and comment procedures (e.g., McCubbins, Noll, and Weingast, 1987; Gailmard and Patty, 2017), and *ex post* monitoring, such as oversight hearings (e.g., McCubbins and Schwartz, 1984; Bawn, 1995). Taking bracketing seriously implies that the proper institutional structure depends on how the agency tends to bracket the relevant decisions.

Ex ante controls might be more effective as the agency's bracketing becomes narrower, because such controls force the agency to consider factors or options it might not otherwise. High profile examples of such controls in the US federal government include the Administrative Procedure Act of 1946,[10] which established the modern rulemaking process and requires agencies in many cases to both solicit public comment and take these into account before rendering a final decision (i.e., the "notice and comment process"), and the National Environmental Policy Act of 1969,[11] which required that most government decisions be evaluated in terms of their environment impact.

---

[10] 60 Stat. 237.   [11] 83 Stat. 852.

Ex post control mechanisms should alter agency behavior only to the degree that their use is considered credible by the agency. This is less likely for decisions made within a narrower temporal bracket. Thus, narrow temporal bracketing may be one of the central causes of bureaucratic failures such as witnessed in the Deepwater Horizon oil spill and the Flint, Michigan water crisis. Narrow bracketing is accordingly a justification for bureaucratic "internal controls" such as hierarchies and multilevel review.

CENTRALIZATION. Agencies are made up of many individual decision-makers with varying independent authorities. Some have argued that central-ization of decision-making can increase accountability because it mitigates coordination problems and fosters preference alignment and credibility between principal and agent (Gailmard and Patty, 2012a; 2019). Taking bracketing seriously in such a setting suggests an additional rationale for centralization and coordination of decision-making: different individuals, or teams of individuals, who tend to make different kinds of decisions will not necessarily bracket their decisions in the same way. The ethnographic analysis by Feldman (1989) demonstrates how different offices within the Department of Energy used different categorical brackets when making policy decisions and, similarly, illustrates how centralization can, in the right conditions, partially merge these various brackets. The possibility of different brackets within a policy-making organization offers one justification for "standard operating procedures" in the form of common rubrics and formulas for evaluating policy alternatives.

In the current-day US Federal government, temporal bracketing is reinforced by various centralizing institutions, including the handling of the regular appro-priations processes by the Office of Management and Budget (OMB), periodic audits of government programs by bodies such as the GAO, and the regulatory review processes coordinated by the Office of Information and Regulatory Affairs (OIRA). Categorical bracketing through centralization is promoted by institutional actors such as Congressional Parliamentarians (King, 1997) and, within bureaucratic agencies, agency leadership and executive reorganization.

SPECIALIZATION. Expertise is a key ingredient of accountability (Gailmard and Patty, 2012a), and this provides a justification for task specialization in the form of dividing authority for different decisions between different teams of individuals (e.g., Ting, 2002). Almost by definition, dividing up responsibility for various tasks and outcomes between various agents will affect how these agents bracket their choices. This reality provides additional insight into why it is often difficult for teams of agents with different specialized responsibilities to work together (e.g., Coglianese, 1997). Specifically, brackets tend to be both idiosyncratic and "sticky": agents with differing day-to-day responsibilities will not necessarily make decisions in the same way, even when presented with the same information and extrinsic incentives. For example, the analysis by Feldman (1989) demonstrates that bracket incongruence can lead to polarization and paralysis.

Specialization in policy-making comes in various forms and can lead to both categorical and temporal bracketing in a variety of ways. Many forms of specialization in organizations both public and private are transparent examples of categorical bracketing: one group of agents is charged with evaluating the proper minimum price for a regulated good while another is given responsibility for determining the minimum quality that might be offered on the market. However, categorical bracketing can occur through specialization in more subtle ways. From a sociological/psychological perspective, the mere labeling of an organizational unit might induce categorical bracketing.

With respect to temporal bracketing, specialization can occur through outsourcing of decisions to sub-governmental or non-governmental actors whose time horizons differ from those of career bureaucrats or elected representatives. Similarly, specialization through assignment of various intermediate decisions to groups of actors can lead to both temporal and categorical bracketing. A famous example of this can be observed in the struggles between economists and lawyers within the Federal Trade Commission and Department of Justice in the 1970s and 1980s (e.g., Eisner, 1991). Because agency economists understandably tended to focus on economic impacts of antitrust enforcement while agency lawyers tended to focus on the legal issues, their analyses often gave different weights to long-term and short-term policy considerations.

Oversight and Temporal Bracketing

Temporal bracketing interacts with and reinforces temporal biases such as the *primacy* and *recency* effects. When recalling sequentially provided information, individuals tend to better recall those that occurred very early (primacy effect) and very late (recency effect) in the sequence. These biases can have large implications for planning. For example, the recency effect is very much in line with the old saw that "there is a tendency in many armies to spend the peace time studying how to fight the last war." More generally, individuals will tend to collect and frame their information with respect to their expectations regarding the outcomes upon which others will judge the quality of their decisions and choices. This can lead to various forms of path dependence (e.g., Page, 2006), particularly as individuals try to infer from previous evaluations when and how future evaluations will be carried out.

OVERSIGHT CRITERIA. This possibility suggests a need for periodic evaluations of agents' decisions, but such a structure can potentially narrow the reviewed agents' temporal brackets. For reasons both procedural and instrumental in nature, systematic review is often carried out using explicit, or at least predictable, criteria. A criterion is predictable not only if it is defined in terms of diagnostic information and is known to the agents: it also requires that the agents have an understanding about how their various potential choices will affect the diagnostic information. In line with the discussion of interdependence above, unpredictable criteria have the potential to reduce individual motivation and commitment to the organization. On the other hand, predictable criteria are sometimes prone to manipulation. In practice, the best criteria represent a balancing of predictability and non-manipulability.

OVERSIGHT AND NARROWING AGENTS' BRACKETS. Regarding the bidirectional relationship between brackets and incentives alluded to at various places above, bracketing by agents can circumscribe the impacts and effectiveness of oversight within an organization because both categorical and temporal bracketing by an agent will tend to narrow the agent's bracket, limiting the information he or she considers when making his or her decisions. Accordingly, narrower bracketing will tend to simultaneously decrease the set of criteria that are controllable *and* foreseeable by the decision-maker. Along these lines, more precisely and narrowly defined roles and responsibilities may have ambiguous effects on accountability. On the one hand, narrow bracketing will lead to decision-making that overlooks relevant externalities (for example, hindering coordination within the organization). On the other hand, narrowing the bracket can provide clarity and feelings of efficacy that can amplify intrinsic motivations and reduce attempts to manipulate evaluation schemes.

Bracketing, Goals, Planning, and Change

Many theories of organizations treat the organization in stasis with respect to its purpose(s). The missions of long-lived organizations typically change over time, though of course this is usually a very gradual (or at least rarely occurring) process. On a general level, there has been much less attention paid to accountability during times of change, or restructuring (but see Olsen, 2015). However, such a focus is especially called for if one wants to understand how altering accountability mechanisms will actually affect decision-making.

Taking a step back and considering the multiple interested actors involved in most public policy-making situations, it becomes clear that actors with competing interests might ultimately compete to influence decision-makers' brackets. This dynamic brings to mind the struggles for autonomy by and within bureaucratic agencies (e.g., Carpenter, 2001). As described above (p. 253), an agent's bracket is not necessarily tied to his or her innate preferences or motives. Accordingly, competition to influence the decisions of a policy-maker might be more easily achieved by altering his or her bracket than by alternative mechanisms such as replacing the policy-maker.

The goals of a government agency can change over time for various reasons, ranging from technological change/obsolescence to politically induced change, to bureaucratic/organizational shifts in policy-making, such as mission creep, and/or various forms of "drift," including "bureaucratic drift" (McCubbins, Noll, and Weingast, 1987), "coalitional drift" (Shepsle, 1992), and "epistemic drift" (Shapiro and Guston, 2006). When a change in goals occurs, then the optimal accountability mechanisms will tend to change as well. The risk of such change is inherently visited upon the agents, insofar as there is a time delay between their individual efforts and assessment. Combined with the inefficiency of risk when attempting to align the incentives of risk-averse agents with those of the organization, this provides a rationale for phenomena such as insulation and incrementalism. An example of incrementalism through bracketing is evaluating (say) monthly performance relative to the average required to meet an annual goal set earlier. In terms of bracketing, such an evaluation system creates incentives for decision-makers to mimic the taxi cab drivers' behaviors documented by Camerer et al. (1997). From an incrementalism standpoint, such a system might lead to the previous year's performance and next year's target to be evaluated according to how frequently individuals "met the targets" of the monthly performance evaluations.

Such a system also insulates individuals working within it by virtue of tending to reduce the risk they bear regarding any extrinsic incentives awarded through the monthly evaluations. In many policy settings, such insulation/insurance results from the law of large numbers – and this fact partially indicates the degree to which such bracketing will tend to reduce the risk visited upon the evaluated individuals: when the random determinants of performance across time periods are both small in magnitude relative to the performance goals and, more subtly, only weakly correlated across time, then narrow bracketing/incremental evaluation will tend to provide good incentives for the individuals working subjected to them.

On the other hand, broadly bracketed choice can increase the systemic risk emanating from the decision-maker's errors predicting latent relevant factors. This is partly because the breadth of an agent's temporal or categorical bracket will tend to correlate with the (temporal and/or categorical) scope of the impact of the agent's decisions. Few would propose that it is optimal for an eighteen year-old to make serious, committed decisions regarding his or her financial planning and career path over the remainder of his or her life. After all, preferences change and people often learn more about how the world works as they get older.

BRACKETING AND REFORM. When sudden change occurs and negative outcomes follow, one key point of investigation should be the bracketing used by decision-makers prior to the change. Three practical questions that can guide this investigation include:

1. Were decision-makers not allowed to and/or incapable of considering all of the relevant alternatives?
2. Were improper criteria applied evaluating the choices?
3. Were important criteria ignored?

Generally, the first question – though not "simple" in many cases – is the simplest of the three to answer. As alluded to above (p. 253), regret about failure to consider an alternative is in some sense more consistent with bracketing than other traditional "mistakes" within a rational choice perspective, and evidence of this is often available in public policy settings. Given the ubiquity of subjective decision-making even in the most technical policy areas and the nature of bureaucratic paper trails, evidence about the second and third questions is somewhat less common. However, the potential need to consider these two questions suggests an additional value of record-keeping in public policy settings: these records can help individuals detect when and how they are bracketing their decisions.

If the answer to any of these questions is "yes," then sub-optimal bracketing is possibly part of the cause of the negative outcomes. If bracketing is part of the problem, the next set of questions one should ask include the following:

1. What is/are the structure(s) of the bracket(s)?
2. Why do the decision-makers apply the brackets they do?
3. Do all relevant decision-makers share a common bracketing of the problem?

The answer to the first question can reveal aspects of the policy problem that were incorrectly believed to be less or more important than they actually are (one possible example is the debate and mixed messaging about face masks in mitigating the spread of COVID-19). When bracketing occurred but the structure of the bracket can not be explained by the decision-maker's subjective assessment of the details of the policy problem, the importance of the answers to second question is increased, because it is more likely that the decision-maker's bracket(s) are induced by structural details of the policy-making process.

From an institutional perspective, the second question may revolve around some of the institutional factors mentioned above (e.g., *ex ante/ex post* controls and/or oversight). Institutional reformers are well-served to keep in mind that the various institutional layers do not necessarily work in isolation – the effects of a reform today might affect the efficacy of other, earlier reforms.

Finally, the third question represents the most difficult of the three to answer conclusively. One practical reason for this is that it is relatively uncommon for individuals to write down their beliefs about how their colleagues bracket their decisions, particularly in real-world settings in which there are many other relevant decision-makers. More generally, a mismatch of brackets within an organization is in a sense "just another example" of a *coordination problem*. Accordingly, reforming the institutional structure to better coordinate individual choices might help alleviate some mis-match between individuals' brackets.

Complementing the empirical questions of how bracketing actually works are normative questions such as "what *should* brackets look like?" I now turn to some speculation regarding this question before concluding.

What Is the Optimal Bracket?

In a classic decision theoretic sense, broad bracketing is clearly optimal in simple settings in which a single decision-maker must choose an option from some set. In this classical setting, broad bracketing is required to ensure that the decision-maker can properly account for all complementarities and conflicts between the various choices. Accordingly, I briefly describe some factors that might suggest reasons to prefer a narrow bracket to a broad one.

1. **Direct Costs of Evaluating Alternatives.** The most obvious potential advantage of a narrow bracket is a reduction of the policy-maker's decision costs. These costs encompass a variety of factors, including the direct costs of information collection and information processing. When policy is the product of decisions by multiple policy-makers with heterogeneous brackets, narrowing their brackets can yield a secondary coordination benefit when the narrowing of their brackets bring the policy-makers' brackets more in line with each other.
2. **Behavioral Biases.** Narrow bracketing can help mitigate other cognitive biases such as self-control problems or misperception of correlation and/or interaction between the alternatives under consideration (e.g., Read, Loewenstein, and Rabin, 1999, 192). Similarly, when there are multiple policy-makers with heterogeneous brackets, narrowing these brackets can mitigate the coordination problems that result from such biases affecting different policy-makers' decisions in different ways.
3. **Credible Commitments and Strategic Effects.** It is common for policy-makers to be subject to external actors' attempts to affect the set of choices and/or their desirability to the policy-makers in question through various activities such as lobbying and campaign donations. The impact of these activities and, in equilibrium, their occurrence may be affected by the policy-makers' brackets. While temporal and/or categorical bracketing can each mitigate the influence of future bribes or punishments that could mitigate the principal's ability to influence the policy-maker, this limitation could benefit the principal overall if the narrow bracketing also reduces the influence of external actors with goals contrary to the principal's.
4. **Clarified Oversight.** Some choices may be less informative about underlying facts that the principal(s) find relevant. A narrow bracket can increase the efficacy of oversight by mitigating adverse selection. In both cases, the principal advantage of a narrow bracket is circumscribing the decision-maker's choice set so as to better leverage diagnostic information.

The Limits of Bracket Manipulation

Political accountability of bureaucrats operates through multiple layers. In the most salubrious situation, unelected civil servants are held accountable by elected politicians and courts (who might be elected or unelected), and elected politicians are held accountable by the voters. The ways by which voters hold elected representatives accountable (for example, regular elections, term limits, etc.) affect how these representatives bracket their decisions about how to monitor and reward or punish the civil servants. That said, in many public policy-making settings, the ability to shape decision-makers' brackets is typically necessarily limited because the bracketing of the civil servants who are making policy decisions are partially determined by the timing and nature of the diagnostic information collected, and selective rewards offered, by the principals who are charged with holding the agents accountable.

For example, broadening the policy-makers' brackets may be infeasible because policy-makers may react to their perceptions of how the principal will utilize diagnostic information and selective rewards. The impact of this type of strategic behavior is particularly potent when considering bureaucratic agencies overseen by a sovereign legislature. For example, even if Congress suggests that Agency *A* is immune to budget cuts for the next twenty years, this "promise" is constantly subject to revision: poor performance in the interim can be punished by Congress in spite of the promise.

Furthermore, if the agents have brackets that shape their individual and collective decisions, then it is reasonable to suppose that their principals will also have their own brackets. Because these brackets may affect the comparisons made, and inferences drawn, by the principals when choosing how to reward and/or punish the policy-makers, the agents' perceptions of the principals' brackets may themselves affect how the agents bracket decisions.

The potential impacts of bracketing by principals are visible in responses to policy crises and/or mishaps. That is, the decisions that are reviewed *ex post* are typically not randomly selected. Rather, in line with the logic behind fire alarm oversight discussed above, oversight often occurs "when something went wrong." If choices tend to be reviewed only if they were made in a sequence of choices that led to a policy failure, then agents will tend to make their decisions with an eye toward potential blame avoidance. This reality suggests a constructive role for (low cost) continuous evaluation attached to low stake rewards – such evaluation systems mitigates the worries leading to blame avoidance strategies and can strengthen selection effects and intrinsic motivations such as organizational identification and professionalism.

Conclusions

Political accountability is, at its heart, about achieving congruence between the interests of the people and the decisions made by their government officials. Much work has focused on how to align the incentives of these officials with those of the citizens. Already a very difficult challenge, incorporating the notion of choice brackets – that is, accounting for constrained, imperfect decision-making processes by the individuals responsible for policy-making – would seem at first blush to complicate matters even more. However, not only is it important to confront the challenge, it is also important to pause and recognize that choice brackets might have salutary effects in the pursuit of accountability. For example, a narrow bracketing might effectively better align the "effective" incentives of the agent with those of the principals. Similarly, bracketing is not the only cognitive limitation in real decision-making. That is, from an empirical standpoint, overly broad bracketing can lead to other pathologies, such as calculation errors, cognitive exhaustion, and indecision/paralysis.

Accordingly, it is important to keep the notion of bracketing in mind when evaluating the performance of both the agents and the accountability mechanisms within which the agents are working. Selective rewards and diagnostic information are central to aligning agents' incentives with those of their principals, but the effects of these tools are conditioned by the agents' choice brackets – these tools can work only to the degree that their effect on the agents' incentives are reflected *within* the agents' brackets. Even more provocatively, the agents' brackets may themselves be altered by details of the accountability mechanisms, such as the timing of review and rewards and how the agents' choices are reflected in measures of the agents' performances. As hopefully indicated by the brief consideration of real-world accountability mechanisms, there are many directions for both theoretical and empirical research into the bidirectional relationship between bracketing and institutional design.

PART IV

OUTSIDE THE PUBLIC EYE? PRIVATE INTERESTS AND POLICYMAKING

12

Legislator Advocacy on Behalf of Constituents and Corporate Donors: A Case Study of the Federal Energy Regulatory Commission

Eleanor Neff Powell, Devin Judge-Lord, and Justin Grimmer

The extent to which corporate campaign contributions influence elected officials is a central question in American politics. Much of the academic research in this area has focused on whether campaign contributions influence legislators' roll-call votes. These numerous studies have produced somewhat mixed results. On the whole, however, the answer appears to be no: that, most of the time, campaign contributions don't influence legislator behavior in the context of a roll-call vote. The literature's focus on detecting a potential influence of money on roll-call votes is unsurprising given the availability of roll-call voting data. Still, the availability and visibility of roll-call votes also make them a poor vehicle for those seeking to quietly influence government decisions without drawing scrutiny from journalists, activists, or constituents.

Compared to the intense scrutiny of roll-call votes, scholars have paid much less attention to behind the scenes congressional advocacy and oversight activities, such as when legislators write letters or emails to government bureaucrats urging them toward or against some decision.[1] While these letters are technically subject to federal open records laws, the disclosure process is often slow and laborious, meaning that, in practice, these letters rarely see the light of day and are highly unlikely to draw public scrutiny. Thus, securing a letter of support from an individual legislator may be a preferred vehicle for those seeking to quietly influence specific government decisions through campaign contributions.

This chapter uses the letters that legislators write directly to federal agencies to deeply examine their relationships with one agency – the Federal Energy Regulatory Commission (FERC). We assess the extent to which legislators' letters to FERC are related to constituents' concerns or corporate campaign

---

[1] This has begun to change in the last few years with recent studies by Mills and Kalaf-Hughes (2015); Ritchie (2017); Lowande (2019); Lowande, Ritchie, and Lauterbach (2018); Judge-Lord, Grimmer, and Powell (2018).

contributions. Specifically, we investigate whether campaign contributions from political action committees (PACs) linked to corporations in the energy sector are correlated with the number of letters that legislators write to the Commission on behalf of those companies. In essence, this is a question of who are the principals that legislators are advocating for: constituents or corporate donors? We find that Republicans and those who receive money from the energy sector write relatively more letters to FERC on behalf of energy companies but not on behalf of constituents. In contrast, Democrats write comparatively more often in opposition to energy companies.

To some extent, these results capture a general focus on energy issues; the overall number of letters a legislator writes to FERC – not just pro-business letters – is positively correlated with energy-sector campaign contributions both in particular electoral cycles and legislative sessions and over a legislator's career. Yet, there is evidence that elected officials who receive more money from the industry in a cycle write more on behalf of companies than against them in the following legislative session. Legislators that receive more money from the energy sector do pay more overall attention to energy issues, but they are also more likely to take a supportive position.

Additionally, while most constituent letters advocate against proposed energy projects, most non-constituent letters advocate in favor of named businesses. Campaign contributions are much stronger predictors of pro-business advocacy than other kinds of attention to energy issues, such as energy-related constituency service or advocacy against energy projects.

WHY STUDY LESS VISIBLE LEGISLATOR ADVOCACY TO BUREAUCRATIC AGENCIES

Attempting to study the influence of campaign contributions on political outcomes is fraught with methodological and observational challenges. As two of us (Powell and Grimmer) have written previously, two of the primary challenges to studying the influence of money on the most visible form of congressional behavior (roll-call votes) are legality and visibility (Powell and Grimmer, 2016). Regarding legality, as the United States Office of Government Ethics (2013) describes, if something of value is given, offered, or promised with the intent "to influence any official act," it is illegal behavior on the part of the contributor. Similarly, on the recipient side, if a public official demands, seeks, receives, or accepts an item of value, it is illegal behavior on the part of the legislator. Given threats of prosecution and jail time, we might expect both contributors and politicians to avoid public actions that could be construed in such a way.

And even if an action is legal, it might still create the appearance of impropriety and therefore create an incentive for legislators to obscure it. To the extent that both campaign contributors who might be seeking favors and elected officials who seek campaign contributions are concerned about appearances, we might expect elected officials to avoid taking visible public actions that could be viewed as corrupt. Rather, both the elected officials and contributors should prefer actions that achieve the same end but through less observable means.

As we elaborate in the following section, much of the research on money in politics has focused on highly visible outcomes such as roll-call votes – the least likely places that these actors would want to connect themselves. In contrast, congressional letter-writing to bureaucratic agencies is much less visible and thus a promising place to look for the influence of money in politics. These letters, which we have obtained through labor-intensive Freedom of Information Act requests and web scraping, are not easily accessible to the public, and both legislators and campaign contributors may reasonably assume that these documents will never be subject to public scrutiny.

It is also reasonable to assume that constituents would be unlikely to hold a legislator accountable for a letter that may influence a bureaucratic agency to take some action that may result in a policy outcome undesirable to a constituent. This complicated sequence of actions would serve to substantially reduce what Arnold called the "traceability" of the action – that is, the ability of a citizen to connect a policy outcome back to an individual legislator (Arnold, 1990). First, as Carpenter and Libgober discuss in Chapter 14 of this volume, government agency decisions often lack traceability – attentive interest groups (and thus citizens) are often unable to trace policy outcomes to agency decisions. Second, as Frances Lee examines in Chapter 9 in this volume, legislators in today's Congress continue to use procedural tactics to reduce the traceability of bills, which make it more difficult for citizens to hold legislators accountable. Likewise, because direct legislator communication with government agencies usually escapes public attention, citizens are unlikely to link executive-branch decisions to legislators, even in the rare cases where they are aware of agency decisionmaking.

A further reason to focus on letters that legislators write directly to federal agencies rather than on the more oft-studied roll-call votes is that many government decisions that affect businesses are made by agencies rather than Congress. If legislators aim to help a donor, their oversight powers may thus often be more useful than their legislative powers. As an independent commission with broad discretion over policy, permitting, and enforcement ranging from price controls on electricity markets to the construction of interstate natural gas pipelines, FERC decisions have major consequences for energy companies.

Legislator letters are better for studying the potential influence of campaign donations because of their specificity and the autonomy with which legislators can write a letter. Roll-call votes are often noisy signals because legislation often addresses multiple issues. It may be difficult to assess whether a legislator supported legislation because it helped a donor or for some other reason.

Additionally, if a link exists between campaign donations to specific legislators and the behavior of those legislators, we are more likely to see it where legislators have the most latitude. Whereas floor votes are on legislation crafted by increasingly powerful party leaders (see Drutman's Chapter 13 in this volume for a review), legislators have more autonomy in letter writing. This autonomy allows legislators to substitute direct advocacy to the bureaucracy for legislative work when the politics of their chamber prevents them from pursuing their policy goals through legislation (Ritchie, 2017). The specificity and autonomy of legislator letters make them an ideal place to look for the influence of campaign donations.

Finally, before reviewing previous research on the influence of money in American politics, we must add a necessary note of caution about the conclusions we can draw in this chapter. This project is an observational study that looks at the correlation between campaign contributions and attempts to influence the Federal Energy Regulatory Commission through legislative letters. We are limited by our data and can only use cross-sectional designs. That said, our results suggest interesting patterns that deserve to be interrogated with data that enables more robust research designs.

WHO ARE LEGISLATORS SERVING? CONSTITUENTS OR CORPORATE DONORS?

In this chapter, we're primarily focused on understanding what motivates legislators when they write advocacy letters to the Federal Energy Regulatory Commission. Are they writing on behalf of constituents (voters) as a form of constituency service? Or are they writing on behalf of corporate interests, and in particular corporate entities that have given them campaign contributions?

Theory: Why Legislators May Advocate for Constituents?

To understand why legislators may write letters on behalf of constituents (i.e., performing constituency service), we turn to the broader literature on what motivates Members of Congress? The classic answer comes from Mayhew (1974). In *Congress: The Electoral Connection*, Mayhew argues that re-election is the primary (or at least the proximate) motivation because it is a necessary step to achieve other goals (such as policy or power within Washington). Constituency service activity has traditionally been viewed as a way to improve one's re-election prospects by assisting individual (or groups of) constituents.

As Cain, Ferejohn, and Fiorina (1984) and Cain, Ferejohn, and Fiorina (1987) elaborate, constituency service helps to build a member's "personal vote." Indeed, in their survey of congressional staffers, Cain, Ferejohn, and Fiorina's (1987) found that the overwhelming majority of staffers believed that constituency service activity has electoral payoffs. Mayhew (1974) and

Cain, Ferejohn, and Fiorina (1987) theories about the re-election benefits of constituency service would suggest that we should see legislators advocating on behalf of constituents to FERC. But the traditional absence of systematic constituency service data, means that until now we've rarely had the opportunity to study them empirically.

Theory: Why Legislators May Act on Behalf of Corporate Donors?

Conversely, the high price of modern congressional campaigns may also mean that re-election-minded legislators may also be acutely aware of the need to serve their campaign donors. While constituency service – helping individual voters – may incrementally (voter by voter) improve a legislator's electoral prospects, the campaign contributions a legislator receives can be used in a myriad of ways to potentially boost a legislator's campaign. While the political science literature disagrees on the impact of campaign spending and political campaigns more generally on electoral outcomes, few politicians would dispute the widely held view among political practitioners that campaign funds help members win re-election.

In line with Arnold's (1979) argument of the anticipated benefits of particularistic spending, elected officials have two kinds of incentives. Elected officials have incentives to advance the interests of potential donors. Projects authorized by FERC may have direct financial benefits to a legislator's district, providing an opportunity to claim credit (Arnold, 1979; Grimmer, Westwood, and Messing, 2015). Likewise, projects are opportunities for businesses to profit, and thus an opportunity for elected officials to demonstrate their value to potential corporate funders. Within the set of potential energy projects, it is reasonable to expect that elected officials will advocate those in their district and those of potential donors.

The Uneven Evidence for the Influence of Money in American Politics

Extensive scholarship examines the influence of money on American politics. And yet, there is only mixed evidence that money influences the legislative process. The literature has demonstrated that donors appear to contribute in ways consistent with short-term access seeking (Snyder, 1992; Romer and Snyder, 1994; Powell and Grimmer, 2016; Barber, 2016; Fouirnaies and Hall, 2018).

Yet, the evidence that legislators undertake actions explicitly for donors is limited. There are some exceptions. First, scholarship on contributions to congressional committees finds that corporations donate to pivotal legislators' congressional committees ((Powell and Grimmer, 2016); Berry and Fowler, 2015). In addition to showing that donors appear interested in short-term access-seeking and contribute to those members influential in policy areas relevant to their business interests, work by Kalla and Broockman (2016) shows that donors are more likely to get meetings with key members of Congress.

This finding is again consistent with this short-term access-seeking behavior. Yet, there is a considerable gap between taking a meeting with a donor and actually advancing their interests. Overall, this literature fails to connect contributions to specific actions by legislators.

Scholars have also investigated whether campaign contributions influence roll-call votes in Congress (For a canonical review, see Ansolabehere, Snyder, and Ting, 2003). Although the findings aren't entirely consistent in this area, the vast majority of studies fail to find an impact of campaign contributions on roll-call voting. Given that both campaign contributors and elected officials may be concerned by issues of legality and visibility, highly visible roll-call votes are an unlikely place to find a correlation between campaign funding and legislator behavior.

There is relatively little work specifically examining the links between campaign contributions, legislators, and the bureaucracy.[2] This is surprising because it is an intuitive location to look for campaign donors seeking influence; these less visible areas of policymaking are where we would expect to find corporate influence (Hall, 1996). Further, bureaucrats have a strong incentive to reply to legislators' requests. They have this incentive because legislators have both oversight powers over federal agencies and because legislators can influence agencies' budgets. And as a result, we expect that donors may contribute to legislators to subsidize their efforts creating a relationship between campaign donations and behavior. Thus letters from legislators to bureaucrats may be a promising potential avenue for those seeking to quietly influence government policy in a given area in that the letters are unlikely to receive public scrutiny and often involve relatively obscure federal agencies that aren't well known or understood by the public.

WHY STUDY THE FEDERAL ENERGY REGULATORY COMMISSION?

Like many agencies within the federal bureaucracy, The Federal Energy Regulatory Commission (FERC) makes policy and enforcement decisions that have major consequences for jobs, lives, profits, and the cost of the commodities it regulations. FERC regulates electricity markets, oil and gas pipelines, hydropower projects, and liquified natural gas export projects. The Commission's decisions have major implications for business profits and the consumers they serve. For example, because many natural gas pipelines cross state lines, FERC largely controls pipeline market entry. Similarly, because electricity grids are regional, conflicts between electric-generating companies and state regulators or regional transmission organizations are often appealed

---

[2] One notable exception is Gordon and Hafer (2005), which develops a formal model of the strategic and signaling complexity of these relationships and finds that large corporate donors overseen by the Nuclear Regulatory Commission are both less compliant and less monitored by the bureaucracy.

to FERC. FERC regulations and their application thus impact the prices that consumers pay for electricity, the reliability of the electric grid, and the ability of new companies to enter markets largely controlled by FERC-authorized and regulated monopolies.

In many ways, FERC is a hard case to find congressional influence. It was designed to be largely insulated from political influence. FERC is self-funding. It is authorized to collect revenue by the Federal Power Act (FPA) and the Omnibus Budget Reconciliation Act of 1986. These revenues fully offset FERC's appropriations, potentially making FERC more independent from Congress than agencies who must compete for limited tax revenue.

FERC is also more independent from presidential power than most agencies, further insulating it from political negotiations between Congress and the President. While technically in the Department of Energy, FERC is structured as an independent non-partisan commission. The five commissioners are appointed to staggered five-year terms, and no more than three can be from any one party. A majority of the Commission at any given time may not have been appointed by the sitting president, and even when the president has appointed a majority, the Commission may not support the administration's priorities. For example, in 2018, the Commission, a majority of whom were appointed by President Trump, rejected the administration's proposal to provide special support for coal and nuclear power plants by requiring consumers to pay higher rates for electricity from these sources.

Yet, like many agencies, FERC receives hundreds of letters from Members of Congress each year. Because FERC's decisions are so consequential to energy company profits, its record-keeping for external communication is meticulous, presenting a particularly good opportunity for a case study of congressional letter-writing where we can be confident that that the data are relatively free from the selection problems that plague records of congressional correspondence with other federal agencies.

LETTER WRITING AND FOIA DATA

To examine the relationship between campaign contributions and letter-writing activity, we assemble a new dataset of legislator-agency contacts covering a wide array of government agencies and the broadest time frame to date. We submitted over 400 Freedom of Information Act (FOIA) requests for all records of communication from Members of Congress and their staff to all cabinet departments, their component agencies, and thirty-four independent agencies for the period from 2007 to 2018. We also used web scraping to gather all publicly available records. For some agencies, like FERC, that have more careful document retention, the combination of FOIA requests and web scraping yielded a longer time frame. In this chapter, we analyze all letters written to FERC between January 1, 2000, and December 31, 2018. The other agencies included in the data presented in Figure 12.1 generally have data for 2007 and 2018.

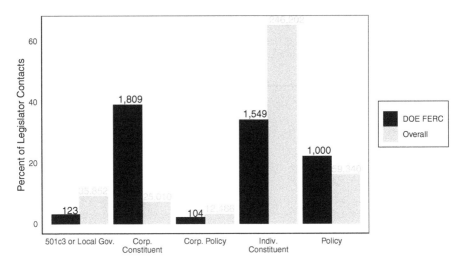

FIGURE 12.1 The distribution across types of congressional requests FERC vs. all agencies

The x-axis shows our four categories of letters: 501c3 (i.e. non-profit) or local government, corporate constituent, individual constituent, and policy. The y-axis shows the percentage of letters that were of that type. The black bars are for letters written to FERC (which is a subsidiary of the Department of Energy) and the gray bars are for the overall averages across all agencies that we have previously coded. The numbers on top of each bar represent the total number of letters represented by the percentages.

As of August 2020, all departments except for the State Department have provided records to us, though the majority of Department of Justice components have not yet released records to us. As for independent agencies, we are waiting on records from the SEC, FLRA, CFPB, CIA, and Appalachian Regional Commission. The remaining twenty-eight independent agencies have provided records, though some are still in the process of reviewing and releasing additional records. Of these, eighteen have been sufficiently cleaned and coded. All of the FERC data have been carefully cleaned and hand-coded. In all, we have filed 421 FOIA requests, yielding 487,890 observations.

Upon receiving records, we extracted names matching variations on the names of members of Congress and matched them to other datasets such as ideology scores (Lewis et al., 2018), committee membership (Stewart and Woon, 2017), and committee oversight (Lewis and Selin, 2012). We also made a considerable effort to verify and update committee membership data.

In this chapter, we draw on both general patterns of legislator letter-writing across all agencies and particularly on letters sent to the Federal Energy Regulatory Commission. For the Federal Energy Regulatory Commission, we obtained all 7,600 letters received by FERC and marked "congressional" since 1990. Most, but not all of these, are from Members of the US Congress. For this chapter, we focus on 6,230 of these letters from 2000 to 2018. Many of these letters are co-signed, which for the purposes of this chapter (identifying patterns in contacts between legislators and FERC), we are treating as equivalent to writing the letter. Including the co-signed letters yields 6,001 member-level observations for 2000–2018 that we have thus far connected to campaign donations from the energy sector. In the Appendix, we include examples of FERC letters.

WHAT ARE CONGRESSIONAL LETTERS TO FERC ABOUT?

First, we identify the interests on whose behalf members of Congress advocated. We classify letters into four categories: (1) Constituency Service on behalf of an individual, (2) Constituency Service on behalf of a for-profit Corporation, (3) Letters on behalf of a nonprofit or local government, and (4) letters about policy issues. To classify such a large volume of letters, we relied on a combination of hand-coding and some inductively developed automated coding rules applied to letters that were not classified by human coders.[3] For example, letters that mention "rulemaking" were automatically classified as policy unless a human coder classified them differently.

We consider constituent service as broader than casework. For example, we coded Senator Rubio asking the IRS for special treatment for residents of hurricane-affected parts of Florida as "Individual Constituent Service." We note these "hard cases" to illustrate the boundaries of our coding scheme. Most contacts were more easily parsed into either individual casework or policy work related to hearings, regulations, and legislation.

Classifying letters addressed to each agency allows us to compare patterns of congressional advocacy targeting FERC to congressional letter-writing targeting other agencies. Figure 12.1 shows how letter-writing to FERC compares to letter-writing to all other agencies. To interpret the figure, across all agencies, over 70% of letters were written on behalf of constituents (144,162 letters), but for FERC, only about 35% of their letters were written on behalf of constituents (1,459 letters). Across all agencies, most letters are written on behalf of individual constituents, followed by letters on behalf of local governments or nonprofits, followed by policy-related letters, and finally letters on behalf of corporate constituents (Judge-Lord, Grimmer, and Powell, 2018).

In contrast to the broader patterns we observe in letter-writing to all agencies, we find very different patterns of letter-writing to FERC. We observe much less individual constituent service and advocacy on behalf of local governments and nonprofits and much greater levels of corporate advocacy and policy-related work. Notably, across all agencies, letter-writing on behalf of corporate constituents is the least common form of letter-writing activity, nearly 45% of the letters to FERC are on behalf of individual for-profit corporations.

---

[3] For details on coding, see the online appendix to this chapter.

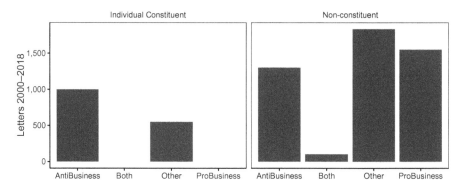

FIGURE 12.2 What types of letters are supportive of businesses?
The left panel shows letters written to FERC on behalf of individual constituents. The right panel shows letters written to FERC on behalf of non-constituents. The bars show what those letters were arguing for, broken down into four categories: against a named business (Antibusiness), in favor of a named business (Probusiness), both for and against named businesses (Both), and Other (other is a catch-all category that may include advocating for or against specific regulations which may benefit (or harm) a business, but no business names were mentioned in the letter.

We can learn more by considering not just on whose behalf the letter is written but also what the letter is advocating for or against. Figure 12.2 provides strong evidence that most constituent letters are advocating against businesses rather than in favor of businesses. In contrast to the constituent letters, most non-constituent letters advocate in favor of named businesses.

WHICH MEMBERS ATTEMPT TO INFLUENCE FERC?

We begin our exploration of which legislators attempt to influence the Federal Energy Regulatory Commission by examining the legislators most active in their communications with FERC. These figures use data from 2000 to 2018. Figure 12.3 shows the most active legislators and their letter-writing activity over time (2000–2018). As the bottom panel of Figure 12.3 shows, Rep. Virgil Goode was one of the most active House letter-writers to FERC.[4] Interestingly, his letter-writing activity was largely focused on FERC with over 67% of his total letters (across all agencies) written to FERC. During the period when he wrote the most letters, electric utility companies (which are overseen by FERC) were one of his greatest sources of campaign contributions. The letters Rep. Goode wrote to FERC illustrate the challenge of linking issues discussed in the letters to campaign contributions. Rep. Goode's letters mention the Smith

---

4 Also of note is that Rep. Goode is one of the relative few party-switchers in recent congresses. He switched from a Democrat to Independent prior to the 2000 election and then switched from Independent to Republican prior to the 2002 election.

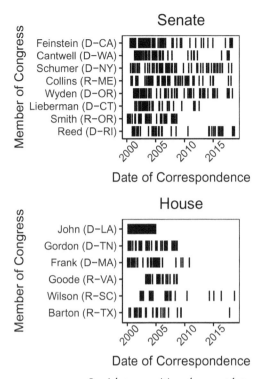

FIGURE 12.3 Legislators writing the most letters to FERC

The top panel shows the Senators who wrote the most letters to FERC and the bottom panel shows the Representatives who wrote the most letters to FERC. Each hash mark indicates the legislator wrote a letter on that date. Note that many members listed in the table weren't in the chamber for the entire period, so blank stretches at the end or beginning of the line may indicate the member was out of office during that period.

Mountain Project and Appalachian Power, a subsidiary of and a project related to American Electric Power (AEP).

Variation in Advocacy for Constituents and Business by Party and Majority Status

One striking feature of legislator advocacy to FERC is that Democrats and Republicans behave differently, and they behave differently when they're in the Majority versus when they're in the Minority. When Republicans controlled the Majority, they wrote approximately 60% of their letters to FERC on behalf of named businesses. In contrast, when the Republicans were in the Minority, those ratios flip, and they wrote nearly 70% of their letters on behalf of constituents.

We observe very different letter-writing patterns for the Democrats. When the Democrats are in the Majority, they write approximately 65% of their letters on behalf of constituents – notably different than Republicans in the Majority who were primarily advocating on behalf of companies while in the Majority. When Democrats lose majority status, their advocacy behaviors change; they write more than half of their letters on behalf of businesses. While both parties change their behavior when they move from the Majority to the Minority, the change in behavior is substantially greater for Republicans.

The variation by majority status is largely explained by changes in pro-business advocacy. The overall volume of letters on behalf of individual constituents is relatively consistent across parties and congresses. In contrast, where Republicans were in the Majority and Democrats in the Minority, both parties made a higher volume of requests on behalf of businesses.

To further interrogate the relationship between party and majority status, Figure 12.4 shows how legislators advocating to FERC on behalf of business and individual constituents varies by party, whether the legislator was in the Majority or Minority and whether the legislator was a member of the president's party. Interestingly, neither the volume of pro-business advocacy nor the ratio of advocacy on behalf of individuals and companies varies by the party of the president's administration. Figure 12.4 shows consistency in the percentage of letters from each party when the president is a co-partisan and when the president is not. For example, the top-right two plots show that when Republicans were in the Majority, they did similar (higher) levels of advocacy

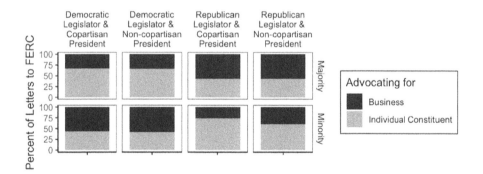

FIGURE 12.4 Who writes on behalf of constituents vs. business? By legislator party, majority status, and president partisanship

The two plots in the upper left corner show the percentage of advocacy on behalf of corporations and individuals for Democrats while they were in the Majority of their chamber. The far upper left plot shows when the legislator was a member of the president's party, and while the plot closer to the middle shows when the legislator was not a member of the president's party. The upper right-hand plots show the proportions of advocacy on behalf of corporations and individuals for Republicans while they were in the Majority. The far-right upper plot shows when the legislator was not a member of the president's party, and the plot closer to the middle shows when the legislator was a member of the president's party. The lower plots show the same proportions for when Democrats and Republicans were in the Minority.

on behalf of businesses under both Democratic and Republican presidents. Likewise, the bottom-left two plots show that when Democrats were in the Minority, they did similar (higher) levels of advocacy on behalf of businesses under both Democratic and Republican presidents.

In any given Congress, a legislators' letters on behalf of individuals are often driven by many constituent's reactions to one or two specific energy projects. It only takes one proposed energy project to generate a large volume of constituent mail. For example, in the 107th Congress, when Democrats were a majority in the Senate, Senator Bob Graham (D-FL) sent twenty-two letters to FERC requesting FERC's response to constituent concerns. Many were on behalf of individuals in his district who were upset by a pipeline expansion proposed by Florida Gas Transmission (an Enron Affiliate). Similarly, in the 110th Congress, when Republicans were in the Minority in the Senate, Richard Lugar (R-IN) sent nineteen letters to FERC requesting that FERC respond to his constituents' concerns, all of them opposing the proposed Rockies Express gas pipeline. In the same Congress, Representative Arcuri (D-NY) sent FERC ten letters, all relaying concerns from constituents about the proposed Millennium Pipeline Project. While these members were from different parties and different states, the pattern of constituent advocacy was the same; many constituents were all upset about the same project.

In contrast, when legislators write to FERC on behalf of businesses, each letter usually represents a different company or project. A large volume of pro-business letters thus represents advocacy on behalf of a large number of companies and projects. For example, in the 115th Congress, when Republicans held a majority in the House, Representative Mooney (R-WV) wrote twelve letters on behalf of businesses, each advocating for a different oil or gas pipeline project. Most of the companies were not located in Mooney's district, and several projects were not even in West Virginia. For example, Mooney advocated for three pipeline proposals from TransCanada, a major Canadian oil and gas company that controls 25% of the North American gas transportation market. Mooney also advocated for Enbridge's proposed pipeline in Michigan and Ohio.

While these data suggest that, during this period, both Democrats and Republicans do more pro-business advocacy when Republicans control the chamber, we want to be careful about the conclusions we draw from this limited observational data. One potential explanation could be that there are more proposed energy projects when Republicans are in the Majority and thus more pipelines and other projects for which legislators from both parties may advocate. This would explain higher levels of pro-business advocacy by both Democrats and Republicans when Republicans are in the Majority. Future research should examine this potential relationship and, likewise, the puzzling lack of relationship between legislator advocacy and partisan control of the White House and FERC.

DEMAND DRIVEN LETTER-WRITING?

One of the challenges of our approach to studying legislative letter-writing to federal agencies is that we don't observe the demand for letters from constituents or businesses. In an ideal world, we would account for the level of constituent demand for legislator advocacy. However, since our project covers both the US House and the US Senate, we can take advantage of the large differences in state population to proxy for the demand for letter-writing from constituents. For example, in 2018, the most populous state of California had a population of 39,557,045, while the least populated state of Wyoming had a population of only 577,737 (Wikipedia, 2019). Thus California's population is approximately sixty-eight times that of Wyoming, and it is not unreasonable to assume that California's senators receive more requests for constituency service than Wyoming's senators.

In our broader research across federal agencies, we typically see senators from larger states doing more constituency service than senators from smaller states. Figure 12.5 shows average Senate letter-writing by state population. We observe this positive relationship between state population and Senate letter-writing to all agencies. The bottom panel shows the relationship between state population and only Senate letter-writing to FERC.[5] Comparing the two panels, we see a weaker relationship between a state's population and letter-writing to FERC than we observed in the agency-wide data as a whole.

To more clearly highlight what states show the highest level of senatorial letter-writing, Figure 12.6 shows the number of Senate letters to FERC by state. As we saw in Figure 12.5, there is only a weak relationship between state population and senatorial letter-writing to FERC. The left-hand panel shows that while some senators from highly populated states write a lot of letters, such as senators from California and New York, other highly populated states such as Florida barely register. Once we adjust for state population (a rough proxy for constituent demand) and turn our attention to the right-hand panel in Figure 12.6, we see that Senate letter-writing from California and New York no longer stands out.

After adjusting for state population, we see that the most active letter-writing Senate delegations hail from Maine, Vermont, Wyoming, Rhode Island, and Montana. While some of these population-adjusted state leaders may be a surprise, others seem consistent with the role the energy sector plays in each state's economy. For example, Wyoming is per capita the top energy-producing state in the country with substantial reserves of oil and natural gas (Wyoming State Geologic Survey, 2019). Western state officials and their congressional delegations are also known to be particularly active on electricity grid policy, where there have recently been high-profile conflicts between state regulations and FERC regulations (personal correspondence with Ben Serrurier, Senior Manager of Market Development at an electric power developer).

---

5 Note the differences in y-axis scales between the two panels of this figure.

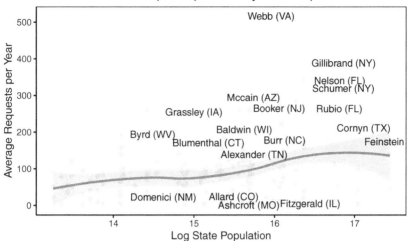

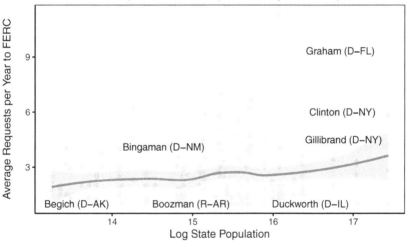

FIGURE 12.5 State population and senate letter-writing

The top panel shows average Senate letter-writing to all agencies by state population, and the bottom panel shows the average Senate letter-writing to FERC by state population. The figures include a lowess smoothing trend line and 95% confidence intervals.

THE RELATIONSHIP BETWEEN ADVOCACY AND CAMPAIGN CONTRIBUTIONS

We focus on the relationship between Political Action Committee (PAC) contributions from the energy sector to a legislators campaign and the legislator's letter-writing activity to FERC. We identify relevant PACs using industry codes

Total Number of Contacts from Members of the Senate | Contacts Per 100,000 Residents from Members of the Senate

Total Contacts   25 50 75 100 125

Contacts Per Capita   25 50 75

FIGURE 12.6 FERC contacts from senators by state

The left panel shows the total number of FERC contacts from senators by state. The right panel shows the contact per million residents from senators by state. Lighter colors show greater letter-writing activity.

assigned to each PAC by the Center for Responsive Politics. Given our focus on the Federal Energy Regulatory Commission and the jurisdiction of that Commission, we include in our totals all political action committees that the Center for Responsive Politics classifies as linked to companies in the Oil, Gas, or Energy sector, excluding those involved in energy extraction or manufacturing (since FERC does not regulate extraction). We create an industry-specific total of PAC contributions to a given member in an election cycle. Collectively this covers 428 PACs in the energy sector, which we then match to their PAC contributions received by each Member of Congress.

Figure 12.7 shows the average amount a member received in each election cycle from all energy sector PAC contributions combined. The figure reveals that the average legislator receives considerable support for their campaigns from energy-sector PACs. To put these numbers in perspective, in 2016 the average winning House race cost $1.5 million and the average winning Senate race cost $12 million, thus the over $700,000 the average Republican received from energy PACs is a substantial element of the party's fundraising base (Center for Responsive Politics, 2021).

Figure 12.8 shows the dramatic cross-party variation in support from the energy industry: Democrats received substantially less money from the energy sector. For example, in the 2012 election cycle, Democrats received approximately a third of what Republicans did from the energy sector.

We also observe substantial inequality across energy-sector PACs in how much money they contribute to congressional campaigns. Figure 12.9 highlights the money that the ten PACs that comprise the top 2% of energy PACs. The most active energy-sector PAC in the 2012 cycle was the Bechtel Company PAC, which contributed well over half a million dollars to members of Congress

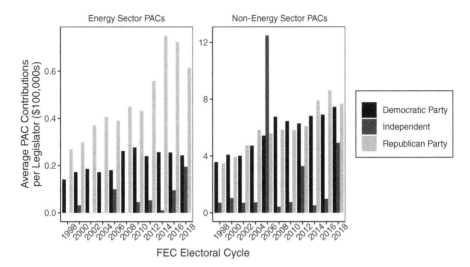

FIGURE 12.7 Average energy sector PAC contributions per member per cycle

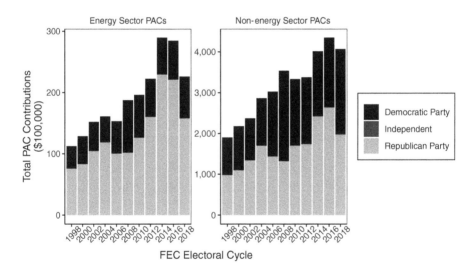

FIGURE 12.8 Cross-party differences in campaign contributions from energy sector PACs (left) and non-energy sector PACs (right)

Note y-scales differ.

in that cycle. The energy-sector PACs with the largest contributions in the 2018 cycle were the National Rural Electric Cooperative, Koch Industries, and Exxon. These differences across PACs and the often diverging goals of competing companies suggest that linking specific PACs to the companies and

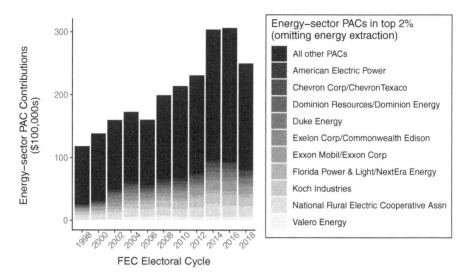

FIGURE 12.9 Unequal money across energy sector PACs

The ten PACs that comprise the top 2% of energy PACs (omitting energy extraction) contribute a disproportionate share of the energy industry's contributions. The contribution activity of those PACs across election cycles is highlighted in individual shades.

projects mentioned in the congressional letters to FERC may be a promising area for future research. In the concluding section, we discuss how we plan to pursue this line of research.

Having established that energy sector political action committees spend substantial sums of money on congressional campaigns, we now ask whether member-level variation in campaign funding from the energy sector is correlated with variation in legislator's letter-writing to FERC. The dependent variable in each model is the number of letters written by a legislator in a congress, either on behalf of energy-sector businesses, opposing energy-sector businesses, on behalf of individual constituents, or all of the above (i.e., the "type" of letter). Figure 12.10 displays bivariate campaign contribution and letter-writing regression results. We observe a positive relationship for overall letter-writing to FERC per cycle and pro-business letter-writing to FERC per cycle. The results show a somewhat weaker relationship between anti-business letter-writing to FERC and no evidence of a relationship between constituent letters and campaign contributions. In terms of the magnitude of the effect size, the model suggests that a member who receives $100,000 dollars in contributions from energy sector PACs writes 0.09 more pro-business letters to FERC in the following Congress compared to a legislator who receives no energy-sector PACs donations.

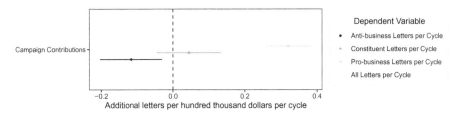

FIGURE 12.10 Bivariate models: Campaign contributions and letter-writing to FERC

These figures show the point estimate and 95% confidence intervals for the energy industry PAC contributions on letter-writing activity to FERC. Each color represents a different dependent variable (a different type of letter). The full regression tables for this model are in Table 12.C.1 in the Appendix.

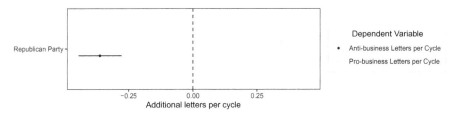

FIGURE 12.11 Bivariate models: Party membership and letter-writing to FERC

These figures show the point estimate and 95% confidence intervals for being a Republican legislator on letter-writing activity to FERC. Each shade represents a different dependent variable (type of letter). The full regression model is available in Table 12.C.2 in the Appendix.

Turning from campaign contributions to party membership, we observed large partisan differences in letter-writing activity earlier in this chapter in Figure 12.4. In Figure 12.11, we see a bivariate model looking at the relationship between being a Republican and writing letters to FERC.[6] The results in Figure 12.11 show stark partisan differences in letter-writing, with Republicans writing significantly more pro-business letters than Democrats and writing many fewer anti-business letters than Democrats.

Next, we bring both party membership and energy industry PAC contributions into a multivariate model predicting letter-writing activity to FERC. Figure 12.12 shows the point estimates and 95% confidence intervals for the coefficients in the multivariate model with both party and energy industry PAC contributions.[7] By including both legislator party and energy industry campaign contributions, we see that energy industry contributions

---

[6] The full regression model is available in Table 12.C.2 in the Appendix.
[7] The full regression table is available in Table 12.C.5 in the Appendix.

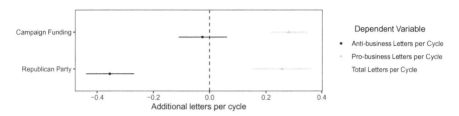

FIGURE 12.12 Multivariate models: Campaign contributions, party, and letter-writing to FERC

These figures show the point estimate and 95% confidence intervals for the coefficients in the multivariate model. Each shade represents a different dependent variable (type of letter). The full regression table is available in Table 12.C.5 in the Appendix.

positively predict total letter-writing and pro-business letters, while they do not appear to affect anti-business letters. Again, we find that Republicans write fewer anti-business letters than Democrats.

Figure 12.13 shows the predicted number of letters that a member of Congress writes to FERC in a Congress given the level of PAC contributions they received from the energy sector in the previous cycle. Because many members do not write to FERC at all, these averages are small. The top panel of Figure 12.13 shows a steep increase in the average number of letters to FERC on behalf of an energy company for both Democrats and Republicans as the level of PAC contributions (the y-axis) increases. The bottom panel of Figure 12.13 shows little increase in the number of letters to FERC in opposition to an energy company for Democrats and no increase for Republicans as the level of PAC contributions (the y-axis) increases.

Figure 12.14 shows the predicted probability that a member of Congress writes to FERC in a Congress given the level of PAC contributions they received from the energy sector in the previous cycle. The top panel of Figure 12.14 shows a steep increase in the probability of writing to FERC on behalf of an energy company for both Democrats and Republicans as the level of PAC contributions (the y-axis) increases. The bottom panel of Figure 12.14 shows little increase in the probability of writing to FERC in opposition to an energy company for Democrats and no increase for Republicans as the level of PAC contributions (the y-axis) increases. The slight positive relationship between energy-sector PAC contributions and letters to FERC opposing energy companies or projects is likely due to a latent interest in energy issues or a prevalence of energy projects in one's district. The much greater correlation between energy PAC contributions and advocating on behalf of businesses may reflect latent interests or district characteristics but also likely reflects the impact of energy-sector campaign funding.

The findings in this section provide new insights into the relationship between elected officials and PACs. Our results demonstrate that there is a

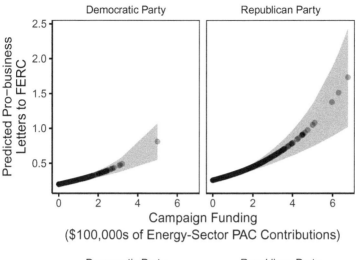

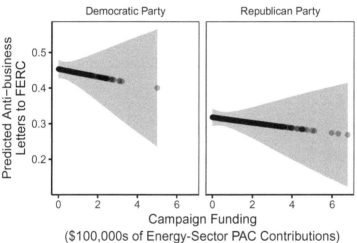

FIGURE 12.13 Predicted number of letters to FERC

These figures show the predicted values and 95% confidence intervals from the multivariate model of the number of pro-business letters (top) and anti-business letters (bottom). The left panels show the predicted number of pro-business and anti-business letters per Congress from Democrats at the range of PAC contributions received by candidates in our data. The right panels show the predicted number of pro-business and anti-business letters from Republicans for the same values. The full regression table is available in Table 12.C.5 in the Appendix.

strong correlation between PAC donations and the behavior of legislators. Of course, our results cannot demonstrate that there is a quid pro quo between legislators and PACs. Rather, our evidence shows that there are relationships between legislators and PACs. Legislators receive donations from PACs, and these same legislators advocate for companies at FERC.

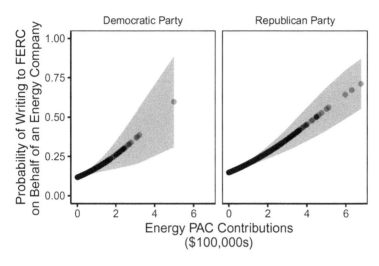

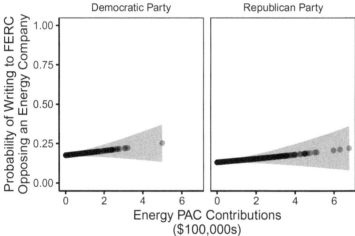

FIGURE 12.14 Predicted probability of writing to FERC

These figures show the predicted probability and 95% confidence intervals for a logit model that is identical to the multivariate Poisson model, but estimating whether a member wrote to FERC in a given Congress rather than the number of letters. The top panel shows the predicted probability of writing on or more pro-business letters per Congress at the range of PAC contributions received by candidates in our data. The bottom panel shows the predicted probability of writing one or more anti-business letters for the same values.

CONCLUSION

In this deep dive into legislator relationships with one government agency, we find evidence consistent with the expectation that energy industry campaign contributions lead to more pro-business letters to FERC. We believe this chapter represents a starting point for what we can learn about legislator motivations and the impact of money on congressional and bureaucratic relations. In future work, we hope to expand our analysis to other agencies where corporate money may shape advocacy behavior. We also hope to look at the impact of the legislator's letters on the actions taken by the agency – in particular, we hope to focus on the speed of the review by FERC as an outcome, as this is often what companies seek in these requests.

Future research could also investigate other forms of interest group activity (both in the form of other types of campaign contributions such as super PACs and independent expenditures, as well as other reasons why legislators may advocate for corporations. For example, the correlation we find between corporate campaign donations and legislator advocacy may indicate much broader and more complex relationships between elected officials and corporations. For example, donations are likely one part of broader lobbying efforts. In turn, specific lobbying efforts are only one part of the dense relationship between corporations and elected officials resulting from the revolving door between legislators and congressional staffers and corporate lobbying initiatives.

One of the most promising areas of future research is connecting company-specific campaign contributions to FERC letters. On the surface, it would seem that it would be relatively straightforward to link political action committees associated with individual companies to the companies that legislators mention in letters to FERC. The Federal Election Commission's rules require that the PAC's name include the full name of the connected organization (sponsoring company or organization) must appear in the name of the SSF. However, one challenge in this industry area is that if a linked organization has parent companies or subsidiaries, those names may not be included in the name of the PAC. Thus we need to connect the companies to their subsidiary/parent companies. Furthermore, the letters to FERC often only mention the name of an energy project that is being developed by a company and do not always include the full sponsoring company in the letter. So to be complete, we need to link parent companies, subsidiary companies, and related energy projects.

As an example of the challenge of connecting corporate PACs to companies and projects mentioned in FERC letters, consider the Williams Company. The Williams Company is a Fortune 500 energy company based in Tulsa, Oklahoma, whose primary business is natural gas, but also has subsidiary parts that cover petroleum and electricity generation (Bloomberg, 2019). The Williams Company PAC has been an active contributor to congressional campaigns in recent cycles. In the 2016 election cycle, the Williams Company PAC contributed $392,000 to congressional candidates, with 7% going to Democrats and 93% to Republicans.

Connecting these contributions to letters written by members of Congress on behalf of the company is more challenging. The Williams Company also owns the Transcontinental Pipeline Company, the Transcontinental Gas Company, and the Transco Pipeline Company. Furthermore, they're the company behind a large number of projects such as the Atlantic Sunrise Project, and the Northeast Supply Enhancement (NESE) Pipeline, among many others. Unfortunately, for our purposes here, the name Williams doesn't appear in their subsidiary companies. Nor does the name Williams appear in the energy projects undertaken by the company. To attempt to link parent companies that have corporate PACs that make campaign contributions like the Williams Company to the projects and subsidiary companies mentioned in the letters, we plan to draw on a combination of news reports and company filings with the Securities Exchange Commission.

While the projects we have outlined here comprise an ambitious research agenda, we believe they represent a collection of concrete steps that will help advance our knowledge in this area. Moreover, we believe that taken together, we can use them to better understand the relationships between legislators and bureaucrats.

12.A SAMPLE LETTERS TO THE FEDERAL ENERGY REGULATORY COMMISSION

SUSAN M. COLLINS
MAINE

United States Senate
WASHINGTON, DC 20510-1904

COMMITTEES
HOMELAND SECURITY AND
GOVERNMENTAL AFFAIRS,
Ranking Member
ARMED SERVICES
SPECIAL COMMITTEE
ON AGING

PO Box 655
Bangor, ME 04402
April 28, 2008

Mr. Mark Whitenton
Director, Division of Congressional and
Federal Energy Regulatory Commission
888 First Street, NE, Room 11H
Washington, DC 20426

Fax: (202) 208-2106

Dear Mr. Whitenton:

Senator Collins has been contacted by ▉▉▉ Agent for Wilsons on Moosehead Lake in Greenville Junction, ME with a request for assistance. ▉▉▉ expressed concern that Florida Energy and Light is attempting to take over the driveway of his business and make it a public way. ▉▉▉ states that turning the driveway into a public way would cause his business great hardship and asked that the Federal Energy Regulatory Commission intervene on his behalf.

Senator Collins has a strong desire to be responsive to constituent requests; with this in mind, I have taken the liberty of providing a copy of ▉▉▉ letter to Senator Collins to you. Please review this matter and provide any appropriate assistance to assure that his concerns are addressed.

Thank you for your help; if you have any questions, or need additional information, please do not hesitate to contact me at (207) 945-0417.

Sincerely,

Deidre Anderson

Deidre Anderson
Staff Assistant to
Susan M. Collins
United States Senator

FIGURE 12.A.1 Example of constituency service letter. This is a constituency service letter written by Senator Susan Collins (R-ME) to FERC on April 28, 2008

ALEX X. MOONEY
2ND DISTRICT, WEST VIRGINIA

FINANCIAL SERVICES COMMITTEE
SUBCOMMITTEE ON
CAPITAL MARKETS AND
GOVERNMENT SPONSORED ENTERPRISES
SUBCOMMITTEE ON
MONETARY POLICY AND TRADE

Congress of the United States
House of Representatives
Washington, DC 20515-4802

CHARLESTON OFFICE:
405 CAPITOL STREET
SUITE 514
CHARLESTON, WV 25301
(304) 925-5964

MARTINSBURG OFFICE:
300 FOXCROFT AVENUE
SUITE 102
MARTINSBURG, WV 25401
(304) 264-8810

WASHINGTON OFFICE:
1232 LONGWORTH HOUSE OFFICE BUILDING
WASHINGTON, DC 20515
(202) 225-2711

http://mooney.house.gov

2017 OCT 19 P 3:10

FEDERAL ENERGY
REGULATORY COMMISSION

October 12, 2017

Neil Chatterjee
Chairman, Federal Energy Regulatory Commission
888 First Street, NE
Washington, DC 20426

RE: Dominion Energy
       Supply Header Project
       Docket No. CP15-555-000

Dear Chairman Chatterjee,

I am writing to express my support for the Dominion Energy, Supply Header Project that is passing through West Virginia and will improve the transmission of natural gas throughout the region.

With your recent appointment, there are many shovel ready projects that will be of great benefit to West Virginia. I know you share my concern regarding the significant backlog of project approvals—and I know you will work diligently to get these projects moving forward.

These projects in and around West Virginia stand to create over 49,000 good-paying jobs and will help jumpstart the economy in the region.

I hope that the Commission will ensure that local landowner and community interests will be carefully vetted to ensure that the project is completed in a safe and efficient manner.

I support the Dominion Energy, Supply Header Project project and hope you will act swiftly to approve this important project.

Sincerely,

Alex X. Mooney
Member of Congress

PRINTED ON RECYCLED PAPER

2017- 00100

FIGURE 12.A.2 Example of energy project advocacy. This is a letter written by Rep. Alex Mooney (R-WV2) to FERC on October 12, 2017

Senator Bob Graham

Florida Governor 1979-1987   US Senator 1987-2005

September 30, 2014

Mr. Phillip D. Moeller
Commissioner
Federal Energy Regulatory Commission
888 First Street, N.E.
Washington, D.C. 20426

RE: Sabal Pipeline PF14-1

Dear Commissioner Moeller,

It has been brought to my attention that in a recent report submitted into the official docket (Access No. 20140910-5159) Sabal Trail has included the following statement located under the Routing/Alternatives Update Section of their report:

"Sabal Trail evaluated the requested changes in the proposed pipeline route on Graham properties and an acceptable route was developed."

While access was granted to Sabal Trail to conduct civil, environmental and cultural surveys, I would like the record to reflect that Graham Angus in no way supports the route proposed across farm property and has made no such requests or agreements with Sabal Trail regarding this matter.

I appreciate your attention to my concerns and look forward to your confirmation that the matters addressed in this letter have been correctly reported.

Sincerely,

Bob Graham

CC: Acting Chairman Cheryl A. LaFleur
       Commissioner Norman C. Bay
       Commissioner Tony Clark

FIGURE 12.A.3 Example of personal business interest. This is a letter written by former Senator Bob Graham (R-FL) to FERC on September 30, 2014, nearly a decade after retiring from the US Senate

12.B APPENDIX: EXAMPLES OF FERC LETTERS

To give readers a sense of the activities FERC regulations and the types of issues raised in congressional letters to the agency, this section presents a selection of examples.

Example of Energy Project Advocacy

As we explore in detail below, many legislator letters to FERC advocate on behalf of an energy project or another corporate interest. In recent years, one of the legislators most focused on advocating for energy-related projects was Rep. Alex Mooney (R-WV). Rep. Mooney was elected to Congress in 2014 and has spent considerable time advocating for energy projects in West Virginia. In the lead-up to the 2016 congressional elections, the Charleston Gazette-Mail wrote an article highlighting the money he had received from energy companies and the approvals those companies were seeking from FERC for various projects under consideration. They wrote, "Dominion is trying to get the Atlantic Coast Pipeline, which would run through national forests in West Virginia, approved by the Federal Energy Regulatory Commission. Columbia Pipeline Group is hoping to have three interstate pipeline projects of its own approved by the same federal agency" (Brown, 2016, 4). Indeed, our data show that Mooney wrote to FERC more than any other agency, always on behalf of energy projects, mostly pipelines.

In 2015 Rep. Mooney wrote on behalf of Columbia's Mountaineer XPress Project and Atlantic Coast Pipeline ACP project. In 2017, he wrote on behalf of the Dominion Energy Supply Header Project, National Fuel Gas Distribution Corporation's Northern Access Project, Transcontinental Gas Pipe Line Company's Atlantic Sunrise Project, Columbia Gas Transmission's proposed Eastern Panhandle Expansion Project, Columbia's WB Xpress Project to build new compressor stations. In addition to the tens of thousands of dollars these companies spent on Mooney's campaign, the parent companies of these projects spend millions of dollars on lobbying (Kim, 2018).

Figure 12.A.2 in the Appendix shows one of the letters written by Rep. Mooney advocating for energy projects. In this case, the letter clearly connects both the name of the project and the name of the company involved with the project. Many letters lack that linkage and list only the project name, leaving us to draw those linkages. Later in this chapter, we discuss how we make those connections across projects, subsidiary companies, and parent companies.

Example of Constituent Service Letter

Another frequently seen type of legislator advocacy to FERC is a constituency service letter – a letter in which the member advocates on behalf of a constituent. Figure 12.A.1 in the Appendix shows an example of this type of letter. In this case, we observe Senator Susan Collins (R-ME) advocating on behalf of a constituent who is concerned that Florida Energy and Light is "attempting to take over the driveway of his business and make it a public way."[8]

Example of Personal Business Interest

In some cases, legislators appeared motivated by personal business concerns. For example, in 2014, former Florida Senator and Governor Bob Graham wrote to FERC regarding an issue that affected his family's farming business.[9] The full text of this letter is in Figure 12.A.3 in the Appendix.

---

[8] Certain passages of this constituency service letter in Figure 12.A.1 have been blacked out. In this case, as we frequently observe in these letters, the constituent's name and personal information have been redacted for privacy reasons.

[9] See http://miamilakes.com/AboutGraham/Overview.aspx for a discussion of Senator Graham's relationship to the farm in question.

12.C APPENDIX: REGRESSION RESULT TABLES

TABLE 12.C.1 *Bivariate models: Campaign contributions and letter-writing to FERC. Bivariate Poisson Regression models predicting letter-writing activity to FERC using campaign contributions from the energy industry*

	Letters to FERC			
	Total (1)	Pro-business (2)	Anti-business (3)	Constituent (4)
Campaign Contributions (per 100k)	0.204*** (0.018)	0.322*** (0.032)	−0.117*** (0.044)	0.044 (0.045)
Republican	0.016 (0.015)	−1.492*** (0.030)	−0.926*** (0.025)	−1.373*** (0.030)
Observations	5,997	5,997	5,997	5,997
Log Likelihood	−12,606.460	−4,212.596	−6,183.930	−4,795.028
Akaike Inf. Crit.	25,216.930	8,429.191	12,371.860	9,594.055

Note: *p <0.1; **p <0.05; ***p <0.01.

TABLE 12.C.2 *Bivariate models: Party and letter-writing to FERC. Bivariate Poisson Regression models predicting letter-writing activity to FERC using Legislator's Party*

	Letters to FERC	
	Pro-business (1)	Anti-business (2)
Republican	0.347*** (0.052)	−0.361*** (0.042)
Constant	−1.551*** (0.040)	−0.797*** (0.028)
Observations	5,997	5,997
Log Likelihood	−4,228.850	−6,150.971
Akaike Inf. Crit.	8,461.700	12,305.940

Note: *p <0.1; **p <0.05; ***p <0.01.

TABLE 12.C.3 *Bivariate models: Logged campaign contributions and letter-writing to FERC. Bivariate Poisson Regression models predicting letter-writing activity to FERC using logged energy industry campaign contributions*

	Letters to FERC	
	Pro-business (1)	Anti-business (2)
Log Campaign Contributions	0.027*** (0.009)	−0.061*** (0.006)
Constant	−1.601*** (0.087)	−0.435*** (0.051)
Observations	5,997	5,997
Log Likelihood	−4,247.016	−6,135.061
Akaike Inf. Crit.	8,498.032	12,274.120

Note: *p <0.1; **p <0.05; ***p <0.01.

TABLE 12.C.4 *Career Bivariate models: Campaign contributions and letter-writing to FERC over a member's entire career. Bivariate Poisson Regression models predicting letter-writing activity to FERC using energy industry campaign contributions*

	Career Average Letters to FERC	
	Pro-business (1)	Anti-business (2)
Career Total Campaign Contributions (per 100k)	0.018*** (0.004)	0.005 (0.005)
Constant	−1.561*** (0.067)	−1.189*** (0.059)
Observations	1,306	1,306
Log Likelihood	−Inf.000	−Inf.000
Akaike Inf. Crit.	Inf.000	Inf.000

Note: *p <0.1; **p <0.05; ***p <0.01.

TABLE 12.C.5 *Multivariate models: Predicting different types of letter-writing activity. Multivariate Poisson Regression models predicting letter-writing activity to FERC*

	Letters to FERC					
	Total		Pro-business		Anti-business	
	(1)	(2)	(3)	(4)	(5)	(6)
Campaign Contributions (100k)	0.243***	0.401***	0.282***	0.260***	-0.025	0.113
	(0.018)	(0.034)	(0.034)	(0.093)	(0.044)	(0.072)
Republican	-0.207***	-0.134***	0.258***	0.250***	-0.354***	-0.292***
	(0.026)	(0.029)	(0.054)	(0.062)	(0.044)	(0.052)
Campaign Contributions × Republican		-0.211***		0.025		-0.207**
		(0.041)		(0.100)		(0.091)
Constant	0.104***	0.062***	-1.618***	-1.612***	-0.791***	-0.822***
	(0.018)	(0.020)	(0.041)	(0.047)	(0.029)	(0.032)
Observations	5,997	5,997	5,997	5,997	5,997	5,997
Log Likelihood	-12,573.380	-12,560.840	-4,200.879	-4,200.848	-6,150.805	-6,148.318
Akaike Inf. Crit.	25,152.760	25,129.690	8,407.759	8,409.696	12,307.610	12,304.640

Note: *p <0.1; **p <0.05; ***p <0.01.

13

Organized Interests, Policymaking, and Congressional Accountability

Lee Drutman

In 1990, Congress went on a binge of landmark bipartisan lawmaking: The Clean Air Act, The Americans with Disabilities Act, The Immigration Act of 1990, and The Budget Enforcement Act of 1990. All four bills reflected a serious, bipartisan, evidence-based, committee-driven process, and did a reasonably good job of responding to a diffuse public interest.

The year 1990 also marked the publication of R. Douglas Arnold's classic, *The Logic of Congressional Action*, a thoughtful and multi-faceted explanation of why Congress is sometimes responsive to a broad and inattentive public, but why it more often generates policies demanded by narrow and attentive publics, also known as "special interests." This was a book that asked the big question: is it possible for American representative government to reflect the concerns and interests of diffuse and at best semi-engaged citizens? Or is our system doomed to respond to the organized over the un-organized, to reward intensity of preference over distribution of preference?

Much has changed in the structure and organization of congressional action since 1990. Congress has become much more polarized and party-driven; partisanship has become a more dominant force in American politics; organized interests now spend much more money on politics; and the relentless media environment has imposed much more constant scrutiny on the actions of Congress. Does the same "logic" hold today in a very different Congress?

In this essay, I'll argue that while much has changed, the same basic logic holds. Narrow, organized interests still have a distinct advantage over diffuse, unorganized interests. But that advantage has grown. On balance, the Congress of today is more favorable towards narrow, attentive publics, compared to the Congress of the 1980s that Arnold based his "logic" on.

THE BASIC "LOGIC"

Simultaneously pessimistic and optimistic, *The Logic of Congressional Action* could be read both as playbook for would-be public-spirited political entrepreneurs, and a reminder that such entrepreneurs were always setting out against long odds. But as the book's case studies showed, the odds were not insurmountable. And if one were to draw carefully on the lessons of the analysis, perhaps these odds could even be improved.

All policies distribute costs and benefits. Often, the benefits (or costs) are narrowly distributed, while the costs (or benefits) are widely distributed. Because of this uneven distribution, "attentive publics" (aka special interests) are more likely to mobilize for political action, and reward or punish individual representatives based on their legislative behavior. By contrast, those who might be harmed by such policies were usually not organized or attentive enough to make similar credible threats. As a result, the attentive would normally triumph over the inattentive.

Attentive, organized interests also had another advantage: policy design. By cloaking their advantages in the green eyeshade language of tax legalese like depreciation allowances, and by burying and diffusing the costs at the end of complicated and indirect causal chains, they undermined accountability. They offered their allies in Congress the cloak of obscurity and plausible deniability, while leaving potential opponents with the unenviable challenge of having to lay out the steps of policy mechanisms too convoluted to be easily decipherable.

But while the more diffuse "inattentive publics" might have lacked the hectoring and credible threats of the "attentive publics," they had one advantage. They stood as a large (albeit latent) force waiting to be mobilized. In the next election, a challenger might come along and focus on an incumbent's support for a corporate giveaway or previously obscured indirect tax hike. Thus, as members of Congress worked through their voting calculus on any given economic issue, they weighed two competing perspectives: on one side the certain but small retribution from the narrow attentive publics, on the other, the uncertain but potentially large retribution from the inattentive publics.

The more that incumbent members feared a challenger or an instigator might activate the latent inattentive public into noticing the harm at the next election, the more likely the incumbent would stand up to that narrow interest and just say no. The more incumbents thought nobody would care, the more they would just go along with the narrow interest. This calculus was never easy, and the likelihood of the issue being salient depended on many factors, including: How perceptible the effects might be; whether there would be any identifiable government actions; how directly that member might actually be held responsible; whether anybody might actually care enough if they found out how they had voted on the issue; how many people might be affected, and, most importantly, how skilled that challenger or instigator might be in raising the issue, and telling a compelling story about it.

For would-be political entrepreneurs looking to enact public-interest policies and triumph over narrow interests, the same calculus held, but in the reverse. To enact a public-interest policy, success depended on making sure the benefits were clear, up front, salient, widely distributed, and easily traceable so that supporting incumbents would get the credit for supporting it, and be blamed for opposing it. This was a process that demanded talent – plenty of obstacles stood in the way.

This analysis had two underlying components, one of which has proven more timeless, the other more time-bound. The timeless piece of the analysis is that policy design matters – support for a policy depends on the distribution, salience, and timing of costs and benefits, and policy success and sustainability depends on clever policy design. The more time-bound piece of the analysis is that incumbent members' electoral fates can depend on their individual policy records, separate of their parties.

When *Logic of Congressional Action* was published, voters did not support congressional candidates entirely along predictable partisan lines (as they largely do today). This left room for elections to hinge on candidates' support for specific policies. Incumbent performance mattered. And because partisan voting was less predictable, more elections were potentially competitive (Campbell and Jurek, 2003; Abramowitz, Alexander, and Gunning, 2006). This meant more members could credibly fear a potential general election challenger, who might hold them accountable for their policymaking records.

These competitive and uncertain electoral conditions helped attentive publics because it meant that their support (whether in campaign contributions or reliable turnout) might be pivotal. These conditions helped inattentive publics for the same reason. Mostly, though, they created more uncertainty for incumbent members of Congress, and created a real sense that the policy portfolios incumbent members developed might actually matter in their re-election. And given that the potential for big losses tends to weigh more heavily in our minds than narrow gains, the unpredictable role policy could play in a given election probably worked somewhat to the benefit of diffuse inattentive publics.

Given these circumstances, the potential existed for inattentive publics to sometimes win out, and for good public policy to triumph as a result. Reflecting this, one could read in the political science of the time a broader optimism that genuine, public-spirited political entrepreneurship was not only possible, but becoming more prevalent. To take the collective judgment of leading works on the policy process at the time, such as Polsby (1985) and Derthick and Quirk (1985), perhaps it was just a matter of combining politics and problems and solutions when the "window of opportunity" came along, and framing the issue in such a way that the benefits and costs were clear to the public, and it was indeed possible for general interests to triumph over concentrated interests. In the hopeful telling of Landy and Levin (1995, 7), for example, not only did policy matter more. There was now a genuine "concern for the substantive

goodness of policy. Those who can persuasively assert that they have invented
the better mousetrap can claim political attention. Ideas, and those who
have mastered them, come to play a larger role than they would in pure
preference politics."

MAKING CONGRESS MORE ACCOUNTABLE

In the concluding pages of *Logic*, Arnold worried that the individualized
nature of congressional accountability posed a challenge for the ability of
inattentive citizens to hold lawmakers accountable. Following the standard
wisdom of political science, he thought stronger parties would improve political
accountability:

> The complexity of the incumbent performance rule and the inequitable distribution
> of information required for its proper use make this a far less effective mechanism
> for controlling government than the party performance rule. This fact usually impels
> political scientists to close with a call for strengthening parties. If only we had strong
> parties (they argue), then government would be more responsive, responsible, and
> accountable. (Arnold, 1990, 274)

But reflecting the collective wisdom of the era, he didn't see much of a
prospect for anything other than the fractured, decentralized parties that had
been the norm in American politics for many decades.

Logic makes an important distinction between the "incumbent performance
rule" and the "party performance rule." Both are forms of retrospective voting.
That is, citizens look back at the performance of incumbents and parties and
decide whether to keep things as they are or make change. But they use different
decision rules for accountability. The party performance rule is obviously less
demanding. Citizens need to assess only two things: which party is in control,
and whether conditions are moving in a positive direction.

By contrast, the incumbent performance rule is more complicated. In addition to discerning whether conditions are moving in a positive direction, voters
must evaluate legislators on their contributions to these conditions. To do
so, voters must possess some understanding of the policymaking process and
how enacted policies affect observed outcomes. In reality, few citizens have
the patience or diligence to do this. But, at least in theory, they don't have to.
Incumbents, challengers and interested groups do it for them. And then citizens
can use this information to evaluate incumbent performance.

But how well does this challenger accountability mechanism really work?
Again, it depends. As Arnold noted, many policies are hard to trace, especially
when they have later-order effects, and it's almost impossible to hold anybody
accountable for inaction. Causal chains are confusing under even the best
circumstances. And incumbents have plenty of other tricks, like securing federal
spending for local projects, to help them get re-elected.

In principle, at least the party performance rule should be easier. But at the
time, given the lack of party unity, it was hard to hold parties accountable

when they didn't have clear party brands. Moreover, as Arnold observed, the party performance rule requires unified government. Otherwise, under divided government, which party should be blamed or held accountable? Party performance makes less sense. Still, the basic theory of party performance (i.e., responsible party government) has an alluring appeal. When citizens can judge the performance of government based on party performance, the accountability should be clear and direct.

Arnold also explored two prospective voting rules – "the party position rule" and "the candidate position rule." These require considerably more information than the retrospective rules, since citizens must not only know where the parties and candidates stand but the consequences of such policies. Yet, as Arnold noted, the party position rule did seem to account for a fair amount of voting in Congressional elections. Arnold's other suggestion for improved accountability was a little less openness and transparency. The logic here is that the more recorded votes, the more open meetings, and the more open rules, the more opportunities for narrow attentive publics to make particularistic demands each step of the process. Particularistic amendments only serve to empower special interests. The fewer, the better. "The key," concludes Arnold (1990, 275), "is to ask legislators to stand up and be counted on the broader policy issues, issues for which the general effects overshadow the group and geographic effects."

And yet, the underlying challenges remain. Policy design is often complicated. And attentive publics are attentive for a reason: they have more at stake; they care more. The more power is diffused and decentralized, the more it winds up in the hands of narrow interests, who care enough to participate *everywhere*.

But, by historical standards, the quarter of a century leading up to 1990 was arguably the most public-spirited quarter of a century the US Congress ever generated. Even if on balance, narrow interests triumphed more often than diffuse interests, by comparative historical standards, diffuse interests were doing as well as they ever had.

WHAT'S DIFFERENT NOW?

Much has changed since 1990. Here I'll focus on three changes relevant to the analytical framework of Arnold (1990) and other seminal works on policy-making of that era (e.g., Polsby, 1985; Derthick and Quirk, 1985): increased partisan polarization; increased spending on lobbying and campaigns; and increased transparency, largely through more media scrutiny.

Partisan Polarization

Let's start with the increased partisan polarization. As Egan and Prior in Chapter 4 as well as Lee in Chapter 9 argue in this volume, Congress has become much more partisan, polarized, and centralized. Today, both parties are as far apart as they've ever been, and partisan antipathy has reached new heights

(Hare and Poole, 2014). Politics is much more nationalized (Hopkins, 2018). And very few voters employ anything like the incumbent performance rule, evaluating the performance of individual members. National partisan brands drive the electoral fates of individual members far more than their individual records. And in a top-down Congress, it's very hard for individual members to distinguish themselves from their party anyway, even if voters still took individual records into consideration.

The development of highly partisan national parties is arguably the most significant change in American politics over the last several decades, and as a result, scholars have written millions of words both chronicling and explaining the sorting and hardening of partisan lines. As with most important changes in complex social systems, there is no single cause, but many interacting forces that feed back on each other in a recursive, interacting, dynamic process (Drutman, 2020).

Are there any mitigating forces left? In Chapter 6 of this volume, Canes-Wrone and Kistner find strong local newspaper coverage helps improve the ideological fit between members and their districts, at least a little bit. However, although their analyses include ones with district fixed effects, the evidence is ultimately based on association and therefore leaves open the possibility newspaper coverage is correlated with greater accountability rather than it. causing the improved correspondence. Moreover, their results suggest that the relationship between challengers' positions and electoral performance has decreased alongside the decline in local newspaper staffing and coverage; indeed, at the lowest levels of observed coverage, challengers pay no price for ideological extremism. These results are consistent with a word in which the potential mediating effect of newspapers no longer holds, at least in the same way.

Clinton, Sances and Sullivan (Chapter 2 in this volume) provide compelling evidence that when representatives take issue stances at odds with their districts, constituents tend to rate their representatives less favorably. But the prevalence of partisan voting, independent of candidate approval, is further proof of how little the incumbent performance rule now applies. Consider the case of Mitch McConnell. In a statewide poll, only 39% of Kentuckians approved of McConnell. Yet McConnell easily cruised to victory in Kentucky, defeating Amy McGrath 58% to 38%. True, McConnell's unpopularity led him to underperform Trump, who defeated Biden 62% to 36%. But for about 96% of Kentucky Republican voters, it was straight Republican – consistent with the nationalization of partisanship.

In theory, the increased focus on party and the centrality of partisan voting should strengthen the party performance rule, as clearer partisan stands make it easier for voters to see differences. But two conditions undermine this. The first is simple: the prevalence of divided government. As Arnold (1990) pointed out, divided government undermines party performance accountability. It's hard to know which part to punish (or reward) under divided government.

The second is more complex. In these polarized times, partisan voter loyalty now approaches blind following, deeply coloring even perceptions of the economy (Lenz, 2012; Achen and Bartels, 2016). When voters become attached to parties as extensions of themselves, as many now do, they are not well equipped to evaluate party performance. So whatever accountability more coherent parties might provide in theory, it has been beclouded by near-automatic partisan voting loyalties that undermine accountability.

At a time when incumbents could more easily distinguish themselves from the party brands, weaker partisan attachments might have made it easier for citizens to treat incumbents dispassionately on their record alone. But, again, the challenge of tracing the impact of an individual members' contributions in a complex political system was far more overwhelming. Whatever heuristic benefit today's clearer partisan labels may have given inattentive publics, the commensurate high-stakes partisan teamsmanship has robbed voters of the independent judgment necessary to take advantage.

Organizationally, the more open, committee-based (and even subcommittee-based) processes of Congress in the 1980s (and before) created space for more productivity and more creative problem-solving. There were simply more venues and moves for public-spirited entrepreneurial lawmakers with policy visions to build coalitions on an issue-by-issue basis, and, without a partisan calculus putting a powerful thumb on the scale of almost every issue, "persuasion" still mattered, both on a member-to-member level, and on a mass public basis. As Congressional processes have become centralized, there are fewer opportunities for would-be policy entrepreneurs (Wawro, 2000; Drutman, 2016).

Finally, the nationalized and distinct party brands that have accompanied polarization have changed the nature of political competition. When national party brands were weaker, individual congressional races operated more as independent races, in which particular issues (often local issues) varied depending on the candidates. Again, in the *Logic of Congressional Action*, this threat of competition created an important accountability mechanism pushing incumbents to respond to the threat of inattentive publics who could be mobilized by a challenger. But as fewer and fewer individual congressional races are still competitive, and national factors have swamped local factors, the potential accountability mechanism inherent in the incumbent performance rule has vanished.

In theory, the more vibrant national partisan competition that replaced the hyper-individualized campaigning of the 1970s should have produced more accountability. Democrats and Republicans should have strived to work more on behalf of inattentive publics, knowing that their national brands were at stake. And rhetorically, they have. But rhetoric and substantive policy accomplishments are not the same.

Because the last three decades have been defined by close competition for control of national institutions, with narrow majorities cycling back and forth

Lee Drutman

between Democrats and Republicans, politics has become especially zero-sum. Partisans on both sides have devoted far more energy to demonizing each other than they have to passing legislation, in hopes of winning the rare unified control that might allow them to pass their priorities (Lee, 2016).

Certainly, Democrats used unified control in 2009–2010 to enact two major landmark pieces of legislation that benefited diffuse inattentive publics – The Affordable Care Act, and the Dodd-Frank Act. But both pieces of legislation reflect the challenges and perils of major lawmaking in this environment. The Affordable Care Act has been challenged at every step of the way, as Republicans have tried to undermine it, and its durability depended on a single vote from a mercurial senior senator (John McCain). The Dodd-Frank Act has slowly been whittled away through regulatory capture,[1] and Congressional Republicans have even repealed a few parts of it.

Of course, each little chip away at the financial regulatory structure is, by itself, a low salience issue with a complex causal chain (e.g., see Carpenter and Libgober, Chapter 14 in this volume). For example, when Republicans (and some Democrats) approved legislation to loosen the threshold size for banks being deemed "systemically important" and thus freed many banks from the required oversight that such a designation required,[2] few paid much attention, and even those who did pay attention subsequently forgot, except for the affected banks. Maybe several years down the road, another financial crisis will hit, and hindsight will consider this to have been a mistake. But by then, the causal chain will be so obscured that accountability will be impossible.

But why did such a rollback even pass? Why, at a time when Congress is able to pass very little of substance, did this issue rise to the top of the agenda, and even win some modest bipartisan support? That takes us to the next big transformation of Washington over the last three decades, the growth of lobbying and the increasing power of money.

More Lobbying and More Need for Campaign Money Combine with Polarization for Less Accountability

Since the 1980s, the lobbying and campaign finance environment has transformed. Certainly, imbalances have always existed between concentrated, attentive interests (primarily businesses) and diffuse, inattentive interests (e.g., Schattschneider, 1960; Schlozman, Verba, and Brady, 2012). But over the

[1] Lee Drutman, "What the Banks' Three-Year War on Dodd-Frank Looks Like," July 22, 2013, http://sunlightfoundation.com/feature/dodd-frank-3-year/; Gary Rivlin, "How Wall Street Defanged Dodd-Frank," *The Nation*, April 30, 2013, www.thenation.com/article/174113/how-wall-street-defanged-dodd-frank.

[2] Alan Rappeport and Emily Flitter, "Congress Approves First Big Dodd-Frank Rollback," *New York Times*, May 25, 2018, sec. Business, www.nytimes.com/2018/05/22/business/congress-passes-dodd-frank-rollback-for-smaller-banks.html; Drutman, "What the Banks'"; Rivlin, "How Wall Street Defanged."

last three decades, concentrated, attentive business interests have poured ever greater amounts of money into lobbying and campaigns, creating an even greater imbalance. Lobbying has become more sophisticated and ubiquitous, and policy has become more complex. This imbalance has, on balance, helped attentive, organized interests (Drutman, 2015).

This growing resource imbalance interacts with partisan polarization in complex ways. First, as polarization has produced more gridlock, the lobbying efforts necessary to build coalitions and pass new policies have grown more complicated and elaborate. Well-financed attentive interests are most likely to have the resources to successfully hire enough lobbyists on both sides to steer the necessary bipartisan agreement.

Second, because today's committee assignments come with fundraising responsibilities, donors have more power over agenda-setting.[3] Parties have national brands to maintain, certainly, which might push them to support more general interest. But in contested, partisan times, parties have become more focused on winning the fundraising wars, which pushes them towards policies that benefit their organized donors over their more inattentive voters. After all, voters can be rallied on behalf of partisan teamsmanship in the emotional binary politics of electioneering.

Third, broadening of conflict and raising the salience of otherwise narrow technical issues now comes with the cost of making an issue partisan, since all salient issues in today's policies become partisan issues. But when issues become partisan, the likelihood of them succeeding is tremendously reduced. This creates a real problem for general interest policy advocates, who want to change policy. But it does create an advantage for general interest policy advocates who want to maintain the status quo.

Fourth, polarization has generated more gridlock, which makes the status quo even harder to change (McCarty, Poole, and Rosenthal, 2006). The additional friction in the system that polarization generates means even more "policy drift" (Hacker, Pierson, and Thelen, 2015). To the extent that attentive interests already have advantages, those advantages are harder to change (e.g., Baumgartner et al., 2009).

Fifth, because Congress is usually unable to resolve issues, policymaking winds up in the domain of regulatory agencies. Though bureaucrats may have more policy expertise, they lack the potential electoral accountability mechanism (the latent, diffuse, inattentive public that might be activated come Election Day) that in theory makes Congress more responsive. And because organized, attentive interests have devoted ever more resources to lobbying, they are better equipped to pressure regulatory agencies, where diffuse interests are least likely to be effective, both because they lack the higher level of expertise required to participate and because the techniques that diffuse-interest

---

[3] Issue One, "The Price of Power" (Issue One, 2017), www.issueone.org/wp-content/uploads/2017/05/price-of-power-final.pdf; Powell and Grimmer (2016).

instigators might use (mobilizing public opinion, organizing phone calls) are least likely to be effective. Specific regulatory rules are even more complex, because their causal chains are more indirect than those in broader legislation, which is more likely to embody general distributive and fairness principles, or at least be framed in these ways for voters. Carpenter and Libgober (Chapter 14 in this volume) address these themes in their analysis of organized interests and administrative policymaking.

Sixth, the centralization of congressional leadership that has accompanied polarization has led to less opportunity for bills to come up through the committee process and commensurately less investment in committee staffing (as committees have become less important). Since congressional committees have always housed the most substantive policy expertise, the decline of committees has led to an overall decline in policy expertise in Congress. This lack of policy expertise has largely benefited narrow, attentive interests, who are most able to fill the gaps. This information subsidy gives them additional influence – largely because they can supply necessary policy details, but also because they can skew the political analysis, through targeted polling. The broader decline in congressional capacity has empowered lobbyists generally as the new keepers of expertise and policy knowhow. And since narrow concentrated interests spend the most on lobbying, this has benefited narrow concentrated interests.

Even if lawmakers want to work on behalf of general, inattentive interests because of their own policy preferences, it is much harder to do so today. There are fewer "legislative subsidies" available on the general interest side, and far more potential opposition to getting anything done (Hall and Deardorff, 2006). This is partially due to polarization, partially due to the fact that all existing policies have their beneficiaries, and the more big attentive beneficiaries benefit, the better organized they typically are to defend it.

To be sure, there are still occasional moments of genuine cross-partisan political entrepreneurship, like the First Step Act, the criminal justice bill that passed on the 115th Congress, which took major steps to move the criminal justice system towards less punishment and more rehabilitation.[4] But more typical of the limited number of bills that become law these days is the "Music Modernization Act," which passed in 2018 and improved royalties and licensing for songwriters and producers in the digital age. The bill passed unanimously, but with little fanfare.[5] The attentive publics (e.g., artists, producers, labels, and streaming services) had negotiated the deal amongst themselves before coming to Congress.[6]

---

4 www.washingtonpost.com/politics/trump-to-sign-bipartisan-criminal-justice-bill-amid-partisan-rancor-over-stopgap-spending-measure/2018/12/21/234f9ffc-0510-11e9-b5df-5d3874f1ac36_story.html?utm_term=.16e153dc1deo. On general productivity of Congress, see: www.pewresearch.org/fact-tank/2019/01/25/a-productivity-scorecard-for-115th-congress/.
5 www.rollingstone.com/music/music-news/trump-signs-music-modernization-act-736185/.
6 www.insideradio.com/what-the-music-modernization-act-means-for-radio/article_bd460db8-7b62-11e8-bca5-6b726ba70551.html.

Presumably, consumers will ultimately pay a little more. No group represents a diffuse collective of music consumers, so this analysis was not part of the debate. And the issue was too picayune to show up in campaigns, especially since both parties supported it, and perhaps it was perfectly fine public policy (songwriters should be paid, right?). A bill like this, where industry and/or professional association actors work out their own deal, provide a big "legislative subsidy" to the lawmakers who advance the bill, and don't trigger any public opposition or partisan tripwires, can still pass in today's Congress.

In short, the changing lobbying environment has interacted with the changed organization of Congress to benefit narrow interests far more over the past three decades.

More Media Scrutiny, More Transparency, Less Space for Deliberation

If one lesson of the *Logic of Congressional Action* was that a little less transparency might generate more public-interest policy (because narrow interests were more likely to take advantage of the more open process), it was a lesson that good government advocacy groups, who claimed to be working on behalf of inattentive publics, ignored. Instead, they generally advocated for more openness and transparency in the political process, and more disclosure, on the theory that the more information the public had, the more it could put pressure on lawmakers and hold them accountable. Certainly, by 1990, most of the modern-era transparency developments had been put in place, such as The Freedom of Information Act (1966), the Government in the Sunshine Act of 1976, and the introduction of C-Span in 1979 for the House, expanding to the Senate in 1986.

Yet the bigger change in recent decades has been not the formal procedures, but the informal expectations and spotlights, and the transformation of political journalism, particularly in the age of social media. Minute-by-minute developments on Capitol Hill today are subject to more constant scrutiny than ever before, with more Washington-based journalists staking out "scoops" to tweet out and then publish ahead of their competitors. Call this the "Politico-ization" of Washington journalism. The demand for this blow-by-blow policy process news is fueled by the growing cast of lobbyists and other actors attempting to influence policy, as both readers and advertisers. The supply for this news is fueled by the growing number of communications directors and public relations specialists hired by individual members to boost their boss's status, and by members and staffers who see leaking to the press as a way to manipulate the coverage and hence the outcome of any process.

In theory, there is nothing preventing individual members of Congress from getting together behind closed doors and working deals out. Indeed, this happens plenty. However, it is harder to do today not because of the formal transparency processes, but because there are both more journalists on the lookout for secret cabals, and more staffers and members who see leaking as a way to steer the outcomes.

As Huber and Tucker (Chapter 8, in this volume) note, it is true local newspapers have closed down their Washington offices. Yet at the same time, the number of Washington-based reporters has increased, largely driven by niche, digital publications.[7] It is easier than ever for citizens to follow the details of Washington policymaking, should they wish to. It is also easier for citizens to follow their individual Senators and representatives, should they wish to, through social media and news alerts. But consistent with the claims of Huber and Tucker, it is much harder to get *independent* coverage focused on individual Senators and representatives, undermining individual-member accountability. This development certainly exacerbates the partisan nationalization of politics, which has become such a central filtering and processing mechanism for any and all political information.

Partisan polarization also interacts with transparency. Both parties have their hardline anti-compromise factions, who would like to blow up any bipartisan compromises. To the extent that they hear of developments, they have an incentive to bring them out into the open, where the delicate negotiations might fall apart. Additionally, because lawmaking processes are more centralized and top-down today, fewer members of Congress are involved. This creates more resentment among individual members, who are largely cut out of the process. This gives them an incentive to leak, should they come into possession of some valuable information.

Given the other two factors discussed in this essay (increased partisan polarization, and the growth of lobbying and campaign finance), the proposition that less transparency would improve responsiveness to inattentive publics is certainly debatable, and I count myself on the somewhat dubious side of the hypothesis. But it's also the case that increased transparency has failed to deliver on any of its promises. Information is not neutral. It must be interpreted. In an era of partisan polarization and increasing distrust, more information just feeds and fuels existing narratives.

TAX REFORM: NOW AND THEN

To observe how the logic of congressional action has changed, let's consider the politics of tax reform in 1986 as compared to 2017. The Tax Reform Act of 1986 was widely seen as a triumph of general interests over particularistic interests. Many factors came together. Tax unfairness became a salient issue, thanks in part to a widely read Citizens for Tax Justice report that highlighted the large number of companies paying nothing in taxes. The unique talents and motivations of Senators Bill Bradley and Robert Packwood, congressman Dan Rostenkowski, and even president Ronald Reagan all played an important role.

---

7 Pew Research Center, "Today's Washington Press Core More Digital, Specialized." December 3, 2015, www.pewresearch.org/journalism/2015/12/03/todays-washington-press-corps-more-digital-specialized/.

As Arnold (1990, 213) summarized, "Coalition leaders worked to persuade citizens, legislators, and the press that the current tax system was both inequitable and inefficient and that everyone would profit from a system with lower rates and fewer tax preferences."

The parties were competing to own tax reform, but whatever rivalry existed, it didn't add up to denying the other side a potential victory. At the time, it appeared that Democrats had a lock on the House, but many Democrats also represented districts that had voted for Reagan. It appeared that Republicans might have a lock on the presidency. Neither Democrats nor Republicans were holding out for unified control in Washington. Instead, members wanted to show their constituents they were working together, and individual members (most notably Packwood) were looking for issues on which they could get re-elected.

The quality of the staff also mattered. As Birnbaum and Murray (1988) wrote in their history of the tax reform bill, "The hardworking tax staffs, both on the tax committees and in the personal offices of the tax writers themselves, were among the Swiss guard of aides on the Hill." Likewise, Malbin (1980) highlighted the competence of the Joint Tax Committee staffers, noting they could provide members with "more help understanding complex tax issues than [the members] could possibly get from their ever changing cadre of legislative assistants." Thus, while Senator Packwood may have had the inspiration to do tax reform with a 25% top marginal tax rate by skewering a whole lot of tax loopholes, he relied on the Joint Committee, with its forty-strong team of economists, lawyers, and accountants, to do much of the actual writing and number-crunching.

Finally, the process mattered. The Senate Finance Committee famously shut its doors, and deliberated in a safe space, where lobbyists couldn't watch their every move. There, they could work out a secret, revenue-neutral deal and then come out locking arms with plausible deniability about any provision should any lobbyist harass them later. As Senator Packwood put it: "When we're in the sunshine, as soon as we vote, every trade association in the country gets out the mailgrams and their phone calls in twelve hours, and complains about the members' votes. But when we're in the back room, the senators can vote their conscience." In Arnold's theoretical terms: "Coalition leaders had to weaken the traceability chain for group costs either by eliminating the identifiable actions that produce costs or by making legislators' individual contributions as nearly invisible as possible" (219). In today's Washington, the idea of a committee actually deliberating in secret and working out a bipartisan agreement seems improbable.

Tax policy since 1986 has largely followed the logic of narrow interests triumphing over general ones. Whatever loopholes the 1986 act cleared away, subsequent incrementalist low-salience legislating added back in. According to a 2005 report from the President's Advisory Panel on Federal Tax Reform: "Since the 1986 tax reform bill passed, there have been nearly 15,000 changes

to the tax code – equal to more than two changes a day. Each one of these
changes had a sponsor, and each had a rationale to defend it. Each one was
passed by Congress and signed into law." In 2011, the IRS' own ombudsman
estimated the length of the US tax code to be 3.8 million words – or about
6.5 times the length of the famous Russian novel War and Peace. "Taxes"
dominates lobbying reports, year after year.[8]

In 2017, Republicans again took up tax reform. The Tax Cuts and Jobs
Act of 2017, like the 1986 bill, relied on closed-door drafting. But this was
done not to cut out lobbyists and narrow interests, but rather to bring them in,
allowing them to shape the bill, with provisions scribbled in by hand at the last
minute.[9] (Given limited congressional staff capacity, little would have gotten
written without considerable outside help). As a *New York Times* analysis of
the lobbying around the bill described:

Business lobbying heavyweights, including the U.S. Chamber of Commerce and the
Business Roundtable, had pushed hard for the signature reform in the overhaul –
drastically lowering the corporate tax rate to 21 percent from today's 35 percent rate.
But they also prevailed in extracting additional changes from the conference committee,
including the repeal of a corporate alternative minimum tax that had been included,
unexpectedly, in the Senate bill.
The Business Roundtable, desperate to remove the corporate alternative minimum tax,
worked behind the scenes, calling lawmakers and raising concerns about how it would
effectively kill the ability of companies to utilize the prized research and development
tax credit. Lawmakers got the message quickly, lobbyists said. "There was a clear
understanding within a short period of time that this was a problem," said one business
association official.[10]

In an analysis of the "winners and losers" of the bill, the *Washington Post*
listed "Big Corporations," "People with money in the stock market" and "rich
kids" as the biggest winners.[11] All of these have lots of lobbyists.[12] The biggest
losers included, "The 13 million Americans who won't have health insurance."
And "The poor." These groups have very few lobbyists. The most aggressive
lobbying company, for example, was Comcast, whose lobbyists succeeded in
getting a provision to allow for full-immediate expensing of new equipment
costs, and preserved the full deduction of advertising costs.[13]

[8] Drutman/Furnas "Untangling the webs of tax lobbying," https://sunlightfoundation.com/
2013/04/15/tax-lobbying/.
[9] See, e.g., www.nytimes.com/2017/12/15/us/politics/lobbyists-tax-overhaul-congress.html,
www.politico.com/story/2018/01/02/tax-overhaul-paydays-for-k-street-261668.
[10] www.nytimes.com/2017/12/15/us/politics/lobbyists-tax-overhaul-congress.html.
[11] www.washingtonpost.com/news/wonk/wp/2017/12/01/winners-and-losers-in-the-senate-gop-
tax-bill-a-running-list/.
[12] See, e.g., www.reuters.com/article/us-usa-companies-lobbying/u-s-business-group-lobbying-
surged-as-tax-reform-took-shape-idUSKBN1FC09H; www.vox.com/policy-and-politics/2017/
12/7/16709586/republican-tax-bills-lobbying.
[13] www.washingtonpost.com/news/wonk/wp/2017/12/01/winners-and-losers-in-the-senate-gop-
tax-bill-a-running-list/.

And rather than pass in broad bipartisan fashion, the bill passed both the House and the Senate on a narrow party-line vote, using the reconciliation process in the Senate to get around the filibuster. This wasn't the grand bargain of 1986. It was a partisan effort Republicans put together that mostly benefited their wealthiest donors. (For a larger discussion of the Tax Reform bill, see Lee, Chapter 9 in this volume.)

Perhaps the plausible electoral politics for Republicans was that by juicing the economy with lots of corporate tax cuts and some up-front middle-class tax cuts, the bill would prove popular and help Republicans win the 2018 midterms. Hence, Republicans did take policy design seriously. But the bill was underwater from the start in popularity, and Republicans did little to market it and run on it, instead opting for an immigration-heavy message, while Democrats focused on healthcare. The 2018 election was largely decided as a partisan referendum on President Trump.

To be sure, it may still be possible for Congress to enact broad, bipartisan policy in the public interest on occasion. As noted earlier, some would consider the First Step Act to be a successful example of Congress working in a broad general interest across party lines. But a close reading of the legislative process around the bill also reveals years of complicated partnership building across unusual "transpartisan" coalitions in ways that appear somewhat sui generis to criminal justice (Dagan and Teles, 2016; Hurlburt and Polimedio, 2016). More likely, Congress will continue to struggle to achieve broad bipartisan general interest compromises, with a few occasional partisan breakthroughs, even as the list of public problems demanding national legislative solutions continues to expand (Binder, 2015).

CONCLUSION

In the broadest sense, the basic logic of congressional action identified by Arnold (1990, 73) still holds. In the battle between inattentive and attentive publics, "the advantage surely belongs to the attentive." But today, in a more partisan time, the mechanisms are somewhat different. Individual lawmakers now have less opportunity and less incentive to distinguish themselves based on policy contributions.

In theory, more coherent, distinct parties save voters from having to wade through the complexities of using the incumbent performance rule to assess their representatives' specific and traceable contributions, and correspondingly, reduces the incentives and pressures on individual lawmakers to anticipate the concerns of potentially pivotal inattentive publics. And since there are not only fewer pivotal inattentive publics, but also fewer individual elections close enough for pivotal inattentive publics to matter, individual members are in one sense more liberated than ever to vote as they please. Yet the party performance rule demands unified government and semi-nonpartisan judgment to actually hold parties accountable for their performance, and our current politics generates lots of divided government and precious little nonpartisan judgment. Moreover, partisan gridlock means that most salient public problems become irresolvable partisan fights, while Congress primarily legislates only on low-salience issues on which attentive publics are unified and without opposition.

The lobbying landscape has also transformed. Narrow, attentive publics are now at a greater advantage than ever before. Part of this is the sheer numbers – they outspend their competitors by large multiples. But part of it is also the political environment. It is harder than ever to win by expanding the scope of conflict, because expanding the scope of conflict makes issues partisan, and partisan issues rarely succeed. And when Congress is in partisan gridlock, mostly the status quo gets preserved, and policy is adjudicated in regulatory agencies, where the latent preferences of inattentive publics hold no threat of electoral loss, and policy expertise matters more.

The earlier era had its problems. The current era is worse. It appears we have not yet found a political arrangement in the United States in which inattentive publics can consistently triumph over attentive publics, in which diffuse interests can consistently triumph over concentrated interests. It remains an open question whether such a consistent triumph is possible in American politics – or perhaps any system of representative democracy.

But certainly, under some rules and conditions, inattentive publics have a better chance than in others. One lasting legacy of the *Logic of Congressional Action* ought to be the nuanced way in which it directs us to the conditions under which diffuse interests are more likely to triumph over concentrated interests, in which broad interests can triumph over narrow ones. We may have yet to achieve such a politics. But that doesn't mean we can't keep working towards it.

14

Administrative Politics with Clear Stakes and Venues: Strategic Commenting upon Federal Reserve Debit Card Regulations*

Daniel Carpenter and Brian Libgober

Because regulation confers benefits and imposes costs, it carries unavoidable redistributive consequences. Many scholars argue that these consequences drive the politics of regulation (Stigler, 1971; Peltzman, 1976). Certainly, the distributive consequences of regulation are a major concern to firms as they engage in legislative lobbying, a well-studied phenomenon. Much less studied has been firms' interventions in regulatory rule-making, particularly through direct lobbying of the regulatory agency as it develops its rules. In this chapter, we provide an in-depth description of the politics of rule-making including direct administrative agency lobbying, in the case of one prominent rule, the so-called Durbin Rule. The Durbin Rule, mandated by the landmark Dodd-Frank banking legislation enacted in the wake of the 2008 financial crisis, required the Federal Reserve Board to regulate fees for debit card transactions. The financial stakes for financial institutions, retailers, and consumers were enormous. The Fed's attempts to write a rule provoked a storm of political activity.

Our theoretical framework highlights two characteristics of potential rules as perceived by firms: the rule's *mechanism clarity* and its *venue clarity*. The former refers to uncertainty about the rule's effects on the firm. The latter refers to uncertainty about who is responsible for the policy and the extent of their discretion. The Durbin Rule was unusual because the consequences

*The authors gratefully acknowledge the support of the Washington Center for Equitable Growth and Social Policy Program, the Kauffman Foundation, the Russell Sage Foundation, and the Radcliffe Institute for Advanced Study at Harvard. We also gratefully acknowledge our research assistant Eric Fegan, as well as substantive feedback from Steve Ansolabehere, Colleen Baker, Pamela Ban, Howell Jackson, Daniel Moskowitz, David Moss, Steve Rashin, Jon Rogowski, Jennifer Selin, Neil Shephard, Ken Shepsle, Jim Snyder, Margaret Tahyar, Paul Tucker, Craig Volden, Wendy Wagner, Philip Wallach, Susan Yackee, Kevin Young, and Luigi Zingales. All errors, omissions and interpretations remain ours alone.

of any variant were clear to the affected parties. Also clear was the identity of the regulators and their discretion. Under those circumstances, we posit the following:

- Direct lobbying of administrative agencies should be increasing in the discretion those agencies have in choosing policy (venue clarity), while decreasing in the uncertainty with which interests can link the agency's discretionary choice to their expected benefits and costs (mechanism clarity).
- When mechanism clarity and venue clarity are combined with a policy parameter choice that is explicitly zero-sum, we should observe counterlobbying dynamics (one constituency or coalition of constituencies lobbying for an increase in the relevant parameter, and a counter-coalition arguing for a decrease in the parameter.
- If direct administrative lobbying is effective, then observable policy benefits should appear for those who lobbied, as opposed to those who did not.[1]

A single case cannot truly assess these predictions, but it can illustrate them. We study the entire rule-making process, using a wealth of qualitative data. In addition, by analyzing the impact of proposed rules on firms' stock prices, we can gauge quantitatively who won (or stood to win) during the process. The result is a vivid portrait of the politics of rule-making by administrative agencies.

MECHANISM CLARITY, VENUE CLARITY, AND THE DURBIN RULE

Economic Problem and Legislative Action

Debit cards emerged in the 1970s as a way of solving a transaction problem. Retailers who accept payment in check or credit worry that the purchaser will not ultimately pay. Consumers with bad credit face high costs in using such cards. Others believe credit undermines financial self-discipline. Prior to debit, payment alternatives had major drawbacks. Cash transactions introduce physical transportation costs and theft risks. Wire-transfers traditionally require substantial effort to arrange. Debit cards, however, allow retailer and consumer to arrange a bank transfer with a simple swipe. In 2009, there were 37.9 billion debit card transactions in the United States worth 1.4 trillion dollars (Federal Reserve System, 2010).

During a card transaction, most of the action occurs off-stage. First, a card reader contacts the merchant's bank, which will attempt to acquire the necessary funds. This "acquiring" bank contacts the "issuing" bank that gave the consumer the debit card. If the issuer approves, the acquirer signals the retailer,

---

[1] We forgo a causal analysis in this paper, though see (Libgober, 2020a) for a detailed and exhaustive examination that rules out a range of competing explanations for differential changes in firm valuation.

who delivers possession of the good. Issuer and acquirer will not, however, directly exchange funds. Rather, they will each have "settlement accounts" with another intermediary, a "network provider" such as Visa or Mastercard. The network provider combines all incoming and outgoing transactions for each account and makes necessary adjustments. "Interchange" fees are what the issuer earns for its service, "network" fees are what the network earns, "discount" fees are what the acquirer earns, and the merchant "pays" all these fees by receiving less than the consumer was charged. A merchant who anticipates these costs may raise prices for consumers. Importantly, the issuing bank does not set its own fee. Rather, the networks compete for the business of the issuing banks, who could choose to give their clients Mastercards, Visas, or other network cards, depending on which interchange fee was higher.[2]

The debit card system had less to do with the financial crisis than the agenda of Assistant Senate Majority Leader Dick Durbin (D-IL). Durbin portrayed himself as a consumer-advocate, tirelessly opposing big finance. Critics have noted Durbin's "knack for delivering on the retail industry's top priorities" (French and Sloan, 2013). At a Judiciary Committee hearing on July 19, 2006, Durbin learned troubling facts. The average American family paid $231 in interchange fees annually, three times the rates in Australia or Canada. Visa's rules governing fees were 1,300 pages long, not available publicly, and allegedly forbade issuers from contracting with American Express or Discover for network services. Following this hearing, Durbin repeatedly offered legislation addressing these market imperfections, without success.

In July of 2009, the Retail Industry Leaders Association invited twenty large retailers to a conference in Washington, DC. Their goal was deciding how to make the most of Dodd-Frank (Mattingly and Schmidt, 2011). The retailers decided to mobilize small-business owners against swipe fees, eventually assembling an email list with more than 20 million contacts. In some cases, they were even more direct, flying small business owners into DC to meet individually with twenty-one Senators. In the midst of the floor debate regarding the Dodd-Frank Act, Durbin offered an amendment that would have the Federal Reserve set debit card fees in such a way that they be "reasonable and proportional." The financial service industry later claimed that this legislative move had taken them by surprise. Indeed, the amendment was carried 64-33 without any Senator taking the opportunity to debate Senator Durbin on the merits.

Administrative Policy: Proposals, Delays, and Revisions

As enacted, Section 1075 of Dodd-Frank was ambiguous. Informed observers argued the Board's implementation could ban interchange fees entirely or issue unenforceable "guidance" for Visa and Mastercard describing what they should

---

[2] Evans and Schmalensee (2005) offer a nice history of this market.

charge.[3] Ultimately, the Federal Reserve would take a middle-path, setting a price cap on interchange fees. Importantly, Section 1075 exempted "small" issuers with fewer than 10 billion in total assets. Only the top 1% of issuers were directly subject of regulation. Nevertheless, estimates suggest big issuers represented over 70% of the market (Evans, Chang, and Joyce, 2015, 62). Given the strong possibility that top-tier norms might spread, the more than 12,000 second-tier issuers had substantial stake as well. Section 1075 also included provisions aimed at promoting increased competition by prohibiting "network exclusivity" arrangements and incentivizing fraud-prevention. Final regulations were due no later than nine months after enactment on July 21, 2010, a tight time-line. As a kicker, some provisions became effective on July 21, 2011. Failure to issue rules would allow stakeholders to enforce the law in court, potentially leading to judicial intervention on agency turf.

On December 16, 2010, the Board proposed a rule implementing the Durbin amendment. They suggested two possible formulas for defining a reasonable interchange fee, and asked for comment on which to enact. Under the first, up to seven cents per transaction was permissible. If the issuer wanted more, it would need to establish its average variable costs per transaction were higher than seven cents. Nevertheless, this increase could not exceed $0.12. Mathematically,

Per Transaction Interchange Fee
$$\leq \max\{\min\{\text{Average Variable Costs}, \$0.12\}, \$0.07\} \quad (A)$$

The second alternative was a simple price cap at $0.12 per transaction:

$$\text{Per Transaction Interchange Fee} \leq \$0.12. \quad (B)$$

The proposal also suggested two approaches to incentivizing fraud-prevention. Under the first, card issuers could charge more to offset the costs of using specific technologies known to prevent fraud. Under the second, an issuer could charge more to offset the costs of running a fraud-prevention program that satisfied Board-specified standards. It also described two approaches to network competition. One would require a card issuer to accept transactions over at least two non-affiliated networks, regardless of whether the network relied on PINs or signatures for authorization. Since most merchants cannot accept PIN transactions, this alternative would not greatly induce network competition. The other alternative would require issuers to carry at least two networks for both PIN *and* signature transactions, a much tougher requirement.

Despite its plans, the Board would find itself receiving comments for longer than the usual sixty days from publication in the Federal Register. Over 11,000 letters were sent to the Board about the rule. Most were form responses that contributed minimally to debate (Mendelson, 2012). Nevertheless over 1,500 comments were unique, and hundreds were submitted by associations,

---

[3] In order to simplify presentation, links to primary source material referenced without citation are reserved for the Appendix.

organizations, or firms. On March 29, 2011, Chairman Bernanke informed oversight committees in Congress that the Fed would miss its legal implementation deadline of April 21st, but was committed to completing rulemaking before the July 21st legal effective date.

On June 29, 2011 the Federal Reserve approved a final rule implementing the network competition and interchange fee portions of the Durbin Amendment. Interchange fees would follow this formula:

$$\text{Per Transaction Fee} \leq \$0.21 + 0.0005 \times \text{Cost of Transaction.}$$

This formula represented a massive reversion to the pre-legislative status quo. According to the proposed rule, the average interchange fee in 2009 was 23 cents for PIN transactions and 56 cents for signature transactions, or 44 cents overall (75 FR 81725). The final rule would entail no reduction in rates for PIN networks relative to 2009. The rule would hit signature debit cards harder, but the bite was a fraction of what the Board had first proposed. As for network competition, the Board implemented the weaker alternative A, which was "universally preferred" by issuers and network providers (Staff Memo, June 29, 2011).

The Board issued a separate interim final rule addressing fraud. Tentatively, they would allow $0.01 in additional fees for those who ran a suitable fraud-prevention program. The Board indicated openness to comments on whether to require specific technologies or adjust the incentive-fee. On July 27, 2012, the Board confirmed its interim approach. Senator Durbin described the Fed's implementation of fraud-prevention as "incompatible with both the plain text and intent of Section 1075" (Durbin Letter, September 30, 2011).

Proposal Development

Table 14.1 outlines the stages of an archetypal proposal-development process according to the published procedures of the Board (Federal Reserve Board, 1979), which are similar to the procedures of other agencies. The process begins by forming a team to work on writing the regulation. Next, the agency begins the task of formulating the regulatory problem, in particular developing an account of the primary and secondary goals of regulation, identifying important stakeholders, and developing a blueprint of what data collection and analysis steps they will need to complete before publishing a proposal. The agency will then acquire necessary data, analyze it, and in the final phase formulate policies based on this data and analysis. One should not assume rule development

TABLE 14.1 *Stages of rule development*

Phase I	Phase II	Phase III	Phase IV	Phase V
Team Formation	Problem Definition	Data Collection	Analysis	Policy Selection

processes always conform neatly to this archetype. Indeed, insider accounts suggest that hardly anyone pays attention to these internal guidance documents (West, 2009). For presentational purposes, however, the development of the Durbin Rule appears to have fit the archetype relatively well.

As others have noted, the debit card rule involved a fundamentally "new set of responsibilities for the Federal Reserve" (Open Board Meeting, December 16, 2010), more akin to utilities regulation than bank supervision. Although the Board's staff are experts on payment systems, most of their prior work concerned institutional banking and not retail. To understand retail systems, the staff would depend on outside interests such as card issuers, network providers, merchants, and consumer groups. Without it, they would not know how to begin formulating their regulatory task, let alone solving it. Two days after Dodd-Frank was enacted, staff from the Division of Reserve Bank Operations and Payment Systems (DRBOPS) met with Visa to discuss implementation of the Durbin amendment. Visa's presentation emphasized three key themes: the large number of stakeholders that depended on debit, the usefulness of these services, and the complexity of the field at play. For example, Visa noted that interchange policies are calibrated biannually and discriminate between features such as whether the transaction is face-to-face, online, or a recurring payment, for example because the risk profiles of each transaction necessitate different authorization procedures. Their powerpoint did not explicitly mention the Durbin Amendment or its interpretation at any point. Thematically and informationally similar presentations were given by Mastercard, Bank of America, JP Morgan, and others. No presentation by a major issuer or network explicitly addressed policy selection issues before October 4th, precisely when the agency was shifting from data acquisition to data analysis. The lobbying of these largest regulated players demonstrated sophisticated situational awareness about where the staff were in the rule development process and what information the agency was most likely to actually use.

On August 5th, DRBOPS staff met with Visa to discuss a potential survey of issuers to identify costs, an indication that staff were moving from problem formulation to data acquisition. Visa's presentation focused on the methodology behind the issuer benchmark studies that Visa "has been evolving ... for more than three decades." Although the staff may have wanted to benefit from Visa's prior experience, the design of the survey instrument had significant distributive implications. For example, it is notable that the sample population focused on the 131 institutions with 10B+ in assets. While these institutions were the only ones subject to the cap, representatives of the 12,000 smaller issuers believed their fates were linked to the bigger issuers. As Mary Dunn, deputy counsel at the Credit Union National Association, emphasized to DRBOPS Chief Louise Roseman during an August 6 phone call, "higher interchange fees to small issuer ... may not be accommodated in the marketplace if interchange fees to large issuers are much lower." The decision not to collect data about the, likely higher, costs of the smaller banks represented a significant bet by the

Federal Reserve that either (a) a two-tiered market would form or (b) if a single-tiered market were maintained, then the effect on smaller entities was not a significant component of the Board's regulatory problem. The failure to address the impact of regulation on smaller banks would later produce significant political blow-back, illustrating the pivotal importance of even subtle issues in rule development. Also noteworthy is that the small issuers advocacy at the earliest stage was focused on policy selection, at a time when the majority of the staff's meetings suggest they were focused on how to collect data. The small issuers lobbying did not demonstrate the same situation sense as the biggest financial institutions.

The survey was fielded between September 13 and October 12. After September 13, the Board changed gears in two ways. High-level officials were deployed to sell the agency's process to the regulated industry. In the last half of September, Director Roseman, Governor Tarullo, and two other associate directors gave presentations about the Board's process to the American, Maryland, and Indiana Bankers Associations, respectively, apparently answering questions but not actively soliciting information. Additionally, the board began to receive presentations from retail interests for the first time. On September 15, the Board met with Craig Wildfang, lead counsel in a 7.5 billion dollar class-action anti-trust suit against major issuers and network providers. Wildfang presented himself as an available resource, offering to share 60 million pages of materials uncovered via litigation or connect the Board with other lawyers representing retail interests. On October 13, the staff had its first significant meeting with consumer groups, almost three months after its first meeting with Visa. These groups argued that Durbin should require "par clearance," or de minimis exchange fees, the same as checks. There is no evidence in the logs that anyone had previously advocated this viewpoint, *after* the survey was fielded. If consumers had persuaded staff that zero was the reference point, not the cost of providing the service, it is likely that a different and harsher proposed rule would have emerged. Nevertheless, since the agency had already invested a great deal in estimating service provision costs, it is unlikely that the no fee position was seriously considered.

As October turned to November, the Board began receiving communications targeting the specifics of interpretation and rate setting. A key point to understand about the arguments that were made is that the more capacious the definition of cost, the larger the potential revenue for financial institutions. Commerce Bank, for example, gave presentations describing hundreds of distinct marginal costs in providing debit cards. The Clearinghouse, a bank trade association, sent a letter on November 1 arguing fees should include "all costs incurred … plus a return on capital," and that anything less was a violation of the Constitution's takings clause. Oliver Ireland, Visa's attorney and senior partner at Morrison and Forrester, argued that the Board should allow "non-variable" costs related to the provision of debit cards, and also raised the takings issue. Celebrated University of Chicago economist Kevin

Murphy submitted his own views, at the behest of Bank of America, on what "incremental costs" should mean: any costs that vary with the number of debit transactions, and also floated the notion that the amendment might only require guidance. Georgetown Law School's Steven Salop, at the behest of a retail coalition, submitted a white paper describing how the Board could issue a rule saying debit cards should clear at par, unless the issuer could establish to the regulator that the fee would "clearly lead to likely consumer benefits" (Merchants Payment Coalition Letter, November 2, 2010). Since he believed this standard was unmeetable by most issuers, fees would as a practical matter equal o.

Although it is impossible to conclusively determine what influence these meetings had on the Board purely from the logs, taken together they suggest a multiplicity of reasons for efficacy. The firms that participated earliest had significant opportunities to shape the staff's formulation of its regulatory problem and data collection strategy (Naughton et al., 2009). The largest financial institutions like Visa were given many opportunities to contribute in this fashion, in part because they possessed information that was helpful for formulating a plan for issuing a reasonable regulation (McCarty, 2017), in this case experience with running similar surveys. At the same time, these interests may have succeeded to some degree in influencing the staff's values and perspective on the subject matter being regulated. Many interest groups that participated later in the process subsidized the production of policy more favorable to their interests by describing specific language to include in the regulation and providing economic, legal, or policy rationales for their preferred approach (Hall and Deardorff, 2006). Meetings also allow for saber-rattling about legal claims that stakeholders might make post-finalization (Yackee, 2006). Meetings at all stages plausibly allowed regulator to gauge the intensity and range of preferences among stakeholders. Conversely, early meetings allowed interests the opportunity to experiment with different kinds of arguments, perhaps learning through these encounters where the regulatory might budge. More speculatively, outside advocacy may have also contributed to the decision to give further study to the fraud-prevention issue, an exercise of agenda control (Yackee, 2012). Although these reasons for influence are likely to reveal themselves in proposed rules, many might prove durable across the months and years that rulemaking requires.

Zero-Sum Politics, Commenting, and Free Riding

The debate visible from post-notice meetings and written comments was similar to what occurred earlier. Yet the conflict was louder and broader. Over 11,000 comments were submitted to the regulatory docket, the vast majority from community banks, credit unions, and small business owners. Most of these letters engaged sincerely, but not very substantively, with the proposed rule. The CFO of North Georgia Bank wrote that his bank "projects that the proposed changes will reduce non-interest income by over 10%." The owner of a Mister Bagel franchise wrote that "Credit card companies are getting richer and richer on the backs of small business owners ... Support small business owners by supporting the cap on debit fees."

The more substantively meaningful engagement involved a smaller set of core market participants, advocacy organization, and policy experts. Many, but not all, of these actors had been involved in rule development. Georgetown's Steve Salop had a meeting with Janet Yellen to explain the no-fee position, which Craig Wildfang also wrote a long letter to support. Visa, Mastercard, JP Morgan, and other regulated firms recapitulated their position. Yet their advocacy had a different tone. They did not emphasize complexity and value, but rather distortions and and perverse consequences for underrepresented interests. For example, the first fault Mastercard found with the proposal was the "fail[ure] to consider the consequences the Proposal would have on key payment system constituencies, including consumers, community banks and credit unions." Consumer advocates' role in the rulemaking, to this point lackluster, now became ambiguous. On January 7, 2011, general interest organizations such as AARP met with Governor Tarullo to explain why they had taken no formal position on the rule. The Consumer Federation of America wrote to explain their concerns about the effects on retail consumers and debit card users. They also noted that based on data from their member credit unions, the costs of providing debit cards was above the cap the Federal Reserve had set based on data from larger institutions. It is notable that this interest group held itself out as having comparable expertise in designing cost surveys as Visa, but was not active in rule development.

Many substantive comments emerged from interest groups that had not previously participated. Associations of Lumber Dealers, Air Carriers, Grocery Store Owners, and others wrote to ask the Board to tighten the fee. Numerous members of Congress, as well as a State Banking Commission, wrote to defend the interests of local banks. A smattering of big firms in retail and banking who had not yet participated, such as PNC Bank to McDonalds, now sent letters. These comments often reiterated previously identified concerns. However, some noted important issues that had not received enough attention. For example, a number of firms claimed that complying with the network exclusivity requirements would prove difficult to impossible on the Board's proposed timetable (HSBC Letter). A number of companies also wrote to note that they were outside the regulatory perimeter of the proposed rule, and insisted that the Board keep it that way (American Express Letter, ISIS Letter). Both requests were granted in the final rule.

To show that the zero-sum nature of the fee constraint and the high traceability of interests' welfare to the parameter choice induced a qualitatively and quantitatively different kind of lobbying, we examine commenting on the Durbin Amendment in context of other Dodd-Frank rules. Figure 14.1 shows the total number of comments received by the two rules on debit card regulation

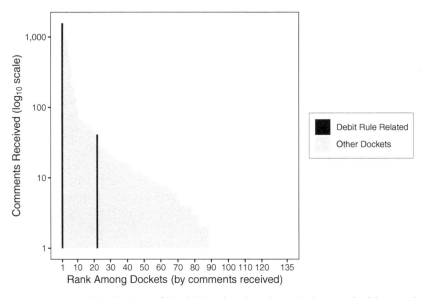

FIGURE 14.1 Distribution of Dodd-Frank rulemaking dockets ranked by number of comments received

Bars indicate the dockets for the first NPRM (left) and for the interim rule (right).

as part of the overall (ranked) distribution of the number of commenters for all rules issued under Dodd-Frank. The debit card fee constraint rule was the single most commented-upon rule in all of Dodd-Frank, and the fraud prevention and fee adjustment rule was also in the top third of rules. This is so in spite of the fact that by any plausible reckoning, the Volcker Rule and other capital standards regulations clearly carried greater aggregate economic impact than did the debit card rules. Because a general measure of "traceability" across rules is elusive, we use this case-centered approach for demonstrative purposes.[4]

Beyond the sheer number of commenters, our theoretical perspective also suggests that the distribution of commenters should look different for the debit card rules. Given the staggering qualitative heterogeneity of rules, this is a complicated undertaking, so we focus our analysis on those aspects of the commenters that involve non-financial and non-bank organizations. To measure the concentration of comments within industrial categories, we compute a Herfindahl index of the concentration of commenting activity in one industrial category; lower values of the index imply a lower level of concentration and, in turn, a greater diversity of commenters based on breadth of economic interest. We find that the Herfindahl index of commenters across

---

[4] We do not attempt any statistical analysis of this distribution, as the point seems demonstrated sufficiently by the primary rank of the debit card fee rule.

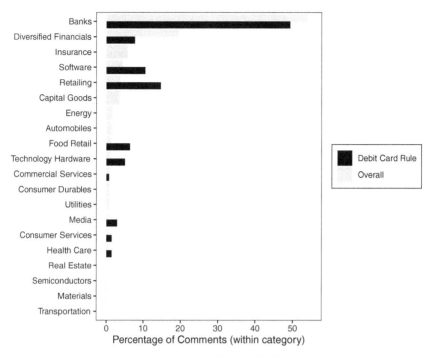

FIGURE 14.2 Proportion of comments from publicly traded companies according to global industrial classification system industry group

all Dodd-Frank rules is 0.303, but for the Durbin Amendment rules it is 0.255. A skeptical reading might simply claim that this is because the debit card rule brought non-bank (or non-financial-services firms) into play, but if we restrict the sample of commenters to non-bank firms, we observe an all-Dodd-Frank HHI of 0.185, while we observe a Durbin-related HHI of 0.154. Here too, our evidence is suggestive rather than statistical, again because of the difficulty of producing a cross-rule measure of mechanisms and venue clarity. Yet among the population of Dodd-Frank commenters that includes banks, as well as among that population that excludes them, the Durbin-related rules attracted a greater diversity of commenters than did other rules (consult Figure 14.2).[5]

---

[5] We think, however, that this measurement exercise would form an excellent research agenda for the next generation of Arnold-inspired regulatory politics scholars. We would start with the cautionary note that just examining the degree of quantification involved in a rule would be an insufficient place to start, as quantification might raise the degree of traceability if in fact several organizations collaborate to the parameter choice, and or if the parameter-choice problem involves beforehand the determination of a number of other parameters and functionals that feed in to the final choice (as, say, the calculation of costs and benefits for a particular rule might depend heavily upon separable decisions about discount rates, or estimates of the cost of a statistical life).

Although the breadth and depth of engagement by retail and banking interests was profound, what is arguably more remarkable is the extensive free-riding. The vast majority of small issuers, who were presumably in positions similar to North Georgia Bank, did not submit comments. Most of the largest banks *also* did not submit comments. If one were to speculate why, one would have to assume it had to do with their belief that the trade association would lobby on their behalf, and so too would other organizations that were similarly affected. Yet this argument could easily prove too much. Why did *any* firms participate in rulemaking, besides oligopolists such as Visa or Mastercard? The self-selection mechanisms at play here remain perplexing. The extent of free-riding raises the serious possibility that both our aggregate commenting measures and our commenter concentration measure *understate significantly* the degree of diverse and high-intensity commenting and influence activity on the debit card rules.

Off-Stage Action and Aftermath

While some financial institutions and retailers were engaging the Board, others were advancing their interests elsewhere. Shortly after the rule proposal, a banking consortium gave the Electronics Payment Coalition (EPC) a starting budget of 11 million dollars to build grass-roots support for repealing the Durbin amendment (Mattingly and Schmidt, 2011). One use of these funds was to run ads in the DC Metro. They also hired high-power congressional lobbyists. To Republicans , lobbyists described typical big government interference in well-functioning markets. To Democrats, they talked about access to banking services. Besides more conventional lobbying and media engagement, some banks also sought to mobilize their clientele. JP Morgan notified Disney Rewards customers that they were discontinuing the program, citing a "new law known as the <u>Durbin</u> Amendment (emphasis in original) (Mattingly and Schmidt, 2011).

On February 17, 2011, Chairman Bernanke and Governor Raskin appeared before Senate and House oversight committees, respectively. While the questioning was polite, doubts about the amendment were palpable. "[A] move from 45 cents down to 12 cents, that is a glaring 73 percent reduction. Is that fair?" asked Representative Scott (D-GA). Representative Hensarling (R-TX) was more blunt: "I just wonder how 7-Eleven would feel if the Federal Reserve came with a rule that said you can only recover incremental cost of selling a Slurpee." A repeated theme in bipartisan questioning was the effect of regulation on community banks. "Is there any way to actually ensure that community banks and credit unions are exempted in practice from this provision?" asked Senator Tester (D-MT). Bernanke did not defend the rule vigorously, saying that there were no guarantees and giving two reasons why the small-issuer exemption might not work. Tester turned to Bernanke's co-witness, FDIC Chairwoman Bair, to ask if delaying the Federal Reserve's implementation would make sense. "Yes," she replied, "Look, there are legitimate policy arguments on both sides of this, but it was done very quickly."

Tester would join Senator Corker (R-TN) in offering a bill to delay the implementation of the debit card interchange regulation, in order to allow further study. The retail coalition reacted with alarm, once again footing the bill for local retailers to meet with their representatives in Washington. Tester-Corker would eventually get fifty-four votes, which was insufficient to overcome a filibuster.

While some representatives from finance went to Congress, others went to court. TCF Bank filed suit on October 12, 2010 in the District of South Dakota, seeking a declaration that the Durbin Amendment was unconstitutional even before the rule was proposed (McGarity, 2012). Although the case was described by observers as a "Hail Mary," it attracted many amicus briefs from interested parties on both sides (Serres, 2011). The court refused to enjoin the rule because it did not believe TCF would win on the merits, a position that was affirmed on appeal.

Interestingly, following the issuance of the final rule, the *retailers* felt themselves sufficiently aggrieved that they sought judicial review. They wanted to correct the doubling of the fees and the weak competition requirement (NACS v. Board, DC Cir., 2014). The retailers' case was stronger. Indeed, the district court in DC would give them summary judgment, finding the Board's interpretation of the statute "utterly indefensible." The Board was ordered to correct its mistakes by not allowing compensation for costs that were not truly incremental, and also imposing a strong network competition requirement (NACS v. Board, D.D.C, 2013). Nevertheless, on appeal, a unanimous circuit court held that the Durbin Amendment was drafted ambiguously and the agency was entitled to make the rule it wanted. The merchants appealed the reversal to the Supreme Court, but certiorari was denied.

ASSET PRICE ANALYSIS OF THE DEBIT CARD RULE

The Market Anticipates and Responds to the Proposed Rule

Although the details of policy implementation were varied and technical, they represented big money for market participants, who were well-incentivized to pay attention. Contemporaneous accounts of business journalists and equity analysts attest that the market reacted strongly to these regulations. Dozens of examples are cataloged in Evans, Chang, and Joyce (2015), an inter-day event study analysis of debit regulations that also found significant market impacts. The direction of these effects were as expected: the proposal hurt debit providers and the final rule helped. Nevertheless, it is worth clarifying how and why markets were able to register these facts within hours *if not minutes* of regulatory announcement.

Over the summer of 2010, debit providers convinced markets that the Durbin amendment was not so ominous as it initially seemed. In a teleconference with analysts, Visa's CEO said the regulatory risk was "minimal," since only interchange fees would be capped, not network fees. Analysts agreed. "What is at stake [for Visa] is the 6.7 basis points of volume fees," wrote one, so as long as cuts are not "draconian" enough to cause an exodus from debit cards, the fundamental business model of Visa would remain strong (Janney Capital markets, May 19, 2010). A Morgan Stanley note from September 20 also read the tea-leaves on the Board's extensive engagement with industry during the rule-development phase: "[The Board seemed] very intent on learning more about the industry and avoiding unintended consequences." Analysts who covered card issuers instead of networks agreed that regulated entities would adjust, for example by cutting costs or imposing minimum balance requirements.

On December 9th, the Board notified the public that the debit card proposal would receive a vote at the next Open Meeting, scheduled for 2:30pm on the 16th. The meeting would have a live-stream and staff summary and rule text disseminated shortly before. Analysts sent last minute advice to their clients. A December 15th report from JP Morgan Equity Research was typical:

Our sense is that the market is pricing in (1) ... that regulators will not require multiple signature networks on debit cards ... and (2) a 50% reduction in debit interchange rates. If consensus is right, a modest relief rally is likely ... The bad case is if signature debt can no longer be exclusive. **We would be incrementally more negative on both stocks if signature debit cards can no longer be exclusive to one network** ... This is a low probability (< 20%) risk, but it can't be ignored. (Huang and Smith, 2010)

Notably, these analysts, who covered Visa and Mastercard, were more concerned about the complex network competition provisions than the easier to parse rate formula. Around or shortly after the start of the meeting, the same analysts at JP Morgan sent their clients a single-page alert, entitled "More Negatives than Expected." The first bullet-point emphasized that both hard and soft exclusivity requirements were still under consideration, while the second emphasized an 80–90% cut to interchange fees, much worse than prior consensus. Figure 14.3 shows the price of key stocks on the afternoon of December 16. Visa, the leading network-provider, lost 10% of its market valuation in less than an hour. JP Morgan, a prominent issuer, bore a less severe, but still significant 1.5% loss over the same time domain. Walmart, a retailer, found its stocks climbing significantly. The reaction for Discover, an alternative network to Visa, was more mixed. For Discover, more competition and lower fees meant a bigger proportion of a shrinking pie.

Market analysts continued to watch the rule development process and form their expectations accordingly. On June 22nd, the Board notified the public that they would meet at 3:30pm on the 29th, with materials posted online shortly before. Equity analysts again simplified the task of interpreting the

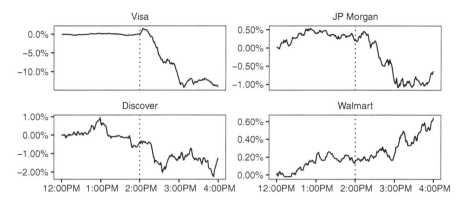

FIGURE 14.3 Percentage returns for key stocks on afternoon of NPRM, December 16, 2010
Webcast of Open Board meeting was scheduled at 2:30pm, with staff memo and rule released shortly before. Vertical dots indicate 2:00pm.

announcement by providing valuation models under a variety of regulatory scenarios. Analysts at Jeffries described market expectations.

> The consensus expectation is for the interchange fee to be increased to the $0.15–$0.20 range in the final rules, from $0.12 in the proposed rules … [While we believe] multiple signature/multiple PIN would prove very cumbersome for the industry to implement, and further … our checks have indicated that there is a greater chance that the Fed will go with the much simpler single signature/unaffiliated PIN scenario, the final outcome of the Fed's rulemaking process remains unclear. (Kupferberg and El-Assal, 2011)

The final rule was better for debit providers on both counts. Figure 14.4 shows how the price of Visa, JP Morgan, Discover, and Walmart responded on the afternoon of June 29. Shortly after 3:00pm, Visa's share price increased almost 10%, leveling off around 15% higher before market close. The +1% and +2% reactions for JP Morgan and Discover were also symmetric reversals of what happened at proposal. Walmart's reaction was negative, as expected.

The Market Reacts to Finalization

The policy issues raised by the Durbin rule were sufficiently complex that the Federal Reserve would ultimately finalize two separate rules in response to its initial proposal of December 12, 2010. The first one addressed the reasonableness of fees (76 *FR* 139) and the other addressed fraud-prevention standards (77 *FR* 46258). Because we require intra-day trading data, we can only examine the second of these rules for firm-specific differences in returns, as the final rule for the first regulation was not announced during trading hours. However, we describe the aggregate, inter-day change in issuers' stock prices below as illustrative of the stakes involved.

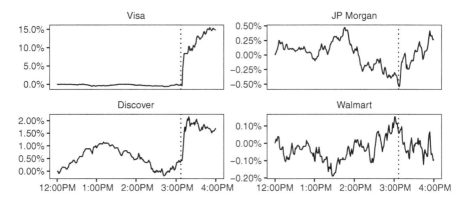

FIGURE 14.4 Percentage returns on afternoon of finalization, June 29, 2011
Webcast of Open Board meeting was scheduled at 3:30pm, with staff memo and rule released shortly before. Vertical dots indicate 3:07pm.

We focus on the fraud-prevention standards component of the rule, which was announced at noon on July 27, 2012. First, we analyze the market performance of four publicly traded companies between 11:00am and 1:00pm that day: Apple, BlackRock Financial, American Express, and Capital One Financial. Apple and BlackRock serve as our placebos, since the future profitability of neither electronics manufacturers nor investment managers seems obviously connected to debit card fees.[6] Indeed, neither firm commented. By contrast, payment processors like American Express and Capital One were directly concerned and both submitted comments that discussed the issue of fraud-prevention standards. We briefly summarize the issues at stake in rulemaking in order to identify how we should expect the market to react for those two firms.

The Durbin Amendment allows issuers to charge additional transaction fees reimbursing the issuers for fraud-prevention costs. The two key issues at stake in rulemaking were the size of the fees and what kinds of fraud prevention measures would qualify. The proposed rule did not set a maximum fee and outlined two possible approaches to qualification: (1) a rules-based approach that would require the adoption of certain technologies and (2) a more flexible approach based on standards. American Express, Capital One, and many other issuers submitted letters requesting high-fees and flexible qualification standards. Merchants wanted lower fees and less flexible qualification standards. The interim final rule of June 29, 2011 adopted a 1% fee and provisionally established a standards-based approach. The outcome was a clear victory for the issuers. As the National Association of Convenience Stores lamented,

---

[6] Apple certainly does have *some* exposure through its chain of retail stores. However, its 2011 10-K makes clear that the Apple Store is a relatively small component of its business, with 88% of sales deriving from other sources.

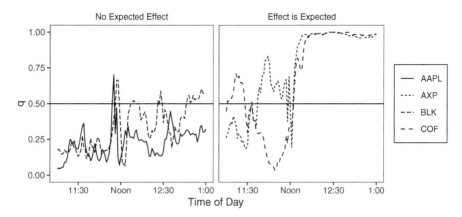

FIGURE 14.5 $\hat{Q}^k_{i\omega(j)}$ for two firms benefitting in expectation and two firms in expectation not affected.

"the Rule lacks any mechanism to ensure that issuers receiving the fraud prevention adjustment are actually preventing fraud." Senator Durbin himself sent a letter to the Federal Reserve insisting that the Board "must address the shortcomings of the interim final rule by implementing a final rule that requires actual compliance with effective fraud prevention steps in order for a fee adjustment to be allowed." For their part, Capital One and other issuers sent comments supporting the interim rule. The final rule largely confirmed the approach of the interim rule, including the 1% fee and non-prescriptive qualification standards. As proof-positive of their displeasure, retailers sued the Board over the rule. For our purposes, the important point is that we should expect a favorable market reaction for representative issuers Capital One and American Express.[7]

Figure 14.5 shows the change in price for each stock relative to its price at noon on July 27, 2012. The price path for Capital One and American Express both indicate notable upward jumps shortly after noon, while Apple and BlackRock do not. In order to emphasize the magnitude of these jumps, the illustration also shows what would have been observed at noon on each of the previous 100 days. Against this 100 day benchmark, the price paths of Apple and BlackRock are unremarkable before and after noon. While American Express and Capital One are also quite typical between 11:00am and noon,

[7] The interim final rule was released too late in the day to permit for the intra-day measures we use. Yet payment processor stocks rose strongly in the following trading day. See Glenn Schorr, "Volcker Rule Due Out Soon: Hopefully More Bark Than Bite," October 6, 2011; http://xa .yimg.com/kq/groups/17389986/555239495/name/NOmura+US+Bank+%26+Brokers .pdf. We examine only the July 2012 rule here, which suggests that our estimates of commenter benefits are, if anything, underestimated, as some of the market reaction favorable to payment processors took place over a year beforehand.

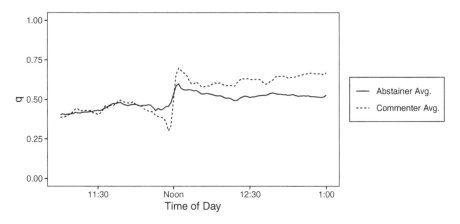

FIGURE 14.6 Illustration of common trends among commenters and abstainers prior to rule announcement: Debit card final rule announcement, July 2012

after the first few minutes the returns are higher than would have been observed on previous days, and stay that way throughout the hour.

Figure 14.6 shows what happens when we separately average the reactions of US financial firms that commented on the Durbin rule and those that abstained. We focus on using quantile returns, the construction of which is described in more detail in the appendix of (Libgober, 2020a). In contrast with the variability of firm-level returns (see Figure 14.5), returns that are averaged across several firms are quite stable. Indeed, for abstainers, these returns are essentially flat around 0.5.[8] Second, note that before noon the two paths are similar. Around the announcement time the returns of the commenters become more volatile. By 12:15pm the difference between the curves is apparent and remains stable over the hour.

While we have thus far used the Debit Card rule to emphasize the logic of our empirical method, the case also fills out the larger story that emerges from looking across the entire set of rules. The retention of the interim rule's outcomes represented a preservation of policy wins for card-issuing banks. In particular, it allowed issuers the right to "tax" retail transactions for costs that were largely illusory, at least according to the merchants and Senator Durbin. For producers, preserving these wins were crucial. The burden of these fees for most merchants was small. For some large retailers, like Amazon or Best Buy, the little burdens may have been enough to justify commenting, but even for them the 1% fee hardly represents an existential threat to their business. Indeed, bank letters were notably more numerous and more detailed than

---

[8] Note that there is some evidence that *abstainers* stock experienced a positive response as well at noon, consistent with the notion that some banks materially gained by "free-riding" on others' commenting activity.

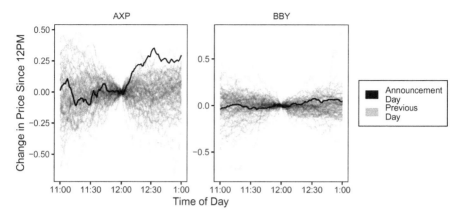

FIGURE 14.7 Returns to final rule for American Express and Best Buy 2012

the merchants at both the proposal and interim final rule stage. Consumer advocates were hardly represented at all. As an illustration of how well commenting financial firms did relative to commenting non-financial firms, American Express experienced returns near the top of its quantile returns distribution while a representative merchant (Best Buy) saw flat stock returns (see Figure 14.7).[9]

This case study demonstrates that increased mechanism clarity can be observed in the rapidity of market responses to the event of rule issuance. Public deliberation allows interested observers to identify a finite set of possible alternatives and their consequences. One of the two major outcomes was partially capturable in a number – the retention of the one cent adjustment. The other major issue was only slightly harder to understand, standards versus specific technologies. The Fed's press release makes clear which way the rule went on both issues, and so does the rule's preamble. Unsurprisingly, the market reaction to the debit card rule was immediate and sustained. Indeed, the differential returns experienced by commenting firms are observable very quickly after final rule announcement, as commenters saw returns at the 60th percentile of ranked returns after just five minutes ($\hat{\beta} = 0.1000$ (0.0374), $p = 0.008$). Average returns after the first hour were highly correlated at $\rho = 0.55$ ($p < 0.001$) with the returns in the first five minutes.

Lessons from the Final Rule on Maximum Interchange Fees

The final rule on maximum interchange fees was issued on June 29, 2011. The rule was highly anticipated and, from all accounts, anxiety-provoking.

---

[9] Amazon's stock rose in the aftermath but that rise had started fifteen minutes before the final rule for reasons unrelated to the rule.

In the proposed rule, issued December 16, 2010, the FRB suggested a maximum interchange fee of 12 cents per debit card transaction. Payment processor firm stocks fell by 7% immediately after the announcement. Comments soon flooded the FRB from payment processors. The letter of American Express (sent February 22, 2011) was indicative of financial institution comments. It combined a dual legal argument (that the EFTA did not give the Fed authority to impose a price cap upon debit card transactions, along with the argument that no cost-benefit analysis or economic impact analysis had been done) with an economic argument that the price caps would be inefficient, damaging both to consumer welfare as well as producer welfare. Here firms mobilized not only legal expertise but also industrial organization expertise. American Express contracted with Princeton economist Robert D. Willig, who wrote a memorandum arguing that "if the price-setting or price-capping mechanism described in the NPRM were applied to American Express, the result would be seriously damaging to the Company's prepaid business and ... ultimately to merchants and consumers."[10]

The final rule represented a medium among the competing demands. A price cap upon interchange fees was kept, but was raised from 12 cents to 21 cents, as well as five basis points of the transaction amount. Payment processor firms immediately saw a 5% increase in stock price. [11]

The trajectory of debit-card rulemaking was closely watched by equity traders (as evidenced from the intra-day movements) and, what is even clearer, by equity market analysts. This not only because of the stakes involved and the zero-sum nature of the policy choice, but also because the debit card rules were some of the first rules that went through the notice-and-comment process under Dodd-Frank rulemaking (this is especially so for highly significant, economically influential rules). In an important and influential memo written in October 2011, as traders eagerly anticipated the proposed rule for the Volcker Rule that would prohibit proprietary trading by bank holding companies subject to limited (but highly significant) exceptions, Nomura Securities analyst Glenn Schorr drew directly upon the evolution of the Durban amendment rules to make forecasts on the shaping of the Volcker Rule. If the Fed's recent behavior was any guide, Schorr suggested, the proposed rule would seem strict and burdensome, but that in the longer run, the rule would be weakened during the Fed's response to the notice-and-comment process. His evidence came directly from the stock prices of payment processor firms.

---

[10] Willig, "Avoiding Misapplication to American Express of the Proposed Debit Card Interchange Fee Rules: An Economic Assessment," February 22, 2011, p. 3; www.federalreserve.gov/SECRS/ 2011/March/20110303/R-1404/R-1404_022211_67230_584162046602_1.pdf.

[11] A "first" Final Rule was announced over a year earlier, then subsequently revised; Board of Governors of the Federal Reserve System, "Federal Reserve issues a final rule establishing standards for debit card interchange fees and prohibiting network exclusivity arrangements and routing restrictions," June 29, 2011; www.federalreserve.gov/newsevents/pressreleases/ bcreg20110629a.htm.

What Schorr's analysis of the payment processors' stock prices shows is that rulemaking, more than any other factor, induced the greatest one-day ("discontinuous") swings in payment processors' firm values over a nearly one-year period. While the proposed rule triggered losses in firm value in December 2010, these were regained by the time of the final rule announcement, and the one-day rise after the final rule announcement (or 5%) gained back over 70% of the losses incurred by the proposed rule. Although we lack intraday evidence on this final rule (having been revealed after trading hours), it is clear that the rule moved in the direction desired by the commenting payment processors, and that the *inter-day* stock price movements reflect this return to commenting.

Yet the context of the Schorr memo tells us something else. First, private equity traders and the analysts who inform them see these intra-day stock price movements as informative of the benefits and costs to firms from regulatory rules. Second, Schorr *explicitly used the trajectory of asset prices in response to the Durbin Rule as a lesson for traders wishing to follow the Volcker Rule.* This suggests, first, that equity markets were not as well accustomed to the process of rulemaking under Dodd-Frank as they would be later on (which fact supports our assumption as to the non-anticipability of the rules and events assumed in our analysis) and, second, that the pattern of costly proposed rule, followed by comments, followed by conditional amelioration of the costs of the rule, is a more general pattern that equity analysts see at work in much rulemaking in the financial sphere (see Libgober, 2020b for a general model that endogenizes the costliness of the initial proposed rule).

INFLUENCE OR LEARNING OR BOTH? ALTERNATIVE EXPLANATIONS

One challenge in interpreting these results concerns how to understand the mechanism by which the notice-and-comment process shaped changes in policy. Different political and industrial observers likely learned that the political coalition supporting the draft rule had weakened during the notice-and-comment process, and observers may also have detected a greater role for economists vis-à-vis lawyers (Katzmann, 1980) as the debate unfolded. Whether our statistical results reflect agency learning about the rule, as opposed to a story about political influence, is not entirely clear, and the evidence retains some ambiguity on this point.

While some degree of learning often occurs during the notice-and-comment process, the contours of this process in particular suggest that learning alone provides a poor explanation for the totality of the results we observe. The first reason is that there was considerable opportunity for learning at the legislative stage. The Durbin rule was a surprise to no one – it was authorized as a plank with the statue itself – and it occasioned considerable lobbying of members of Congress. Once the statute had passed and the administrative stage was reached, moreover, the strength of the political coalition mattered far less to the final outcome. The second is that there was also interaction between affected parties and the Federal Reserve directly well before the publication of the proposed rule.[12] The existence of the Durbin Amendment in statute and the pre-notice-and-comment meetings cast doubt on the existence of significant policy uncertainty remaining at the notice-and-comment stage, which is when we observe significant firm-specific asset price changes. Those changes, finally, correspond directly to those who commented, which is a more direct and simpler explanation than changes in policy uncertainty (which would require much greater theorization), and which would likely have led to more generalized influence activities. While firm-specific influence may have carried policy information, the timing of asset price changes suggests that the particular effect was realized during the notice-and-comment process, as firm asset prices would already have captured previous policy changes and reductions in uncertainty.

CONCLUSION: WHAT DEBIT CARD RULEMAKING TELLS US ABOUT REGULATORY POLITICS

The idea of *explicitly redistributive* political influence over bureaucracy – theoretically pioneered in (Arnold, 1979) – usefully steps apart from the all-too stale debates over principal-agent and bureaucratic control problems and points instead to a world that has received little study in the social sciences: the abundant, little measured and highly significant attempts to influence administrative policy by targeting administrative actors themselves. The notice-and-comment provisions of the Administrative Procedures Act (APA) provide merely the best-observed features of this process. Important studies have demonstrated that direct meetings with rulemakers are also plausibly influential in moving policy, perhaps more than in the notice-and-comment process itself (Krawiec, 2013; Libgober, 2020a). Important qualitative accounts also point to meetings with policymakers (the "13 bankers" case being just one example) where the issue at hand concerns not rulemaking but enforcement (Johnson and Kwak, 2010).

The battle over debit cards comprises, to be sure, only one case. Chapter 12 by Powell et al. in this volume, for example, highlights regulatory policy making with direct and extensive lobbying of the agency by members of Congress,

---

[12] These include FRB staff meetings meetings during the pre-notice-and-comment period with American Express in August 2010 (www.federalreserve.gov/newsevents/rr-commpublic/amex_20100803.pdf and www.federalreserve.gov/newsevents/rr-commpublic/amex_20100816.pdf), with the ABA's Card Policy Council in September 2010 (www.federalreserve.gov/newsevents/rr-commpublic/ABA_council_meeting_20100922.pdf), and with Mastercard in October 2010 (www.federalreserve.gov/newsevents/rr-commpublic/mastercard_meeting_20101004.pdf) and November 2010 (www.federalreserve.gov/newsevents/rr-commpublic/mastercard_meeting_11162010.pdf).

rather than primarily by organized interest groups.[13] That said, no other Dodd-Frank rule attracted as much attention in the notice-and-comment process, and the various interests in play also marshaled a diverse range of academic and legal analyses. Whenever administrative rulemakers engage in the direct choice of explicit policy parameters, and perhaps when the costs are implicit but more easily estimable and traceable, direct lobbying of administrative actors should follow.

A truly general account of high-clarity regulatory politics should comprise an important agenda for the next generation of political scientists. The case study here can be extended to other cases, as well as to cross-policy studies where the variable of traceability is more systematically measured, and where influence activities are structured both formally and informally. Finally, theories that endogenize mechanism clarity and venue clarity in the administrative realm – when clearer decisions are left to agencies and when they are retained by Congress itself – should provide a fruitful research agenda for theorists and empiricists alike.

---

[13] Chapter 13 by Drutman in this volume helps put the tactics of the Electronic Payment Coalition in context.

15

Conclusion: Assessing Contemporary Accountability

Charles M. Cameron, Brandice Canes-Wrone,
Sanford C. Gordon, and Gregory Huber

Any attempt to assess the *overall* impact of political accountability of government performance in the United States immediately founders on a host of conceptual, measurement, and inferential problems. The authors of the thirteen previous chapters have pursued a different approach, each providing a unique perspective on some facet of political accountability and representation in the contemporary USA. They represent a significant diversity of methodological approaches, with quantitative analysis, experiments, qualitative case studies, and formal theory all making appearances. Likewise, they vary considerably in their substantive focus, with some shedding light on the behavior of voters, others on various sets of public officials, and still others on special interests. A few chapters take a synthetic approach and consider all three.

At the same time, what unites these chapters into a coherent research program is their focus on some of the volume's major recurrent themes: how does the behavior (actual or anticipated) of voters and other private actors such as special interest groups inform the decisions of policymakers? And to what extent do recent developments suggest a need to reevaluate classic accounts of political accountability?

In this conclusion, we endeavor to tie together what the substantive chapters have to say on these themes, and on the subject of political accountability more generally. We do so with reference to four key questions:

- Accountability *of whom*?
- Accountability *to whom*?
- Accountability *for what*?
- Accountability *on the basis of what information*?

For each of these questions, we describe some of the key lessons provided in the volume's pages, and comment on whether they point in the direction of significant change in the nature of democratic accountability given recent changes in the political landscape. We then conclude by offering some tentative conclusions and directions for future research.

FOUR RECURRENT QUESTIONS, AND SOME TENTATIVE ANSWERS

Agents: Accountability *Of Whom?*

Perhaps owing to the expertise of the volume's contributors, the public officials garnering the most attention in this volume's pages are members of Congress. It's important to point out, however, that this is not the *exclusive* focus. In Chapter 14, Carpenter and Libgober's focus on the Fed's rulemaking process reminds us of the importance of considering political accountability in bureaucracy; likewise, Chapter 11 by Patty and Chapter 10 by Cameron and Gordon suggest broadening our focus to public officials in the non-legislative branches of government. Viewed in this light, Chapter 12, Powell et al.'s analysis of legislative correspondence with the Federal Energy Regulatory Commission (FERC), suggests that we need not only be concerned with the accountability of FERC to Congress but also of legislators to their constituents.

Even when focusing exclusively on Congress, it is important to recall Shepsle's (Shepsle, 1992) famous adage that "Congress is a they, not an it," and consider what this means when asking about accountability *of whom*. As Egan and Prior note in Chapter 4 of this volume, legislators may be evaluated with respect to their own individual performance (e.g., through position-taking, as in Chapter 2 by Clinton et al. or Chapter 6 by Canes-Wrone and Kistner, or through local interests, as in Chapter 12 by Powell et al.), or the performance of their respective parties, as discussed in the essays on the challenges of lawmaking in a polarized era by Drutman (Chapter 13) and Lee (Chapter 9). Drutman argues that a consequence of increasing partisan homogenization and polarization has been a displacement of the individual legislator as object of evaluation by the legislative party. As the evidence provided by Clinton et al., Canes-Wrone and Kistner, and Powell et al. suggests, however, this displacement is far from complete.

Principals: Accountability *To Whom?*

Any description of the behavior of public officials must not only assess *whether* they are accountable but also *to whom* they are accountable. A critical distinction between political accountability relationships and the accountability relationship between, say, an employer and employee, is that public officials invariably answer to more than one principal. And *which* of those principals will, owing to the economy of incentives faced by elected officials, wield the most leverage over them may vary according to the informational and institutional context. The standard list of principals is well known: median general election voters, median primary voters, organized interests, campaign contributors, local economic elites, and wealthy individuals.

A number of the contributors to this volume help to flesh out the "to whom" question, shedding light on both the economy of incentives and the full "cast of characters" to consider, in order to arrive at a more textured understanding.

As Bawn et al. note in Chapter 5, local parties or groups sometimes play a key role in reducing uncertainty both for other groups and for voters by throwing their support behind candidates that represent their own idiosyncratic interests. While reducing uncertainty may benefit voters, it comes at the potential cost of undermining accountability to the electorate more generally. Note that in their account, the overlap between party elite and organized interests is often considerable, so the local party elite may resemble an interest group coalition that (in some sense) has captured the party's candidate selection mechanism.

In Chapter 12, Powell et al., in their analysis of congressional correspondence to FERC, note that *which* constituents legislators tend to advocate on behalf of with the Commission depends critically on both the partisanship of the official and majority control of Congress, with different legislators writing letters supportive of consumer or business interests. Hence, Powell et al. help to describe how the nature of legislator responsiveness is moderated by partisan facts on the ground.

Several other chapters explore how macropolitical changes may have changed political accountability relationships over time. What, for example, has affected the relative leverage of special interests versus the general electorate in influencing politician behavior? According to Drutman, the increased polarization of Congress has, if anything, *strengthened* the hand of interest groups: gridlock has put a premium on the value of costly lobbying to pass new policies; donors have greater power over agenda setting than previously; and partisan acrimony undermines lawmaking in the general interest.

An additional factor that affects the leverage of different principals is the decline of local media. Canes-Wrone and Kistner note that reductions in local media coverage undermine the electoral penalty for ideologically extreme challengers. To the extent that their cross-sectional findings might be applied to more general secular trends in the American media landscape, the global result may be an overall decline in the fealty of legislators to the ideological centers in their districts.

Actions and Outcomes: Accountability *For What*

The third recurrent question concerns the *what* of accountability relationships: what do principals ultimately care about when evaluating incumbents? The major contribution of Arnold (1990) is to demarcate the contours of these objects of concerns, drawing critical distinctions between costs and benefits, policies with general versus particular effects, and policies with short versus long term consequences. As Egan and Prior note, the critical issue is what legislators *think* voters want. Some of the chapters in this volume have further fleshed out some critical distinctions with reference to this question.

In their analysis of voter evaluations of congressional voting, for example, Clinton et al. find that while partisanship exerts an independent effect on voter evaluations of candidates, issues continue to matter, at least in salient cases like repeal of the Affordable Care Act. In their discussion of the Durbin Rule, Carpenter and Libgober focus on the distribution of costs and benefits across different interests and its implications for investments by private interests in steering the regulatory process. At a more conceptual level, Patty discusses features of institutional design that bracket categories of outcomes for evaluation by principals.

Two chapters discuss the consequences of partisan polarization for policy outcomes that speak to change in the "what" dimension of accountability. Drutman argues that the empowerment of special interests makes it more difficult for Congress to pursue broad policy changes in the national interest. And Lee, while acknowledging important similarities in coalition building in the present versus previous eras, concedes that polarization creates constraints in the availability of coalition partners, making broad legislative successes less likely.

Information: Accountability *On the Basis of What?*

The final recurrent question when assessing the state of political accountability in the contemporary United States concerns information: as Patty puts it, what are the *diagnostic criteria* for evaluating the performance of (political) agents?

Information is a critical feature of the relationships described in the substantive chapters. Some of the authors consider the nature of the information to which voters have access. Chapter 7, by Carnes, for example, laments the lack of information on the backgrounds of candidates, arguing that this may compromise descriptive representation. Cameron and Gordon describe incentives of third party actors ("sentinels") to strategically withhold or share information about incumbent performance, potentially distorting the behavior of incumbents to the detriment of democratic accountability.

Other chapters consider how voters process the information provided to them. Key among these is Chapter 3 by Patashnik et al., whose experiments reveal that citizens make more efficient use in evaluating incumbent performance when provided with contextual information ("yardsticks"), that they are prone to negativity bias in their evaluations, and that they are strongly predisposed against policies that concentrate costs in a narrow segment of the citizenry.

What has changed in the availability of diagnostic information with which to evaluate incumbents? As noted above, the lessons from Canes-Wrone and Kistner's piece speak to declining local media coverage. In Chapter 8, Huber and Tucker provide a comprehensive perspective on changes in technology of news provision, noting not only the decline of local media coverage but also the advent of cable news, social media, and mass streaming platforms.

They are reticent, however, to point to any firm conclusions regarding the welfare consequences of technological changes: although it is possible that incumbent legislators may take fewer actions focused on their districts, it is also possible that doing so could shift their electoral strategies from seeking small-bore local victories for which to claim credit to helping achieve broad-based partisan policy victories. Whether such a shift would be good or bad for voters depends in part on assumptions regarding voters' policy preferences.

VOTERS AND PUBLIC OFFICIALS: AN ASSESSMENT

As we stated in the Introduction chapter, a primary goal of this volume has been to integrate empirical and theoretical advances in the study of the behavior of both voters and public officials into a more comprehensive understanding of political accountability.

Let us begin with the voters. It would seem that a first-order requirement for voters to punish public officials for holding positions inconsistent with their attitudes, or for performing poorly in office, is that voters know something about those positions or performance. Since the 1960s, however, a recurrent question in political science concerns whether voters have adequate information or knowledge to do so. Early work by Miller and Stokes (1963) and Converse (1964) articulated reasons for skepticism; and the skeptical view has seen a resurgence of late in the form of advocacy of "epistocracy" (e.g., Brennan, 2016). A countervailing line of inquiry, starting with Key (1966), disputes this bleak assessment.

The chapters in this volume flesh out the role of the voter in political accountability in ways that are informative to this ongoing debate. One theme that emerges concerns *conditional responsiveness*. Clinton et al., for example, demonstrate that voters evaluate their representatives on their issue positions, *at least for highly salient issues*. Canes-Wrone and Kistner document voter responsiveness to candidate positions, *conditional on the availability of rigorous news coverage*.

A second theme that emerges is the importance of voter cognition. Patashnik et al. point to the importance of information not just about incumbent performance but also appropriate benchmarks for comparison. Egan and Prior discuss how partisan-motivated reasoning might diminish the accuracy of voters' performance evaluations.

A better understanding of these themes can lead to a more comprehensive account of the behavior of public officials. As Patty notes, temporal bracketing, which affects not just the existence but also the timing of diagnostic information available to voters, can play an important role in structuring the incentives of incumbents. Viewed in this light, one can interpret challenger and interest group behavior with respect to the provision of verifiable information to voters as a form of strategic bracketing, with important implications for incumbent accountability.

Taking a step back, the chapters in this volume provide a nuanced understanding of the role of increased partisan polarization in moderating political accountability. As has long been noted, party labels can provide an important heuristic for voters to make reasonably well-informed decisions in the voting booth. As the parties have grown more distinct, this has doubtless made the selection problem easier. By the same token, the critical importance of forestalling primary challenges may have increased the leverage of primary electorates and interest groups at the expense of the electorate more broadly. This is a takeaway of the essays by Drutman on lawmaking in a polarized era and by Bawn et al. on the influence of group and local interests in the candidate selection process.

Likewise, changes in the media landscape such as those described by Huber and Tucker may be a double-edged sword. On the one hand, voters have unprecedented access to cheap political information. On the other hand, the decline of local news coverage shifts the focus of the accountability relationship from the legislator as an agent of local interests to an agent participating in a national team in the form of a political party. This, like other factors, may give legislators more incentive to focus on national (partisan) policymaking at the expense of effort on behalf of locally relevant issues, but whether this is good or bad for voters depends on the relative returns to this different allocation of effort.

REFORM?

The findings of these chapters raise the question of whether particular policy reforms might increase democratic accountability and the representation of voters' preferences. A thorough discussion of policy reforms is well beyond the scope of this brief conclusion, but it is worth highlighting that there are active debates in the academic and policy worlds about how to increase the influence of the public – including the inattentive public – and reduce the influence of organized interests in elections, legislative policymaking, and agency decision-making. Such potential reforms span electoral procedures, campaign finance, regulation of the media, and lobbying. But a few such examples include ranked choice voting, requirements regarding the sources and timing of campaign contributions, changes to antitrust regulations regarding traditional and social media conglomerates, and restrictions on lobbying by recent government officials.

The chapters here are not designed to evaluate specific proposals, but offer evidence and insight into the ways in which politicians are held accountable in the contemporary political and media environments. Importantly, many of the chapters highlight that dynamic adaptation by all actors affected by a reform must be considered when evaluating any institutional change. For example, as Bawn et al. describe, groups and parties adapt to a variety of primary electoral institutions, some of which were designed to increase voters' influence. Likewise, Lee shows how despite the large institutional changes in Congress, coalition-builders use many of the same techniques today as in earlier eras. At the very least, it is likely that substantial reforms will evoke changes in the behavior of legislators, parties, organized interests, and perhaps even voters, all of which may produce outcomes far different from what those who enacted reforms sought in the first place. The evidence here provides a foundation upon which potential reforms can be evaluated as well as suggests new research questions that could further our understanding of existing accountability dynamics.

DIRECTIONS FOR FUTURE RESEARCH

In light of the contributions of this volume for what we do know about the nature of in the contemporary USA, it is also useful to highlight areas where future research seems warranted. Most chapters already present ideas related to their specific topics, so here we focus on a few cross-cutting issues that combine the findings of multiple chapters. For instance, Bawn et al. argue that groups, including local parties, are central to the selection of legislative primary victors, that the groups support members who will pursue the groups' policy goals, and that these goals may not align with those of the general electorate. Other chapters, including Clinton et al. and Canes-Wrone and Kistner, find that at least under some circumstances, voters will hold members accountable for their policy actions. Together, the chapters suggest the need for research on the extent to which legislators pursue the goals of the major group(s) who supported their primary candidacy and how this behavior relates to future electoral dynamics.

A related set of questions concerns the implications of changes in electoral accountability and the media for policymaking. The chapter by Drutman argues that private interests now have more of the upper hand relative to diffuse interests than in recent eras. Without directly disputing this claim, Lee's chapter paints a slightly more optimistic picture. Going even further, some research outside this volume suggests important legislation continues to be produced at a pace comparable to that in earlier eras (e.g., Mayhew, 2019), albeit without categorizing whether this important legislation represents diffuse interests. Drutman's claims clearly fit with the conventional wisdom regarding changes in partisanship and the media. At the same time, it is also possible that as the media has become more partisan and competitive, the incentives to report on conflict rather than on cooperation have increased. Open questions for the literature include whether important legislation that represents diffuse interests has declined over time as well as the extent to which patterns of media reporting on contested versus bipartisan legislation have changed.

Finally, a host of cross-cutting questions are associated with Huber and Tucker's suggestion for research that tracks consumers' online news diets. For example, how do these news consumption patterns relate to partisan-motivated reasoning? In districts where the local news is weak, are citizens more likely to engage in the type of partisan-motivated reasoning analyzed in Egan and Prior? Likewise, how does online news consumption in a district relate to a member's policymaking activity, including their interactions with the bureaucracy?

Analyzing these sorts of large, synthetic questions is enormously challenging given the need for expertise in what have become somewhat isolated areas of study within the US Politics subfield, to say nothing of the ever-present difficulties of making strong causal claims. While synthetic accounts can be extremely valuable, a natural approach likely to yield the highest returns is to break these larger questions down into more manageable components. The research program that these components add up to will invariably present the synoptic view that it is difficult for any one study to sufficiently provide. At the same time, it is critical that we not lose site of the broader context, which informs the features of the environment we choose to focus our attention on, while animating our interest in these topics in the first place.

Bibliography

Abernathy, Penelope Muse. 2018. *The Expanding News Desert*. Chapel Hill, NC: The University of North Carolina Press.

Abramowitz, Alan I., Brad Alexander, and Matthew Gunning. 2006. "Incumbency, Redistricting, and the Decline of Competition in U.S. House Elections." *Journal of Politics* 68 (1): 75–88.

Achen, Christopher H., and Larry M. Bartels. 2016. *Democracy for Realists*. Princeton, NJ: Princeton University Press.

Adler, E. Scott, and John D. Wilkerson. 2008. "Intended Consequences." *Legislative Studies Quarterly* 33 (1): 85–112.

Ahler, Douglas J., and David E. Broockman. 2018. "The Delegate Paradox." *Journal of Politics* 80 (4): 1117–1133.

Akerlof, George A. 1970. "The Market for 'Lemons'." *The Quarterly Journal of Economics* 84 (3): 488–500.

Aldrich, John H. 2011. *Why Parties? A Second Look*. Chicago, IL: University of Chicago Press.

Allcott, Hunt, Luca Braghieri, Sarah Eichmeyer, and Matthew Gentzkow. 2020. "The Welfare Effects of Social Media." *American Economic Review* 110 (3): 629–676.

Allison, Graham T. 1969. "Conceptual Models of the Cuban Missile Crisis." *American Political Science Review* 63: 689–718.

Altman, Alex. 2014. "The U.S. Chamber of Commerce is Saving the GOP Establishment at the Ballot Box." *TIME*.

Anderson, William D., Janet M. Box-Steffensmeier, and Valeria Sinclair-Chapman. 2003. "The Keys to Legislative Success in the U.S. House of Representatives." *Legislative Studies Quarterly* 28 (3): 357–386.

Ansolabehere, Stephen, and Philip Edward Jones. 2010. "Constituents' Responses to Congressional Roll-Call Voting." *American Journal of Political Science* 54 (3): 583–597.

Ansolabehere, Stephen, James M. Snyder Jr., and Michael M. Ting. 2003. "Bargaining in Bicameral Legislatures." *American Political Science Review* 97 (3): 471–481.

Arnold, R. Douglas. 1979. *Congress and the Bureaucracy*. New Haven, CT and London: Yale University Press.
    1981. "Legislators, Bureaucrats, and Locational Decisions." *Public Choice* 37 (1): 107–132.
    1990. *The Logic of Congressional Action*. New Haven, CT and London: Yale University Press.
    1993. "Can Inattentive Citizens Control Their Elected Representatives?" In *Congress Reconsidered*, ed. Lawrence C. Dodd and Bruce I. Oppenheimer. 5th ed. Washington, DC: CQ Press, pp. 401–416.
    2004. *Congress, the Press, and Political Accountability*. Princeton, NJ: Princeton University Press.
    2017. "The Electoral Connection, Age 40." In *Governing in a Polarized Age: Elections, Parties, and Political Representation in America*, ed. Alan S. Gerber and Eric Schickler. New York, NY: Cambridge University Press, pp. 15–34.
Ashworth, Scott. 2012. "Electoral Accountability." *Annual Review of Political Science* 15 (1): 183–201.
Ashworth, Scott, and Kenneth Shotts. 2011. "Challengers, Democratic Contestation, and Electoral Accountability." Presented at the Annual Meeting of the American Political Science Organization.
Bafumi, Joseph, and Michael C. Herron. 2010. "Leapfrog Representation and Extremism." *American Political Science Review* 104 (3): 519–542.
Balko, Radley. 2013. *Rise of the Warrior Cop*. Philadelphia, PA: PublicAffairs.
Barber, Michael J. 2016. "Donation Motivations." *Political Research Quarterly* 69 (1): 148–159.
Barber, Michael, and Jeremy C. Pope. 2019. "Does Party Trump Ideology?" *American Political Science Review* 113 (1): 38–54.
Barbera, Pablo, Simon Munzert, Andrew Guess, and JungHwan Yang. n.d. "Paying Attention to Attention." Working Paper.
Baron, David P., and John A. Ferejohn. 1989. "Bargaining in Legislatures." *American Political Science Review* 83 (4): 1181–1206.
Bartels, Larry M. 1996. "Uninformed Votes." *American Journal of Political Science* 40 (1): 194–230.
    2000. "Partisanship and Voting Behavior, 1952–1996." *American Journal of Politcial Science* 44: 35–50.
    2002. "Beyond the Running Tally." *Political Behavior* 24 (2): 117–150.
    2008. *Unequal Democracy*. Princeton, NJ: Princeton University Press.
Baumgartner, Frank R., Jeffrey M. Berry, Marie Hojnacki, David C. Kimball, and Beth L. Leech. 2009. *Lobbying and Policy Change*. Chicago, IL: University of Chicago Press.
Bawn, Kathleen. 1995. "Political Control versus Expertise." *American Political Science Review* 89 (1): 62–73.
Bawn, Kathleen, Martin Cohen, David Karol, Seth Masket, Hans Noel, and John Zaller. 2012. "A Theory of Political Parties." *Perspectives on Politics* 10 (3): 571–597.
Baylor, Christopher. 2017. *First to the Party*. Philadelphia, PA: University of Pennsylvania Press.
Beim, Deborah, Tom S. Clark, and John W. Patty. 2017. "Why Do Courts Delay?" *Journal of Law and Courts* 5 (4): 199–241.
Beim, Deborah, Alexander V. Hirsch, and Jonathan P. Kastellec. 2014. "Whistleblowing and Compliance in the Judicial Hierarchy." *American Journal of Political Science* 58 (4): 904–918.

Bendix, William. 2016. "Bypassing Congressional Committees." *Legislative Studies Quarterly* 41 (3): 687–714.

Bentley, Clyde H. 2008. "Citizen Journalism: Back to the Future?" Paper presented at the Carnegie-Knight Conference on the Future of Journalism, Cambridge, MA, June 20–21.

Bernhard, William, and Tracy Sulkin. 2018. *Legislative Style*. Chicago, IL: University of Chicago Press.

Berry, Christopher R., and Anthony Fowler. 2015. "Cardinals or Clerics?" *American Journal of Political Science* 60 (3): 692–708.

Besley, Timothy, and Anne Case. 1995. "Incumbent Behavior." *The American Economic Review* 85 (1): 25–45.

Binder, Sarah. 2015. "The Dysfunctional Congress." *Annual Review of Political Science* 18 (1): 85–101.

Birnbaum, Jeffrey H., and Alan S. Murray. 1988. *Showdown at Gucci Gulch*. New York, NY: Vintage.

Bisgaard, Martin. 2015. "Bias Will Find a Way." *Journal of Politics* 77 (3): 849–860.

Bloomberg. 2019. "Company Overview of the Williams Companies, Inc." www.bloomberg.com/research/stocks/private/snapshot.asp?privcapId=390225. Date Accessed: May 8, 2019.

Boatright, Robert G. 2014. *Congressional Primary Elections*. London, UK: Routledge.

Bonica, Adam. 2014. "Mapping the Ideological Marketplace." *American Journal of Political Science* 58 (2): 367–386.

   2016. "Database on Ideology, Money in Politics, and Elections." https://data.stanford.edu/dime.

   2018. "Inferring Roll-Call Scores from Campaign Contributions Using Supervised Machine Learning." *American Journal of Political Science* 62 (4): 830–848.

Bonica, Adam, and Gary W. Cox. 2018. "Ideological Extremists in the U.S. Congress: Out of Step but Still in Office." *Quarterly Journal of Political Science* 13 (2): 207–236.

Boydstun, Amber E., Alison Ledgerwood, and Jehan Sparks. 2019. "A Negativity Bias in Reframing Shapes Political Preferences Even in Partisan Contexts." *Social Psychological and Personality Science* 10 (1): 53–61.

Brady, Henry E., and Paul M. Sniderman. 1985. "Attitude Attribution." *American Political Science Review* 79 (4): 1061–1078.

Brennan, Jason. 2016. *Against Democracy*. Princeton, NJ: Princeton University Press.

Broockman, David E. 2016. "Approaches to Studying Policy Representation." *Legislative Studies Quarterly* 41 (1): 181–215.

Broockman, David E., and Daniel M. Butler. 2017. "The Causal Effects of Elite Position-Taking on Voter Attitudes." *American Journal of Political Science* 61 (1): 208–221.

Brown, Andrew. 2016. "WV Republican Congressmen's Funding Dwarfs Challengers'. October 1, 2016." *Charleston Gazette Mail*.

Bullock, John G. 2011. "Elite Influence on Public Opinion in an Informed Electorate." *American Political Science Review* 105 (3): 496–515.

Bullock, John G., Alan S. Gerber, Seth J. Hill, and Greg A. Huber. 2015. "Partisan Bias in Factual Beliefs about Politics." *Quarterly Journal of Political Science* 10 (4): 519–578.

Burden, Barry C. 2007. *Personal Roots of Representation*. Princeton, NJ: Princeton University Press.

Bussing, Austin, Will Patton, Jason M. Roberts, and Sarah A. Treul. 2020. "The Electoral Consequences of Roll Call Voting." *Political Behavior*. https://doi.org/10.1007/s11109-020-09615-4

Butler, Daniel M., Adam G. Hughes, Craig Volden, and Alan E. Wiseman. 2019. "Do Constituents Know (or Care) about the Lawmaking Effectiveness of Their Representatives?" Working Paper.

Cahn, Emily. 2014. "For Democrats, It's Déjà Vu in California's 31st District." *Roll Call* May 14. https://rollcall.com/2014/05/14/for-democrats-its-deja-vu-in-californias-31st-district/.

Cain, Bruce E., John A. Ferejohn, and Morris P. Fiorina. 1984. "The Constituency Service Basis of the Personal Vote for U.S. Representatives and British Members of Parliament." *American Political Science Review* 78 (1): 110–125.

Cain, Bruce, John Ferejohn, and Morris Fiorina. 1987. *The Personal Vote*. Cambridge, MA: Harvard University Press.

Caliendo, Stephen M., and Charlton D. McIlwain. 2006. "Minority Candidates, Media Framing, and Racial Cues in the 2004 Election." *Harvard International Journal of Press/Politics* 11 (4): 45–69.

Camerer, Colin, Linda Babcock, George Loewenstein, and Richard Thaler. 1997. "Labor Supply of New York City Cabdrivers." *The Quarterly Journal of Economics* 112 (2): 407–441.

Campbell, Angus, Phillip E. Converse, Warren E. Miller, and Donald E. Stokes. 1960. *The American Voter*. Chicago, IL: University of Chicago Press. Unabridged Edition, Midway Reprint Series.

Campbell, James E., John R. Alford, and Keith Henry. 1984. "Television Markets and Congressional Elections." *Legislative Studies Quarterly* 9 (4): 665–678.

Campbell, James E., and Steve J. Jurek. 2003. "The Decline of Competition and Change in Congressional Elections." In *Congress Responds to the Twentieth Century*, ed. Sunil Ahuja and Robert E. Dewhirst. Columbus, OH: Ohio State University Press, pp. 43–72.

Canes-Wrone, Brandice. 2015. "From Mass Preferences to Policy." *Annual Review of Political Science* 18 (1): 147–165.

Canes-Wrone, Brandice, David W. Brady, and John F. Cogan. 2002. "Out of Step, Out of Office." *American Political Science Review* 96 (1): 127–140.

Canes-Wrone, Brandice, Michael C. Herron, and Kenneth W. Shotts. 2001. "Leadership and Pandering." *American Journal of Political Science* 45 (3): 532–550.

Canes-Wrone, Brandice, and Michael R. Kistner. 2022. "Out of Step and Still in Congress? Electoral Consequences of Incumbent and Challenger Positioning across Time." *Quarterly Journal of Political Science* 17 (3): 389–420.

Canes-Wrone, Brandice, William Minozzi, and Jessica Bonney Reveley. 2011. "Issue Accountability and the Mass Public." *Legislative Studies Quarterly* 36 (1): 5–35.

Carmon, Irin. 2014. "Women in 2014: A Turning Point for Women in Politics?" *MSNBC* January 9. www.msnbc.com/msnbc/2014-turning-point-women-politics-msna243841.

Carnes, Nicholas. 2013. *White-collar Government*. Chicago, IL: University of Chicago Press.

  2018. *The Cash Ceiling*. Princeton, NJ: Princeton University Press.

Carnes, Nicholas, and Noam Lupu. 2019. "What Do Voters Think about the Descriptive Underrepresentation of the Working Class?" Working Paper.

Carpenter, Daniel P. 2001. *The Forging of Bureaucratic Autonomy*. Princeton, NJ: Princeton University Press.

Carson, Jamie L., and Ryan D. Williamson. 2018. "Candidate Ideology and Electoral Success in Congressional Elections." *Public Choice* 176 (1): 175–192.

Caughey, Devin, James Dunham, and Christopher Warshaw. 2018. "The Ideological Nationalization of Partisan Subconstituencies and the American States." *Public Choice* 176 (1): 133–151.

Caughey, Devin, and Christopher Warshaw. 2019. *Electoral Penalties for Ideological Extremism in US Federal and State Elections*. MIT Typescript.

Center for Responsive Politics. 2021. "Election Trends: Total Cost of Election 1998–2020." www.opensecrets.org/elections-overview/election-trends. Date Accessed: September 10, 2021.

Chen, Anthony. 2019. "In the Private Interest?" In *Can America Govern Itself?*, ed. Frances Lee, and Nolan McCarty. New York, NY: Cambridge University Press.

Chinoy, Sahil, and Jessia Ma. 2019. "How Every Member Got to Congress." *New York Times*.

Chong, Dennis, and James N. Druckman. 2010. "Dynamic Public Opinion." *American Political Science Review* 104 (4): 663–680.

Clark, Tom S., and John W. Patty. 2021. "Equilibrium Ripeness." Working Paper.

Clinton, Joshua D. 2006. "Representation in Congress." *Journal of Politics* 68 (2): 397–409.

Clinton, Joshua D., and Ted Enamorado. 2014. "The National News Media's Effect on Congress." *The Journal of Politics* 76 (4): 928–943.

Coffé, Hilde, and Elizabeth Theiss-Morse. 2016. "The Effect of Political Candidates' Occupational Background on Voters' Perceptions of and Support for Candidates." *Political Science* 68 (1): 55–77.

Coglianese, Cary. 1997. "Assessing Consensus." *Duke Law Journal* 46 (6): 1255–1349.

Cohen, Marty. 2019. *Moral Victories in the Battle for Congress*. Philadelphia, PA: University of Pennsylvania Press.

Cohen, Marty, Hans Noel, and John Zaller. 2004. *Local News and Political Accountability in House Elections*. UCLA Typescript.

Conroy, Meredith, Sarah Oliver, Ian Breckenridge-Jackson, and Caroline Heldman. 2015. "From Ferraro to Palin." *Politics, Groups, and Identities* 3 (4): 573–591.

Converse, Philip E. 1964. "The Nature of Belief Systems in Mass Publics." In *Ideology and Discontent*, ed. David E. Apter. New York: Free Press of Glencoe, pp. 206–261.

Cook, Timothy E. 1986. "House Members as Newsmakers." *Legislative Studies Quarterly* 11 (2): 203–226.

 1988. "Press Secretaries and Media Strategies in the House of Representatives." *American Journal of Political Science* 32 (4): 1047–1069.

Cormack, Lindsey. 2016. "Extremity in Congress." *Legislative Studies Quarterly* 41 (3): 575–603.

Cox, Gary W., and Matthew D. McCubbins. 2005. *Setting the Agenda*. New York, NY: Cambridge University Press.

Cross, Frank B., and Emerson H. Tiller. 1998. "Judicial Partisanship and Obedience to Legal Doctrine." *The Yale Law Journal* 107 (7): 2155–2176.

Curry, James M. 2015. *Legislating in the Dark*. Chicago, IL: University of Chicago Press.

2017. "Here's Why Senate Republicans Are Being So Secretive with Their Oba-macare Repeal Plan." March 2. Vox.com. www.vox.com/mischiefs-of-faction/2017/3/2/14793124/republican-obamacare-replacement-secret.

Curry, James M., and Frances E. Lee. 2019. "Non-Party Government." *Perspectives on Politics* 17 (1): 47–65.

2020a. *The Limits of Party*. Chicago, IL: University of Chicago Press.

2020b. "What Is Regular Order Worth?" *Journal of Politics* 82 (2): 627–641.

Dagan, David, and Steven Teles. 2016. *Prison Break*. New York, NY: Oxford University Press.

Dahl, Robert A. 1971. *Polyarchy*. New Haven, CT: Yale University Press.

Darr, Joshua P., Matthew P. Hitt, and Johanna L. Dunaway. 2018. "Newspaper Closures Polarize Voting Behavior." *Journal of Communication* 68 (6): 1007–1028.

Derthick, Martha, and Paul J. Quirk. 1985. *The Politics of Deregulation*. Washington, DC: Brookings Institution Press.

DiSalvo, Daniel. 2012. *Engines of Change*. New York, NY: Oxford University Press.

Dolan, Kathy. 2004. *Voting for Women*. Boulder, CO: Westview Press.

Dominguez, Casey B. K. 2011. "Does the Party Matter?" *Political Research Quarterly* 64 (3): 534–544.

Downs, Anthony. 1957. *An Economic Theory of Democracy*. New York, NY: Harper.

Drutman, Lee. 2015. *The Business of America is Lobbying*. New York, NY: Oxford University Press.

2016. *Political Dynamism*. Washington, DC: New America.

2020. *Breaking the Two-Party Doom Loop*. New York, NY: Oxford University Press.

Dunaway, Johanna. 2008. "Markets, Ownership, and the Quality of Campaign News Coverage." *Journal of Politics* 70 (4): 1193–1202.

Egan, Patrick J. 2013. *Partisan Priorities*. New York, NY: Cambridge University Press.

2020. "Identity as Dependent Variable." *American Journal of Political Science* 64 (3): 699–716.

Eggers, Andrew C., and Marko Klašnja. 2019. "Wealth, Fundraising, and Voting in the U.S. Congress." Working Paper.

Eisner, Marc Allen. 1991. *Antitrust and the Triumph of Economics*. Chapel Hill, NC: University of North Carolina Press.

Ellis, Christopher, and James A. Stimson. 2012. *Ideology in America*. New York, NY: Cambridge University Press.

Erikson, Robert S., Michael B. MacKuen, and James A. Stimson. 2002. *The Macro Polity*. New York, NY: Cambridge University Press.

Erikson, Robert S., and Gerald C. Wright. 2017. "Voters, Candidates, and Issues in Congressional Elections." In *Congress Reconsidered*, ed. Lawrence C. Dodd and Bruce I. Oppenheimer. 11th ed. Thousand Oaks, CA: CQ Press, pp. 61–88.

Eulau, Heinz, and Paul D. Karps. 1977. "The Puzzle of Representation." *Legislative Studies Quarterly* 2 (3): 233–254.

Evans, David S., Howard Chang, and Steven Joyce. 2015. "The Impact of the U.S. Debit-card Interchange Fee Regulation on Consumer Welfare." *Journal of Competition Law and Economics* 11 (1): 23–67.

Evans, David S., and Richard Schmalensee. 2005. *Paying with Plastic: The Digital Revolution in Buying and Borrowing*. Cambridge, MA: MIT Press.

Evans, Diana. 2004. *Greasing the Wheels*. New York, NY: Cambridge University Press.

Fearon, James D. 1999. "Electoral Accountability and the Control of Politicians." In *Democracy, Accountability, and Representation*, ed. Adam Przeworski, Susan C.

Stokes, and Bernard Manin. Cambridge Studies in the Theory of Democracy. Cambridge, UK: Cambridge University Press, pp. 55–97.

Federal Reserve Board. 1979. "Rulemaking Procedures." *Federal Reserve Bulletin* January, 15: 137.

Federal Reserve System. 2010. 2010 Federal Reserve Payments Study. Technical report Federal Reserve System.

Feldman, Martha. 1989. *Order without Design.* Stanford, CA: Stanford University Press.

Fenno, Richard F. Jr. 1978. *Home Style.* New York, NY: Harper Collins.

 1977. "U.S. House Members in Their Constituencies." *American Political Science Review* 71 (3): 883–917.

Ferejohn, John A. 1974. *Pork Barrel Politics.* Palo Alto, CA: Stanford University Press.

 1986. "Incumbent Performance and Electoral Control." *Public Choice* 50 (1/3): 5–25.

Fiorina, Morris P. 2016. "The (Re)Nationalization of Congressional Elections." Hoover Institution Essays on Contemporary American Politics, Series No. 7.

Fiorina, Morris P., Samuel J. Abrams, and Jeremy C. Pope. 2010. *Culture War?* 3rd ed. Boston, MA: Longman.

Fogarty, Brian J. 2008. "The Strategy of the Story." *Legislative Studies Quarterly* 33 (3): 445–469.

 2013. "Scandals, News Coverage, and the 2006 Congressional Elections." *Political Communication* 30 (3): 419–433.

Fouirnaies, Alexander, and Andrew B. Hall. 2014. "Financial Incumbency Advantage." *Journal of Politics* 76 (3): 711–724.

 2018. "How Do Interest Groups Seek Access to Committees." *American Journal of Political Science* 62 (1): 132–147.

Fowler, Linda L., and Robert D. McClure. 1988. *Political Ambition.* New Haven, CT: Yale University Press.

Fox, Justin, and Richard Van Weelden. 2012. "Costly Transparency." *Journal of Public Economics* 96 (1–2): 142–150.

Freeder, Sean, Gabriel S. Lenz, and Shad Turney. 2019. "The Importance of Knowing What Goes with What." *Journal of Politics* 81 (1): 274–290.

French, Lauren, and Steven Sloan. 2013. "Dick Durbin, Retailers' BFF." *Politico.* April 30. www.politico.com/story/2013/04/dick-durbin-looking-to-become-retailers-bff-090801.

Gailmard, Sean. 2014. "Principal Agent Theory and Accountability." In *The Oxford Handbook of Public Accountability*, ed. Mark Bovens, Robert E. Goodin, and Thomas Schillemans. Oxford, UK: Oxford University Press, pp. 90–105.

Gailmard, Sean, and John W. Patty. 2012a. "Formal Models of Bureaucracy." *Annual Review of Political Science* 15: 353–377.

 2012b. *Learning While Governing.* Chicago, IL: University of Chicago Press.

 2017. "Participation, Process and Policy." *Journal of Public Policy* 37 (3): 233–260.

 2019. "Giving Advice *vs.* Making Decisions." *Political Science Research & Methods* 7 (3): 471–488.

Gaines, Brian J., James H. Kuklinski, and Paul J. Quirk. 2007. "The Logic of the Survey Experiment Reexamined." *Political Analysis* 15 (1): 1–20.

Gavazza, Alessandro, Mattia Nardotto, and Tommaso Valletti. 2019. "Internet and Politics." *Review of Economics Studies* 86 (5): 2092–2135.

Gentzkow, Matthew, and Jesse M. Shapiro. 2006. "Media Bias and Reputation." *Journal of Political Economy* 114 (2): 280–316.

George, Lisa M., and Joel Waldfogel. 2006. "The New York Times and the Market for Local Newspapers." *American Economic Review* 96 (1): 435–447.

Gerber, Alan S., Eric M. Patashnik, and Patrick D. Tucker. 2022. "How Voters Use Contextual Information to Reward and Punish Credit Claiming, Legislative Performance, and Democratic Accountability." *Journal of Politics* 84 (3): 1839–1843.

Gershon, Sarah Allen. 2012. "Press Secretaries, Journalists, and Editors: Shaping Local Congressional News Coverage." *Political Communication* 29 (2): 160–183.

Gilens, Martin. 2001. "Political Ignorance and Collective Policy Preferences." *American Political Science Review* 95 (2): 379–396.

2012. *Affluence and Influence*. Princeton, NJ: Princeton University Press.

Gilens, Martin, and Benjamin I. Page. 2014. "Testing Theories of American Politics." *Perspectives on Politics* 12 (3): 564–581.

Gilovich, Thomas, Dale Griffin, and Daniel Kahneman, eds. 2002. *Heuristics and Biases*. New York, NY: Cambridge University Press.

Gneezy, Aldo, and Aldo Rustichini. 2000. "A Fine Is a Price." *Journal of Legal Studies* 29 (1): 1–18.

Goldenberg, Edie N., and Michael W. Traugott. 1987. "Mass Media in U.S. Congressional Elections." *Legislative Studies Quarterly* 12 (3): 317–339.

Goldstein, Rebecca, Michael Sances, and Hye Young You. 2018. "Exploitative Revenues, Law Enforcement, and the Quality of Government Service." *Urban Affairs Review* 56 (1): 5–31.

Gooch, Andrew, and Gregory A. Huber. 2020. "How Issue Positions Affect Candidate Performance: Experiments Comparing Campaign Donors and the Mass Public." *Political Behavior* 42 (2): 531–556.

Gordon, Sanford C., and Catherine Hafer. 2005. "Flexing Muscle." *American Political Science Review* 99 (2): 245–261.

Gordon, Sanford C., and Gregory A. Huber. 2007. "The Effect of Electoral Competitiveness on Incumbent Behavior." *Quarterly Journal of Political Science* 2 (2): 107–138.

Green, Donald P., Brad Palmquist, and Eric Schickler. 2002. *Partisan Hearts and Minds*. New Haven, CT: Yale University Press.

Green, Matthew, and William Deatherage. 2018. "When Reputation Trumps Policy." *The Forum* 16 (3): 419–440.

Griffin, John D., Brian Newman, and David W. Nickerson. 2019. "A God of Vengeance and of Reward?" *Legislative Studies Quarterly* 44 (1): 133–162.

Grimmer, Justin. 2013. *Representation Style in Congress*. New York, NY: Cambridge University Press.

Grimmer, Justin, Solomon Messing, and Sean Westwood. 2012. "How Words and Money Cultivate a Personal Vote." *American Political Science Review* 106 (4): 703–719.

Grimmer, Justin, Sean Westwood, and Solomon Messing. 2015. *The Impression of Influence*. Princeton, NJ: Princeton University Press.

Groseclose, Tim, and Nolan McCarty. 2001. "The Politics of Blame." *American Journal of Political Science* 45 (1): 100–119.

Grossmann, Matt, and David A. Hopkins. 2016. *Asymmetric Politics*. New York, NY: Oxford University Press.

Guess, Andrew M., Brendan Nyhan, and Jason Reifler. 2019. "Fake News Consumption and Behavior in the 2016 U.S. Presidential Election." Working Paper.

Hacker, Jacob S., Paul Pierson, and Kathleen Thelen. 2015. "Drift and Conversion." In *Advances in Comparative-Historical Analysis*, ed. James Mahoney and Kathleen Thelen. New York, NY: Cambridge University Press.

Hall, Andrew B. 2015. "What Happens When Extremists Win Primaries?" *American Political Science Review* 109 (1): 18–42.

2019. *Who Wants to Run?* Chicago, IL: University of Chicago Press.

Hall, Andrew B., and Chloe Lim. 2018. "Ideology and News Content in Contested U.S. House Primaries." Working Paper.

Hall, Andrew B., and Daniel M. Thompson. 2018. "Who Punishes Extremist Nominees?" *American Political Science Review* 112 (3): 509–524.

Hall, Richard L. 1996. *Participation in Congress.* New Haven, CT: Yale University Press.

Hall, Richard L., and Alan V. Deardorff. 2006. "Lobbying as Legislative Subsidy." *American Political Science Review* 100 (1): 69–84.

Hamilton, James. 2004. *All the News That's Fit to Sell.* Princeton, NJ: Princeton University Press.

Han, Hahrie, and David W. Brady. 2007. "A Delayed Return to Historical Norms." *British Journal of Political Science* 37 (3): 505–531.

Harbridge, Laurel. 2015. *Is Bipartisanship Dead?* New York, NY: Cambridge University Press.

Hare, Christopher, and Keith T. Poole. 2014. "The Polarization of Contemporary American Politics." *Polity* 46 (3): 411–429.

Hassell, Hans J. G. 2017. *The Party's Primary.* New York, NY: Cambridge University Press.

Hassell, Hans J. G., and J. Quin Monson. 2016. "Representational Inconsistency." *Congress & the Presidency* 43 (2): 206–226.

Hayes, Danny, and Jennifer L. Lawless. 2015. "As Local News Goes, So Goes Citizen Engagement." *Journal of Politics* 77 (2): 447–462.

2016. *Women on the Run.* New York, NY: Cambridge University Press.

2018. "The Decline of Local News and Its Effects." *Journal of Politics* 80 (1): 332–336.

Healy, Andrew, and Gabriel Lenz. 2014. "Substituting the End for the Whole." *American Journal of Political Science* 58 (1): 31–47.

Herrnson, Paul S. 2012. *Congressional Elections.* 6th ed. Washington, DC: CQ Press.

Hess, Stephen. 1991. *Live from Capitol Hill!* Washington, DC: The Brookings Institution.

Highton, Benjamin. 2019. "Issue Accountability in US House Elections." *Political Behavior* 41 (2): 349–367.

Hill, Seth J., and Gregory A. Huber. 2017. "Representativeness and Motivations of the Contemporary Donorate." *Political Behavior* 39 (1): 3–29.

2019. "On the Meaning of Survey Reports of Roll Call 'Votes'." *American Journal of Political Science* 63 (3): 611–625.

Hindman, Matthew. 2011. "Less of the Same: The Lack of Local News on the Internet." Washington, DC: FEC Report.

Holmström, Bengt. 1979. "Moral Hazard and Observability." *The Bell Journal of Economics* 10: 74–91.

Hopkins, Daniel J. 2018. *The Increasingly United States.* Chicago, IL: The University of Chicago Press.

Huang, Tien-tsin, and Reginald L. Smith. 2010. V/MA: Fed Rules Tomorrow. Technical report.

Hurlburt, Heather, and Chayenne Polimedio. 2016. Can Transpartisan Coalitions Overcome Polarization? Technical report. New America: Washington, DC.

Isenstadt, Alex. 2013. "GOP Establishment Frets over Alabama Contender." *Politico.* November 4. www.politico.com/story/2013/11/alabama-primary-tea-party-dean-young-bradley-byrne-99286_Page2.html.

Jacobs, Ben. 2013. "Alabama's Republican Runoff Election May Predict the Party's Future." *The Daily Beast.* July 11. www.politico.com/story/2013/11/alabama-primary-tea-party-dean-young-bradley-byrne-99286_Page2.html.

Jacobson, Gary C. 1989. "Strategic Politicians and the Dynamics of U.S. House Elections, 1946–1986." *American Political Science Review* 83 (3): 773–793.

2015. "It's Nothing Personal." *Journal of Politics* 77 (3): 861–873.

2021. "The Presidential and Congressional Elections of 2020." *Political Science Quarterly* 136 (1): 11–45.

Jacobson, Gary C., and Jamie L. Carson. 2019. *The Politics of Congressional Elections.* 10th ed. Lanham, MD: Rowman & Littlefield.

Jacobson, Gary C., and Samuel Kernell. 1983. *Strategy and Choice in Congressional Elections.* 2nd ed. New Haven, CT: Yale University Press.

Jessee, Stephen A. 2012. *Ideology and Spatial Voting in American Elections.* New York, NY: Cambridge University Press.

Jewell, Malcom E. 1983. "Legislator-Constituency Relations and the Representative Process." *Legislative Studies Quarterly* 8 (3): 303–337.

Johnson, Simon, and James Kwak. 2010. *13 Bankers.* New York, NY: Pantheon.

Judge-Lord, Devin, Justin Grimmer, and Eleanor Neff Powell. 2018. "Unequal Representation." Unpublished Working Paper. Presented at the American Political Science Association 2018 Annual Meeting.

Kahn, Kim Fridkin. 1994. "The Distorted Mirror." *Journal of Politics* 56 (1): 154–173.

Kahneman, D., and A. Tversky. 1979. "Prospect Theory." *Econometrica* 47 (4): 263–291.

Kalla, Joshua L., and David E. Broockman. 2016. "Campaign Contributions Facilitate Access to Congressional Officials." *American Journal of Politcial Science* 60 (3): 545–558.

Kane, John V., and Benjamin J. Newman. 2019. "Organized Labor as the New Undeserving Rich?: Mass Media, Class-Based Anti-union Rhetoric and Public Support for Unions in the United States." *British Journal of Political Science* 49 (3): 997–1026.

Karol, David. 2009. *Party Position Change in American Politics.* New York, NY: Cambridge University Press.

Katzmann, Robert A. 1980. *Regulatory Bureaucracy.* New York, NY: Cambridge University Press.

Key, V. O. Jr. 1961. *Public Opinion and American Democracy.* New York, NY: Alfred A. Knopf.

1966. *The Responsible Electorate.* Cambridge, MA: Belknap Press of Harvard University Press.

Khanna, Kabir. 2019. "Do Facts Speak for Themselves? Causes and Consequences of Partisan Bias in Factual Beliefs." Doctoral dissertation, Princeton University.

Kim, In Song. 2018. "LobbyView: Firm-level Lobbying & Congressional Bills Database." Working Paper. http://web.mit.edu/insong/www/pdf/lobbyview.pdf.

Kinder, Donald R., and D. Roderick Kiewiet. 1981. "Sociotropic Politics." *British Journal of Political Science* 11 (2): 129–161.

King, David C. 1997. *Turf Wars: How Congressional Committees Claim Jurisdiction.* Chicago, IL: University of Chicago Press.

Kirby, Brendan. 2013. "Dean Young vows to be 'Ted Cruz congressman,' but pro-Cruz PAC backs Byrne." *AL.com.* November 4. www.al.com/live/2013/11/dean_young_vows_to_be_ted_cruz.html.

Kirkland, Patricia. 2019. "The Business of Being Mayor." Working Paper.

Krawiec, Kimberly D. 2013. "Don't 'Screw Joe the Plummer'." *Arizona Law Review* 55: 53–103.

Krehbiel, Keith. 1998. *Pivotal Politics.* Chicago, IL: University of Chicago Press.

Kupferberg, Jason, and Ramsey El-Assal. 2011. Visa, Inc. Technical report Jeffries.

Lacy, Stephen. 1987. "The Effects of Intracity Competition on Daily Newspaper Content." *Journalism Quarterly* 64 (2–3): 281–290.

Landa, Dimitri, and Dominik Duell. 2015. "Social Identity and Electoral Accountability." *American Journal of Political Science* 59 (3): 671–689.

Landy, Marc K., and Martin A. Levin, eds. 1995. *The New Politics of Public Policy.* Baltimore, MD: Johns Hopkins University Press.

Lawless, Jennifer L., and Richard L. Fox. 2005. *It Takes a Candidate.* New York, NY: Cambridge University Press.

Lee, Frances E. 2016. *Insecure Majorities.* Chicago, IL: University of Chicago Press.

Lenz, Gabriel. 2012. *Follow the Leader?* Chicago, IL: University of Chicago Press.

Levendusky, Matthew S. 2009. *The Partisan Sort.* Chicago, IL: University of Chicago Press.

Levy, Dena, and Peverill Squire. 2000. "Television Markets and the Competitiveness of U.S. House Elections." *Legislative Studies Quarterly* 25 (2): 313–325.

Levy, Ro'ee. 2021. "Social Media, News Consumption, and Polarization." *American Economic Review* 111 (3): 831–870.

Lewis, David E., and Jennifer L. Selin. 2012. "ACUS Sourcebook of United States Executive Agencies." *Administrative Conference of the United States.*

Lewis, Jeffrey B., Keith Poole, Howard Rosenthal, Adam Boche, Aaron Rudkin, and Luke Sonnet. 2018. "Voteview: Congressional Roll-Call Votes Database."

2022. Voteview: Congressional Roll-Call Votes Database. https://voteview.com/.

Libgober, Brian. 2020a. "Meetings, Comments, and the Distributive Politics of Rule-making." *Quarterly Journal of Political Science* 15 (4): 449–481.

2020b. "Strategic Proposals, Endogenous Comments, and Bias in Rulemaking." *Journal of Politics* 82 (2): 642–656.

Lodge, Milton, and Ruth Hamill. 1986. "A Partisan Schema for Political Information Processing." *American Political Science Review* 80 (2): 505–520.

Lowande, Kenneth. 2019. "Politicization and Responsiveness in Executive Agencies." *The Journal of Politics* 81 (1): 33–48.

Lowande, Kenneth, Melinda Ritchie, and Erinn Lauterbach. 2018. "Descriptive and Substantive Representation in Congress." https://sites.lsa.umich.edu/lowande/wp-content/uploads/sites/581/2018/06/dr-v2.pdf. Date Accessed: August 20, 2018.

Lowi, Theodore J. 1979. *The End of Liberalism.* New York, NY: Norton.

Lucas, Jennifer C. 2017. "Gender and Race in Congressional National News Media Appearances in 2008." *Politics & Gender* 13: 569–596.

Malbin, Michael. 1980. *Unelected Representatives.* New York, NY: Basic Books.

Maltzman, Forrest, and Lee Sigelman. 1996. "The Politics of Talk." *Journal of Politics* 58 (3): 819–830.

Martin, Gregory J., and Joshua McCrain. 2019. "Local News and National Politics." *American Political Science Review* 113 (2): 372–384.

Masket, Seth. 2004. "A Party by Other Means." Doctoral Dissertation, Department of Political Science, University of California at Los Angeles.

2011. *No Middle Ground*. Ann Arbor, MI: University of Michigan Press.

Maskin, Eric, and Jean Tirole. 2004. "The Politician and the Judge." *American Economic Review* 94 (4): 1034–1054.

Mason, Lilliana. 2018. *Uncivil Agreement*. Chicago, IL: University of Chicago Press.

Mattingly, Phil, and Robert Schmidt. 2011. "How Wal-Mart Swiped JPMorgan in $16 Billion." *Bloomberg Technology* June 28, 2011.

Mayhew, David. 1974. *Congress: The Electoral Connection*. New Haven, CT: Yale University Press.

2019. "Updates to Divided We Govern." https://campuspress.yale.edu/davidmayhew/datasets-divided-we-govern/, Date Accessed: December 15, 2021.

McCarty, Nolan M. 2017. "The Regulation and Self-Regulation of a Complex Industry." *Journal of Politics* 79 (4): 1220–1236.

McCarty, Nolan, Keith T. Poole, and Howard Rosenthal. 2006. *Polarized America*. Cambridge, MA: MIT Press.

McCarty, Nolan, and Eric Schickler. 2018. "On the Theory of Parties." *Annual Review of Political Science* 21: 175–193.

McChesney, Robert Waterman, and John Nichols. 2011. *The Death and Life of American Journalism*. Philadelphia, PA: Nation Books.

McConnaughy, Corrine M., Ismail K. White, David L. Leal, and Jason P. Casellas. 2010. "A Latino on the Ballot." *The Journal of Politics* 72 (4): 1–13.

McConnell, Christopher, Yotam Margalit, Neil Malhotra, and Matthew Levendusky. 2018. "The Economic Consequences of Partisanship in a Polarized Era." *American Journal of Political Science* 62 (1): 5–18.

McCubbins, Mathew, Roger Noll, and Barry Weingast. 1987. "Administrative Procedures as Instruments of Political Control." *Journal of Law, Economics, and Organization* 3 (2): 243–277.

McCubbins, Mathew D., and Thomas Schwartz. 1984. "Congressional Oversight Overlooked." *American Journal of Political Science* 28 (1): 165–179.

McDermott, Monika L. 2005. "Candidate Occupations and Voter Information Shortcuts." *The Journal of Politics* 67 (1): 201–219.

McDonald, Jared, David Karol, and Lilliana Mason. 2019. "An Inherited Money Dude from Queens County: How Unseen Candidate Characteristics Affect Voter Perceptions." *Political Behavior* 42.3 (2020): 915–938.

McGarity, Thomas. 2012. "Administrative Law as Blood Sport." *Duke Law Journal* 61: 1671.

McGrath, Robert J. 2013. "Congressional Oversight Hearings and Policy Control." *Legislative Studies Quarterly* 38 (3): 349–376.

McIlwain, Charlton D. 2011. "Racialized Media Coverage of Minority Candidates in the 2008 Democratic Presidential Primary." *American Behavioral Scientist* 55 (4): 371–389.

Mendelson, Nina A. 2012. "Should Mass Comments Count?" *Michigan Journal of Environment and Administration* 1 (1): 173–183.

Merl, Jean. 2014. "Hilda Solis backs Eloise Gomez Reyes for Gary Miller's House seat." *Los Angeles Times*. February. 24. www.latimes.com/local/political/la-me-pc-solis-reyes-20140224-story.html.

Merrill, Richard A. 1978. "Regulating Carcinogens in Food." *Michigan Law Review* 77 (2): 171–250.

Milgrom, Paul. 2008. "What the Seller Won't Tell You." *The Journal of Economic Perspectives* 22 (2): 115–132.

Miller, Gary J. 2005. "The Political Evolution of Principal-Agent Models." *Annual Review of Political Sciences* 8: 203–225.

Miller, Gary J., and Andrew B. Whitford. 2016. *Above Politics*. New York, NY: Cambridge University Press.

Miller, L. Keith, and Robert L. Hamblin. 1963. "Interdependence, Differential Rewarding, and Productivity." *American Sociological Review* 28 (5): 768–778.

Miller, Warren E., and Donald E. Stokes. 1963. "Constituency Influence in Congress." *American Political Science Review* 57 (1): 45–56.

Mills, Russell, and Nicole Kalaf-Hughes. 2015. "The Evolution of Distributive Benefits." *The Journal of Economics and Politics* 22 (1): 35–58.

Moe, Terry M. 1985. "The Politicized Presidency." In *The New Direction in American Politics*, ed. John E. Chubb and Paul E. Peterson. Washington, DC: The Brookings Institution, pp. 235–271.

Mondak, Jeffery J. 1995a. "Newspapers and Political Awareness." *American Journal of Political Science* 39 (2): 513–527.

1995b. *Nothing to Read*. Ann Arbor, MI: University of Michigan Press.

Morelli, Massimo, and Richard Van Weelden. 2013. "Ideology and Information in Policymaking." *Journal of Theoretical Politics* 25 (3): 412–439.

Moskowitz, Daniel J. 2021. "Local News, Information, and the Nationalization of U.S. Elections." *American Political Science Review* 115 (1): 114–129.

Moynihan, Donald P. 2008. "The Normative Model in Decline?" In *Public Service Motivation: State of the Science and Art*, ed. Annie Hondeghem and James L. Perry. Oxford, UK: Oxford University Press, pp. 247–267.

Mummolo, Jonathan. 2018. "Militarization Fails to Enhance Police Safety or Reduce Crime but May Harm Police Reputation." *Proceedings of the National Academy of Sciences* 115 (37): 9181–9186.

Mummolo, Jonathan, Erik Peterson, and Sean Westwood. 2021. "The Limits of Partisan Loyalty." *Political Behavior* 43 (3): 949–972.

Munger, Kevin, Patrick J. Egan, Jonathan Nagler, Jonathan Ronen, and Joshua Tucker. 2020. "Political Knowledge and Misinformation in the Era of Social Media." *British Journal of Political Science* 52 (1): 107–127.

Murphy, Tim. 2013. "GOP Congressional Candidate Told Gay Citizens to Go 'Back to California'." *Mother Jones*. November 4. www.motherjones.com/politics/2013/11/dean-young-bradley-byrne-alabama-gay/.

Nakanishi, Masao, Lee G. Cooper, and Harold H. Kassarjian. 1974. "Voting for a Political Candidate under Conditions of Minimal Information." *Journal of Consumer Research* 1: 36–43.

Napoli, Philip M., Sarah Stonbely, Kathleen McCollough, and Bryce Renninger. 2017. "Local Journalism and the Information Needs of Local Communities." *Journalism Practice* 11 (4): 373–395.

Naughton, Keith, Celeste Schmid, Susan Webb Yackee, and Xueyong Zhan. 2009. "Understanding Commenter Influence During Agency Rule Development." *Journal of Policy Analysis and Management* 28 (2): 258–277.

Nielsen, Poul A., and Donald P. Moynihan. 2017. "Romanticizing Bureaucratic Leadership?" *Governance* 30 (4): 541–559.

Niven, David, and Jeremy Zilber. 1998. "What's Newt Doing in People Magazine?" *Political Behavior* 20 (3): 213–224.

Noel, Hans. 2014. *Political Ideologies and Political Parties in America.* New York, NY: Cambridge University Press.

Nyhan, Brendan, Eric McGhee, John Sides, Seth Masket, and Steven Greene. 2012. "One Vote Out of Step?" *American Politics Research* 40 (5): 844–879.

Olsen, Johan P. 2015. "Democratic Order, Autonomy, and Accountability." *Governance* 28 (4): 425–440.

Paarlberg, Laurie E., and Bob Lavigna. 2010. "Transformational Leadership and Public Service Motivation." *Public Administration Review* 70 (5): 710–718.

Page, Scott E. 2006. "Path Dependence." *Quarterly Journal of Political Science* 1 (1): 87–115.

Patashnik, Eric M. 2008. *Reforms at Risk.* Princeton, NJ: Princeton University Press.

Patty, John W. 2007. "The House Discharge Procedure and Majoritarian Politics." *Journal of Politics* 69 (3): 678–688.

Patty, John W. and Elizabeth Maggie Penn 2020. "Identity and Information in Organizations." *Journal of Political Institutions and Political Economy* 1 (3): 379–416.

Paulos, John Allen. 1988. *Innumeracy.* New York, NY: Hill and Wang.

Peltzman, Sam. 1976. "Toward a More General Theory of Regulation." *Journal of Law and Economics* 19 (2): 211–240.

Peskowitz, Zachary. 2019. "Ideological Signaling and Incumbency Advantage." *British Journal of Political Science* 49 (2): 467–490.

Peters, Ellen. 2012. "Beyond Comprehension." *Current Directions in Psychological Science* 21 (1): 31–35.

Peterson, Erik. 2017. "The Role of the Information Environment in Partisan Voting." *Journal of Politics* 79 (4): 1191–1204.

2021a. "Not Dead Yet." *Political Behavior* 43 (1): 339–361.

2021b. "Paper Cuts: How Reporting Resources Affect Political News Coverage." *American Journal of Political Science* 65 (2): 443–459.

Pew Research Center. 2019. "Newspapers Fact Sheet." www.pewresearch.org/journalism/fact-sheet/local-newspapers/.

Pierce, Richard J. Jr. 2009. "What Factors Can an Agency Consider in Making a Decision." *Michigan State Law Review* 2009 (1): 67–88.

Pierson, Paul. 2001. "The Prospects of Democratic Control in an Age of Big Government." In *Politics at the Turn of the Century*, ed. Arthur M. Melzer, Jerry Weinberger, and M. Richard Zinman. New York, NY: Rowman & Littlefield, pp. 140–161.

Pitkin, Hanna F. 1967. *The Concept of Representation.* Berkeley, CA: University of California Press.

Polsby, Nelson W. 1985. *Political Innovation in America.* New Haven, CT: Yale University Press.

Poole, Keith T., and Howard Rosenthal. 1991. "Patterns of Congressional Voting." *American Journal of Political Science* 35 (1): 228–278.

Powell, Eleanor Neff, and Justin Grimmer. 2016. "Money in Exile." *Journal of Politics* 78 (4): 974–988.

Prendergast, Canice. 2003. "The Limits of Bureaucratic Efficiency." *Journal of Political Economy* 111 (5): 929–958.

Prior, Markus. 2006. "The Incumbent in the Living Room." *The Journal of Politics* 68 (3): 657–673.

2007. *Post-Broadcast Democracy*. New York, NY: Cambridge University Press.

2013. "Media and Political Polarization." *Annual Review of Political Science* 16 (1): 101–127.

2018. *Hooked*. New York, NY: Cambridge University Press.

Prior, Markus, Gaurav Sood, and Kabir Khanna. 2015. "You Cannot Be Serious." *Quarterly Journal of Political Science* 10 (4): 489–518.

Rahn, Wendy. 1993. "The Role of Partisan Stereotypes in Information Processing about Political Candidates." *American Journal of Political Science* 37 (2): 472–496.

Read, Daniel, George Loewenstein, and Matthew Rabin. 1999. "Choice Bracketing." *Journal of Risk and Uncertainty* 19 (1–3): 171–197.

Ritchie, Melinda N. 2017. "Back-Channel Representation." *Journal of Politics* 80 (1): 24.

Roberts, Jason M., and Stephen C. Roberds. 2002. "Are All Amateurs Equal?" *Politics & Policy* 30 (3): 482–501.

Robertson, Campbell, and Eric Lipton. 2013. "In Alabama Race, a Test of Business Efforts to Derail Tea Party." *The New York Times*. October 31. www.nytimes.com/2013/11/01/us/politics/in-alabama-race-a-test-of-business-efforts-to-derail-tea-party.html.

Rogers, Steven. 2019. "Coattails, Raincoats, and Congressional Election Outcomes." *Political Science & Politics* 52 (2): 251–255.

Romer, Thomas, and James M. Snyder, Jr. 1994. "An Empirical Investigation of the Dynamics of PAC Contributions." *American Journal of Political Science* 38 (3): 745–769.

Rosse, James N. 1980. "The Decline of Direct Newspaper Competition." *Journal of Communication* 30 (2): 65–71.

Rugaber, Walter. 1974. "Congress Clears Auto Safety Measure Eliminating Seat Belt Interlock System." *The New York Times*. October 16. www.nytimes.com/1974/10/16/archives/congress-clears-auto-safety-measure-eliminating-seat-belt-interlock.html.

Schaffner, Brian F. 2006a. "Local News Coverage and the Incumbency Advantage in the U.S. House." *Legislative Studies Quarterly* 31 (4): 491–511.

2006b. "The Political Geography of Campaign Advertising in U.S. House Elections." *Political Geography* 25: 775–788.

Schaffner, Brian F., and Mark Gadson. 2004. "Reinforcing Stereotypes?" *Social Science Quarterly* 85 (3): 604–623.

Schaffner, Brian F., and Patrick J. Sellers. 2003. "The Structural Determinants of Local Congressional News Coverage." *Political Communication* 20 (1): 41–57.

Schattschneider, Elmer Eric. 1960. *The Semi-Sovereign People*. New York, NY: Holt, Rinehart and Winston.

Schickler, Eric. 2016. *Racial Realignment*. Princeton, NJ: Princeton University Press.

Schiller, Wendy J. 1995. "Senators as Political Entrepreneurs." *American Journal of Political Science* 39 (1): 186–203.

Schlozman, Daniel. 2015. *When Movements Anchor Parties*. Princeton, NJ: Princeton University Press.

Schlozman, Kay Lehman, Sidney Verba, and Henry Brady. 2012. *The Unheavenly Chorus*. Princeton, NJ: Princeton University Press.

Schudson, Michael. 2010. "Political Observatories, Databases and News in the Emerging Ecology of Public Information." *Daedalus* 139 (2): 100–109.

Schwartz, Mildred A. 1990. *The Party Network*. Madison, WI: University of Wisconsin Press.

Serres, Chris. 2011. "Limits on Debit Card Fees on Trial." *Minneapolis Star Tribune*, February 21. www.startribune.com/minnesota-soldier-s-lawsuit-challenges-citibank/116633613/.

Shapiro, Stuart, and David Guston. 2006. "Procedural Control of the Bureaucracy, Peer Review, and Epistemic Drift." *Journal of Public Administration Research and Theory* 17 (4): 535–551.

Shepsle, Kenneth A. 1992. "Congress Is a 'They,' Not an 'It': Legislative Intent as Oxymoron." *International Review of Law and Economics* 12 (2): 239–256.

Shleifer, Andrei. 1985. "A Theory of Yardstick Competition." *Rand Journal of Economics* 16 (3): 319–327.

Sides, John H., Michael Tesler, and Lynn Vavrek. 2018. *Identity Crisis*. Princeton, NJ: Princeton University Press.

Sinclair, Barbara. 2016. *Unorthodox Lawmaking*. 5th ed. Washington, DC: CQ Press.

Smith, Steven S. 2014. *The Senate Syndrome*. Norman, OK: University of Oklahoma Press.

Snyder, James M. Jr. 1992. "Long-Term Investing in Politicians." *Journal of Law & Economics* 35 (1): 15–43.

Snyder, James M. Jr. and David Strömberg. 2010. "Press Coverage and Political Accountability." *Journal of Political Economy* 118 (2): 355–408.

Snyder, James M. Jr., and Michael M. Ting. 2002. "An Informational Rationale for Political Parties." *American Journal of Political Science* 46 (1): 90–110.

    2003. "Roll Calls, Party Labels, and Elections." *Political Analysis* 11 (4): 419–444.

Society for Civil Engineers. 2017. 2017 Infrastructure Report Card: Infrastructure Scores a D+. Technical Report Society for Civil Engineers.

Soroka, Stuart N. 2014. *Negativity in Democratic Politics*. New York, NY: Cambridge University Press.

Squire, Peverill. 1988. "Who Gets National News Coverage in the U.S. Senate?" *American Politics Quarterly* 16 (2): 139–156.

Stewart, Charles III, and Mark Reynolds. 1990. "Television Markets and U.S. Senate Elections." *Legislative Studies Quarterly* 15 (4): 495–523.

Stewart, Charles III, and Jonathan Woon. 2017. "Congressional Committee Assignments, 103rd to 115th Congresses, 1993–2017." November 17, 2017.

Stigler, George J. 1971. "The Theory of Economic Regulation." *The Bell Journal of Economics and Management Science* 2 (1): 3–21.

Stracke, Rudi, Rudolf Kerschbamer, and Uwe Sunde. 2017. "Coping with Complexity." *European Economic Review* 98: 264–281.

Straus, Jacob R., and Matthew E. Glassman. 2016. "Social Media in Congress." *Congressional Research Service Report*. http://fas.org/sgp/crs/misc/R44509.pdf. Date Accessed January 30, 2020.

Sulkin, Tracy. 2011. *The Legislative Legacy of Congressional Campaigns*. New York, NY: Cambridge University Press.

Sunstein, Cass R. 2001. *One Case at a Time*. Cambridge, MA: Harvard University Press.

Taber, Charles S., and Milton Lodge. 2006. "Motivated Skepticism in the Evaluation of Political Beliefs." *American Journal of Political Science* 50 (3): 755–769.

Tausanovitch, Chris, and Christopher Warshaw. 2017. "Estimating Candidates' Political Orientation in a Polarized Congress." *Political Analysis* 25 (2): 167–187.

2018. "Does the Ideological Proximity between Congressional Candidates and Voters Affect Voting in U.S. House Elections?" *Political Behavior* 40 (1): 223–245.

Taylor, Jessica. 2013. "Will It Be Ruin or Resurgence for the Tea Party in Alabama Race?" *MSNBC*. October 23. www.msnbc.com/the-daily-rundown/ruin-or-resurgence-tea-party-alabama-msna193771.

Terkildsen, Nayda, and David F. Damore. 1999. "The Dynamics of Racialized Media Coverage in Congressional Elections." *Journal of Politics* 61 (3): 680–699.

Thaler, Richard. 1985. "Mental Accounting and Consumer Choice." *Marketing Science* 4 (3): 199–214.

Thomsen, Danielle. 2019. *Dropout Decisions in US House Elections*. UC Irvine Typescript.

Tidmarch, Charles M., and John J. Pitney, Jr. 1985. "Covering Congress." *Polity* 17 (3): 463–483.

Tiefer, Charles. 2016. *The Polarized Congress*. Lanham, MD: University Press of America.

Ting, Michael M. 2002. "A Theory of Jurisdictional Assignments in Bureaucracies." *American Journal of Political Science* 46 (2): 364–378.

Trussler, Marc. 2020. "Get Information or Get In Formation." *British Journal of Political Science* 51 (4): 1529–1549.

Tversky, Amos. 1972. "Elimination by Aspects." *Psychological Review* 79: 281–299.

Tversky, Amos, and Daniel Kahneman. 1991. "Loss Aversion in Riskless Choice." *The Quarterly Journal of Economics* 106 (4): 1039–1061.

United States Department of Justice. 2015. "Investigation of the Ferguson Police Department." Report of the Civil Rights Division, March 4.

United States Office of Government Ethics. 2013. "18 U.S.C. 201: Bribery of Public Officials and Witnesses." www.oge.gov/displaytemplates/statutes regulationsdetail.aspx?id=77. Date Accessed: April 4, 2013.

Utych, Stephen M. 2019. "Man Bites Blue Dog." *Journal of Politics* 82 (1): 392–396.

Vinson, Danielle. 2003. *Local Media Coverage of Congress and Its Members*. Cresskill, NJ: Hampton Press.

Volden, Craig, and Alan E. Wiseman. 2014. *Legislative Effectiveness in the United States Congress*. New York, NY: Cambridge University Press.

Wawro, Gregory. 2000. *Legislative Entrepreneurship in the U.S. House of Representatives*. Ann Arbor, MI: University of Michigan Press.

Weaver, Vesla M. 2007. "Frontlash." *Studies in American Political Development* 21 (2): 230–265.

Weber, Max. 1946. "Economy and Society." In *Max Weber: Essays in Sociology*, ed. H. H. Gerth and C. Wright Mills. New York, NY: Oxford University Press.

Weissberg, Robert. 1978. "Collective vs. Dyadic Representation in Congress." *American Political Science Review* 72 (2): 535–547.

West, William F. 2009. "Inside the Black Box." *Administration & Society* 41 (5): 576–599.

Wikipedia. 2019. "List of U.S. States by Population." https://simple.wikipedia.org/wiki/List_of_U.S._states_by_population. Date Accessed: May 6, 2019.

Wilson, James Q. 1980. *The Politics of Regulation*. New York, NY: Basic Books.

1989. *Bureaucracy*. New York, NY: Basic Books.

Witko, Christopher, and Sally Friedman. 2008. "Business Backgrounds and Congres-
    sional Behavior." *Congress & the Presidency* 35: 71–86.
Wolton, Stephane. 2019. "Are Biased Media Bad for Democracy?" *American Journal of
    Political Science* 63 (3): 548–562.
Woon, Jonathan, and Jeremy C. Pope. 2008. "Made in Congress?" *Journal of Politics*
    70 (3): 823–836.
Wyoming State Geologic Survey. 2019. "Wyoming's Energy Resources." www.wsgs.wyo
    .gov/energy/energy. Date Accessed: May 9, 2019.
Yackee, Susan Webb. 2006. "Sweet-talking the Fourth Branch." *Journal of Public
    Administration Research and Theory* 16 (1): 103–124.
    2012. "The Politics of Ex Parte Lobbying." *Journal of Public Administration Research
    and Theory* 22 (2): 373–393.
Zaller, John R. 1992. *The Nature and Origins of Mass Opinion.* New York, NY:
    Cambridge University Press.
    2003. "A New Standard of News Quality." *Political Communication* 20 (2): 109–130.

Author Index

Subject Index

For EU product safety concerns, contact us at Calle de José Abascal, 56–1°,
28003 Madrid, Spain or eugpsr@cambridge.org.